A Tragedy
in
Several Acts.

A Recovery
in
Righteousness
and
Glory!

A Bible Story ... in History.

Written that Israel may fulfill Lev 26:40-42 KJV.

Jewish Chronicles

How the Jewish Nation Will Turn in Faith
to Rabbi Jesus of Nazareth, Well
Before the Second Coming!

What Bible History and Secular History
tells us about the Jews, and
Where this is headed.

A Spiritual History.

Neal Fain

AngleofEntry .com
Learning for the Journey

Cover Design by Neal Fain
The cover illustration is of Ezekiel 37, Israel rises from the dead,
by Gustave Doré
ISBN 978-0-9786866-7-3 © 2020, 2024 by Neal Fain

Library of Congress Control Number 2018910208

The King James Version KJV is the default translation of this volume.

Preface

***If one does not understand the history of the Jews, they do not
understand World history, nor where it is headed.***

This is book about Bible prophecy as it relates to the Jews, and about how
these things have, and are, working out in history, and how this *will* work out,
as told by Bible prophecy, both Old Testament and New Testament. This is my
third volume about Bible prophecy, and how it relates to our modern world.
And yes, Jesus is many times referred to as "Rabbi" in Scripture, although it is
sometimes translated as "Master."

A simple story is here: The Old Testament story of unfaithful Israel ... a story which has not yet ended. The flirtations of the descendants of Abraham with
other gods has gone on unabated from the time of Isaac and Jacob, even to our
own times. This in turn has led to multiple nefarious paths which have led to
destruction for both the Jews, and for other peoples. The modern Jews have
nowhere found their roots. They are still lost to them.

For most of America this is a story they have never known, of a people
whom they have never really known. They were here ... we met them, fought
with them, or *against* them, on a political or an intellectual or religious stage, dined
with them ... did business with them ... but never really knew them. This book is
so we can know them, and turn this obstinate people to their own Savior, their
own true Messiah, Jesus of Nazareth, the Christ, the Savior also of the world.

No, this is not really about eschatology, last things. Rather this is about our
world as it is now, and in the future, but well before the end in human terms.
This is about some major breaks in continuity for the Jews, from the time of
Moses to today. The view of prophecy reflected here is the same as in my first
two books: *Prophecy Principles,* and *Revealing the Christian Age.* They are the proper background for this work. However, this volume will stand on its own, inso-
far as it deals with particular issues. I said in the Introduction to *Prophecy
Principles*, that "Whole books have been and will be written on what is here only
chapters," and the same is true here. This is about what was only mentioned in
passing in "A "Post-Millennial" or "Pre-Millennial" World?"" in *Prophecy Principles*. There are two particular issues here: "other spirits," and the physical descendants of Abraham, the Jews; and the place of each in the end of the ages in
which we are placed. As has been showed previously, there are still some Biblical "types" to come in history, and some of these are discussed here.

A central contention here is that the main things you need to learn about
the Jews, you can learn from the Bible. The things you need to understand to
both beware and be undeceived and to be ready to act appropriately, are all to
be seen and understood from Scripture, in both the Old Testament and the
New Testament. This book will point out some of these things, and how they

relate to the last 2,000 years of history. Jewish Chronicles. The essentials are all yours to read and study and understand and to act. This is an overview, noting salient facts and turns in history, and for the future.

A note perhaps should be added. I do not think there is anything which is proved here, which can cannot be proved from other Scriptures or from other lines of documentation, generally speaking from Jewish sources. If you were a European writing of these things, you would probably have even better documentation available. Or even better yet, if you could read Hebrew, or Yiddish written in Hebrew characters. While the American reader may not have access to many of these sources, the European will probably also have access to the American sources. In the end there was far more quality material than could be used, and the problem in writing became one of culling material, and selecting a smaller set of issues to deal with.

This is not really about any secret things. There are secret things concerning our subject, but not as such in this book. I have tried to stick with publicly available materials which are available to the general English reader, or in a few isolated cases, consulted in a university or seminary library. Almost all of the non-biblical documentation you see here I have tried to gather as best I could from publicly available Jewish sources. Likewise, all of this and more can proved from other publicly available Jewish sources, which are abundant. *This book is about things which are known, but not widely, and not widely acknowledged.*

So what is the objective? As with my previous volume, it is that all of us, both Jews and Gentiles, may have the information we need, so that we might be able to better order our lives in light of the currents of history in our age. That we might be like the men of Issachar "who understood the times, with knowledge of what Israel should do," 1Chron 12:32.

You, the reader, and I are partners in this research. I will present the evidence as clearly as I am able. I will try to evaluate it as we go along, and perhaps even if we come to different conclusions on some parts, we will still see at the end the need for national repentance among the Jews, as also among ourselves, and even if dimly at present, I hope we can all look together for better days among the Jews, and all of us. I make no special claims for the Index, but I hope it will prove useful to the reader.

And what was my greatest discovery in this research? It seems the severe time of stress for the Jews, which will produce their repentance and turning to Jesus of Nazareth, will begin with a severe widespread persecution of Christians! These are Biblical/prophetic things which clearly have not happened yet.

I must ask your indulgence as a reader. I often speak here of the sins of a people important in history. These *never* apply to *all* of the individuals, just as it is with the common faults of other peoples. "We speak not as enemies, but as friends that dare to tell the truth." pg 277. May you be blessed in your reading!

Preface to the Second Edition, 2024

I have felt for sometime that the end of this book was not pointed enough as to what all of this will mean for the Jews, and their place in history and in Christianity for the end of our present age. I felt some of the theological points in the end sections, while true and pertinent, were not as important as giving a fuller picture of the good things these events will bring to the Jews. What you see here is a partial rewrite of Sections **VI. "As It Was Against Your Fathers,"** **1Sam 12:15**, and **VII. The Great Break: Israel Turns to Her Great Prophet**. Part of the problem is there is so much Scriptually to say about these times which are "soon" coming up. I think these changes will make the end of this volume more readable. Added use of the World English Bible has been made. Also there have been minor editorial changes here and there.

Neal Fain, August, 2024

About the Quotes

I have tried as best as possible to handle the citations for quotes within the text, while still trying to preserve readability. There are a few true footnotes, but I have tried to keep them to a minimum. There is a Select Bibliography at the end of the book. I have chosen to use the King James Version (KJV) as the default translation. Where the KJV is mystifying, or even down right confusing to the modern reader, I have chosen to use a combination of the New King James Version (NKJV), and the New American Standard Bible, 1995 edition (NASB). I consider the NASB to be the most accurate overall, of our modern translations, and its strength really shows up in the prophets. Spelling of Bible names and places follows the NASB. Bible chapters are cited in full, as for instance, "Genesis 12". Precise quotes are abbreviated, as for instance "Gen 1:31" (see the list of abbreviations on page xi). Citations of other translations include The New International Version, 1984 (NIV), and the English Standard Version (ESV).

For clarity with the *secular* quotes and my non-standard citation method, I have used quote marks even with indented quotes. See also the Bibliography.

For quotes of the old standard *A Hebrew and English Lexicon of the Old Testament*, by Brown, Driver, and Briggs I have sometimes used the abbreviation "BD&B." For the new standard, *Hebrew Aramaic Lexicon of the Old Testament*, by Koehler, and Baumgartner, I have sometimes used the abbreviation "HALOT."

For the handful of Yiddish terms I have used *The New Joys of Yiddish*, by Leo Rosten, as my spelling standard, and for English *The Oxford New American Dictionary*. The spelling of Hebrew names and words in current English literature is unfortunately all over the place, with the transliterations often depending both on how the author pronounces Hebrew, and how he pronounces English! Further, at times the same author will use different systems in different books! In the quotes I have tried to preserve the original spellings, and in my comments I often had to make choices, trying to note variations when they might confuse the reader.

Other Works: Ancient Jewish historian Flavius Josephus' *Antiquities of the Jews*, is quoted as *Antiquities*, and his *Wars of the Jews*, is quoted as *Wars*, giving the standard Book and chapter and section numbers. I have used William Whiston's old translation as the most available. Gibbon's *Decline and Fall of the Roman Empire* is quoted using his standard Volume, Chapter and Part numbers.

I have used the abbreviations BC for Before Christ and AD for Anno Domini, the Christian era. Our Lord and Master deserves to be so honored.

I should note that the English word "gentile" really is an obsolete translation which should be abandoned. In both Hebrew and Greek it is really just another translation for the word "nation." Some of the newer translations have made some moves to clearer translation here, but like this present work, it has been incomplete. The need to communicate in currently used Biblical and Jewish religious terms has led me to reluctantly continue the use of "gentile" at times.

I clearly do not agree with the late Jewish tradition that Yahweh is best honored by never saying His name. Would you like to be "honored" that way?

Lastly, Jesus was named after Joshua the son of Nun, which in Hebrew is *Yehoshua* יְהוֹשֻׁעַ. In Ezra and Nehemiah a popular shortened form of this name was *Yeshua* יֵשׁוּעַ, Ezra 2:36, Neh 11:26, etc. (Like Jonathan, John, Johnnie, Jon, etc. in English.) *Both* are translated as *Iāsous* Ἰησοῦς, in the Greek translations of the Old Testament. In Greek Jesus name is *Iāsous* Ἰησοῦς. My read, perhaps wrongfully, is that probably both forms of this Hebrew name were current in the first century. In modern Hebrew Jesus is translated as *Yeshua* יֵשׁוּעַ.

Special Thanks

Special thanks must be given to my proofreaders: Alice Stoffel, a teacher and librarian and a busy mom; my youngest daughter Alicia Hickman; and my good friend from my Alaska days, Allen Houtz, all of whom have very sharp eyes, and made many constructive critical comments on parts of the text. However all of the mistakes which remain are mine, whatever their nature.

Lastly I must give special thanks to my wife Cecilia, who has patiently endured nearly eleven years of me being buried in research, writing, and revising. Without her endurance these works would never have been possible.

This was composed using OpenOffice, final graphics handling was with GIMP image processing, and layout and typesetting were done using Scribus.

*We must first see what **has** happened,*
*so we can understand what **will** happen,*
*so we will **do** what we must **do**.*

Both Jew and Gentile!

Bible Abbreviations

1Chron	1 Chronicles	Jer	Jeremiah
1Cor	1 Corinthian	Jn	John
1Jn	l John	Job	Job
1Kgs	1 Kings	Joel	Joel
1Pe	1 Peter	Jonah	Jonah
1Sam	1 Samuel	Jos	Joshua
1Thes	1 Thessalonians	Jude	Jude
1Tim	1 Timothy	Judg	Judges
2Chron	2 Chronicles	KJV	King James (or also
2Cor	2 Corinthians		called Authorized) Version, 1611
2Jn	2 John	Lam	Lamentations
2Kgs	2 Kings	Lev	Leviticus
2Pe	2 Peter	Lk	Luke
2Sam	2 Samuel	Mal	Malachi
2Thes	2 Thessalonians	Mic	Micah
2Tim	2 Timothy	Mk	Mark
3Jn	3 John	Mtt	Matthew
Acts	Acts	Nah	Nahum
Amos	Amos	Neh	Nehemiah
Col	Colossians	NASB	New American Standard, 1995
Dan	Daniel	NET	New English Translation, 2005
Deut	Deuteronomy	NIV	New International Version, 1984
Eccl	Ecclesiastes	NKJV	New King James Version, 1982
ESV	English Standard Version 2001	Num	Numbers
		Obad	Obadiah
Eph	Ephesians	Phil	Philippians
Esth	Esther	Philem	Philemon
Ex	Exodus	Prov	Proverbs
Ezek	Ezekiel	Psa	Psalms
Ezra	Ezra	Rev	Revelation
Gal	Galatians	Rom	Romans
Gen	Genesis	Ruth	Ruth
Hab	Habakkuk	Song Sol	Song of Solomon
Hag	Haggai	Titus	Titus
Heb	Hebrews	WEB	World English Bible
Hos	Hosea		February, 2017
Isa	Isaiah	Zech	Zechariah
Jas	James	Zep	Zephaniah

I. The Call From Other Spirits

> [10] But the LORD *is* the true God; he *is* the living God, and an everlasting king: at his wrath the earth shall tremble, and the nations shall not be able to abide his indignation. [11] Thus shall ye say unto them, The gods that have not made the heavens and the earth, even they shall perish from the earth, and from under these heavens.
> Jer 10:10-11 KJV

The first confrontation with other spirits occurred early after man's creation. Man was in an ideal situation at first. Yes, there was already sin in the universe, and rebellion against the Lord our God, but it had not reached man. Mankind was still pure and innocent. Man had received incredibly great blessings, and great responsibilities, and this was all of mankind. Like many of the great Bible stories, it begins in the garden.

> [28] And God blessed them, and God said unto them, Be fruitful, and multiply, and replenish the earth, and subdue it: and have dominion over the fish of the sea, and over the fowl of the air, and over every living thing that moveth upon the earth. [29] And God said, Behold, I have given you every herb bearing seed, which *is* upon the face of all the earth, and every tree, in the which *is* the fruit of a tree yielding seed; to you it shall be for meat. [30] And to every beast of the earth, and to every fowl of the air, and to every thing that creepeth upon the earth, wherein *there is* life, *I have given* every green herb for meat: and it was so.
>
> [31] And God saw every thing that he had made, and, behold, *it was* very good. Gen 1:28-31 KJV

Man was given authority over all of creation, was given a perfect place to live—a garden, a paradise. Man was also given work to do (to till and keep the garden) and a mate as a companion and helper.

Then came the fall—the seduction of mankind—through the woman, by that great liar and deceiver, the serpent, the great adversary of all that is good and wholesome, also called the devil or Satan. Man was ruined and started to die. The access which he might have had to the tree of life was now denied. The creation itself now came under a curse because of man's sin, Gen 3:17. Man was sent out of the garden to earn his living in adverse circumstances. Provision was already being made for the redemption of man. Through the woman had come the fall, and through the woman would also come the Redeemer. First though, it seems that man must learn what this is all about; he must come face to face with what are the real effects of refusing to obey the LORD our God.

The downhill slide was fast and furious. The second generation produces mankind's first murderer. Shortly, we have polygamy and vices of every sort. In a mere 1600 years or so (without the later restraining influence of the organized punishment of lawlessness—what we call civil government) the situation was intolerable to the Lord. Most of mankind had completely ruined themselves, following the whims of their demonic masters. Things had become so bad, the violence so great, that the Lord our God destroyed the earth as it had existed. It was a tragedy of overwhelming proportions, reshaping the earth and its valleys and mountains to near their present state, and forever putting more distance between man and that pristine environment in which he and the animals had first lived. It seems the purpose was to destroy that which could no longer be reformed, and to lay the foundations of a godly seed. The foundations of what we now call civil government were laid in the death penalty, and a community duty was laid on men to punish the evil doer. This expanded the lengths to which men could grow and prosper. Once again man began to fill the earth, and to pursue his work of subduing and managing it.

Now a man by the name of Serug became the father of Nahor in Gen 11:22, and he lived a total of 230 years. Men were not living as long, not as long as their fathers had, but it was still a long time compared to us. The world-wide flood was in the recent past. Despite this, Satan was still at work, and men's inclinations still ran downhill. First, men tried to stay together, in opposition to God's desire that they scatter and fill the earth. So the Lord scrambled the brains of men by family so they could no longer speak the same language, and men started to scatter, Genesis 11. Then to further separate things, the earth was divided in Peleg's time, Gen 10:25. This seems to be speaking of our present continents.

The environment no longer supported some of our larger creatures, nor the extended life-span enjoyed by the early fathers. A dismaying decline in lifespans occurred over the next few hundred years, until it reached near our present limits. God did not seem to think that wicked men needed, or deserved, to live as long as formerly. Even so, man's tendencies were still down and not up, even with the addition of community discipline. There was still the need to further the foundations of the seed of woman.

Nahor in time became the father of Terah, and Terah became the father of Abram, in Gen 11:24-26. Terah was also the father of another Nahor, and Haran, and Haran became the father of Lot, Gen 11:27. So Haran and Abraham were brothers. Then Lot's dad Haran died in Ur of the Chaldees (what we would call Babylon), according to Gen 11:28. This family subgroup started moving, Gen 11:31-32. It seems that Genesis 12 goes on to tell why they started moving.

The Lord told Abram to leave his own country, Gen 12:1. Ur of the Chaldees was in the those days a highly developed place. But what was Canaan in those days? Nothing! A backwater! Now in the original call of Abram, he did not even know where he was going. God just told him to leave his own country and go to where God would show him, Heb 11:8. At a time when "social security" was in having relatives to care for you in your old age, this old man, the 75 year old Abram, left his family "security," to go; he knew not where! By faith Abram lived as an alien in a foreign land, lived as a migrant, lived on a "green card" in Canaan, Heb 11:9. A faithful first century Jew named Stephen spoke of these things in Acts 7:2-5. Look carefully, because Abram did not receive in his lifetime the promises from his obedience to God. It was all for the future! The Lord promised He would make a great nation of Abram, and make him a blessing to "all the families of the nations," Gen 12:2-3. God will bless whoever blesses Abram and curse whoever curses him! God has made a decision up front that He would bless Abram. God knew how Abram would turn out, and so He chose him, Gen 18:19. So Abram left his homeland on a promise he would never see in his earthly lifetime and was faithful to the promise, which he could not see! You can call this many things, but it was not living for this present world! Abraham is called the father of the faithful. Would you leave at age 75 to go you know not where? They did take all they could, Gen 12:5. Then when Abram got to Canaan, God appeared to him again and made him a promise of that land, Gen 12:6-7.

There is much to tell about Abraham (the Bible tells us a great deal) and not all of it is by any means flattering. One Jewish author said about the prophets, they were men "with a nature like ours." You do not have to be perfect for God to love you. You can be an ordinary, miserable, fallible human being and have God love you, and even protect you! Rom 5:6. The Messiah died for the ungodly! The ungodly! That is broad enough to take in you and me. One would hardly die for a righteous man, but maybe for a good man. But the Messiah died for us while we were still sinners, Rom 5:7-8, much like Abraham.

Faith does not require perfection. It does require following and repenting, as we go along. Then comes the key. It is not flawless execution, or a certain carefully calculated ritual. Some years later, still with no off-spring, the Lord took Abram outside to show him all of the stars and dared him to count them. The Lord said that Abram's off-spring would be like the number of the stars. Then Abram believed the LORD His God, and the Lord counted this belief as a replacement for sinless perfection, Gen 12:6. It was not by a certain canny and powerful ritual, but by faith. It is accounting terminology which is being used here, in both the Old and New Testaments. A landlord may reckon some work in the place of some rent due, so God decides to reckon confidence and trust in Him, as righteousness. As it says in Rom 4:22 NASB, "Therefore IT WAS ALSO CREDITED TO HIM AS RIGHTEOUSNESS." God is laying the foundations for a salvation by faith, through the Messiah who was to come. God decides to do these things through "the seed," the descendants, of Abraham. Abraham, though imperfect like us, decides to believe God (not just believe in God, but instead to actually believe what God says), and to follow in faith, so

> And in thy seed shall all the nations of the earth be blessed; because thou hast obeyed my voice. Gen 22:18 KJV

The descendants developed. First, through Isaac, then through Jacob, whose name was later changed to Israel. So, of course, Israel's children became ... well ... uh ... the children of Israel. God is working to produce a holy seed. God bless our relatives, we love them. We care for them, but they like us have many short comings and faults, faults with which we can often become infected. God seems to be trying to separate Abraham from what another Jewish author described as the "useless way of life handed down by your forefathers." Even so, marriage partners come from somewhere, and the influence of our mates may become an eternal asset to us ... or a snare. Some very good things, and some very noble traits developed from this Abrahamic posterity, and also some very worldly traits. God was trying to separate a people from the deadly practices of mistaking other spirits as God or gods, or of assuming that God has the likeness of some man or beast or fish or reptile, and that an image of His supposed likeness has some special powers of connection to deity. All of these are detestable to the True and Living God.

Even so, separation from bad ideas and practices does not come easily, does it? How many of us have found that playing with fire left us burned, or at least, badly scorched? We are left with desires to play with fires which we know are harmful, but which produce a glow that we love. Along side the desires for better things, eternal things, we find a tugging from our lower nature which often bedevils us all the rest of our lives.

That is the way it was with "Israel" also. Some of the separating happened early and directly. When Rebekah was pregnant with twins from her husband Isaac, the Lord foresaw the development of the boys, and

> And the LORD said unto her, Two nations *are* in thy womb, and two manner of people shall be separated from thy bowels; and *the one* people shall be stronger than *the other* people; and the elder shall serve the younger. Gen 25:23 KJV

Before the events had come to pass, God chose Jacob as the vessel for the holy seed, and rejected Esau. As He said by one of His later prophets,

> [2] ... *Was* not Esau Jacob's brother?" saith the LORD: yet I loved Jacob, [3] And I hated Esau, and laid his mountains and his heritage waste for the dragons of the wilderness. Mal 1:2-3 KJV

Another Hebrew author says none of us should be "a fornicator or profane person as Esau." It is easy to see that this "seed" was never about mere physical reproduction. Also it can be seen from history that the physical seed had their share of problems struggling with the useless ways inherited from their fathers. Despite trying to produce a holy seed which only worshipped the True and Living God, and which avoided images, they lapsed early and often.

According to Joshua the entire family had "served other gods," in ancient times, Jos 24:2. When Jacob was running from his father-in-law Laban, his wife

Rachel left only after stealing her dad's household idols, and later lied about the matter to complete the theft, Gen 31:34-35. Rachel however was not the only one leaving with some idols, and later when Jacob was trying to clean up his act to be acceptable before the Lord his God, he told his family and all of those with him to purify themselves, and give him all of their idols, and Jacob hid them under an oak tree in the region, Gen 35:2-4.

The prophet Amos said that even when Israel was in the wilderness, separated from Egypt and national slavery, many still carried on the secret worship of other gods.

> [25] Have ye offered unto me sacrifices and offerings in the wilderness forty years, O house of Israel? [26] But ye have borne the tabernacle of your Moloch and Chiun your images, the star of your god, which ye made to yourselves. Amos 5:25-26 KJV

It is in these ways made clear that this was not just an occasional falling back to bad habits, but a persistent and stubborn clinging to spirits which are no gods, and which also persistently brought God's judgement on them in their personal and national lives, as it has and does, even to this day.

> Therefore will I cause you to go into captivity beyond Damascus, saith the LORD, whose name is The God of hosts. Amos 5:27 KJV

Joshua pleaded with them in his day, to be faithful to the Lord.

> Now therefore fear the LORD, and serve him in sincerity and truth; and put away the gods which your fathers served on the other side of the flood, and in Egypt; and serve ye the LORD. Jos 24:14 KJV

Joshua then sternly warned them that they would not be able to serve the Lord, because,

> "[19] ... he is a jealous God; he will not forgive your transgression nor your sins. [20] If ye forsake the LORD and serve strange gods, then he will turn and do you hurt, and consume you, after that he hath done you good. [21] And the people said unto Joshua, Nay; but we will serve the LORD. Jos 24:19-21 KJV

Then Joshua pointed out that they were witnesses against themselves, and they agreed that they were.

In this way began a painful history of spiritual duplicity and sin in what should have been a shining record of faith and glory. As our teenage dallying with sin often produces bondage to bad habits which pursue us for the rest of our natural lives, so these sins have pursued the descendants of Jacob.

Warfare with Other Spirits

Indeed, We Are Not Alone.

Other Spirits do exist according to the Jewish prophet John son of Zebedee, and not all of them are faithful to God, 1Jn 4:1. There has been, and it is documented, a revolt in the universe before man came. It was revolt against the Lord our God's very authority. It was a revolt into which our species has been drawn. So yes, there are other spirits, other beings, in the universe. Again, we really are not alone. However, only Yahweh God is to be worshipped.

> [2] I *am* the LORD thy God, which have brought thee out of the land of Egypt, out of the house of bondage. [3] Thou shalt have no other gods before me. [4] Thou shalt not make unto thee any graven image, or any likeness *of any thing* that *is* in heaven above, or that *is* in the earth beneath, or that *is* in the water under the earth: [5] Thou shalt not bow down thyself to them, nor serve them: for I the LORD your God, *am* a jealous God, visiting the iniquity of the fathers upon the children unto the third and fourth *generation* of them that hate me; [6] And shewing mercy unto thousands of them that love me, and keep my commandments. Ex 20:2-6 KJV

Not even angels are to be worshipped, and faithful angels reject such worship. When the prophet John, who was mentioned above, attempted in reverence to worship the glorious angel who had given him such incredible revelations, he was rebuked.

> [8] And I John saw these things, and heard *them*. And when I had heard and seen, I fell down to worship before the feet of the angel which shewed me these things. [9] Then saith he unto me, *See thou do it* not: for I am thy fellowservant, and of thy brethren the prophets, and of them which keep the sayings of this book: worship God. Rev 22:8-9 KJV

This point is repeatedly made, for instance, in Rev 19:9-10. The "angels" are just created beings, just as we are, and although they are of a higher order than we are, they too are supposed to be mere servants of the Lord our God. In fact, the worship of other created beings, including even angels will bar you from eternal life. So the Apostle Paul warns,

> Let no one keep defrauding you of your prize by delighting in self-abasement and the worship of the angels, taking his stand on *visions* he has seen, inflated without cause by his fleshly mind, Col 2:18 NASB

Under Moses' law, whoever sacrifices to other "gods" is to be put to death, Ex 22:20, and idols (literally images) are not to be made or worshipped, Ex 20:4. Really, images are nothing in themselves, but bits of wood, bone, metal, plastic, or stone of one kind or another.

> [4] As concerning therefore the eating of those things that are offered in

sacrifice unto idols, we know that an idol *is* nothing in the world, and that *there is* none other God but one. ⁵ For though there be that are called gods, whether in heaven or in earth, (as there be gods many, and lords many,) ⁶ But to us *there is but one* God, the Father, of whom *are* all things, and we in him; and one Lord Jesus Christ, by whom *are* all things, and we by him. 1Cor 8:4-6 KJV

What then are all of these other "gods" which men sometimes worship? They are worshipping and making sacrifices to demons.

> "They sacrificed to demons, not to God,
>> *To gods* they did not know,
>> To new *gods*, new arrivals
>> That your fathers did not fear." Deut 32:17 NKJV

This is not an isolated teaching in Scripture. When the psalmist describes Israel's descent into debauchery, he frames it this way:

> ³⁶ They served their idols,
> Which became a snare to them.
> ³⁷ They even sacrificed their sons
> And their daughters to demons,
> ³⁸ And shed innocent blood,
> The blood of their sons and their daughters,
> Whom they sacrificed to the idols of Canaan;
> And the land was polluted with the blood.
> ³⁹ Thus they were defiled by their own works,
> And played the harlot by their own deeds. Psa 106:36-39 NKJV

None of this *ever* indicated that *all* of Israel was involved in such black deeds. Even when Judah was at one of her low points in the 7th century BC, she still produced some incredibly faithful young men, like Daniel during the first exile. **However, there was enough of this occurring to again and again bring judgement on the nation as a whole** ... even including the Daniels. Still, the worship of demons was by no means confined to the Jews. A Hebrew writer of the first century AD described pagan worship in this way:

> ¹⁹ What am I saying then? That an idol is anything, or what is offered to idols is anything? ²⁰ Rather, that the things which the Gentiles sacrifice they sacrifice to demons and not to God, and I do not want you to have fellowship with demons. ²¹ You cannot drink the cup of the Lord and the cup of demons; you cannot partake of the Lord's table and of the table of demons. ²² Or do we provoke the Lord to jealousy? Are we stronger than He? 1Cor 10:19-22 NKJV

Notice that it is easy to be involved with demons and not realize what you are doing. Also another key fact needs to mentioned. The LORD is still really and truly God, and the spirits, all the spirits, are under God's overseeing control, as indeed we are. When Job is to be tempted, Satan has to ask permission to tempt and try Job, Job 2:4-6. Later, Satan wanted to tempt Peter, but he could not just do this on his own, and Peter was told,

> [31] The Lord said, "Simon, Simon, behold, Satan asked to have you, that he might sift you as wheat, [32] but I prayed for you, that your faith wouldn't fail. You, when once you have turned again, establish your brothers." Lk 22:31-32 WEB

These rebellious spirits are more powerful than men. They are malicious, and they despise and hate men. Despite all of that, the Lord has allowed them some time in life, even as He has us. However, they, like us, are subject to the Lord of Hosts and, though they might wander, in the end must submit to Him.

Traffic With Other Spirits.

The Lord our God is the One we are to seek and worship and serve. He is the One who holds all power and authority, and from whom all others derive their power and authority. Even so, at times many have been tempted to seek power or authority or riches from other sources, either fleshly or ethereal. God has had something to say about such practices. In the law of Moses there is extensive legislation concerning such things.

The Canaanites of old had long been involved in such detestable practices. When these things happen, the Lord generally gives those involved time to reconsider their actions, to turn, to repent. Then if they will not turn from these vile practices, our God will at last deal with these things, and bring men's corruptions down on their own heads. When the Lord was talking to Abraham in Canaan, these things were well advanced with the Canaanites. God was going to deal with these things, as He always does. God tells Abram that He is going to give Abram's descendants the land of Canaan, but not for a few hundred years.

> [15] And thou shalt go to thy fathers in peace; thou shalt be buried in a good old age. [16] But in the fourth generation they shall come hither again: for the iniquity of the Amorites is not yet full.
> Gen 15:15-16 KJV

There is more than one interesting concept in this passage. For instance, the Lord foresees how things will develop in the future, and at some point or other a man's or a nation's sins may become more than God will bear, and we may "fill up" the full measure of our sins. So when Moses was laying out the rules on these matters, he brings up the conduct of the Canaanite nations.

> "When you come into the land which the LORD your God is giving you, you shall not learn to follow the abominations of those nations."
> Deut 18:9 NKJV

These are not just rules for the Israelites, but for everyone who visits or passes through their land because these things can ruin a country.

> [26] 'But as for you, you are to keep My statutes and My judgments and shall not do any of these abominations, *neither* the native, nor the alien who sojourns among you [27] (for the men of the land who have been before you have done all these abominations, and the land has become defiled);' Lev 18:26-27 NASB

The land had become defiled, and it was about to be cleansed ... by putting to death the evil doers. Then the Lord starts outlining what is forbidden.

> "There shall not be found among you *anyone* who makes his son or his daughter pass through the fire, *or one* who practices witchcraft, or a soothsayer, or one who interprets omens, or a sorcerer,"
> Deut 18:10 NKJV

"To pass through the fire" is a Bible term for human sacrifice. Among some of the Canaanite cults, especially the Baal and Asherah cults, the ultimate expression of devotion to one's "god" was to sacrifice your own child in a sacrificial fire to your god. Human sacrifice is something that has shown up from time to time in history, especially in degenerate civilizations, or those in serious decline, but at times even among other groups. If murder automatically carries its own burden (and it does), so does human sacrifice to multiplying powers we can scarcely conceive. It is indeed abominable, both to God and to men, whether practiced by Canaanites, Carthaginians, Romans, Celts, Aztecs, or the people of modern New Guinea. Among the Canaanites and later among the Jews, it clearly seems to have been the babies of one's own family.

Next, mentioned in Deuteronomy 18, is "divination" NASB ("fortune telling"): predicting the future through augury or reading omens (reading stars, tea leaves, the palms of your hands, chicken soup, or whatever). Wherever you read of these things, there is always the implication that all things are related to each other. More details of the theory of these things will be discussed later, but it is implied that if the stars change, that also changes the tea leaves, the bumps on your head, the entrails of an animal (or a person), and it also changes what will happen to you, or happen in your life. So the theory is that by reading what is happening to any one thing in the universe, you can discover what will happen to all other things. This *assumed **theory*** is often referred to "As above, so below."

Among the implications of augury or omens are that the universe is one vast mechanical sort of system, in which there is a rigid determinism to everything. That there is an essential unity to the universe that is not readily seen. If you take these theories seriously, it means a determinism which is beyond comprehension. It also means that we are just very sophisticated "machines" that can only bounce around and react, but who in fact really have absolutely NO free will at all, not even a free thought. Generally though, these implications are in the background, with people acting out a fantasy of finding out what the future holds, and then attempting to act so as to change it, or to co-opt it!

It is true that *some* things in "nature" are related. It is true, for instance, that if your body changes, then probably your excrement will also change (scatology, the study of excrement). It is true that the Lord our God overrules all of both the physical and the spiritual world. But these theories of divination are without any real foundation, and the future is dependent on what the Lord God decides will happen, and what He *allows* you or I or others to do or say or decide. The practice of such things is another of those "detestable things" in the sight of our God. Our universe is NOT merely a large mechanical clock, and the Lord, and you and I, can and *should* and *do* make moral decisions in this universe.

One of the Hebrew words for divination is *nahash* נָחַשׁ, and it can refer to either what we might call the reading of signs, or what we might call an enchantment, a spell, a hypnotic spell, cast on someone either with or without drugs. It is translated both ways in many of our mainline English translations. *Nahash* נָחַשׁ is also the basic word for a serpent or snake, and indeed, you cannot disassociate Satan from these things, wherever you meet them in history or in life. One Hebrew phrase in Deut 18:10 for "interprets omens" NASB is *mi-na-hesh* מְנַחֵשׁ, or literally "from the serpent." The associations involved go directly to depths of Satan and the occult, even from the first. Some of the other associations involved are given in Leviticus.

> 26 "You shall not eat *anything* with the blood, nor shall you practice divination or soothsaying. 27 You shall not shave around the sides of your head, nor shall you disfigure the edges of your beard. 28 You shall not make any cuttings in your flesh for the dead, nor tattoo any marks on you: I *am* the LORD.
> 29 "Do not prostitute your daughter, to cause her to be a harlot, lest the land fall into harlotry, and the land become full of wickedness."
> Lev 19:26-29 NKJV

The next thing spoken of in Deuteronomy 18 is sorcery or witchcraft, what we might call "magic," that is the worshipping or seeking the power or aid of other spirits. Webster defines magic as, "The use of power gained from the assistance or control of evil spirits ...". *The New Oxford American Dictionary* defines what we might call religious (?) magic as "the power of apparently influencing the course of events by using mysterious or supernatural forces ..." This is one of the key concepts here. The idea is to secure the help of "other spirits." The other spirits may be thought of as "gods," or as angels or even acknowledged as being demons. The magician or sorcerer is then sometimes praying to (or more often attempting to manipulate or sometimes even attempting to command) these "other spirits." The latter would only be by a magician who is very, very sure of himself, or who thinks he has the power to "rig" the situation, in order to accomplish whatever is desired.

Like much legislation throughout history, the Law of Moses often uses overlapping terms to make sure that the entire is subject is covered. In this case "witchcraft" (NASB) and the last item in Deut 18:10, "a sorcerer," overlap, and this is reflected in our main translations. Using the New American Standard as the basis for these points, one Hebrew word for "witchcraft" is the Hebrew word *anan* עָנַן, from a word that means a cloud, and its use stretches from various forms of divination ("fortune telling"), to various forms of "magic." "Sorcerer" here is from the Hebrew word *kashaph* כָּשַׁף, or as in Deut 18:10 the form is a *mi-kashaph* מְכַשֵּׁף. This is the more regular Old Testament word for what we call a true magician or sorcerer, and it is a basic word for sorcery or magic and seems to come from a root which means to "cut." See HALOT (*The Hebrew and Aramaic Lexicon of the Old Testament*, Koehler and Baumgartner, 2000, Brill, The Netherlands) on כָּשַׁף (*kashaph*).

Sometimes sorcery is merely thought of as a procedural thing. You do certain things, and certain things "happen," and you see such "explanations" throughout magic literature, even to our own times. In Jewish magic, for over two thousand years, the key spirits are sometimes called the Sefirot. The theory will be covered later, but in the book *A Historical Atlas of the Jewish People, From the Time of the Patriarchs to the Present*, (Ed. Eli Barnavi, Shocken Books, NY, 1992), when explaining the Jewish Kabbalistic practice of magic, summarizes the theory as:

"Man is capable, by practicing precise rites, of influencing the Sefirot which determine the span and progress of the

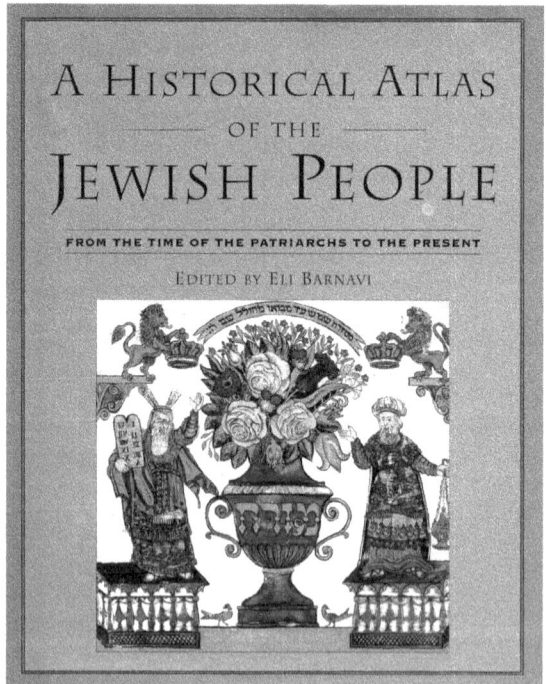

A Historical Atlas of the Jewish People, edited by Eli Barnavi, is written from a liberal / secular point of view, but is a well conceived and executed historical atlas of Judaism, and is useful for an

world." pg 144.

So it is all about who knows the "right" procedures? Oh? Uh-m-m-m.

For many people this is all fraud and nonsense, without a spot of reality in the whole. They say there is no Satan. For sure, the occult is permeated with deceit and pretense. Despite that, is not deceit what Satan is really all about? And the reality? How much is really there? More than you might suspect. Although deceit is the forte, as it was with our ancestors' first forbidden fruit, all of this is not without its power and effects!

This is what we see in the next item in Deut 18:11. It is called casting spells or *hober habar* חָבַר חֹבֵר or more literally, to tie a spell. This is what most would call "hypnosis," with or without drugs, and has been known since extreme antiquity. Scripture does not quibble about the exact way spells are cast, or their supposed "evil" or "good" results. Rather, it treats these things as dangerous and evil in themselves, and tells us,

> For whoever does these things is an abomination to Yahweh: ...

and

> ... but as for you, Yahweh your God has not allowed you so to do.
> Deut 18:12, 14 WEB

Other forbidden activities include serving as "a medium, or a spiritist, or one who calls up the dead," Deut 18:11. A medium (or "channeler" is a term in fashion in America today, although fashions change as necessary to deceive) is, "A person supposed to be susceptible to supernormal agencies and able to impart knowledge derived from them or perform actions which are impossible without their aid ..." Webster. Lev 19:31 says,

> "Give no regard to mediums and familiar spirits; do not seek after them, to be defiled by them: I *am* the LORD your God." NKJV

God promises He will oppose those who turn to such practices,

> "And the person who turns to mediums and familiar spirits, to prostitute himself with them, I will set My face against that person and cut him off from his people." Lev 20:6 NKJV

In other words, in these things men are consulting and seeking the approval of other spirits when they should be consulting and seeking the approval of God. This is unfaithfulness to God, and it is called playing the "harlot" against God. Consulting with the dead is called necromancy. Webster calls this "revealing the future by pretended communication with the spirits of the dead; hence magic in general ..." All of us know there is plenty of fraud here, but I personally would not be as dogmatic as this definition. Consider, from a Biblical point of view, the matter of fact account in 1 Samuel 28. In any account, whether real, or as is admittedly often the case, pretended,

[12] "... whoever does these things is detestable to the LORD; and because of these detestable things the LORD your God will drive them out before you. [13] You shall be blameless before the LORD your God. [14] For those nations, which you shall dispossess, listen to those who practice witchcraft and to diviners, but as for you, the LORD your God has not **allowed** you *to do* so." Deut 18:12-14 NASB (bold emphasis added)

Here we see that practicing these things can cause a people to lose their country! We are only to listen to God's prophets and His special prophet.

"The LORD your God will raise up for you a prophet like me from among you, from your countrymen, you shall listen to him."
Deut 18:15 NASB

'But the prophet who speaks a word presumptuously in My name which I have not commanded him to speak, or which he speaks in the name of other gods, that prophet shall die.' Deut 18:20 NASB

Using language similar to that used by legislators down through history, Scripture defines witchcraft and magic, and all of its various forms and extensions, and then forbids these things to God's people.

"God's" Secrets And the Oral Law.

It was by a powerful and public deliverance that Israel was brought out of slavery in this world, out of slavery in Egypt. Staggering plagues fell on Egypt, ruining the country, and only after severe sufferings was the Egyptian's nation of slaves released. Marvelous deliverances were given to the descendants of Abraham, to both free them and to care for them. Then they were brought to Mount Sinai, to receive God's laws and regulations. The Lord told them,

Ye have seen what I did unto the Egyptians, and how I bare you on eagles' wings, and brought you unto myself. Ex 19:4 KJV

Then the Lord promised to make them a nation of priests.

[5] Now therefore, if ye will obey my voice indeed, and keep my covenant, then ye shall be a ... treasure unto me above all people: ... [6] And ye shall be unto me a kingdom of priests, and an holy nation. These are the words which thou shalt speak unto the children of Israel. Ex 19:5-6 KJV

This is an explicit promise, and one that clearly says that they will not only be a nation *with a* **tribe** *of* priests, rather they shall be a nation which is *as a whole* priests to the Lord, a nation of priests! A promise which clearly was never to be fulfilled in the laws which God revealed through Moses. This promise and many others in the law of Moses, point to the temporary character in the Law of Moses. This was a law which was only to last until a special prophet like Moses was to come. After clearly instructing Israel on the need to abandon the magic, witchcraft, and fortune-telling of the pagans, God promised Israel that further instruction was coming. A prophet who was like Moses was coming.

> [15] Yahweh your God will raise up to you a prophet from the midst of you, of your brothers, like me; to him you shall listen; ...
> [18] I will raise them up a prophet from among their brothers, like you; and I will put my words in his mouth, and he shall speak to them all that I shall command him. Deut 18:15, 18 WEB

It can be seen from these verses alone that God had more to say to Israel, more than He was telling them by Moses. The instructions given through Moses were never intended to be final, or sufficient for an earth-lasting code. Further, God was going to tell them these things through a special prophet "like me," that is to say, "like Moses." To say that the Messiah, the special Anointed One, who is in Greek called the Christ, would be like Moses, is a mouth full. Moses, along with other characteristics, spoke with God directly.

> And the LORD said to Moses, "Behold, I come to you in the thick cloud, that the people may hear when I speak with you, and believe you forever."
> So Moses told the words of the people to the LORD. Ex 19:9 KJV

The people were to consecrate themselves, wash their clothes, abstain from sex ("do not go near a woman," Ex 19:15 NASB), and stand at a distance from the spectacle of God giving instructions to Moses. One holy psalmist spoke of God covering Himself with light as a cloak, Psa 104:2. A first century Jew spoke of God as living in "unapproachable light." That is something a modern can easily understand. Sometimes we cannot even stand bright sunlight in the visible spectrum for very long. Infrared and microwave radiation can cook us, and more than a few seconds of x-rays can kill us. Moses is explicitly a priest, but Israel is NOT! Israel is to stand back while their special priest Moses was given special protection to draw close.

> And it came to pass on the third day in the morning, that there were thunders and lightnings, and a thick cloud upon the mount, and the voice of the trumpet exceeding loud; so that all the people that was in the camp trembled. Ex 19:16 KJV

Moses is a priest, but Israel dare not approach, Ex 19:21. Warn them again lest they die, the Lord told Moses. If they really are priests, they had better make sure they are made holy, that they are consecrated, Ex 19:22. Moses protests that the Israelites have been told that they cannot come up, Ex 19:23. God says that Moses and Aaron may approach, but if the rest come, they will die, so go back and warn them again, which Moses did, Ex 19:24-25. As a result, the promise made that Israel will become a nation of priests, as in Ex 19:6 will never be fulfilled in Moses' Law! Only when the Great Prophet comes, and the law of Moses is fulfilled, and a fuller law is given, is it that these promises will be fulfilled.

> ¹⁸ And mount Sinai was altogether on a smoke, because the LORD descended upon it in fire: and the smoke thereof ascended as the smoke of a furnace, and the whole mount quaked greatly. ¹⁹ And when the voice of the trumpet sounded long, and waxed louder and louder, Moses spake, and God answered him by a voice. ²⁰ And the LORD came down upon mount Sinai, on the top of the mount: and the LORD called Moses *up* to the top of the mount; and Moses went up.
> Ex 19:18-20 KJV

This is a description of an overwhelming experience, but despite all of that, there is one greater than Moses.

> I will raise them up a Prophet from among their brethren, like unto thee, and will put my words in his mouth; and he shall speak unto them all that I shall command him. Deut 18:18 KJV

One whose words will supersede Moses's words, who will give new statutes and ceremonies, and will make it so that Israel will not just be a nation with a tribe of priests, but a nation of priests. Moses says this himself. At that time, anyone who dares to disobey this greater-than-Moses prophet, he will have to answer to God Himself.

> And it shall come to pass, that whosoever will not hearken unto my words which he shall speak in my name, I will require it of him.
> Deut 18:19 KJV

A prophet "like Moses" is full of meaning. It implies One who speaks directly to God, through special position with God. It implies that this prophet is also a lawgiver, and that His coming would be necessary to make Israel a nation of priests. If He is a prophet like Moses, He would also have to be a priest, one who could approach the mercy-seat, above the ark of the covenant, as Moses could and did, to make intercession for the people. It is clear from later prophecies, He was to be of the house of David ... not of the house of Levi, the tribe of priests; so again necessitating a change in the Law which Moses was delivering. This too was known in Moses' day, for Jacob had prophesied of the Messiah, that He was to be of the house of Judah, not of the house of Levi as Moses was. It is an incredible description of prosperity for this Messiah.

> ¹⁰ " The scepter shall not depart from Judah,
> Nor the ruler's staff from between his feet,
> Until Shiloh comes,
> And to him *shall be* the obedience of the peoples.
> ¹¹ "He ties *his* foal to the vine,
> And his donkey's colt to the choice vine;
> He washes his garments in wine,
> And his robes in the blood of grapes.

¹² "His eyes are dull from wine,
And his teeth white from milk. Gen 49:10-12 NASB

It implies that here is a king who will have the obedience of all peoples.

I remember my dad telling me about one of the worst whippings he ever had as a boy. My granddad, "Papa Mac," had a prize watermelon in his field, that he was saving for some local competition. Boys being boys, my dad could not resist playing with and turning this watermelon around, and whoops, he accidentally split this heavy monster! In contrast, this ruler from Judah, who has "the obedience of the peoples," will tie His donkey to His vines, to have the critter eat as he pleases, and will tie a donkey's colt even to the choicest vine in vineyard. He is so rich he washes his clothes in wine, and His robes in the blood of grapes. Even today, try pricing that at your grocery or liquor store.

Clearly, Moses knew that God had put the entire priesthood in the house of Levi in his own day. As the one who put the book of Genesis in its present form, he would surely remember that this ruler-priest who talks to God, would be of the tribe of Judah, and that One is the One who everyone has to listen to ... even above Moses.

So having such a revelation of God's instructions for a nation, how should they be treated? Here also, the commands are clear.

> "You shall not add to the word which I command you, nor take from it, that you may keep the commandments of the LORD your God which I command you." Deut 4:2 NKJV

Again God warned through Moses,

> "Whatever I command you, be careful to observe it; you shall not add to it nor take away from it." Deut 12:32 NKJV

As a prophet also warned,

> Do not add to His words,
>   Lest He rebuke you, and you be found a liar. Prov 30:6 NKJV

Are the commands of Moses inviolable and eternal? No. Will they ever be superseded? Absolutely, and this will be necessary for God's people to become what they really should be. On the other hand, short of being superseded by the new order of the prophet-king, are these laws to be amended at will, either to blunt their intention or increase their scope or effect? Not in any way.

Now a special prophet would come one day who would change Moses' Law, but short of that prophet, that king, who then has authority to amend the Law of Moses? The clear answer is: no one! Not Isaiah, or Amos, nor Jeremiah, or Hosea, or you name them, who were in some ways just like faithful preachers of the gospel age. They might review the foundations of the current covenant. They might also talk about the current habits and sins of the people in light of that covenant, the Law. They might tell the people what would happen if they did not repent and return to obedience to the Lord's commands, but did Isaiah or Jeremiah or Ezekiel or any of the others have authority to change that law, to amend it, to lighten its burden, or expand its scope? Absolutely not! They might explain the true meaning of the command to love your neighbor as yourself, but they could no more "add to the word which I am commanding you, nor take away from it," than any "shlemiel" in the nation could. At least, not and be faithful to God. Were the prophets speaking the very Words of the Lord to the people in an inspired way? Yes! Were they revealing some things to the people which they did not already know? Yes, quite often they were. Did they or anyone short of the great prophet "from among their countrymen like you," have authority to change Moses Law? NO!

No doubt, when new prophets were revealed, the people were often looking, testing, trying to see if this prophet might be the great prophet. When John the Baptist came as the forerunner of the Messiah, we see these reasonings come forward. Men were sent from the chief priests and the scribes and lawyers in Jerusalem to see what his claims were, and he told them, "I am not the Christ."

> And they asked him, "What then? Are you Elijah?"
> He said, "I am not."
> "Are you the Prophet?" Jn 1:21 NKJV

It is clear from the discussion that many did not understand that the Messiah and the Great Prophet were the same. John the Baptist just answered, "No."

> ²⁴ Now those who were sent were from the Pharisees. ²⁵ And they asked him, saying, "Why then do you baptize if you are not the Christ, nor Elijah, nor the Prophet?" Jn 1:24-25 NKJV

Clearly the Pharisees, though confusing many things, understood that the Christ would be baptizing when He came.

What then should be the direction and effect of good priests? The prophet Malachi gives us a lesson on these things.

> ⁵ My covenant was with him of life and peace; and I gave them to him *for* the fear wherewith he feared me, and was afraid before my name. ⁶ The law of truth was in his mouth, and iniquity was not found in his lips: he walked with me in peace and equity, and did turn many away from iniquity. ⁷ For the priest's lips should keep knowledge, and they should seek the law at his mouth: for he *is* the messenger of the Lord of hosts. Mal 2:5-7 KJV

That is what should have happened. But what did happen?

> ⁸ But ye are departed out of the way; ye have caused many to stumble at the law; ye have corrupted the covenant of Levi, saith the Lord of hosts. ⁹ Therefore have I also made you contemptible and base before

all the people, according as ye have not kept my ways, but have been partial in the law. Mal 2:8-9 KJV

The Jews, not every individual, but the group as a whole, did not want to follow God's instructions and laws, and the priests were bowing to custom, and desire, and not to the Word of the LORD. Then we see widely varying strains of heresy arising in Judaism of old. The prophet Isaiah described the situation this way:

> The Lord said, Because this people draw near *to me*, and with their mouth and with their lips to honor me, but have removed their heart far from me, and their fear of me is a commandment of men which has been taught *them*;
> Isa 29:13 WEB

They pretend obedience, but it is only a pretense. They honor God with their words, but in their hearts they seek other things. The little bit of obedience they show is just a series of memorized ceremonies, which are without any substance. Also in this same passage, God outlines how He will deal with the Jews.

> [14] "Therefore behold, I will once again deal marvelously with this people, wondrously marvelous;
> And the wisdom of their wise men will perish,
> And the discernment of their discerning men will be concealed."
> [15] Woe to those who deeply hide their plans from the LORD,
> And whose deeds are *done* in a dark place,
> And they say, "Who sees us?" or "Who knows us?"
> [16] You turn *things* around!
> Shall the potter be considered as equal with the clay,
> That what is made would say to its maker, "He did not make me";
> Or what is formed say to him who formed it,
> "He has no understanding"? Isa 29:14-16 NASB

How then did they deal with these commands, about many of which they had profound disagreement, or maybe they just did not like some particualar commands? In two different ways. **First**, they distorted the law though lawyerly pettifogging deceit and the legal tricks with which every nation on earth has experience. They tried to change what was the obvious the intent of the law into what they thought *should have been* said! Or at least, into whatever they *wanted* to be said. Lawyers being lawyers, they also often subtly changed the law in ways which would give them more influence and power. The prophet Jeremiah described such things, as if men are wiser than God, and points out how far these things are from any real wisdom.

> "How can you say, 'We are wise,
>   And the law of the LORD is with us'?

> But behold, the lying pen of the scribes
> Has made *it* into a lie. " Jer 8:8 NASB

So the covenant given by Moses had become just a legal code. Perhaps a very good one for the times, but still just a legal code. Have you done something wrong? Well, that is not good, but no problem, there is a solution. A certain sacrifice, a donation to the synagogue or the temple, certain prayers worded in certain ways, and then God will be satisfied. All will be well. It may not even matter exactly what you do, as long as you, so to speak, tie it up right legally. The interpretations of the law then slowly began to overtake the law itself, even if with great pretense of fidelity. These perversions over time seemed to need greater protection. It is all well and good to say God will be satisfied with this or that, but what authority do our words really have?

Second, it is at this point that lying traditions arose of other "oral revelations" which were said to be binding. These were traditions from another "revelation" from God. This was, supposedly, an oral revelation from the Lord our God, not a written one. It was presented as being at every point parallel to the written, and superior to the written revelation! These traditions later split into two major branches. *First* it seems the traditions of the elders came to be identified with an original oral revelation. Often this was implied rather than spoken. The effect though was that the traditions of the elders came to have the force of the law of God itself, or really, as has been pointed out, to be superior to the written law, because at its root it was supposedly the inspired "proper" interpretation of the written law! *Secondly*, there was also asserted to exist an oral law that was so holy, so much higher than the written law, that it was never even supposed to be revealed to the average *am ha-aretz* הָאָרֶץ עַם, "the people of the land," the local yokels. So the idea was sown, not just of a secret revelation from Zeus or Isis or Mithra or whomever; but of a secret revelation from the LORD our God Himself. A revelation so high and so holy that it must never be written down, but must be transmitted orally, and never revealed to the common man. So there came to be among the Jews also, an ancient secret tradition. And oh yes! Did I mention? The tendency of the secret revelation is that rule keeping, law keeping, was just for the peons, and not for the Lord's "higher," "more fully instructed," servants. H-h-h-a-a-a-m-m-m! Who would have guessed?

The first of these options—the traditions of the elders—were finally put into a written form beginning in the second century AD and was called the Mishna. This was supplemented by the Gemara, a commentary on the Mishna, and the two of them together formed the Talmud. This has formed the core of Jewish doctrine during the major part of the last 2,000 years.

The ancient secret tradition took on a circuitous (and devious) development. Both claimed superiority to the written law (Genesis through Deuteronomy), with the ancient secret tradition claiming superiority even over the traditions of the elders, and only in the Middle Ages was it supposedly put into writing. Scripture though, emphatically rejects these detours around the written law.

Were there ever secret things? Things which were not told to men? Yes, decidedly so, but such things belong to the LORD God Himself and not to some supposed elite who disdain God's written commands.

> The secret *things belong* unto the LORD our God: but those *things which are* revealed *belong* unto us and to our children for ever, that *we* may do all the words of this law. Deut 29:29 KJV

The commandment is not treated as some out of reach thing, but a thing of faith which can be lived, Deut 30:11-14. It is not some inferior revelation, to be superseded or ignored by the so-called "wise."

> The words of the LORD *are* pure words: *as* silver tried in a furnace of earth, purified seven times. Psa 12:6 KJV

These are blameless concepts which are a shield to the righteous.

> *As for* God, God, His way is perfect
> > The word of the LORD is proven;
> > He is a shield to all who trust in Him. Psa 18:30 NKJV

> [7] The law of the LORD *is* perfect, converting the soul: the testimony of the LORD is sure, making wise the simple. [8] The statutes of the LORD *are* right, rejoicing the heart: the commandment of the LORD *is* pure, enlightening the eyes. [9] The fear of the LORD *is* clean, enduring for ever: the judgments of the LORD *are* true and righteous altogether. [10] More to be desired *are they* than gold, yea, than much fine gold: sweeter also than honey and the honeycomb. Psa 19:7-10 KJV

Or again,

> Every word of God *is* pure: he *is* a shield unto them that put their trust in him. Prov 30:5 KJV

None of this, or many other Scriptures, sound like something which needs amending. One could go on and on about the sufficiency of the revelation made by Moses for the times for which it was revealed. It should not have needed to have been said, but the Lord our God said it through the prophet Isaiah,

> I have not spoken in secret, in a dark place of the earth: I said not unto the seed of Jacob, Seek ye me in vain: I the LORD speak righteousness, I declare things that are right. Isa 45:19 KJV

Implied is that there is nothing here which requires secrecy. These are righteous and upright things, and do not need to be kept in secrecy. Again,

> Come ye near unto me, hear ye this; I have not spoken in secret from the beginning; from the time that it was, there *am* I: and now the Lord GOD, and his Spirit, hath sent me. Isa 48:16 KJV

Similarly then it was with the Great Prophet. He said at His trial,

> "I spoke openly to the world. I always taught in synagogues and in the temple, where the Jews always meet, and in secret I have said nothing." Jn 18:20 NKJV

Once again, the secret things belong to God. So the key thing is to "keep and seek for all the commandments," 1Chron 28:8 KJV, until the time of the Great Prophet.

Like Their Fathers Who Did Not Believe, 2Kgs 17:14

As we come to the end of the wilderness wanderings of the children of Israel, we see Moses summarizing what has happened to Israel, and what will happen to this people chosen by the Lord our God. God had wanted a people for His own possession. God wanted a holy people of His own.

> For thou art an holy people ... ; the LORD thy God hath chosen thee to be a special people unto himself, **above all people** that are upon the face of the earth. Deut 7:6 KJV (*bold emphasis added*)

God had not chosen them because they were a numerous people, because they were few compared to many nations, even of that time. Rather he wanted a holy people, and He was fulfilling the oath He had made to their forefathers, to Abraham, Isaac and Jacob, to bring them out with a mighty hand, to redeem them from their slavery of 400 years, Deut 7:7-8. God was, of course, faithful and cared for them. He had cared for them as an eagle watches over her young, Deut 7:9-11.

His purpose was to deliver men from those spirits which by nature are no gods (Gal 4:8), who did not create the heavens and the earth. These so-called "gods" will perish, Jer 10:11. So it was God alone who acted. Thus, it was only the "us" of creation in Genesis 1 who were involved in the actual creation process.

> So the Lord alone did lead him, and *there was* no strange god with him. Deut. 32:12 KJV

The powerful care of the Lord in the wilderness had been more than sufficient to sustain this body of say three-and-a-half million people in an area which could not otherwise have supported them. The other side is that Israel had been strictly warned not to rebel against the Lord. God's blessing comes with submission and obedience. So they had been told of the angel of the Lord,

> Beware of him, and obey his voice, provoke him not; for he will not pardon your transgressions: for my name is in him. Ex 23:21 KJV

A Stubborn and Rebellious People.

Again when they were about to enter the land, the people were daunted with the fear of man, and the size of the task which was before them. Moses pleaded with them to just obey the Lord, and trust that His instructions were right and would work.

> "Only rebel not ye against the LORD, neither fear ye the people of the land; for they *are* bread for us: **their defence is departed from them,** and the LORD *is* with us: fear them not.
> Num 14:9 KJV (*bold emphasis added*)

The implication of God's overseeing power should not be missed in this verse. If a nation is sustained and protected, it is God who does it; and if they become a prey to others it is also because the Lord, for His reasons, has removed their protection. Despite all of this, and the powerful signs from God which the entire nation had seen, the nation of Israel was still reluctant to trust the Lord. The psalmist Asaph speaks of these things, and pleads with Israel in his own day and summarizes their rebellion.

> [5] For he established a testimony in Jacob, and appointed a law in Israel, which he commanded our fathers, that they should make them known to their children: [6] That the generation to come might know *them, even* the children *which* should be born; *who* should arise and declare *them* to their children: [7] That they might set their hope in God, and not forget the works of God, but keep his commandments: [8] **And might not be as their fathers, a stubborn and rebellious generation**; a generation *that* set not their heart aright, and whose spirit was not stedfast with God. ... [17] And they sinned yet more against him by provoking the most High in the wilderness. ...[40] How oft did they provoke him in the wilderness, and grieve him in the desert! ... [56] Yet they tempted and provoked the most high God, and kept not his testimonies: Psa 78:5-8, 17, 40, 56 KJV (*bold emphasis added*)

The confrontations in the wilderness because of stubbornness and defiance were many. They were warned about "faking" prophecy in order to gain influence over others.

> And that prophet, or that dreamer of dreams, shall be put to death; because he hath spoken to turn *you* away from the LORD your God, which brought you out of the land of Egypt, and redeemed you out of the house of bondage, to thrust thee out of the way which the LORD thy God commanded thee to walk in. So shalt thou put the evil away from the midst of thee. Deut 13:5 KJV

They had multiple confrontations concerning the authorities placed over them. God had chosen Moses and Aaron and his house to be priests to the Lord. Some died in these clashes, and the rest were put to shame. The key was that God had the right and the power to put whoever He wants in charge, both in Israel and the nations. He does whatever He pleases, Dan 4:17. Accepting valid authority over themselves is something many in fleshly Israel have rejected all the way through history. In one of the fights, as evidence of God's choice, He had made Aaron's staff to bud, and Israel was commanded to store the staff by the ark of the covenant as a testimony against those who would rebel against God's choices, Num 17:10. Another time,

> And Moses and Aaron gathered the congregation together before the rock, and he said unto them, Hear now, ye rebels; must we fetch you water out of this rock? Num 20:10 KJV

Moses summarized it this way:

> Ye have been rebellious against the LORD from the day I knew you." Deut 9:24 KJV

Also Moses knew the worst was yet to come in Israel's rebellion against both earthly and heavenly authority.

> For I know thy rebellion, and thy stiff neck: behold, while I am yet alive with you this day, ye have been rebellious against the LORD; and how much more after my death? Deut 31:27 KJV

Another unnamed psalmist summarized it this way.

> [7] Our fathers in Egypt did not understand Your wonders;
> They did not remember
> Your abundant kindnesses,
> But rebelled by the sea, at the Red Sea. ...
> [32] They also provoked *Him* to wrath at the waters of Meribah,
> So that it went hard with Moses on their account;
> [33] Because **they were rebellious against His Spirit**,
> He spoke rashly with his lips. ...
> [43] **Many times He would deliver them**;
> They, however, were **rebellious in their counse**l,
> And *so* sank down in their iniquity.
> Psa 106:7, 32-33, 43 NASB (*bold emphasis added*)

Other summaries are given in the psalms.

> [11] Because they rebelled against the words of God,
>   And despised the counsel of the Most High, ...
> [17] Fools, because of their transgression,
>   **And because of their iniquities, were afflicted**.
> Psa 107:11, 17 NKJV (*bold emphasis added*)

> So He brought their days to an end in futility
> And their years in sudden terror. Psa 78:33 NASB

Only the most severe punishments would begin to bring them to their senses.

> ³⁴ When He killed them, then they sought Him,
> And returned and searched diligently for God;
> ³⁵ And they remembered that God was their rock,
> And the Most High God their Redeemer.
> ³⁶ But they deceived Him with their mouth
> And lied to Him with their tongue.
> ³⁷ **For their heart was not steadfast toward Him,**
> Nor were they faithful in His covenant.
> ³⁸ But He, being compassionate, forgave *their* iniquity and did not destroy *them*;
> And often He restrained His anger
> And did not arouse all His wrath.
> ³⁹ Thus **He remembered that they were but flesh,**
> A wind that passes and does not return.
> ⁴⁰ How often they rebelled against Him in the wilderness,
> And grieved Him in the desert. Psa 78:34-40 NASB (*bold emphasis added*)

Little else would stem their stubborn and perverse nature. So it was that **resistance to authority became a signature trait in physical Israel**. This of course is not speaking of the entire nation, but of common distinguishing traits of the Jews. Traits common enough to be repeatedly commented on by their prophets and leaders, and also by outsiders. Most of the time it was just short of outright anarchy, as in Moses' time. On occasion it actually blossomed into anarchy, much to their own hurt and the hurt of the nation. Nevertheless, over and over it became an identifying trait of the Jews, *even to our own time*s. When they could, they tended to oppose and even destroy authority, to exalt themselves individually. After Moses' time, Israel became intensely dissatisfied with God's direct rule over them through the prophets. They wanted a king just as the gentiles had. The prophet Samuel was their leader at this time, and he was very upset with their request. God told Samuel to listen to the people because they had not rejected Samuel, but the Lord their God Himself, 1Sam 8:6-7. Samuel, however, sternly warned the people, reviewing their history and their dominant characteristics.

> ¹⁴ If ye will fear the LORD, and serve him, and obey his voice, and not rebel against the commandment of the LORD, then shall both ye and also the king that reigneth over you continue following the LORD your God: ¹⁵ But if ye will not obey the voice of the LORD, but rebel against the commandment of the LORD, then shall the hand of the LORD be against you, **as *it was* against your fathers.**
> 1Sam 12:14-15 KJV (*bold emphasis added*)

Later when the new king himself led the way in departing from godliness,

Samuel drew a parallel between rebellion against the rule of God and witch-craft and magic. There is a parallel between refusing the rule of God and seek-ing to manipulate the power of other spirits who have also rebelled against God, and the worshipping of their images.

> For rebellion is as the sin of witchcraft, and stubbornness is as iniquity and idolatry. Because thou hast rejected the word of the LORD, he hath also rejected thee from being king. 1Sam 15:23 KJV

The Lord commented on these things through the later prophets. The prophet Isaiah straddled the time when the Northern kingdom of Israel went into captivity, and he died before Judah went into captivity. The prophet asked them,

> ⁵ Why should ye be stricken any more? ye will revolt more and more: the whole head is sick, and the whole heart faint. ... ²⁰ But if ye refuse and rebel, ye shall be devoured with the sword: for the mouth of the LORD hath spoken *it*. ... ²³ Thy princes are rebellious, and companions of thieves: every one loveth gifts, and followeth after rewards: they judge not the fatherless, neither doth the cause of the widow come unto them. Isa 1:5, 20, 23 KJV

> For Jerusalem is ruined, and Judah is fallen: because their tongue and their doings *are* against the LORD, to provoke the eyes of his glory. Isa 3:8 KJV

> ¹ Woe to the rebellious children, saith the LORD, that take counsel, but not of me; and that cover with a covering, but not of my spirit, that they may add sin to sin ... ⁹ That this is a rebellious people, lying children, children *that* will not hear the law of the LORD; Isa 30:1, 9 KJV

The reader should be reminded, these are not the words of an "anti-Semite" propagandist working for the Czar or the Brown Shirts of the 1930's Germany. These are words of the Jew's own prophets, telling the story of the nature of their inbred ungodliness and rebelliousness. There is too much to quote here, but just reading some of Isaiah is a good education in these mat-ters. God says these are not new problems with the Jews.

> Yes, you didn't hear; yes, you didn't know; yes, from of old your ear was not opened: for **I knew that you did deal very treacherously**, and **was called a transgressor from the womb**.
> Isa 48:8 WEB (*bold emphasis added*)

The end of all these things for the Jews was that instead of God giving them grace, God turned against them and truly became their opponent, as He says in promises to all of us in passages like Prov 3:34 and Jas 4:6.

> But they rebelled and grieved His Holy Spirit;
>   So He turned Himself against them as an enemy,

And He fought against them. Isa 63:10 NKJV

" I have stretched out My hands all day long to **a rebellious people,**
Who walk in a way *that is* not good,
According to their own thoughts;"
Isa 65:2 NKJV (*bold emphasis added*)

As the life of Isaiah spanned the fall and captivity of the Northern kingdom Israel, so the prophet Jeremiah's life spanned the fall and the initial phase of the captivity of Judah. Jeremiah tried everything he could to get the stubborn Jews to change and avoid captivity and exile, all to no avail. He too testified of the character of the Jews.

'Like watchmen of a field they are against her round about,
Because she has rebelled against Me,' declares the LORD.
Jer 4:17 NASB (*bold emphasis added*)

But this people has **a defiant and rebellious heart;**
They have revolted and departed.
Jer 5:23 NKJV (*bold emphasis added*)

²⁷ "I have made you an assayer and a tester among My people,
That you may know and assay their way."
²⁸ **All of them are stubbornly rebellious,**
Going about as a talebearer.
They are bronze and iron;
They, all of them, are corrupt. Jer 6:28 NASB (*bold emphasis added*)

For through the anger of the LORD *it* came to pass in Jerusalem and Judah, till he had cast them out from his presence, that Zedekiah rebelled against the king of Babylon. Jer. 52:3 KJV

Again through the prophet Ezekiel, God reviewed their history.

But the house of Israel rebelled against me in the wilderness: they walked not in my statutes, and they despised my judgments, which *if* a man do, he shall even live in them; and my sabbaths they greatly polluted: then I said, I would pour out my fury upon them in the wilderness, to consume them. Ezek 20:13 KJV

So the Lord was sending Ezekiel to preach to Israel, and this was some 800 plus years after Moses. He emphasized the rebellious nature of the Jews.

³ Then He said to me, Son of man, I send thee to the children of Israel, to a rebellious nation that hath rebelled against me: they and their fathers have transgressed against me, *even* unto this very day. ... ⁵ And they, whether they will hear, or whether they will forbear, (for they *are* a rebellious house,) yet shall know that there hath been a prophet among them.

⁶ And thou, son of man, be not afraid of them, neither be afraid of their words, though briers and thorns be with thee, and thou dost dwell among scorpions: be not afraid of their words, nor be dismayed at their looks, though they be a rebellious house. ⁷ And thou shalt speak my words unto them, whether they will hear, or whether they will forbear: for they are most rebellious. Ezek 2:3, 5-7 KJV

But when I speak with thee, I will open thy mouth, and thou shalt say unto them, Thus saith the Lord God; He that heareth, let him hear; and he that forbeareth, let him forbear: for they *are* a rebellious house. Ezek 3:27 KJV

How bad then were these people of the exile? The Lord testified through the mouth of Ezekiel.

'She has rebelled against My judgments by doing wickedness more than the nations, and against My statutes more than the countries that *are* all around her; for they have refused My judgments, and they have not walked in My statutes.' Ezek 5:6 NKJV (*bold emphasis added*)

It can be seen here that even the Gentiles, the *goyim* גּוֹיִם, the nations, know the basics of God's commands, but that Israel has rebelled against God's commands more wickedly than the nations.

Son of man, thou dwellest in the midst of a rebellious house, which have eyes to see, and see not; they have ears to hear, and hear not: for they *are* a rebellious house. Ezek 12:2 KJV

Eyes but not seeing. Ears but not hearing. They were not willing to forsake the pursuit of other gods, not even for the God who actually brought them up from Egypt.

"But they rebelled against Me and were not willing to listen to Me; they did not cast away the detestable things of their eyes, nor did they forsake the idols of Egypt. Then I resolved to pour out My wrath on them, to accomplish My anger against them in the midst of the land of Egypt. Ezek 20:8 (*bold emphasis added*)

Many other of the prophets spoke of these things. Zephaniah is well worth quoting here.

¹ Woe to her who is rebellious and defiled,
The tyrannical city!
² She heeded no voice,
She accepted no instruction.
She did not trust in the LORD,
She did not draw near to her God.
³ Her princes within her are roaring lions,
Her judges are wolves at evening;

They leave nothing for the morning.
⁴ Her prophets are reckless, treacherous men;
Her priests have profaned the sanctuary.
They have done violence to the law. Zep 3:1-4 NASB

Even her "prophets" are "reckless, treacherous men." After the fact, Daniel confessed the sins of the Jews in Dan 9:5:

We have sinned, and have committed iniquity, and have done wickedly, and have rebelled, even by departing from thy precepts and from thy judgments: KJV

With Political Rebellion and Sedition.

So then, is this just a religious thing? Do they just want to do their own thing in church, in the synagogue? No, it was also political, and the results were political. It was the religious rebelliousness and occult leanings which led to the political rebelliousness. Ezra also testifies to these things, recording that men said of Jerusalem,

¹⁵ ... this city *is* a rebellious city, and hurtful unto kings and provinces, and that they have moved sedition within the same of old time: for which cause was this city destroyed. ...
¹⁹ And I commanded, and search hath been made, and it is found that this city of old time hath made insurrection against kings, and *that* rebellion and sedition have been made therein. Ezra 4:15, 19 KJV

After the return from the exile, Nehemiah had this to say about the Jews:

"But they became disobedient and rebelled against You,
And cast Your law behind their backs
And killed Your prophets who had admonished them
So that they might return to You,
And they committed great blasphemies." Neh 9:26 NASB

The Lord speaking through the mouth of the prophet Malachi in the fourth century BC, had this to say to the priests of the post-exilic period:

A son honoureth his father, and a servant his master: if then I be a father, where is mine honour? and if I be a master, where is my fear? saith the LORD unto you, **O priests, that despise my name.** ...
Mal 1:6 KJV (bold emphasis added)

Malachi talks at length about these problems. Naturally, if the priests show no real respect for the Lord, you can imagine the attitudes of most of the people. Malachi says,

Judah has dealt treacherously,
        And an abomination has been committed in Israel and in
        Jerusalem,

> For Judah has profaned
> The LORD'S holy institution which He loves:
> He has married the daughter of a foreign god. Mal 2:11 NKJV

Once again, God was promising judgement within history, if they do not change.

> ⁵ And I will come near to you to judgment; and I will be a swift witness against **the sorcerers**, and against the adulterers, and against false swearers, and against those that oppress the hireling in *his* wages, the widow, and the fatherless, and that turn aside the stranger *from his right*, and fear not me, saith the LORD of hosts. ⁶ For I am the LORD, I change not; therefore ye sons of Jacob are not consumed.
> Mal 3:5-6 KJV (*bold emphasis added*)

So "sorcerers" were part of the mix of evil, well after the first exile and return, and well before the New Testament period. The Jewish historian Josephus in his *Wars of the Jews*, spoke of how after Malachi's time the Jews were delivered into the hands of the Romans.

> Was it not derived from **the seditions that were among our forefathers**, when the madness of Aristobulus and Hyrcanus, **and our mutual quarrels**, brought Pompey upon this city, and when God reduced those under subjection to the Romans, who were unworthy of the liberty they enjoyed? *Wars*, V, 396 (*bold emphasis added*)

Josephus documents more than the Bible does about the petty rebelliousness and general trouble-making which the Jews took with them everywhere they went. Josephus' histories of the first two centuries BC and the first century AD are a good education on these things. These are things which, in fact, did not go away. A Jewish prophet of the first century called the Jews "An evil and adulterous generation" and "an evil generation," and a "faithless and perverse generation."

There is something worth noting here. None of this has the character of national myths. National myths just do not work that way. Take for instance many of the national myths about America. All the common people of the seventeen and eighteen hundreds are viewed as hard-working, freedom loving, and very dedicated Christians. Their leaders were all noble characters of the highest order, and so on. Now don't get me wrong. I am an American, and I love America. America has many good traits and traditions and laws which are well worthy of emulation world wide, and many of these are constantly emulated worldwide. But the myths of national righteousness? Well, they are just myths. For instance, America of the later 1700's and early 1800's had a strong irreligious streak, and a love of alcohol that was almost unbounded. The per capita consumption of alcohol (taken from Federal tax records, not taking into account illegally manufactured alcohol) was about three or four times as high as it is in America today! Some have even called America of that period an "alcoholic nation." Then religion started to turn habits around with some great revivals in the 1820's and 30's. The alcohol abuse was slowly turning around by the time of the Civil War, but even then it was pretty bad, and more than one Civil War general of both the North and the South was relieved of command because they were drunk on the day of battle! All of this and more is easy to confirm by those willing to look. But none of this is part of the national myth. The Old Testament is not some Homeric Ode of better times of valor and fidelity. It is the unvarnished truth of God, a God who acts in history all along, as presented by His prophets, against rebellious and sinful nations. If you want the myths about the Jews, go to a good secular bookstore. You need not go to Scripture. Scripture is a distressing picture of a perverse and obstinate people, who are loved for the sake of some of their faithful ancestors, Rom 11:28.

Again and again we see the fomenting of revolt and meddling with any group with whom they do not agree. These included the Assassins mentioned in Acts 21:38. It clearly extended into the Roman Empire. Gibbon notes,

> "From the reign of Nero to that of Antoninus Pius, the Jews discovered a fierce impatience of the dominion of Rome, which repeatedly broke out in the most furious massacres and insurrections."
> *Decline ...*, Vol 1, Chapter 16, Part 1

This is a part of Jewish history which many current secular "histories" gloss over. This is not about the many fine men and women of Jewish ancestry down through history and even to today. This is about the character of the people overall, as presented in Scripture and in history.

This has only scratched the surface of what is pertinent in history and in the prophets of old. This very clear testimony should not be undervalued. The Jews have made a forte of fomenting seditions and rebellions all the way down through history, and as will be shown, it continues literally to our own day.

Jews Like Gentiles, Like Sodom, to the Lord.

As we come to 1 Samuel 19 and Psalm 59, the house of David ben Jesse has been chosen to bring the Messiah into the world. King Saul, on the other hand, had repeatedly rejected the Word of the Lord, and now has himself been rejected by the Lord. David will clearly be the next king over Israel, and the house of Saul will be deposed. Saul at this point seriously fears David. Saul knows that God has abandoned him. Further, Saul can clearly see that God is blessing David. Envy and jealously have completely taken over Saul's activities. What is more, now Saul instructs his servants to kill David, 1Sam 19:1.

However, Saul's son Prince Jonathan sincerely admires David and is his close friend and supporter and seeks to help him. Jonathan is no Herod the Great. Worldly position and glory is not everything with him. He is not afraid to be demoted if that is God's desire. Jonathan assembles a plan to pin down his father Saul's intentions, and then to warn David, 1Sam 19:3.

Jonathan met with his father the King and pointed out how much David had helped Saul and his kingdom. David had repeatedly taken his life in his own hands to try to help and support Saul's kingdom, 1Sam 19:4-5. Why sin against a man who has helped you so much? Why try to criminally put him to death? Finally Saul listened and repented, and David was once again brought into the king's court; again went to fight on King Saul's behalf and was spectacularly successful, 1Sam 19:6-8.

Then the evil spirit from God returned to afflict Saul. There is not space to discuss all of these factors, but let us just say for now God has His reasons. He uses even the wicked, both men and angels, to accomplish His purposes. David was again playing the harp to soothe the king. Then jealousy, rage, and fear return to Saul. Saul himself tried one more time to personally kill David, and tried to pin David to the wall with a spear, but David escaped.

Then Saul sent men to watch David's house and to capture and kill him. David's wife, who was Saul's daughter Michal, warned David. David's own father-in-law is trying to kill him. Michal then helped David escape.

It was somewhere in this series of events that David wrote the 59th psalm. The introduction of the psalm tells specifically when this psalm was written. "Deliver me from my enemies," David pleads in Psa 59:1. "Save me from the bloodthirsty men. ," Psa 59:2 WEB.

Notice that the men sent to kill David are elite soldiers in Saul's army. They are what moderns probably would call "special operations personnel." No doubt they think they are doing the right thing. They think that whatever the king tells them to do is right for them to do. They are sent to kill David, an honored and decorated soldier in Saul's army, whom the president (the king) now considers his enemy. Men in special operations work often think that anything that they do is right if the proper authorities are behind them, but it can be seen here that is not true. They can commit murder just like ordinary men. Scripture calls these men "workers of iniquity," Psa 59:2 KJV. It is plain then that even special operations personnel on active duty, can do valid fighting for their country, or they can commit murder. There is plenty of reason for soldiers of any stripe to use their head, and refrain from murder.

"They have set an ambush for my life," David says in Psa 59:3 NASB. Literally so. The Medal of Honor winner, the Iron Cross winner, is being staked out for assassination, and it is wrong! Look at Saul to see how quickly power can move men from sensible and modest to monsters. Now Saul reacts in jealousy and envy at one who has done nothing against him. David calls on God to see all of this and to act in his behalf. David, their objective, is innocent. It is just as the apostle James said about what jealousy and selfish ambition can produce.

¹⁴ But if you have bitter envy and self-seeking in your hearts, do not

boast and lie against the truth. [15] **This wisdom** does not descend from above, but *is* **earthly, sensual, demonic**. [16] For where envy and self-seeking *exist*, confusion and every evil thing *are* there.

Jas 3:14-16 NKJV (*bold emphasis added*)

The Greek word used here is quite literally "demonic," *daimoniōdās* δαι-μονιώδης. That well describes the one who is no longer chosen, and who in jealously is not willing to bow to God's will. All of this is nothing like the Jewish prophet John the Baptist, when he was told that Jesus was also baptizing, and that everyone was running to him. Modestly, John pointed out that no one can receive *anything* unless it is given to him from above! "He must increase, and I *must* decrease," Jn 3:26-30 KJV. So where does that leave Saul and his men?

"Punish all the nations," the *goyim* גּוֹיִם, the gentiles of this world, David pleads in Psa 59:5 NASB ("heathen," KJV). But David is describing his would be assassins, and describes them and their master as goyim, as men of the gentiles opposed to God's holy nation. The word for what many call "gentiles" ("heathen," here in the KJV) and the word for "nations" is the same word in Hebrew (likewise in Greek, the word *ethnos* ἔθνος is translated as both nation and gentile, and sometimes as heathen).

Who are these men of the nations? They are men of Israel who are in Saul's army. "Loyal" soldiers of the King of Israel. What are these evil men of the nations like? David speaks of these men as like howling, prowling dogs in the city, looking for someone to devour, Psa 59:6. They are "black ops" ("black operations," illegal operations) personnel of Saul. They are like belching dogs. Their lips are swords, and they think no one notices the evil that they do, Psa 59:7.

But the Lord laughs at the *goyim*, Psa 59:8. In context this includes many of the armies and soldiers of Israel. "For they are not all Israel who are descended from Israel," Rom 9:6 NASB. There is a difference between those who are physically descended from Israel and those who are part of the Israel of God, Psa 73:1. Those who become like vicious dogs are just *goyim* גּוֹיִם, men of the nations, not men of God. These dogs do not share in the glory of God's Holy Israel, so says the Holy Spirit of God, speaking by the prophet David.

Because of the enemy's strength, David has to pin his hopes on the Lord. He cannot escape the assassination bureau's attempts on his own. He must trust in God. Despite his troubles, David is sure God will let him look with victory on his enemies, because, unlike these goyim he trusts in God.

Punish them in a special way, David says. Don't kill them God! That is not the best way. Instead let them stay around and be punished. Let them be like Israel of old. They sinned against the Lord. Not once, but again and again and again, until the Lord was no longer willing to forgive. At that time, God said in Num 14:11-12.

> [11] Then the LORD said to Moses, "How long will these people reject Me? And how long will they not believe Me, with all the signs which I have performed among them? ... [12] I will strike them with the pestilence and disinherit them, and I will make of you a nation greater and mightier than they." NKJV

Moses then pleaded on their behalf, and the Lord listened to Moses' prayer. Yet there was a penalty to be paid. All of those who had seen God's glory and yet had refused to obey would never see the promised land, which is a "type," a symbol of heaven, Num 14:22-24.

Clearly, the Lord is teaching us that not all of physical Israel are heirs of the promises. *The rest are like the nations which perish.* They are treated as though they were just goyim deserving to perish. The result was they just sort of wasted away in the desert until they were all gone!

In a way, that is the process one can see happening with Saul. He was under judgement after departing from the Lord's commands, but ruled a full 42 years and only then was he killed. Sometimes God just lets us waste away in our sins as part of our proper punishment. The penalties for not keeping the Mosaic covenant included such things.

> [28] The LORD shall smite thee with madness, and blindness, and astonishment of heart: [29] And thou shalt grope at noonday, as the blind gropeth in darkness, and thou shalt not prosper in thy ways: and thou shalt be only oppressed and spoiled evermore, and no man shall save thee. Deut 28:28-29 KJV

All of Deuteronomy 28 is pertinent to our subject, both the details of the blessings of submitting to God, and the far more detailed curses of the law. Some of it is very pertinent to our staying "alive," but wasting away in our sins, being the most fitting punishment for us.

> [65] ... the LORD will give you a trembling heart, failing of eyes, and despair of soul. [66] So your life shall hang in doubt before you; and you will be in dread night and day, and shall have no assurance of your life. [67] In the morning you shall say, 'Would that it were evening!' And at evening you shall say, 'Would that it were morning!' because of the dread of your heart which you dread, and for the sight of your eyes which you will see." Deut 28:65-67.

Let them be caught in their pride David says, let them just waste away. David is speaking by inspiration of Saul and his men.

> [11] Do not slay them, or my people will forget;
> Scatter them by Your power, and bring them down,
> O Lord, our shield.
> [12] *On account of* the sin of their mouth *and* the words of their lips,
> Let them even be caught in their pride,

And on account of curses and lies which they utter. Psa 59:11-12 NASB

A Jewish prophet of the first century put it well, God opposes the proud but exalts the humble, Jas 4:6. Plainly, that does not just apply to the nations, as we see in Psalm 59. David says he will sing of God's strength, and will praise Him all the day, in the midst of his troubles.

The same theme can be seen in other places in the prophets. The LORD tells us through the pen of Isaiah:

> "The ox knows its owner
>   And the donkey its master's crib;
>   But Israel does not know,
>   My people do not consider." Isa 1:3 NKJV

Isaiah is speaking to a people who are spiritually dense. Sadly, the truth of these things continue to our own day, as shall be proved. Isaiah says of the Jews,

> [4] Alas, sinful nation,
>   A people laden with iniquity,
>   A brood of evildoers,
>   Children who are corrupters!
>   They have forsaken the LORD,
>   They have provoked to anger
>   The Holy One of Israel,
>   They have turned away backward.
> [5] Why should you be stricken again?
>   You will revolt more and more.
>   The whole head is sick,
>   And the whole heart faints. Isa 1:4-5 NKJV

Isaiah in his time saw the devastations which occurred during the reign of the godly King Hezekiah. The land itself was mainly desolate, with the exception of Jerusalem, which the Assyrians were never able to take. Isaiah speaks of these ruinous attacks and plundering as a down payment on the sins of the Jews.

> Except the LORD of hosts had left unto us a very small remnant, we should have been as Sodom, and we should have been like unto Gomorrah. Isa 1:9 KJV

So what is the real difference between the Jews and Sodom and Gomorrah? The real difference is that God chose to leave some Jewish survivors, so says the prophet Isaiah speaking by the Holy Spirit of God. Then he goes on to address this Jewish Sodom.

> Hear the word of the LORD, ye rulers of Sodom; give ear unto the law of our God, ye people of Gomorrah. Isa 1:10 KJV

Isaiah is addressing the princes and people of the Jews, and it is the word of the LORD. They are the rulers of Sodom. The people are the people of Gomorrah. The LORD goes on and says to the Jews, Who really asked you to trample my courts? Take your worthless sacrifices away. "I cannot endure iniquity and the solemn assembly," the LORD says in Isa 1:13. The Lord pleads with His people to turn around,

> Learn to do well; seek judgment, relieve the oppressed, judge the fatherless, plead for the widow. Isa 1:17 KJV

What then have the Jews become?

> How is the faithful city become an harlot! it was full of judgment; righteousness lodged in it; but now murderers. Isa 1:21 KJV

This speaks not just of immoral Saul and his henchmen, but of the entire nation of the Jews, and this is even before the Messiah comes. What are the Jews? Hear the Word of the LORD: They have become the great harlot of the prophets. They have spiritually become Sodom and Gomorrah to the LORD. They too are just goyim to the LORD, just like the other sinful nations of the world.

The Jews are no better than the rest of us. The Jews, just like the rest of us *goyim*, must repent and turn to their own Messiah; or ... like the rest of us ... bear the burden of their own sins ... forever!

A Penchant For False Prophecy.

In the pursuit of false gods, and the rejection of whatever the Lord God might want them to do, the Jews developed a readiness to invent whatever sort of religion they might desire at this time or that. Sometimes that just involved twisting the Words of God to their own destruction. At other times, it involved inventing new gods, or "words of God," or whatever was "needed." This is first seen full scale in the times of the kings of Israel and Judah, but it has continued all the way down through history. In a way though, it has always been part and parcel of the occult. I mean, if someones says that they are operating by the great power of Satan, and then they use fraud to prove their point, does that mean that they are not really of Satan? By no means! Satanism is really about fraud and lies. So divination and sorcery and their signs and wonders as described in Deuteronomy 13 and Deuteronomy 18 have always had more than a little fabrication to them. Partially this was to make them seem to work, to please the dupe, the golem, be he royal or of the masses.

If possible, the false prophets may even fool the elect. The false prophet in 1Kings 13 first deceives the true prophet of the Lord, and later delivers the truth to him. The true prophets of the Lord often seemed a little strange to people, a little crazy, a little mad. In 2 Kings 9 Elisha sends one of the "sons of the prophets" to anoint Jehu king over Israel. When the process is finished, Jehu comes out and one of his officers asks him, "Is all well? why came this mad fellow to you?" 2Kgs 9:11 NASB. Ezekiel also seemed a little "mad" at times. Acting weird? Strange? This is one of the easier things to fake or exhibit. Soon there were legions of Jews faking inspiration from the times of the kings onward, all through the Middle Ages, and even into our own time. Often they were trying to vindicate their sect or denomination, and since they are sons of the father of lies, they ever flatter their kings. They are often seen in the ruling group of a country. There are 400 such men surrounding the courts of Ahab the king of Israel. They are pretending to speak, not for foreign gods but for the true God of Israel. When Micaiah, a true man of the Lord, tells Ahab the truth, that he will be killed in the coming battle, one of the false prophets comes forward to rebuke him in the name of the LORD God of Israel.

> [24] Now Zedekiah the son of Chenaanah went near and struck Micaiah on the cheek, and said, "Which way did the spirit from the LORD pass from me to speak to you?"
>
> [25] And Micaiah said, "Indeed, you shall see on that day when you go into an inner chamber to hide!"
>
> [26] So the king of Israel said, "Take Micaiah, and return him to Amon the governor of the city and to Joash the king's son; [27] and say, "Thus says the king: 'Put this fellow in prison, and feed him with bread of affliction and water of affliction, until I come in peace.'"
>
> [28] But Micaiah said, "If you ever return in peace, the LORD has not spoken by me." And he said, "Take heed, all you people!"
>
> 1Kgs 22:24-28 NKJV

So the conflict goes on continually even to our own day. Jeremiah said of his day,

> The prophets prophesy falsely,
> And the priests rule on their *own* authority;
> And My people love it so!
> But what will you do at the end of it? Jer 5:31 NASB

For every large Bar Kokhba type figure, Josephus in his *Wars of the Jews*, records a dozen whose follies never really get off the ground. You hear of "Messianic Jews" in modern times rolling off new prophecies by occult type "automatic writing," like those of old, soon to be forgotten when they fail. But not to worry, we can try again, right?

To get a good idea of the range of this sort of foolishness, consult *The Old Testament Pseudepigrapha*, edited by James H. Charlesworth, 1983, 2 Volumes, Hendrickson Publishers. Much of the scholarship on these books is inconclusive. Many of these "scriptures" are by anonymous authors, of fictitious accounts of Bible stories which are almost as bad as a Cecil B. De Mille epic Bible movie. It is overall an endless procession of invented drivel. If a factual statement is made once in Scripture, it is embellished into a book in pseudo-scripture, and given details one would only get otherwise from a Hollywood script writer, raised to the seventh power, then called a revelation fully equivalent to Word of God.

Take the book of Enoch for instance as seen in *Pseudepigrapha*. (I am not saying that the real Enoch never said anything that was recorded, or that the *Pseudepigrapha* book of Enoch authors do not quote or paraphrase some of it, just as they do other Scriptures.) Much of it almost seems like a parody of Scripture. The authors are well versed in Scripture, and it would seem also in some folklore, and some occult lore. "First Enoch" includes a great deal of well-written pseudo-scripture, seemingly using as sources some Scripture, some folklore, some of what one might call primitive scientific observations, and also some occult speculations, fantasies, dreams, and hallucinations, which are all wrapped up into what might appear to some as "the Word of the Lord." It must be admitted that the author(s) often show themselves as intelligent and understanding readers of Scripture, often clearly showing they understand what was said, and they try to emulate some of the writing styles shown in Scripture, in a verbose sort of way. That there may also have been here some genuinely demonic material cannot on first principles be ruled out, but most of it appears to be pure human fabrication. Can it be called it outright lies? As the Messiah has said, the devil is the father of lies!

It is almost like separating fact from fiction in family stories that have been passed down for generations. Especially when some of the stories came through great uncle Charlie, who was well known for "shooting-the-bull," exaggerating or even inventing stories. It is sometimes hard or even impossible to sort out truth from fiction!

The book called First Enoch is full of strange things. Was Enoch's wife's name really Edna? (Meaning "pleasurable" it would seem.) Was it really? Who knows! But there it is in 1Enoch 85:3. But like in the Talmud itself, to separate genuine oral history from invented foolishness is just about impossible, although it is clear some of both are there.

The fact that some false prophet said something smart in 189 BC (or there about), or quoted something from somewhere else, does not necessarily mean that inspired authors are quoting that false prophet. It is clear that the authors of 1 Enoch have picked up, copied or otherwise used sources (including Scripture, perhaps indeed about Enoch) from all over the place. In pages and pages of nonsense, they also wrote some things which are true even from a Scriptural point of view, and perhaps used bits of real history (written or oral) which are otherwise only known from the New Testament, and oh yes, also from the false prophets!

There is a little bit of everything in these things. The so-called "Sibylline Oracles" for instance are a bizarre mixture of pagan and Jewish and Christian beliefs. Not just paradoxes, but also plain old fashioned contradictions. The modern introduction to the Sibylline Oracle Book 11 says,

> "No one would suggest that all this material was composed by the same author at one time. Rather we have an ongoing tradition that was repeatedly updated." *The Old Testament Pseudepigrapha,* Vol. I, pg432

Some of it is no doubt from gentile writers, but in places it has the clear hand of some Jewish authors or editors.

So the felt need to embellish or change or add to Holy Writ has never seemed to completely leave the Jews. If you read some of the legions of books on the Apocrypha or the so-called "lost books of the Bible," or from aliens from other worlds, Jewish authors disproportionately turn up.

Some of the big failures of false prophets have threatened to destroy the very foundations of Judaism within history. So some major changes were made. The lead in false prophecies was often later given to crypto-Jews or gentile shills, so that failures would not reflect so badly on Judaism. This genre of Jewish activity has never really gone away, and we will run into it over and over again in our story.

"You Have Trusted In Your Way," Hosea 10:13c.

The Bible documents many things it does not explain. These things are then left for us to think about. The Jews have for a long time been willing to go well beyond Scripture to do almost anything which they think will help them survive. This is clear in both macro-looks at the Jews, and also micro-looks. I guess the grounds in Scripture for such things go all the way back to Abraham and Sarah who, in their despair of the LORD making good on His promises of a son, concoct their own plan. Their plan was for Abraham to have a child by a slave woman of Sarah's, Hagar. (Who said surrogate mothers was a new thing?) Of course, this experiment with "helping," would seem to be its own refutation. God did not need any help, and at the right time Sarah herself had a child by Abraham, the promised Isaac. All of their "helping" God, really just ended up being trouble for Abraham, Sarah, the slave woman Hagar, and her son Ishmael; and for the conflict over time between the Ishmaelites and the Israelites.

It seems clear that God was teaching the descendants of Abraham the necessity of family purity in the true religion of the Lord. This seems to have been at least part of the reason for God separating Abraham from Ur of the Chaldees. After that separation, Abraham made a point of telling his servant to never take the young Isaac back to the land of Abraham's birth in Genesis 24. That seems to have been at least part of the reason for God firmly separating Israel later from Egypt and commanding "You shall never return that way," Deut 17:16.

The commandments concerning intermarriage with the Canaanites and other religious groups are very specific.

3 "Nor shall you make marriages with them. You shall not give your daughter to their son, nor take their daughter for your son. 4 For they will turn your sons away from following Me, to serve other gods; so the anger of the LORD will be aroused against you and destroy you suddenly." Deut 7:3-4 NKJV

In this case we have both the command and the reason, a very sensible command, understandable in human terms. The evil effects of the violation of these commands can easily be seen in many places in Scripture (and in the modern world), even in the case of one as wise as Solomon in 1 Kgs 11:2-5, who was in his old age seduced into rank paganism by his foreign wives.

Later these very factors will bring upon the Jews one of the largest disasters for the Jewish people in all of history: their conquest by Assyria and Babylon, the desolation of their country, and then being deported *en masse* from their home country to foreign lands. Their playing with other religions ended up compromising their devotion to the one true God and brought God's anger against them. The description given in 2 Kings 17 is the definitive summary of the factors causing their downfall.

Then on their return a strange dualism in the Jewish attitudes arises. On one hand, there are the factors and attitudes illustrated in the book of Nehemiah. Nehemiah is a cup bearer to the Persian King Artaxerxes, a privileged position, a position of trust, a person who would in part be responsible to defend the King against assassination attempts through poisoning. In chapter one Nehemiah is aware of both what triggered the Jews deportation, and also the sorry state of affairs in Judah at this time. No, the Jews had not yet learned much from the conquest and deportations. In Nehemiah chapter two, he took advantage of his position to request leave to to go Jerusalem to organize the rebuilding of the city. Nehemiah received a commission from the king to do these things and went to Jerusalem to superintend the rebuilding of Jerusalem and to try to sort out the mess they were in. Amidst plenty of serious opposition, the walls of Jerusalem were rebuilt. Nehemiah then began addressing the Jewish sins which were hindering their recovery. The Jews were forcing the poorer brethren to mortgage their property and even their children, charging them usury (that is the term used in Nehemiah 5 for one percent interest), and forcing many of their brethren into slavery. Nehemiah forces them to free the enslaved, return confiscated property, and amend their ways. In chapter 13 he restores observation of the Sabbath and addresses their marriages outside of the faith.

25 And I contended with them, and cursed them, and smote certain of them, and plucked off their hair, and made them swear by God, saying, Ye shall not give your daughters unto their sons, nor take their daughters unto your sons, or for yourselves. 26 Did not Solomon king of Israel sin by these things? yet among many nations was there no king like him, who was beloved of his God, and God made him king

over all Israel: nevertheless even him did outlandish women cause to sin. Neh 13:25-27 KJV

I guess you could call this the original hair-pulling contest in church. The Jews themselves can identify with this sort of tenacity in taking positions. Nehemiah commanded them to divorce their foreign wives. At this point in our English Bible the book of Nehemiah is followed by one of the strangest of books of the Bible, the book of Esther, and one of the most curious turns of teaching in all of Scripture.

One has to ask himself at times the purpose for which things are recorded in Scripture. Not everything recorded is approved. Often times the actions of men are recorded for approval, and for imitation. The phrase Jesus often uses for these things are words like "Have you not read in scripture ..." Nonetheless, sometimes the Word of God is simply telling what happened, not approving what was done. For instance in the treachery of Judas or the denying of Christ by Peter during Jesus' trial, or the fornication of Judah with his daughter-in-law Tamar. The reader is not told these are *not* good examples. It is just assumed.

This is a section of Jewish history when big changes are coming. On one hand, these changes bring an adherence to Moses' Law which is sheer formalism and human tradition in the extreme. Further, it often went hand-in-hand with a covert paganism such as Israel had learned in Canaan and Babylon, and certain new factors of duplicity in dealing with her enemies, and of really trusting in themselves and not in God.

"This Magnificent Tradition." The Crypto-Jews.

Esther is one of the central books to help us understand modern Judaism. Among other things, out of it grew the modern feast of Purim (Esther 9). Curiously, the book of Esther does not even mention God, or the name of God (which is *Yahweh / Yehovah* יהוה, which is often translated as "LORD," in small caps, in many of our modern translations). That alone is unique in a library about God: the Bible. Many argue that they can see the hand of God working in the background, but that can also be argued for Samson's keeping company with a prostitute and the conflict which followed, and many other foolish things throughout history.

In the book of Esther, the King of Persia has had a falling out with his wife the queen. The king is advised to divorce her and seek another queen. Now kings down through history have not led normal lives sexually. They were in many ways often the only "rock stars" around, and have been able to cater to their desires as they pleased, and generally speaking have so indulged themselves. Given the nature and inclinations of men, it has generally been too great a temptation to resist. That being said, for self-indulgence it would be hard to find any greater picture of excess than the kings and emperors of the East, even all the way to modern times, and yes, even the kings of ancient Persia.

The Persian king, called Ahasuerus in Esther 1:1, is known as Xerxes in most of our Western history books. He starts his search for a new queen, a competition for the harem, and guess what? A Persian Jew by the name of Mordecai recommends that his beautiful cousin Esther, an orphan, enter the competition! Then we read

> ... Esther was brought also unto the king's house, to the custody of Hegai, keeper of the women. Esth 2:8 KJV

She was transferred to the best place in the harem, but Esther did not make known her people or her kindred, for Mordecai had instructed her that she should not make them known, Esth 2:10.

I cannot help but be inclined to give Esther some slack in these matters. She is a young woman who is misguided, but perhaps after the confrontation with Haman she was able to openly practice her religion. However, many women of the faith, even young ones, in Old Covenant times and New Covenant times, have chosen death over such compromise. Also notice how different this is from ethics taught by and practiced by Jesus. I know as a young man, and a new Christian, I was terribly upset by how much of Jesus teaching seemed to be designed to make someone a standup target, almost as if you had to stand up and say, 'Here I am, take a shot at me.' There are many passages that demand a public and open stand. For instance,

> Therefore do not be ashamed of the testimony of our Lord, nor of me His prisoner, but share with me in the sufferings for the gospel according to the power of God, 2Tim. 1:8 NKJV

Then there are fearful warnings about doing anything less.

> Whosoever therefore shall be ashamed of me and of my words in this adulterous and sinful generation; of him also shall the Son of man be ashamed, when he cometh in the glory of his Father with the holy angels. Mk 8:38 NKJV

It took me some years to realize that I needed to take such a stand in order to become the man I should become, and that God was able to take care of me. Nehemiah did not need to be told these things, nor Moses or David, nor most of the great champions of God of ancient times. Perhaps though, Abraham and Sarah needed such counsel in Genesis chapters 12 and 20, and Isaac and Rebecca in Genesis 26, although in each case God could and did protect them when the ruse was discovered. Perhaps Mordecai and Esther needed such encouragement.

The Part of Our Wrongs in God's Plans.

Some say that God can only use us if we are near perfect, without defect or blemish, but such ideas are not found in Scripture. In fact, the Lord is presented to us as being able to accomplish His plans no matter what we may do. Do we wish to sin and block God's plans? That is pure foolishness.

> [30] *There is* no wisdom nor understanding nor counsel against the LORD.
> [31] The horse is prepared against the day of battle: but safety *is* of the LORD. Prov 21:30-31 KJV

Or such passages as

> I know that, whatsoever God doeth, it shall be for ever: nothing can be put to it, nor any thing taken from it: and God doeth it, that *men* should fear before him. Ecc 3:14 KJV

And again,

> No weapon that is formed against thee shall prosper; and every tongue *that* shall rise against thee in judgment thou shalt condemn. This *is* the heritage of the servants of the LORD, and their righteousness is *is* me, saith the LORD. Isa 54:17 KJV

You can not prove from Abraham or Isaac or Solomon that God's commands on marriage need improvement, or from any Old Testament saint that hiding our religion has some special virtue. There *are* higher laws that take precedence over lower laws. The supreme law is not survival, but the love of God! Much less can be said for a speculative marrying of "the enemy" so that you may be able to influence later events.

When the Lord uses a wrongdoer to accomplish His purposes, the people involved are still in the end punished for their wrongs. Their evil intentions are turned to God's purposes, but they are held responsible for evil aims. This can be seen in Scripture throughout. For instance, in Isaiah 10 it talks about the role of evil Assyria in the conquering of nations, and the prophets reveal to us that Assyria is accomplishing God's plans: the destruction of evil nations. However this is not anything for which the Assyrian's should take pride. Instead, the Lord says,

> [5] "Woe to Assyria, the rod of My anger
>   And the staff in whose hand is My indignation.
> [6]   I will send him against an ungodly nation,
>   And against the people of My wrath
>   I will give him charge,
>   To seize the spoil, to take the prey,
>   And to tread them down like the mire of the streets.
> [7]   Yet he does not mean so,
>   Nor does his heart think so;

But *it is* in his heart to destroy,
And cut off not a few nations. Isa 10:5-7 NKJV

Look at the picture which we have here. Assyria has in her heart considerable murder, treachery and looting. She is a godless nation and hardly realizes these things are in her heart. For sure, we may not realize the evil which often lurks deep down inside of us. No wonder that Scripture does not encourage us to trust our own heart. Rather, "He that trusteth in his own heart is a fool: but whoso walketh wisely, he shall be delivered." Prov 28:26 KJV.

As you go further into Isaiah 10 all of Assyria's bragging is seen as empty. She is just a tool whom, because of her wickedness, the Lord is using to punish wicked men, and when God is done with her, when Assyria has served her purposes, then the Lord will in turn take care of her.

¹⁵ Shall the ax boast itself against him who chops with it?
Or shall the saw exalt itself against him who saws with it?
As if a rod could wield *itself* against those who lift it up,
Or as if a staff could lift up, *as if it were* not wood!
¹⁶ Therefore the Lord, the Lord of hosts,
Will send leanness among his fat ones;
And under his glory
He will kindle a burning
Like the burning of a fire.
¹⁷ So the Light of Israel will be for a fire,
And his Holy One for a flame;
It will burn and devour
His thorns and his briers in one day. Isa 10:15-17 NKJV

So yes, Assyria is wicked; and yes, she is used by the Lord, and yet she will still be held accountable for her wickedness and punished for the evil of her heart when God is through using her. When it discusses the death of Jesus Christ, the Messiah of the Old Testament, it says that the Jewish leaders and the gentiles were fulfilling "those things which God foretold by the mouth of all His prophets," Acts 3:18 NKJV. Does that make them any less guilty? Hardly, for, "woe unto that man by whom the Son of man is betrayed!" Mtt 26:24 KJV. So God is like the master chess player who can turn the move of the most cunning adversary into something for His benefit, and still in the end hold the adversary accountable for the malice and evil in his heart. God is fully capable and willing to use even evil deeds to accomplish what He desires, although in the end He does hold us accountable for our sins. It is repentance, a change of mind about our sins, that works a great change, 1Jn 1:8-10.

Esther proves to be pivotal in a crisis which later erupts, and as the story unfolds she is able to deliver the Jews from impending catastrophe, even gains approval for them to loot, and kill 75,000 of their enemies, Esth 9:15-17!

And Big Changes Among the Jews

Rabbi Louis Finkelstein in his book *The Pharisees, The Sociological Background of Their Faith*, Jewish Publication Society of America, 1940-5700, Philadelphia, comments in Volume I on the Book of Esther:

> "... the Book of Esther confirms all the more effectively the other evidence of the lack of true religious spirit and trust in God among the pre-Maccabean nobility. ... these patrician land owners believed not in piety and devotion, but in prudence and achievement." pg 219

Amen! But this slipping away into hiding is an age-long thing. In no way did it begin with the Marranos of Spain, or 19th century European Jews. Suetonius mentions that Domitian despised this in the Jews, because Jews of that day would often pose as gentiles to avoid extra taxes. The truth is that they have continually acted as people who have something to hide. This can be seen in many things. For instance, their tendency to write the native language of a land in Hebrew characters.

> "... no matter what the language they use—Hebrew, Arabic, Persian, Spanish, Greek, and even Yiddish—they are written in Hebrew letters." *A Historical Atlas of the Jewish People*, General Editor Eli Barnavi, Schocken Books, NY, 1992, Hachette Literature, pg 90

This is something seen throughout history, leading in some cases even to a third sort of language, like Yiddish. Yiddish, which if I may be allowed to over simplify, is German written backwards with Hebrew letters, and with a sprinkling of words from both Hebrew and other sources. Most European languages are written in a variation of Roman or Greek characters. Hebrew characters, and the Hebrew writing being from right to left, would be enough to foil most gentile attempts to "read their mail," so to speak. Then if you throw in a few code words and perhaps some Jewish lingo, then you have something virtually indecipherable to the nations. So secure that according to historian Nial Ferguson, most of the early Rothschild business correspondence is still secure against most historians, two centuries later, *The House of Rothschild, Money's Prophets, 1798-1848*, Viking, NY, 1998, pg 29. Even so, why? Business secrets? Or it might lead to a hostile reaction? (And this is not just about "orthodox" Jewish practices.) *A Historical Atlas of the Jewish People*, calls this "The custom of concealing texts ..." and speculates on the cause of the "custom," pg 90. Again, these are adaptations to foreign cultures which are not common in history.

The Rise of the Crypto-Jew.

I would be an remiss, if I did not take note of the astonishing depth that such strategies have given the Jews in intelligence matters. Depth that can hardly otherwise be matched ... except by the Lord our God's ability to turn the hearts and souls of men, even the most wicked, to suit His purposes. Here we see an age arise of what the Jews themselves often call "crypto-Jews," that is to say, Jews under cover, hidden Jews, or more innocently, simply Jews who are not noticed.

The phrase "this magnificent tradition," is taken from Jewish historian Cecil Roth's book, *A History of the Marranos*, Shoken Books, NY, Fourth Edition, 1932, pg 297. It refers there to the traditions of Jews going "underground," of Jews posing as gentiles, in order to gain an advantage for the Jews. According to Roth "Crypto-Judaism, in one form or another, is as old as the Jew himself." Roth, *The Morranos*, pg 1. As was already pointed out from Scripture, that is in fact literally true. Roth then pointed out that a Jew could validly save his life by any means, but murder, incest, or idolatry. He is clearly speaking of validity in Jewish tradition, not Scripture.

There is another factor that has aided in these things: the diaspora, the dispersion of the Jews all over the world. This ancient Greek term for dispersing something has been used by the Jews for themselves, and is seen in passages like Jn 7:35 (*diaspora* διασπορά, is the Greek word for dispersion). They have become part of every nation, tribe and tongue on the earth, quite often without losing their identity as Jews. So what we are seeing in the book of Esther is the appearance of a "hidden" arm of Juda-

אוֹטֵנְטֵה טְרִי

אֵין נַזָאִיאִי אִינֵלְצֵסְטִי נַזָאִי פְּיַיו קִי טוּטִי לִי
לִינְגְּוַאִי סַנְטִיפִּיבֶּכְטִי נַזָאִי נִילִי קוֹבֵּנְמֵיֶנְטִי
טוֹאִיאִי אַפְּרֵיסִיבֵּסְטֵי נַזָאִירִי נוֹסְטְרוֹ זָאֵלוֹ
סִירְזוִיזִיאוֹ טוֹאוֹ אִי לוֹנוּבִּי טוֹאוֹ נְרַאֵנִיאִיסַן־
טוֹסוֹפְרֵירִינַזָאִי קִיאַבְּסָטִי אִי דְּיִיסְטִי זָבֵנוֹאִי
רוֹמְבֵּית בֵּית נוֹסְטְרוֹ אִין אַבּוֹרִי . סַבֵּיטִי
פִּיר רְפוֹסַטְיֵנְטוֹ אִי טִינְפּוֹרַאלִי פִּיר אלְנְרֵיעֵי
אִי פֵּסְטִי אֵי טִינְפּוֹרַאלִי פִּיר אַלֵינְרֵיעֵי לַדִירִי
רֵ־לוֹ סַבֵּיטוֹ קֵוִיסוֹ אִי לַדִירִי לַפִּיסְטַרֵד רִי
לאֵצִימִי קֵוִיסְטוֹ טִינְפּוֹדִי לַלִיבִּירְטַדִי נוֹסְטֵרַרֵח
וֹזֵקוֹל־לוֹ סַנְטוֹ זָארִיקוֹרְדוֹ אַלוֹ זֵיסִיר־־יזִי דִי
מֵצְרִים :

דִּית נוֹסְטְרוֹ אֵידִית דִּילִי פַּטְרִי נוֹסְטְרִי
סַלֵנְהַאִי וֵינִנָה אִי יוֹנְיִיאִי סִיאַה
וִידוֹטוֹ אִי סִיאַה פְּיִיאֵינוֹטוֹ אֵי סִיאַה אִינְטִיסוֹ
אִי סִיאַה רְוֵזִיטָאטוֹ אִי סִיאַה אַרִינְקוֹרַדוֹ
לוֹ אַרִינְקוֹרְדוֹ נוֹסְטֵר־־רוֹ אֵי רֵ־לוֹ אַרִינְקוֹרְדוֹ
דִי לִי פַּטְרִי נוֹסְטְרִי לוֹ אַרִינְקוֹרְדוֹ דִי יְרוּשָׁלַם

A Jewish prayer in Italian, but printed iwith Hebrew characters, Bologna, Italy, 1538. As shall be shown, sometimes even religious texts carried sentiments which were bitterly and despitefully against Christianity, or all other nations. Thus the habit to try to conceal everything they could.

ism that parallels the public existence of Judaism. Jews from this time forward often become chameleons: in Persian pagan society they appear as Persian pagans, among Mohammedans as Mohammedans, among Christians as Christians,

without ever exposing their true loyalties except under necessity. These are to-gether very unique reactions to the deportations of the Assyrians and Babyloni-ans, without parallel among the subject peoples of the east. I had to laugh when I read the name chosen by a Jewish con-artist of the last century. He chose for a last name a word meaning "a mirror" in another language. I thought, how ap-propriate, because wherever they have gone, the Jews have become mirrors of whatever they find, a hopefully faithful reflection of their hosts, without really becoming part of their hosts. What a swing vote they have become in whatever has happened. This often became an occasion for misunderstanding the Jews by the naive.

But is it Right to Hide Your Faith?

Nevertheless we come back to the Law of Moses and God's commands to not intermarry with unbelievers. There is not even a hint that Israel should sneak a good-looking Jewish girl into the harem of Pharaoh king of Egypt, into the harem of the king of Assyria, or into the harem of Nebuchadnezzar king of Babylon, so to speak, "just in case." Notice that this mindset is completely at variance with the point of view of Nehemiah in his work to reestablish Jerus-alem, and definitely couldn't be proved as "good" or "right" by the Law of Moses. Should there really be a Christianity which pretends that it does not know or serve the Lord God? Such is unknown in Scripture. A Christian may indeed run to save his life. One Jewish author commented on those saints of the Old Testament of whom it says,

> [37] They were stoned, they were sawn asunder, were tempted, were slain with the sword: they wandered about in sheepskins and goatskins; being destitute, afflicted, tormented; [38] (Of whom the world was not worthy:) they wandered in deserts, and *in* mountains, and *in* dens and caves of the earth. Heb 11:37-38 KJV

Ah yes, all these things they did, but did they pretend that they did not know God to save their skin? Was that an approved device for survival when all else "failed"? Or was it to die rather than deny the Lord who would deliver them? Surely denial was not the view point of Shadrach, Meshach and Abed-nego in Dan 3:16-18. It was not their viewpoint to "fake" the worship of a Baby-lonian image or a so called "Christian" image in order to secure the "survival" of Moses' religion, and the escape of the Jews from extermination. Rather it was to stand firm no matter what. It can be seen from Daniel 3 that God did visibly approve their faith as authentic, and all of this was in the same exile that Esther was later still enduring. Similarly Jesus taught,

> But when they persecute you in this city, flee ye into another: for verily I say unto you, Ye shall not have gone over the cities of Israel, till the Son of man be come. Mtt 10:23 KJV

I cannot help but cringe at some of the ladies Bible classes that seem to promote Esther as a model for young ladies, even though I would be the first to acknowledge that sometimes God uses unlikely instruments to accomplish His purposes. Many, including myself, have had to rethink the significance of the book in instructing Christians. Others first asked me, when was the last time you urged the most beautiful girl in your family to join the harem of a religious adversary, "just in case." Perhaps it is good that many have missed the point of the story, but the Jews did not. I can only shudder in horror as I think of how many young ladies and young men have been sacrificed in such operations down through the centuries. Nero's "wife and mistress, the beautiful Poppaea," was a Jewess and had interceded with Nero on behalf of the Jews (Gibbon's *Decline and Fall of the Roman Empire*, Vol 2, Chapter 16, Part 2). Imagine! Later she was kicked to death by Nero while she was pregnant with his child. Weep you Jewish mothers, who have seen your children so ill used!

Righteousness has different supports and in the long run stronger supports. The LORD of Hosts is His Name! The alternative of course is to give up your own ways and trust the Lord, and "Be faithful until death, and I will give you the crown of life." Especially from Esther forward, this does not seem to be the dominant Jewish mindset.

Viewing Jewish "Assimilation" as a Weapon.

It involves:

- A trusting in themselves and their own plans, which is very much in contrast to trusting the Lord God which was continually preached by the prophets.

- An expertise and depth in what the intelligence agencies call "HUMINT" (or "human intelligence"), that is literally without parallel in all of human history.

In Esther it is plain that "assimilation" was a theological weapon of great power, and one which came to receive the approval of the rabbis. Then did we forget to notice what Purim is really all about? It is about the killing of seventy-five thousand gentiles, Esth 9:16.

Then comes an era of what might call "covert operations" in what is developing into modern Judaism. From this time, the increase of clandestine activities between the Jews and other peoples and especially any potential adversary becomes a signature value, and one definitely seen in Scripture. These are things rarely mentioned in gentiles histories, but they still pop up on the peripheries, and the historical specialists are aware of these things in their domains, yet without having overall perspective. In this way also the Jews were often ideally suited in the world to help whoever they wanted (including themselves) and have a tendency to come out on the winning side. I cannot help but bring to mind Napoleon's famous dictum, and I paraphrase, "The spy is a natural trait-or." Here is great advantage, and also great danger. In international relations for instance, you often cannot help one without hurting another. So Will Durant comments on the English Jews during the late 1700's.

> "Several prominent Jews accepted conversion to Christianity— Sampson Gideon the banker, David Ricardo, Isaac Disraeli the author. The last, besides fathering the incomparable Benjamin Disraeli ..."
> Durant, *The Age of Napoleon*, MJF Books, NY, 1975, pg 360

Benjamin Disraeli of course later became prime minister of Britain. Of their influence during the conflicts with France, Durant writes.

> "The long experience of the Jews in banking and their family connections across frontiers, enabled them to come to the aid of the British government in the Seven Years War and the long duel with France."
> Durant, *The Age of Napoleon*, pg 360-361

It is important note that these things are almost always figured out in the end. The "losers" in these trades have had the tendency to become what the Jews like to call "anti-Semitic." These opportunities to play enemies against each other have frequently been temptations too great to resist, but twenty-four hundred years of clever schemes in commerce, religion, and politics has continually kept them right on the edge of serious trouble, or sometimes in the middle of serious trouble, and always scrambling to keep their balance, as the Jews themselves have noted. So along with these unique reactions to the ancient deportations, have come some unique abilities to wear out their welcome. Later this study will return to the story of the crypto-Jew, but you can clearly see its modern beginnings in the Bible, in the book of Esther. So it has to be asked,

What then is the place of the book of Esther?

What is its rhyme or reason for the faith? It is at its root divergent not only from the great mass of Scripture, but even from the roughly contemporary Ezra and Nehemiah and Daniel. Perhaps it is this: to document what Rabbi Finkelstein noted, a shift away from trusting in God and His plans, and care; to the trusting of the Jews in themselves. The prophet Jeremiah commented on trusting in men, either themselves or others.

> [5] Thus saith the LORD; Cursed be the man that trusteth in man, and maketh flesh his arm, and whose heart departeth from the LORD. [6] For he shall be like the heath in the desert, and shall not see when good cometh; but shall inhabit the parched places in the wilderness, *in* a salt land and not inhabited. [7] Blessed *is* the man that trusteth in the LORD, and whose hope the LORD is. [8] For he shall be as a tree planted by the waters, and *that* spreadeth out her roots by the river, and shall not see

when heat cometh, but her leaf shall be green; and shall not be careful in the year of drought, neither shall cease from yielding fruit. [9] The heart is deceitful above all things, and desperately wicked: who can know it? Jer 17:5-9 KJV

Then one looks for the Jewish attitudes about these things. How do they treat the subject of crypto-Jews? First, let it be recognized that it is a sensitive subject to them. By and large they do not discuss the subject with gentiles. Between themselves they are more candid, but it is still a carefully discussed matter. Respected Jewish historian Cecil Roth, while very pro-Jewish, militantly so when he thinks it is necessary, discusses the subject very openly, as a subject that a serious historian cannot really avoid without doing violence to the records. Further, Roth is obviously very proud of this tradition. The older (19th century) Jewish historian Heinrich Graetz of Germany, on the other hand, while likewise very pro-Jewish, and again, very militantly so when he thinks it is necessary, sparingly uses only the term "secret Jew." He seems to avoid the subject of Esther. When he deals with it, one runs across passages like:

> "To the secret Jews of Hamburg there belonged at that time the beloved and much sought physician, Rodrigo de Castro (born about 1560 at Lisbon, died 1627 or 1628)," *History of the Jews*, Vol 4, pg 686

It is to this day a tender subject because of on one hand the great secret influence this has often given the Jews, and also, perhaps critically today, on the other hand, the tremendous losses of Jews to the gentiles, permanently. That is to say, there were ***many* Jews who "assimilated" in truth, and formally and forever abandoned Judaism and the Jews, and never looked back**. This tendency to lose so many of their crypto-Jews through assimilation strikes sheer terror into the hearts of many leaders and thinkers of the Jews. The threat is that the Jews might be completely extinguished in history through drifting away. So "assimilation" has very much proved to be a double-edged weapon. As it is written:

Whoever digs a pit will fall into it,

And he who rolls a stone will have it roll back on him.

Prov 26:27 NKJV

Then a series of breaks in continuity begin to appear in Judaism.

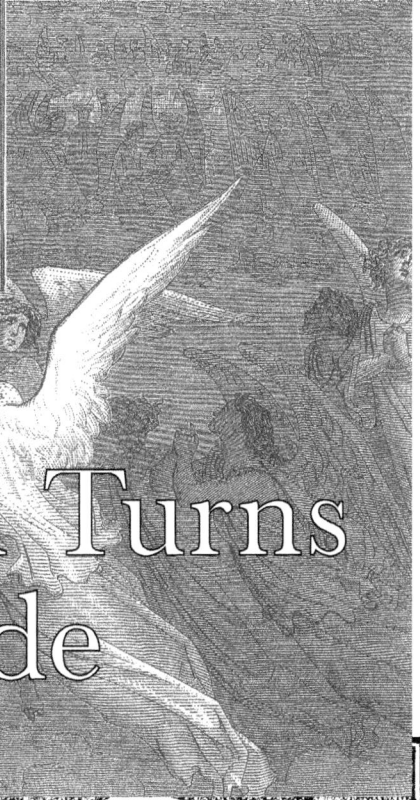

II. Israel Turns Aside

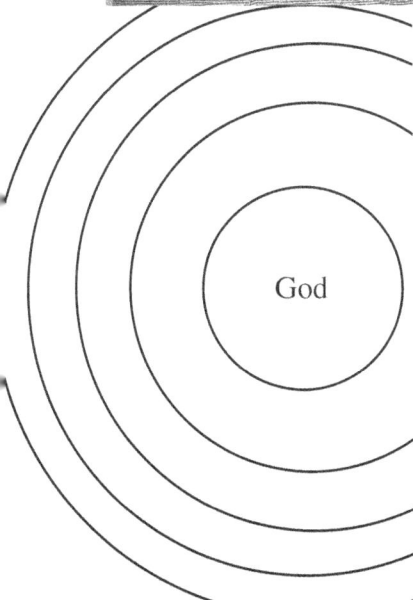

God

"For I know your rebellion and your stubbornness; behold, while I am still alive with you today, you have been rebellious against the LORD; how much more, then, after my death?" Deut 31:27 NASB

Moses Down, Asherah Rises

It was pointed out at the beginning of our story, the call of Abraham, and the nurturing of a special people in the Lord, who were from the first intended to draw mankind toward a purer worship of the One True God and away from the demonic false gods which abound in our world, both then and now. However the Jewish people throughout history have had ample pagan tendencies. A couple of factors contributed to this.

The first difficulty was that paganism was already firmly in place in many of the hearts and minds of the people that originated from Abraham. It was mentioned how false gods were still among household goods of Abraham's grandson Jacob. It has also been shown that even hundreds of years later, in the wilderness, while seeing amazing things, and trying to follow and trust the Lord, there were still hidden in their tents "Sikkuth your king and Kiyyun, your images, the star of your gods which you made for yourselves." Amos 5:26 NASB. They might have been kept around, you might say, "just in case" these gods were "needed." Moses noted, as was showed you earlier, that

> "They sacrificed to demons, not to God,
> To gods they did not know,
> To new gods, new arrivals
> That your fathers did not fear. " Deut 32:17 NKJV

Being perverse and stubborn, and their inclination to accept direction from *no one*, not even the Lord, was another factor at work among these descendants of Abraham. These are not my words, but the descriptive terms which are repeatedly used by the prophets of God to describe Israel. This is spoken of in Scripture from one end to the other. Moses put it as succinctly as anyone.

> [5] "They have acted corruptly toward Him,
> **They are not His children**, because of their defect;
> **But are a perverse and crooked generation**. ...
> [20] "Then He said, 'I will hide My face from them,
> I will see what their end *shall be*;
> **For they are a perverse generation**,
> Sons in whom is no faithfulness. Deut 32:5, 20 NASB (*bold emphasis added*)

Just plain old "cuss-ed stubbornness" it would have been called in the American Old South. Some were faithful but the majority were not. Joshua and others tried to persuade them to be faithful, but again and again they refused. Deut 32:5 (above) puts it as clearly as any passage. *They were not really God's children because of their defect!*

Their proposed faithfulness, in any account, was short-lived. First there were lapses in their duty to fully occupy the land, Judges 1. Soon it was to be said,

> [11] And the children of Israel did evil in the sight of the LORD, and served Baalim: [12] And they forsook the LORD God of their fathers, which brought them out of the land of Egypt, and followed other gods, of the gods of the people that were round about them, and bowed themselves unto them, and provoked the LORD to anger. [13] And they forsook the LORD, and served Baal and Ashtaroth.
>
> Judg 2:11-13 KJV

Baal (*Baal* בַּעַל, meaning master, in the sense of absolute master or lord) was the male deity. Ashtaroth was the female deity, and is often viewed as being another name for the so called "great goddess," who in other passages is called Asherah, or in Egypt Isis. *The Hebrew Aramaic Lexicon of the Old Testament*, Koehler and Bumgarner, 2000 (HALOT) describes her under Ashtaroth (*ashtoret* עַשְׁתֹּרֶת) as the "Canaanite goddess of fertility and warfare" and mentions a correspondence to Astarte. Brown, Driver and Briggs *Hebrew English Lexicon of the the Old Testament* (BD&B) says of Ashtaroth that she is an "ancient Semitic goddess," who has a male counterpart in various countries **and seems to be identified with "various local goddesses ...** as Canaanitish deities." (*bold emphasis added*). The gods and goddesses of the nations often seemed to overlap, or a deity would have one name in one nation and another name in other places. There would often be local variations in description, theol-

Baal as a Sun god.

ogy and worship, but a general essential agreement. The English reader can easily see these things working when comparing the variations and similarities between the Greek and Roman gods.

Ashtaroth/Asherah (if I may be permitted this association) is what we would probably call "mother nature." She was often associated with trees, and so trees were often planted in honor of her (the KJV generally translates *Asherah* as "groves"). HALOT cites Asherah *ashera* אֲשֵׁרָה as "consort of El and mother of the gods," and says we should consult "the Egyptian myth of Astarte." BD&B

calls her,

> "Ashera ... a. a Canaanitish goddess of fortune & happiness; having prophets ... an image ... b. a symbol of this goddess, a sacred tree or pole set up near an altar 1K 16[33]. ... Pl. [plural, nf] asherot אֲשֵׁרוֹת. the goddess Ju 37. b. sacred trees or poles 2Ch 19[3] ..."

Others call her a Phoenician goddess of love. These all seem to be overlapping or *associated* names of goddesses. Putting it in plain English, it might be well to consider these as various names for the same demons. This is perhaps an over simplification to make the overall situation clear. So Moses commanded,

> "You shall not plant for yourself any tree, as a wooden image, near the altar which you build for yourself to the LORD your God." Deut 16:21 NKJV

It seems that Asherah was often represented in a wooden pole (or what might be called a totem pole) carved in a seductive image of her. The worship of Ashtaroth or Asherah was often associated with ritual fornication and prostitution in which the god-

An image of Astarte from nearby Phoenicia.

dess brought blessings in productivity. These things are reflected in Scripture in passages like 1Kgs 15:11-13 about King Asa of Judah:

> [11] Asa did what was right in the sight of the LORD, like David his father. [12] He also put away the male cult prostitutes from the land and removed all the idols which his fathers had made. [13] He also removed Maacah his mother from *being* queen mother, because she had made a horrid image as an Asherah; and Asa cut down her horrid image and burned *it* at the brook Kidron. NASB

Then began a cycle which continues to this day. God would hold out His hands to His people. They would change a little but despise His offers. Then God would send punishments so perhaps they might turn around. They would change a little, but again despise His offers. This cycle could and did continue ... even to this day. When Gideon destroyed the altar to Baal, and cut down the Asherah pole beside it, the Israelites of his city were angry.

> [29] And they said one to another, Who hath done this thing? And when they enquired and asked, they said, Gideon the son of Joash hath done this thing. [30] Then the men of the city said unto Joash, Bring out thy

son, that he may die: because he hath cast down the altar of Baal, and because he hath cut down the grove that *was* by it. Judg 6:29-30 KJV

To the pure, good, and true God, the LORD Yehovah, as a group they paid lip service. To the mother nature "gods" they gave their heart felt devotion, often covertly, but sometimes, as has just been seen, openly. A little later,

> And the children of Israel did evil again in the sight of the LORD, and served Baalim, and Ashtaroth, and the gods of Syria, and the gods of Zidon, and the gods of Moab, and the gods of the children of Ammon, and the gods of the Philistines, and forsook the LORD, and served not him. Judg 10:6 KJV

When the faithful prophet Samuel was urging the Israelites of the 11th century BC to repent, he said.

> ... If ye do return unto the LORD with all your hearts, then put away the strange gods and Ashtaroth from among you, and prepare your hearts unto the LORD, and serve him only: and he will deliver you out of the hand of the Philistines. 1Sam 7:3 KJV

A little later, to secure the kingdom and bring greater faithfulness, the Lord allowed a human king. First Saul was appointed, but later proved unfaithful. Then David was selected, but had not yet been seated by the Lord. Saul at this point knows that God has abandoned him and has said that He will terminate Saul's kingdom. Further, Saul can clearly see that God is blessing David, and envy and jealously have completely taken over Saul's activities. Earlier, Saul instructed his servants to kill David, 1Sam 19:1. They were assassins from Saul, but when they come, David's wife (Saul's daughter Michal) makes excuses for David—saying he is sick. Then a strange thing is seen, knowing the context of the story.

> Michal took the teraphim, and laid it in the bed, and put a pillow of goats' hair at the head of it, and covered it with the clothes. 1Sam 19:13 WEB

Evidently Michal shows them the idol, lying covered up in bed, as if it were David, 1Sam 19:14. Plainly, along with some very good things, some evil religion was still lingering in Israel. There is in the house of Michal, Saul's daughter, and of David, the chosen man after God's own heart, an idol. You cannot tell from this story whether it was David's or Michal's or something just left in the house when David first started living there, and which they have not had time to destroy. This idol is large. The size of a man of that time in Palestine, so perhaps five feet tall. This idol is called a *teraphim* הְּרָפִים. The first teraphim seen in Scripture is in Gen 31:19, when Rachel stole a smaller sized idol from her dad. Later we saw a teraphim in Judg 17:5 when the priest Micah made an idol. Then when the prophet Samuel condemns idolatry in 1Sam 15:23, the word he used for idolatry is teraphim. In our story David's wife makes excuses, and David himself escaped, 1Sam 19:17-18. Even so, here is another story which illustrates how bad the moral situation in Israel really was. Idols were all around, even among God's people.

There is much more to tell from Kings and Chronicles and the prophets, but perhaps Hosea's marriage well illustrates the depths to which Israel has repeatedly sunk.

The Prophet Marries A Prostitute.

Hosea was a prophet for about sixty or so years, from the time of Uzziah, and all the way to the first years of Hezekiah, Hos 1:1. It tells us,

> When the LORD began to speak by Hosea, the LORD said to Hosea:
> "Go, take yourself a wife of harlotry
> And children of harlotry,
> For the land has committed great harlotry
> By departing from the LORD." Hos 1:2 NKJV

It clearly says "prostitute" in the NET Bible. It says a wife of "harlotry" in the NASB, and in the NKJV. It says to take "a wife of whoredoms" in the KJV, that is a wife involved in whoredom. Then it says to have children by harlotry! The Hebrew word that is used here is the word *zanah* זָנָה. The NIV says an adulterous wife. Now the word *zanah* can be used to mean merely an immoral person, someone who sleeps with many people, a promiscuous person. Those who are sexually wild. It also seems to be used of a prostitute, someone who so-called "loves" for money.

When the sons of Israel got really angry about the seduction of their sister, they said, "Should he deal with our sister as with an harlot?" Gen 34:31 KJV, and the Hebrew word is *zanah*. A little later on when Judah went to what he thought was a prostitute, it says "When Judah saw her, he thought her to be an harlot; because she had covered her face." Gen. 38:15 KJV. Again the Hebrew word is the word *zanah*. It later calls her a "temple prostitute" or literally a "holy woman" (*qidesha* קְדֵשָׁה) in Gen 38:21 NASB, because that was how she was dressed. Many pagan religions did have their own prostitutes for "worship." *Zanah* is also the word used for Rahab the harlot. It says there, "they went and came into the house of a harlot (literally, "a woman harlot" *isha zanah* וְאִשָּׁה זוֹנָה) "named Rahab, and lodged there." Jos 2:1 KJV. Why then would the Lord command such a thing as marrying a harlot to His prophet Hosea?

"The land commits flagrant harlotry forsaking the Lord."

The land in Hos 1:2 seems to indicate the land of Israel. In Hos 7:1-5 Hosea calls the king of Israel "our king." So it is the northern kingdom of Israel that is committing harlotry against the Lord.

It is well known that in pagan religions in the ancient world, some of them engaged in various forms of fornication as part of worship, especially of certain gods. So when the women of Moab invited the men of Israel to worship with them, all at the false prophet Balaam's suggestion, it says, "the people began to commit harlotry with the women of Moab," Num. 25:1 NKJV. Paul mentions this as a warning against fornication, 1Cor 10:7-8. Religious fornication is mentioned in other passages, such as in Leviticus 20.

> ⁵ Then I will set my face against that man, and against his family, and will cut him off, and all that go a whoring after him, to commit whoredom with Molech, from among their people. ⁶ And the soul that turneth after such as have familiar spirits, and after wizards, to go a whoring after them, I will even set my face against that soul, and will cut him off from among his people. Lev 20:5-6 KJV

God is sometimes explicitly, and more often implicitly, viewed as the husband of Israel. Going to other religions is being unfaithful to God, is committing harlotry against God, spiritual adultery, Ex 34:15-16 and the above. As we have seen, worshipping these other gods often did involve actual harlotry, religious prostitution.

It was with the goat demons that they often played the harlot, Lev 17:7 NASB. "The devils" it calls them in the KJV. The Lord foretold that Israel would turn to these things after Moses' death.

> And the LORD said unto Moses, Behold, thou shalt sleep with thy fathers; and this people will rise up, and go a whoring after the gods of the strangers of the land, whither they go to be among them, and will forsake me, and break my covenant which I have made with them. Deut 31:16 KJV

Not all of it seems to imply literal fornication with foreign gods, but much of it was literal. Israel was unfaithful with an ephod Gideon made, and it may or may not have included literal immorality, but it was definitely spiritual unfaithfulness to God, Judg 8:27. This went on and on. *They were in essence married to God, and worshipping another god was spiritual adultery.* **Israel was whoring against God!**

So Hosea took the harlot Gomer as a wife, Hosea 1:3. It seems to be talking about an actual woman, a woman who might have been one of these temple prostitutes. Scripture tells us who her dad was, a man by the name of Diblaim. You will hear his story in the judgment. Hosea had a son by her. He was supposed to have "children of harlotry" according to Hos 1:2 NKJV. It says to name this son Jezreel, Hos 1:4. Jezreel means God scatters. Everyone hopes it means "He scatters blessings," but instead He is about to scatter a nation. Jezreel was one of the palaces, the residences, of the kings of Israel. This was where Elijah met Ahab, Jehu, and others. This is where Jehu by direct command brought God's revenge on the house of Ahab as told in 2 Kings 9.

Hosea then had a daughter by Gomer, and later another son. God said to name the boy *Lo-ammi*, which means, "not my people." It seems this boy is a bastard, not even Hosea's son. Hear the Word of the LORD,

> ... Then said *God*, Call his name Loammi: for ye are not my people, and I will not be your *God*. Hos 1:8 KJV

Even in Bible times **MOST of Israel was NOT God's people, and the LORD was NOT their God!**

Israel has Gone Wild, Hosea 4.

Hear the Word of the Lord. There is no faithfulness of any kind in Israel, Hos 4:1-2. The land itself mourns.

> Therefore the land will mourn;
>> And everyone who dwells there will waste away
>> With the beasts of the field
>> And the birds of the air;
>> Even the fish of the sea will be taken away. Hos 4:3 NKJV

Everyone who lives there mourns. Even the animals and the birds are hurting, and even the fish in the streams and the lakes are hurting ... all because of sin. It has been plain from the first that sin hurts the earth itself. Man's environment is ruined, is hurt, all because of sin. That is what can bes seen from the Genesis onward, Gen 3:17b-18.

What are the people of Israel like? They are like people who like to fight with the preacher, Hos 4:4. So what does all of this mean? They will stumble and be destroyed. "... and I will destroy thy mother," it says in Hos 4:5 KJV. You have to ask, what is this about? It may be talking about the wife of Hosea who has returned to harlotry. Or I cannot help but think it is also talking about God will be destroying the "goddess" Asherah, the demon they are worshipping.

Being a priest is about spreading the knowledge of God according to Mal 2:7. God says to the Levites, you congratulate yourself on being a priest of God. But the Lord says through Hosea, you steadfastly refuse to pursue the knowledge of God. What will be the decree of God? You rejected knowledge, and despised lessons in the Word, so God will reject you from being a priest, and I will forget your children.

> [6] My people are destroyed for lack of knowledge: because thou hast rejected knowledge, I will also reject thee, that thou shalt be no priest to me: seeing thou hast forgotten the law of thy God, I will also forget thy children. [7] As they were increased, so they sinned against me: therefore will I change their glory into shame. Hos 4:6-7 KJV

What does that mean? For Hosea the prophet it could have meant that Hosea is not going to take care of Gomer or her illegitimate offspring, born of harlotry. For Israel there may be greater implications. God may be saying, you have not been faithful to Me, and I won't take care of your children! Look at this! This implies that if **YOU** are not faithful, *God may not take care of **your** children!* How do you read it? *Also clearly, these have not been idle words in Israel's history,* from ancient times to modern times.

The priests and the people are both guilty, Hos 4:9. Therefore God is going to punish all of them. They have sought the approval of their fertility gods, so the Lord will make it so they eat but do not have enough, Hos 4:10. Fornication and drunkenness makes you stupid. They consult wooden statutes, and they like to party.

> [11] Prostitution, wine, and new wine take away understanding.
> [12] My people consult with their wooded idol,
>> And answer to a stick of wood.
>
> Indeed the spirit of prostitution has led them astray,
>> And they have been unfaithful to their God.
>
> Hos 4:11-12 WEB

The "*diviner's* wand" in verse 12 indicates falling into the occult practices of reading mystical signs, instead of seeking the knowledge of the Most High God, another sign of immoral religion contrary to the commands of the Law. Where then do all these religious sex parties occur? Hos 4:13 says on the mountains, and the hills, under the shade of trees. God says He is **not** going to punish the women involved in harlotry.

> "I will not punish your daughters when they commit harlotry,
>> Nor your brides when they commit adultery;
>> For the men themselves go apart with harlots,
>> And offer sacrifices with a ritual harlot.
>> Therefore people who do not understand will be trampled.
>
> Hos 4:14 NKJV

God says that in the end they will be ashamed of their lives, **however** *that is not something that is yet seen in physical Israel.* Still the Lord loves His unfaithful wife, Israel. So God uses Hosea to show the love He has for His people. God commands Hosea to take back his unfaithful wife Gomer in chapter 3. Gomer, the harlot who has returned to her harlotry, has gone down hill. She has ended up in slavery. We end up in the slavery of sin, Rom 6:16-17, which is indeed a very real thing. Further often we end up in virtual slavery to our oppressors and exploiters, or even, God forbid, our employers. So Hosea, in order to get his unfaithful wife back, has to buy her out of slavery. She is not worth much as a slave. A good slave was worth 30 shekels of silver according to Moses' Law, Ex 21:32. Gomer though has been ruined by her sins. She is not worth nearly that much.

> [1] Then the LORD said to me, "Go again, love a woman who is loved by

a lover and is committing adultery, just like the love of the LORD for the children of Israel, who look to other gods and love the raisin cakes of the pagans."

^{2} So I bought her for myself for fifteen shekels of silver, and one and one-half homers of barley. Hos 3:1-2 NKJV

This is not the price of a good male slave, nor the price of a good-looking woman. This has only been about the "nicer" (?) aspects of Israel's immorality. The rest of the picture, as shown by the other prophets, turns darker and darker. The prophet Amos speaks of Israel as exploiting their own poor, taking their very clothes as collateral for loans, and then using these same garments to lay with the temple prostitutes.

^{6} Thus says the LORD:
"For three transgressions of Israel, and for four,
I will not turn away its punishment,
Because they sell the righteous for silver,
And the poor for a pair of sandals.
^{7} They pant after the dust of the earth which is on the head of the poor,
And pervert the way of the humble.
A man and his father go in to the same girl,
To defile My holy name.
^{8} They lie down by every altar on clothes taken in pledge,
And drink the wine of the condemned in the house of their god." Amos 2:6-8 NKJV

Their worship also sometimes involved human sacrifice. Such things have been seen from time to time among pagans world-wide, some of the latest being with the Incas and Aztecs in comparatively modern times. These things were already going on in Canaan when Israel entered the land, and such things were expressly forbidden.

Thou shalt not do so unto the LORD thy God: for every abomination to the LORD, which he hateth, have they done unto their gods; for even their sons and their daughters they have burnt in the fire to their gods. Deut 12:31 KJV

Leviticus 20 commands the death penalty for any such worship, and clearly forecasts that such things will even happen in the temple in Jerusalem. The image of the "god" Molech it seems was often made in the form of a furnace, with fire showing behind his eyes and mouth, and his arms stretched out as a grating on which the baby was then placed for burning. It was often called making someone "pass through the fire." The hardness of heart that this would take is mind boggling. Surely these were scary things even in their depravity.

There shall not be found among you any one that maketh his son or his daughter to pass through the fire, or that useth divination, or an observer of times, or an enchanter, or a witch, Deut 18:10 KJV

Of King Ahaz of Judah it says,

But he walked in the way of the kings of Israel, yea, and made his son to pass through the fire, according to the abominations of the heathen, whom the LORD cast out from before the children of Israel. 2Kgs 16:3 KJV

And they caused their sons and their daughters to pass through the fire, and used divination and enchantments, and sold themselves to do evil in the sight of the LORD, to provoke him to anger. 2Kgs 17:17 KJV

Of King Manasseh of Judah it says,

And he made his son pass through the fire, and observed times, and used enchantments, and dealt with familiar spirits and wizards: he wrought much wickedness in the sight of the LORD, to provoke *him* to anger. 2Kgs 21:6 KJV

And of the reforms under good King Josiah of Judah it says,

And he defiled Topheth, which is in the valley of the children of Hinnom, that no man might make his son or his daughter to pass through the fire to Molech. 2Kgs 23:10 KJV

The psalmist summarizes these things Israel did:

36 They served their idols,
     Which became a snare to them.
37   They even sacrificed their sons
     And their daughters to demons,
38   And shed innocent blood,
     The blood of their sons and daughters,
     Whom they sacrificed to the idols of Canaan;
     And the land was polluted with blood.
39   Thus they were defiled by their own works,
     And played the harlot by their own deeds. Psa 106:36-39 NKJV

The prophet Isaiah speaks to the pagans of Israel as the children of an adulterer and a prostitute who are "slaying the children in the valleys under the clifts of the rocks?" Isa 57:3-5 KJV. There is more to read in the same passage, and there is more to quote from the Word of God, but I think this gives an overview.

Now for a long season Israel *hath been* without the true God ... 2Chron 15:3 KJV

Then another question comes to mind.

How long did Asherah worship go on?

The prophet Ezekiel was in the first deportation, and while in Babylon saw in a vision what was still going on in temple in Jerusalem, which was at this point still standing. There were many secret things going on which were contrary to the Lord our God. The Lord said to him,

> ⁹ ... Go in, and behold the wicked abominations that they do here. ¹⁰ So I went in and saw; and behold every form of creeping things, and abominable beasts, and all the idols of the house of Israel, pourtrayed upon the wall round about. ¹¹ And there stood before them seventy men of the ancients of the house of Israel, and in the midst of them stood Jaazaniah the son of Shaphan, with every man his censer in his hand; and a thick cloud of incense went up. ¹² Then said he unto me, **Son of man, hast thou seen what the ancients of the house of Israel do in the dark, every man in the chambers of his imagery?** for they say, The Lord seeth us not; the Lord hath forsaken the earth. Ezek 8:9-12 KJV (*bold emphasis added*)

> ¹⁴ Then he brought me to the door of the gate of the Lord's house which was toward the north; and, behold, there sat women weeping for Tammuz. ¹⁵ Then said he unto me, Hast thou seen this, O son of man? turn thee yet again, and thou shalt see greater abominations than these. Ezek 8:14 KJV

Tammuz being a Babylonian "god," lover of Ishtar, and symbolic of the seasonal death and rebirth of vegetation. So even after the first deportations, these things are going on among the priests even in Jerusalem.

Later when Jeremiah had been dragged to Egypt against his will, *after* the final destruction of Solomon's temple and all of Jerusalem, and the words of the prophets concerning these things had been fulfilled, Judah had still not learned her lessons, even in the dispersion. Jeremiah rebuked them for their sins, and we see their response.

> ¹⁵ Then all the men which knew that their wives had burned incense unto other gods, and all the women that stood by, a great multitude, even all the people that dwelt in the land of Egypt, in Pathros, answered Jeremiah, saying, ¹⁶ As for the word that thou hast spoken unto us in the name of the Lord, we will not hearken unto thee. ¹⁷ But we will certainly do whatsoever thing goeth forth out of our own mouth, **to burn incense unto the queen of heaven, and to pour out drink offerings unto her, as we have done, we, and our fathers, our kings, and our princes, in the cities of Judah,** and in the streets of Jerusalem: for then had we plenty of victuals, and were well, and saw no evil. ¹⁸ **But since we left off to burn incense to the queen of**

heaven, and to pour out drink offerings unto her, **we** have wanted all things, and **have been consumed by the sword and by the famine.** [19] And when we burned incense to the queen of heaven, and poured out drink offerings unto her, **did we make her cakes to worship her, and pour out drink offerings unto her, without our men?** Jer 44:15-19 KJV (*bold emphasis added*)

It is clear that we are talking about top to bottom unfaithfulness to the LORD, and a refusal to turn away from the these things, **even *after* the exile** of both Israel and Judah. So when did these things actually end?

Hosea, after taking Gomer back, lays down some rules for her in Hosea 3. God is planning to redeem Israel, but she is not going to be independent for a long time.

> For the children of Israel shall abide many days without a king, and without a prince, and without a sacrifice, and without an image, and without an ephod, and without teraphim: Hos 3:4 KJV

Not being independent lasted at least up to 1948 and the establishment of Israel. You can even argue that they are not independent even now. They depend on America, and (as much as possible) try to manipulate America into fighting their wars, and ruining their enemies. But God says Israel will finally really turn to God, in many passages like Hos 3:5.

> Afterward shall the children of Israel return, and seek the LORD their God, and David their king; and shall fear the LORD and his goodness **in the latter days**. KJV (emphasis added)

It is easy to argue from Scripture, and from history, that this has not really happened, even to our day. ***But it will happen one day.*** This subject will come up again near the end of this volume.

Here we move on to some of the modern adherents of what might be called, "mother nature," and Jewish author Raphael Patai's book *The Hebrew Goddess*, Third Enlarged Edition, Wayne State University Press, Detroit, 1990. Some of the endorsements speak for the cultural importance of the book to some. On the back cover there is "Critical praise for earlier editions."

> "This brilliant essay on goddess worship in Judaism written by an anthropologist represents a major contribution to comparative religion." James Preston, *Encyclopedia of Religion.*

> "Patai's discussion of the individual metaphors and representations of femininity is based on a thorough knowledge of the primary sources." Dan Ben-Amos, *Journal of American Folklore.*

> "Carefully researched, well-written, and well-illustrated, the book is an interesting and invaluable contribution to Judaic." Martin Cohen, *Library Journal*

The central thesis of the book seems to be on page 1 of the book, just inside the cover. It is a quote from the 12th century AD Jewish book the *Zohar*, which is part of the Jewish Kabbalah.

> *"In the beginning God created ... This God is the Supernal Mother who rides and rises with a triumphant shout." Tiqqune haZohar, 47a*

In other words, Yahweh, the LORD our God, is not the "true" creator god of the Old Testament. Asherah is!

Patai has extensive knowledge of Jewish occult literature and "goddess" lore. He also has a good deal of knowledge about archaeological evidence concerning gods and goddesses of the Middle-East, and some knowledge of Scripture. He is, though, hardly an impartial researcher and writer. He speaks of "The Genius of Idolatry," pg 30. Some actual dates are cited, but then he uses strange phrases like "dated with confidence as deriving from all ages of the Israelite period," pg 39 and often uses phrases like an "informed guess." He does comment that, "The archaeological data ... are disappointing because of their paucity and lack of clarity," pg 35. That is true. It is necessary to constantly read between the lines of both archaeology and Scripture to form a complete picture of what was happening in ancient Israel. Patai even makes admissions like, "The argument of this section must, therefore, remain conjectural," pg 90. Then he makes giant leaps of speculation such as that the supposedly "female" cherubim of the temple statuary "thus symbolized Israel," pg 91; and that the "male" cherubim was originally an idolatrous image of Yahweh, pg 95. He discusses the links between different "goddess" religions and then tells us with a straight face that, "The Virgin Mary ... also belongs to this category of female deities ..." and "Mary bore Jesus to God, and several other sons and daughters to her earthly husband yet she remained "The Virgin,"" pg 140. Although he might deny it, Patai implicitly deals with Judaism as just another polytheistic religion (in a double talk kind of way). Clearly, many Jews would deny this.

Patai points to, no, not a "trinity," but a "tetrad." Shekinah / Matronit "or the Matron" as "the goddess of the Kabbala" and as the "most Jewish, expression of the idea of a goddess." pg 135. He speaks of

> **"the emergence of the Talmudic Shekhinah** ... that of interposing personified mediating entities between God and man. ... as being His attributes or emanations ..." pg 97 *(bold emphasis added)*

He is using Gnostic terminology here, which will be discussed in Section III. As Patai develops his thesis, he comments that

> **"... in the vast compendium of the Talmud**, one finds in it only **one single significant addition** to the realm of religious faith: the loosely sketched, **vague aspects of God's Presence, called *Shekhina* ...**"
> pgs 29-30 *(bold emphasis added)*

Or again,

"post-Biblical Judaism created for itself a new concept of feminine divinity in the figure of the Shekhina ..." pg 98

According to Patai the *Shekinah* (I am following the spelling of the *New Oxford American Dictionary* here, and Patai uses another variation, of which one may find many) is supposed to represent "God's Presence." *In one passage he points to the Shekinah as if it resided in the ark of the covenant*, pg 100. Then he goes on to show how the idea of the Shekinah came to be viewed as feminine and as even what most would call a "goddess," and he carefully builds his case for the Shekinah being either a "god," or a "virtual god," in the way various rabbis treated the Shekinah. Patai says his quotes,

"are sufficient to establish that the idea of two separate divine entities did exist in Talmudic times," pg 106 (*bold emphasis added*)

More about the *Kabbalah* and the Shekinah will come later. Patai provides a convenient way to introduce these subjects and to give the reader some idea of how wide spread these pagan beliefs still are. It would seem that some readers of Patai are zealous adherents.

There are a few points to make. Patai's writing really seems to be that of a devotee, not a scholar, and this is not really an objective treatment. It does contain useful evidence of some religious views, and how these ideas developed in the occult world, but really much of it should be classified as speculative, not really an objective study of the evidence. If this were Christian theological speculation, especially of a "conservative" sort, it would never get a university press to publish it, but see the quotes from the back cover which were cited above. Feminism is very important to the Western Establishment, and this is another phase of their cultural assault on traditional "Western" or Christian values.

Patai *does demonstrate* many of the links between *ancient* "goddess" idolatry, **and Jewish *Kabbalistic* goddess lore of the 12th and 13th centuries AD, and** *today*. **He shows us many of the links between the ancient terminology in "goddess" worship in the occult and modern devotion to the "goddess."** He *does* produce enough evidence to show that **these things have existed in Judaism** *continuously* **since Pre-Christian times!**

So was Asherah the "true" god of ancient Israel, and Moses a liar, or was Yahweh the true God of ancient Israel and Asherah a disastrous fraud? At the end of the day, the realities of Yahweh rest on events of history which cannot be denied, and this is true of both the Old Testament and the New Testament. But Asherah? "She" "rests" on a mist of suppositions which have never proven "her" to be a "god," only at best, dare we say it, *perhaps* a demonic power? Was she actually worshipped as a "goddess"? Obviously so, by some.

So what does Patai really prove? *That the Jews **never** really left all of their bonds to paganism; that they were never completely monotheistic, at least as a group.*

Many are reluctant to admit these truths, but you can also see this in other writings on the subject. For instance Gershom Scholem in his *Jewish Gnosticism, Merkabah Mysticism, and Talmudic Tradition*, New York, The Jewish Theological Seminary of America, 2012. Part of Scholem's stated purpose was to "... to consider the relationship between the Hekhaloth writings and the talmudic tradition, but also ... between these texts and the elements of Gnostic teaching ..." pg 65. Scholem, perhaps much more than any other Jewish author on the subject, is very obviously very zealous to protect the reputation of the Jews both internationally and down through history. He goes out of his way to avoid making really damaging admissions against Judaism. Many Jews, of course, consider the Christian "Trinity" to be the height of foolishness, and that is one of the "reasons" Christianity simply cannot be tolerated by them. But look at Scholem discussing the subject of an angel called "Metatron," who in some occult literature is identified with the angel Michael, and later identified with Jahoel or Michael or with Enoch, *Jewish Gnosticism,* pgs 50-51.

Metatron is called "Jahoel," pg 41 (Should it be "Yahoel"? nf). Then there is discussion of "Metatron as the highest angel who bears, in a way, the name of God is called ... (the Lesser Tetragrammaton)" pg 41. What does that mean? That "Metatron" is a little Adonai/Lord? A little "Yahweh"? A little "god"? Then Metatron is later cited as "Lesser Jaho," pg 43 (or "Yaho"? nf), and later says "Metatron is as much a secret name of the Dynamis ... " pg 47. (Compare this by the way with Patai's discussing of "Matronit "or the Matron"" which has been previously discussed on page 64 of this text.)

In another work, Scholem says the origins of "Metatron" are obscure, but most think it "is short for Metathronisos, i.e. "he who stands besides [sic] the (God's) throne," or "who occupies the throne next to the divine throne."" *Major Trends in Jewish Mysticism*, Schocken Books, NY, 1974, pg 69. The nonsensical discussions go on and on. Jesus the Christ as the Son of God? No way! Metatron as in some way god? Sure? Also notice that Scholem's title *Major Trends in Jewish Mysticism*, implies that Gnosticism/Kabbalism is an ongoing phenomenon in Judaism, which indeed it is.

The picture of the Jews as a group being faithful to Moses' Law is false. Moses, and all the prophets, and the Great Prophet Jesus of Nazareth all testify, they have ***never*** been faithful to the One and Only God *as a group*! Ever! They have been more faithful to Asherah than to the True and Living God, and they have been, all along, paying the price for this. They need to repent. *They need national repentance.*

Even today we are surrounded by hints of covert Asherah worship. The fictional movie *Raiders of the Lost Ark*, is an example. The Nazi villains are able to actually find and seize the "true" "ark of the covenant," and open it, and who does Jewish filmmaker Steven Spielberg have coming out of the open ark to defend it? Lo and behold ... it is a woman! Shades of the Shekinah!

The First Break: Man's Word Rules

Strictly speaking, the Pharisees are our next topic. Some of their influence has already been touched on, but not by their name. The Pharisees were after the systematic coming of the crypto-Jews, but not by much. One of the issues after the return from the first captivity was how to avoid any more deportations. That would actually require living in a pleasing manner before the Lord God, obeying Him from the heart, but there were other approaches.

The problems were huge. Even during the captivity, the prophets Jeremiah and Ezekiel constantly complained of their unfaithfulness. Coming out of the captivity, both Ezra and Nehemiah complained repeatedly of them still failing to observe even the most rudimentary aspects of the Law. The last of the Old Testament prophets, Malachi, similarly warned of the corruption going on throughout the nation, *including* in the priesthood itself. Secular Jewish historian Josephus similarly paints a picture of pervasive unfaithfulness, as do many gentile histories when they touch on the moral condition of the Jews.

This was quite a job, considering the unfaithfulness of Israel. The Pharisees concentrated their work in two areas. One was the formulation of strictly *legal* foundations for righteousness. The second was to act as representatives to work on behalf of the nation, with their generally gentile overlords. Graetz says of their objectives,

> Their opinions were framed, their actions governed by **one cardinal principle—the necessity of preserving Judaism**. The individual and the State were **to be ruled alike by the laws and customs of their fathers**. Graetz, *History of the Jews*, Vol. II, pg 18, Philadelphia, 1893 (*bold emphasis added*)

The key words from the Pharisees point of view was that they were "to be ruled alike by the laws **and customs** of their fathers." In other words, the Word of God was not sufficient. The customs of men were needed as its supplement. And to *survive* was *paramount*.

This presents immediate conflicts with Scripture. In the Law of Moses and the prophets and the psalms, both implicitly and explicitly, the law is sufficient for the things which it deals with and should **NOT** be "supplemented," in any real sense.

> Ye shall not add unto the word which I command you, neither shall ye diminish ought from it, that ye may keep the commandments of the LORD your God which I command you. Deut 4:2 KJV

They are not to add to God's words, nor take away from them. This is seen as *mandatory* in order to be able to "keep the commandments of the LORD your God." Again,

> [5] Every word of God is pure: he is a shield unto them that put their

trust in him. [6] Add thou not unto his words, lest he reprove thee, and thou be found a liar. Prov 30:5-6 KJV

These and a host of other passages do not sound in the least as if the law of God needed to supplemented. Even so, the Pharisees point of view was that the rule was to be by both "the laws and customs of their fathers." Josephus comments on these things among the Pharisees, and the trouble which it caused.

> "What I would now explain is this, that the Pharisees have delivered to the people a great many observances by succession from their fathers, which are not written in the law of Moses; and for that reason it is that the Sadducees reject them and say that we are to esteem those observances to be obligatory which are in the written word, but are not to observe what are derived from the tradition of our forefathers;"
> Josephus, *Antiquities of the Jews*, Book 13, Chapter 10. 6. 297

Rabbi Finkelstein in his book *The Pharisees* is even more adamant about how the Pharisees operated.

> "Customs create exegesis, not exegesis customs." Vol I, pg 131

Some even went further, saying in effect that the Law of Moses could be ignored, but *not* the traditions of the fathers. So viewed candidly, Pharisaism is at its root a heresy from the Law of Moses and the prophets, another apostate denomination of Judaism. It is another form of men trusting in themselves, instead of really trusting in the Lord their God.

There is more to say about this sect of the Jews, of which this can only be an overview. Their personal lives often showed a great deal of personal discipline, even if it was regulated by human rather than by divine rules. They were men who were good at making a "good impression." Josephus says they,

> "... live meanly, and despise delicacies in diet; and they follow the conduct of reason;" *Antiquities* 18.1.3.12

> "... the cities gave great attestations to them on account of their entire virtuous conduct, both in the actions of their lives and their discourses also." *Antiquities* 18.1.3.15

Almost everyone, including Jewish historians Graetz, Finkelstein, and Cecil Roth, point out the Pharisee emphasis on what one might call "theoretically correct" scholarship, (misguided though it often was). Finkelstein says the Pharisees laid "the foundations for a world civilization," *The Pharisees*, Vol I, pg xxx. (A scary thought to many, *including* many Jews.) Even so, many Jews still look forward to a "Pharisee" "world civilization." Still there are some key things to note.

The self-styled righteousness of the Pharisees took some special forms. The term Pharisee, comes from the Greek *pharisaios*, Φαρισαῖος, which in turn seems to come from the Hebrew word *parush* פָּרוּשׁ, "to cut oneself off ... to separate" to make oneself "blameless," "to separate, distinguish," HALOT. Thus one who is separated by special practices. In concept, the term would overlap with the words for "holy," which has the idea of separating something for special use by God. All of which is laudable in general terms, and there were some very fine men among the Pharisees, but a closer look should be taken at the principles on which they based their decisions.

A Human Fence Around the Law.

If you want to see how influential the Pharisees have been—even in our modern religious world, not just among the Jews, but also among both Mohammedans and Christians—you only have to take a look at their concept of building a "fence" around God's laws.

The idea of the "fence" was to set boundaries so far away from violations of the commands of God, so that violations of the law would be practically impossible. If walking twenty miles on the Sabbath day meant you were breaking the Sabbath, then establishing a clear limit way below that would mean you could always be sure of never breaking the law. A fence around the law. A **mandatory** *human* fence.

One of these fences which the Pharisees instituted was the "Sabbath days journey." "Six days shalt thou labour, and do all thy work: ... *in it* thou shalt not do any work," Ex 20:9-10 KJV. Obviously then, a person would not go on a trip on the Sabbath day. Even so, how would you define a "trip," and what would really qualify as forbidden travel. So the Jews invented "a Sabbath days's journey." This was a set distance a person could safely travel on the Sabbath day, without being guilty of "working" on the Sabbath day. This distance was approximately 3/4 of a mile, or about 1,100 meters This became another standard unit of measure used by the Jews, as reflected in Acts 1:12 and other places. So then if you take a walk on the Sabbath day of 1,100 meters, that is fine. If instead you walk 1,200 meters on the Sabbath, you are guilty of breaking the Sabbath and should be put to death. The building of obligatory human fences around God's commands is a heresy which is common among many "Bible believing" Christians and Christian ministers. In trying to "protect" the flock, they readily invent new "rules" for "Christians"—rules not found in the Word of God. The "leaven of the Pharisees" (Mtt 16:6) is all around us in our world.

Perhaps it was not plain at first, but once in place, not only was the Law of Moses binding, but also the fence was binding. In this case, the Sabbath day's journey. The law was amended by custom. The customs of men had been added to the Law of God. Indeed, Deut 4:2 and hosts of other commands had been violated.

However, this is still not the end of the story. For instance, how would you define the beginning of a journey? Does the 1,100 meters begin at your doorway? At the edge of your property? At the edge of your village? Where?

Law, Tradition, and Evasion

Soon dodging the commands of *both* Scripture *and* tradition through legalism became a Pharisee forte. No one was as adept at evading their own rules as the Pharisees themselves. Even the sympathetic treatment given in *McClintock and Strong* mentions some of this:

> "Before the Sabbath commenced (i.e. Friday afternoon), an article of food was deposited by each member in the court selected for the social gathering, so that it might thereby become the common place for all; **the streets were made to form one large dwelling place with different gates, by means of beams laid across on the tops of the houses, and doors or gates put in the front; and meals were put in a house at the end of the distance permitted to walk, in order to constitute it a domicile, and thus another Sabbath-day's journey could be undertaken from the first terminus.** By this means the Pharisees could evade the law, and, like the priests, meet together in any place to celebrate their social meals on the Sabbath, and carry anything that was wanted for its sacred festival, as they had three common meals on the Sabbath."
>
> *McClintock and Strong's Cyclopedia Of Biblical, Theological, and Ecclesiastical Literature*, article, *Phar'isee. (bold emphasis added)*

There were ways to evade the most demanding commands. First century Rabbi Yehoshua severely censured the Pharisee quibbling about when an oath was binding, and when it was not binding.

> "Woe to you, you blind guides, who say, 'Whoever swears by the temple, it is nothing; but whoever swears by the gold of the temple, he is obligated.' You blind fools! For which is greater, the gold, or the temple that sanctifies the gold? 'Whoever swears by the altar, it is nothing; but whoever swears by the gift that is on it, he is a obligated.' You blind fools! For which is greater, the gift, or the altar that sanctifies the gift? He therefore who swears by the altar, swears by it, and by everything on it. He who swears by the temple, swears by it, and by him who was living in it. He who swears by heaven, swears by it, and by the throne of God, and by him who sits on it."

The list goes on and on. With the correct procedure you could evade honoring mom and dad (Mtt 15:4-6). There were (and are) ways to avoid the guilt of incest, murder, mistreating an alien or a foreigner, you name it. All in the name of following the letter of the law.

*So Pharisaism became a system of legal formalities, with the result that the clear intent of God's commands were **often** completely ignored.* Not *all* Jews or even *all* Pharisees agreed with these perversions, **ever!** But this was the dominant system, beginning with the ancient Pharisees, and from their times on it proved an additional pollutant to the great body of Jews. The traditions at first were only passed on verbally from generation to generation. Later, during the third to the sixth centuries AD these traditions were codified and written down in what is now called the Talmud.

Skill in Harsh Politics and Intrigue.

The second objective of the Pharisees was to act as the representatives of the interests of the people before their rulers. These were brutal times of political infighting. The period leading up to the coming of the Christ was filled with continual Jewish rebellions against various gentiles, and against each other. Josephus alone is sufficient to document this. These times were punctuated with things such as the attempted assassination of Herod recorded by Josephus in Book 15, chapter 8 of *Antiquities of the Jews*. Ten Jewish assassins formed a conspiracy to kill Herod, even if it cost them their lives. They ended up being betrayed and killed, and then the spy who betrayed them was murdered by the Jews, cut to pieces and fed "to the dogs." 15.8.4.284ff. Story after story speaks of a political intensity among the Jews which is only equaled in the terrorists and anarchists of modern times.

> "When, therefore, the Jews were come thither, ... there arose a sedition; and the Syrians ... , by the assistance of the Jews, who are men that despise dangers, and very ready to fight upon any occasion."
> *Antiquities* 18.9.9.374

The Pharisees were hardly the only party involved in what I have chosen to call "hard-core" politics. Among other hard core political players in the first century AD were the well known Zealots and the Assassins (literally the daggers, *sikaros* σικάριος, Acts 21:38). But the Pharisees were among the hard-core players. Again,

> "In political conflicts they generally followed democratic principles, and sometimes carried them to an extreme, trusting to their combined influence for success."
> *McClintock and Strong's Cyclopedia* article, *Phar'isee*

The Jewish historian Josephus says more or less the same thing.

> "of the Pharisees ... they had great authority among the Jews, both to do hurt to such as they hated, and to bring advantages to those to whom they were friendly disposed;" *Antiquities* 13. 15. 5. 401

And later,

> "These are those that are called the sect of **the Pharisees, who were in a capacity of greatly opposing kings. A cunning sect** they were,

and soon elevated to a pitch of open fighting and doing mischief."
Antiquities 17. 2. 4. 41 (*bold emphasis added*)

Josephus also emphasizes the Pharisees great skill in manipulation of the public. He says they,

> "have so great a power over the multitude, that when they say anything against the king or against the high priest, they are presently believed."
> *Antiquities* 13. 9. 10. 288

In fact, sometimes it could be said, and it was said of Hasmonean queen Alexandra,

> "while she governed other people, and the Pharisees governed her."
> *Wars of the Jews*, 1. 5. 2. 112

So Pharisaism was from the first *both* religious *and political*. Obviously this is another part of the rebellious character of the Jews, and their inclination to continually foment revolts.

Love of Money and Position.

A couple of things should be noted. The first is the Pharisees very worldly love of money and position, which would go hand-in-glove with politics.

> The Pharisees, who loved money, heard all this and were sneering at Jesus. Lk 16:14 NASB

In Matthew 23 Jesus gave a biting indictment of their sins of loving preeminence while treating others despitefully.

Secondly, for all of their great pretense of protecting the people, the Pharisees were very much elitists and despised the common man. It was considered among the Pharisees that,

> "the garments of an עַם הָאָרֶץ ['man of earth,' or a publican, a sinner, as he is termed in the New Testament, who neglected to pay the tithes and observe the laws of Mosaic purity], defile the Pharisee."
> *McClintock and Strong's Cyclopedia Of Biblical, Theological, and Ecclesiastical Literature*, article, *Phar'isee*. (*bold emphasis added*)

Though the phrase *am ha-arets* עַם הָאָרֶץ, literally the "people of the land," is generally used of the despised gentile nations surrounding Israel, they are pointing out that **these elitist Pharisees** *used the term to describe* **despised fellow Jews**. Notice that these points are made from a *McClintock and Strong* treatment of the Pharisees which is so sympathetic that it more or less accuses Jesus of causing His own death. Such as this can be seen all through Jewish history, even up to and including modern times, especially if you read much of what Jews write for consumption by other Jews.

Rabbi Finkelstein's *The Pharisees*, Vol I, which was written during the early

1940's says more or less the same thing. The "*am ha-aretz*" are discussed as "the people of the soil" and were looked down upon even in the first century, Vol. I, pg 25 "as brutish individuals" boors, the equal to "villains" in England, etc, as "nothing more than "ignorant"" pg 26. He also mentions there was some opposition from "the masses ... to the spiritual mastery of the nobility." pg 19. Still in Volume I, he says, "... the patrician masters of Galilee were upper-class Pharisees of Shammaites ..." pg 61. It was even questioned whether a Pharisee should extend food to these lower class Jews during a famine. All of which is reflected today in Judaism in the conflicts between the rich and the super-rich Jews, and "the lesser brethren," and also the widespread covert snobbishness of many Jews toward all gentiles, and even to many "lesser" Jews.

But the Pharisees were very astute politically, and they were continually in the political intrigues of their times.

Lest it be thought that Jesus had a monopoly on thinking the Pharisees were corrupt, listen to a declamation on the Pharisees sins equal in every respect to the protests of Rabbi Yehoshua:

> "Somewhat earlier a Hillelite writer had spoken of his Shammaitic opponents in the following terms: "Treacherous men, self-pleasers, dissemblers in all their own affairs and lovers of banquets at every hour of the day, gluttons, gourmands ... devourers of the goods [of the poor], saying that they do so on the ground of justice, but in reality to destroy them; complaining, deceitful, concealing themselves lest they should be recognized, impious, filled with lawlessness and iniquity from sunrise to sunset: saying, 'We shall have feastings and luxury, eating and drinking, and we shall esteem ourselves as princes.' And though their hands and their minds touch unclean things, yet their mouth speaks great things, and they say furthermore, 'Do not touch me lest thou shouldst pollute me, in the place where I stand.' "
> Finkelstein, *The Pharisees, Vol I,* pg 98.

Some of the Talmudic comments on types of Pharisees are just plain satirical, although they owe much to these men.

A Willingness to Even Invent Scripture for Political Purposes.

This is not always obvious in the standard brand accounts of the Pharisees, but it is there, and shows up now and then. This was touched on when discussing false prophecy in the last section In a way, this is an outgrowth of dabbling in the occult and is part of that inclination to even "invent" "scripture" when it seemed to be "lacking." The accounts of the trial and death of Rabbi Yehoshua clearly show that both the Pharisees and the Sadducees were willing to deny any inconvenient truth which might prove a barrier to their political and financial aspirations. Truth that collides with ambition is automatically rejected. They are at their root political. So it is little wonder that they too might invent a little prophecy, or be complicit in its invention, if it will serve their purposes. So Josephus relates the Pharisee's pretense as prophets,

> "since they were believed to have the foreknowledge of things to come by divine inspiration, they foretold how God had decreed that Herod's government should cease, and his posterity should be deprived of it; but that the kingdom should come to her and Pheroras, and to their children." *Antiquities of the Jews*, 17.2.4.43

None of which, of course, ever happened, and all of this received its prompt "reward" from Herod himself, as also is recorded by Josephus. So the Pharisees may instantaneously reject any true prophet teaching inconvenient truths, but some will gladly concoct false prophecies if it will serve their political purposes! *So it was that the lowest forms of obstinacy and rejection of truth which caused the original scatterings of Israel and Judah, were continued by the Pharisees.*

Then Judaism Became Pharisaism.

One last thing needs to be said of the Pharisees. In all of the political intrigues and manipulations and mistakes from the second century BC to the second century AD, it was the Pharisees who survived and in the end became dominant among the Jews. The Sadducees power centered around the temple, while the Pharisees power revolved around the synagogue and political manipulations. From the time of the destruction of the second temple in 70 AD, the Pharisees came to dominate Jewish national life.

This is reflected as early as say 95 AD in the Gospel of John. If you look closely, the term "Pharisee" and the term "Jew" are already being used interchangeably. Look closely at the events described in John chapter 8 into John chapter 9.

> Then the **Jews** said to Him, "You are not yet fifty years old, and have You seen Abraham?" Jn 8:57 NKJV

> ... *Jesus* ... saw a man who was blind from birth. ... Jn 9:1 NKJV

> They brought him who formerly was blind to the **Pharisees**. Jn 9:13 NKJV

> But the **Jews** did not believe concerning him, that he had been blind and received his sight, until they called the parents of him who had received his sight. Jn 9:18 NKJV

> His parents said these things because they feared the **Jews**, for the

Jews had agreed already that if anyone confessed that He was Christ, he would be put out of the synagogue. Jn 9:22 NKJV

Then some of the **Pharisees** who were with Him heard these words, and said to Him, "Are we blind also?" Jn 9:40 NKJV

The context is clear. The Apostle John, son of Zebedee, raised as a Jew and probably writing now in the late first century AD, regards the terms "Jew" and "Pharisee" as interchangeable.

McClintock and Strong says basically the same thing.

To state the doctrines and statutes of the Pharisees is to give a history of orthodox Judaism; since Pharisaism was after the return from the Babylonian captivity, and is to the present day, the national faith of the orthodox Jews, developing itself with and adapting itself to the ever-shifting circumstances of the nation.
Pharisee, III. The Tenets and Practices of the Pharisees.

A Historical Atlas of the Jewish People, General Editor Eli Barnavi, Schocken Books, NY, 1992, states this in more restrained terms.

"Rabbinical Judaism, which emerged after the destruction of the Temple, was undoubtedly the progeny of the Pharisees." pg 43

Rabbi Finkelstein is more explicit:

"Pharisaism became Talmudism, Talmudism became Medieval Rabbinism, and Medieval Rabbinism became Modern Rabbinism. But throughout these changes of name, inevitable adaptation of custom, and adjustment of Law, **the spirit of the ancient Pharisee survives unaltered**." Finkelstein, *The Pharisees*, Vol I, (From his "Foreword to First Edition") pg xxi. (*bold emphasis added*)

These traits of the Pharisees, remain signature traits of the Jews to our very own day. Quoting Rabbi Finkelstein one more time:

"the days came when Pharisaism was no longer a part of the Jewish people, but the whole of it;" Vol I, pg 79

It is not just Jesus of ancient times, but you and I, and the Jews of today, who have to deal with Pharisaism.

The Will to Power in The Early Centuries

In the first century AD, it is a completely different world that the Jews live in religiously. The Jewish leadership, although having to live under Roman rule, and having limits on their authority and the span of their power, have a pretty good set up.

The Temple.

Now the Lord's House was supposed to be a house of prayer, Isa 56:7, a place to seek God. David looked forward to coming to God's house in places like Psa 5:6-7. Originally, the priesthood was by birth alone, and limited to the descendants of Aaron. Then Israel had a kingship and things were separate. However, when the Jews came back from Babylon, there was no longer a king. The High Priest often served as chief judge for the Jews, almost like a small king. He was appointed by the pagan emperors and collected taxes for them. So the priesthood became involved with big money.

For instance, for a long time the prevailing price for becoming the High Priest was 300 talents of silver, and a talent was about 20 years pay for a working man. In 175 BC, a priest by the name Jason bid 440 talents to be the High Priest, and he bid another 150 talents for the privilege of building a gymnasium. Where then was he going to get the money, including the extra money? Well, by taxing or cheating his fellow Jews.

The high priests sometimes even confiscated the tithes, which were for all the priests. The Jewish historian Josephus tells about one of the high priests when Jesus was a boy, a man by the name of Ishmael the son of Phabi, who sent out slaves to confiscate the tithes to the Lord. He got all of the grain and produce, and some of the other priests starved, *Antiquities* 20.8.8.179ff. Annas also did the same thing, *Antiquities* 20.9.2.206ff.

Some estimate that as many as two and a half million Jews came to Jerusalem for the feast of Passover. That means that for about two weeks each year, Jerusalem was very crowded. "Hotel rooms" were expensive, food was expensive, and the purchase of an animal to sacrifice was expensive. It was too far from home for most Jews to bring sacrifices with them, so they bought them when they got to Jerusalem. Outside the temple, a pair of doves to sacrifice cost about $45 in our money. Even so, they had to be without fault, and there were priests inside the temple who, for a fee, would examine your dove or your sheep or goat, and certify it as acceptable for sacrifice, but wow! Look! Your bird or goat just bought outside the temple "bazaars" cannot pass inspection. Oh my, oh my! But look, just inside the temple, a pair of doves might be bought for a mere $600 in our money (2020), and they have already been approved! So the Jewish leadership was skinning their own people to make themselves rich.

There was also a two drachma temple tax that all Jewish males were supposed to pay. Two drachmas were about two days wages, and was to be paid only in certain coin—coins without any pagan images. If you didn't have the right kind of money to pay it with, there were moneychangers in the temple, who for about six hours pay, would give you the right kind of coin to pay the temple tax. It has been estimated that 76,000 Jews had to pay this tax, which would be about one hundred-thirty million dollars in our money. These were called the "bazaars of Annas," named after Annas the High Priest. It was a racket! A corrupt money-making racket! It was about getting ahead in life, it was about providing luxury in life, for a select few ... at the expense of the majority of the Jews. John the Baptist started preaching when Annas was the High Priest, according to Lk 3:2. Part of Jesus' trial was before Annas, Jn 18:13, 24. When the apostle Peter preached before the Sanhedrin, Annas was there, according to Acts 4:6.

Then Jesus hits the foundations of current financial power: the temple and its services. Jesus hit them where it hurt the most, in their greed, in their lust for money, in their desire for promotion and luxury. Jewish historian Josephus remarks how fortunate this Annas was (*Antiquities* 20.9.1.197ff), because he served as High Priest for such a long a time, and five of his sons and one son-in-law also served as High Priest. He was no doubt the lead speaker at the Jerusalem lectures and seminars, held in honor by all, as indeed, Josephus held him in honor. It is interesting to see how little many smart men know about what is really important or necessary or lasting or a blessing. Most Christians, knowing what was coming for the Jews and Jerusalem, would hardly call Annas blessed today, but rather a high-living religious con artist, in a fool's world of illusions which were swiftly coming to an end.

In these high dollar/high stakes games, just like in the regular business world, normal rules of right and wrong and morality often go right out the window. When John the Baptist comes preaching, the issue for them is not whether he is the forerunner of Isaiah 40, or the messenger of Malachi chapter three or chapter four. The question for them is: how will this affect our set up? So in Jn 1:19-24 they sent priests and Levites to ask John who he was. Are you the Prophet? Are you Elijah? Are you the Christ? They did not seem to realize that the special "Prophet" of Deuteronomy 18 is the Christ. And if you are not the Christ or Elijah, then why are you baptizing? This is really intriguing in prophetic terms. They realized that the "Elijah" when he would come would baptize, and that the Messiah when He would come would baptize!

Jesus' Threat to the Jewish Establishment.

Jesus was named after Joshua, which in Hebrew is *Yehoshua* יְהוֹשֻׁעַ. Jesus, both early and late in His ministry, hit the temple swindles of the leaders hard. The first cleansing of the temple is in John the second chapter, early in his ministry. Jesus went to the temple and found the "bazaars of Annas" going full blast, selling animals for sacrifice and the money changers ready to sell "approved" coins without pictures of Zeus or Mercury or whoever was on them. He made a whip out of ropes and drove the whole bunch out of the temple area (and this was a large public area), and He dumped the tables of the moneychangers. He told all of them,

> [16] ... "Take these things away! Do not make My Father's house a house of merchandise!" [17] Then His disciples remembered that it was written, *"Zeal for Your house has eaten Me up."* Jn 2:16-17 NKJV

As far as most of the observers were concerned Jesus was nothing more than just another radical Jewish Rabbi (of which there were many) doing a one-man cleanup operation on the temple. So the leaders asked what authority He had or what sign did he offer for these things He was doing. His answer was telling. He said that if they destroyed this temple He would raise it up again in three days. The Jews were stunned. The building of that temple was started in 20 BC by Herod the Great and was still going on! In fact, it was not finished until the year 64 AD, shortly before it was destroyed in the revolt of the late 60's AD. When the Jews protest to Jesus that they had been working to build the temple for forty-six years (Jn 2:20), it meant that these things were happening in the year 26 AD. (Which if Jesus was about thirty years old, as Lk 3:23 indicates, then our calendar is off by four or more years.) However Jesus was really talking about the temple of His body. This was missed even by His disciples until after His resurrection (Jn 2:22), but it can be inferred that this was not lost on the leaders of the Jews. Jesus was instituting a temple made up of much more valuable stones, that is of men.

> you also, as living stones, are being built up a spiritual house, a holy priesthood, to offer up spiritual sacrifices acceptable to God through Jesus Christ. 1Pe 2:5 NKJV

Men were part of his body the church, in the place of a static geographically located facility. This thinking turned up again and again in Jesus' preaching. Jesus told the Samaritan woman in John 4 that the time is close when men will not worship in Jerusalem, but rather "in spirit and in truth," Jn 4:21-24. Such thinking was a clear threat to the Jewish oligarchy. Although this puts us far ahead of our lines of inquiry, this thinking is clearly pertinent in trying to figure out how the great eternal temple of God will be made! Right?

The second cleansing of the temple was in the last week of His ministry and probably sealed His fate as far as the leadership was concerned.

Here are all the ingredients of an unparalleled disaster for the Jews.

The Second Break: Rejecting Their Own Messiah

One God, Multiple Persona

persona noun (pl. **-sonas** or **-sonae**)

the aspect of someone's character that is presented to or perceived by others: her public persona. In psychology, often contrasted with ANIMA.

• a role or character adopted by an author or an actor.

ORIGIN early 20th cent.: Latin, literally 'mask, character played by an actor.' *New Oxford American Dictionary*

Perhaps this is not a good analogy to the persons of the Godhead, but there is a point to be noticed here. A man, an "actor," or "someone," can do this? And the LORD our God *cannot*? That is a foolish idea if you think about it, and as shall be shown from the Old Testament, not a Scriptural one.

It was "us" in the beginning,

And God said, Let **us** make man in **our** image, after **our** likeness: ...
Gen 1:26 KJV (*bold emphasis added*)

Yes it is plural. It is a plural of *asah* עָשָׂה, to do or make or cause to happen, in *our* image *bitzlimenu* בְּצַלְמֵנוּ. But then curiously, or logically, next it says,

So **God** created man in **his** own image, in the image of God created **he** him; male and female created **he** them.
Gen 1:27 KJV (*bold emphasis added*)

This time it is consistently singular. So "us" is making man in "our image" and "God created man **in his own image**." Of course, the prophets point consistently to One God and *only* One God. Isaiah gives plenty of good examples.

"I am the LORD, and there is no other;
    apart from me there is no God.
I will strengthen you,
    though you have not acknowledged me," Isa 45:5 NIV

Then about creation, the Lord says through Isaiah,

Thus saith the LORD, thy redeemer, and he that formed thee from the womb, I am the LORD that maketh all things; that stretcheth forth the heavens **alone**; that spreadeth abroad the earth **by myself**;
Isa 44:24 KJV (*bold emphasis added*)

But "us" and "our" making man in "our" image, in "his" image, is still there, from the very first. The singular God who is from the very first verse called by a plural form, *Elohim* אֱלֹהִים, Gen 1:1, or "God." Some call this a "plural of majesty," but it is still very much a plural. Much more could be quoted. Context shows that this is more than a grammatical curiosity.

Now no one has ever seen God. "God is spirit," Jn 4:24. God Himself says that mortal man cannot see God.

> But," he said, "you cannot see my face, for no one may see me and live." Ex 33:20 NKJV

It was emphasized, "you saw no form."

> "Then the LORD spoke to you out of the fire. **You** heard the sound of words but **saw no form; there was only a voice.**" Deut 4:12 KJV

All Israel heard that voice. Still, *something* was seen, at least at times, for instance when Abraham sat around on a certain day in the ancient past.

> And the LORD appeared unto him in the plains of Mamre: and he sat in the tent door in the heat of the day; Gen 18:1 KJV

The text does not explain it, however it does say that he saw "three men," Gen 18:2, and he ran and bowed to the earth before them, strangers whom he had evidently never seen before. Abraham offers hospitality to the "men" *anashim* אֲנָשִׁים, and they ate fresh made bread and a select calf. During the meal, one of the "men" says that Sarah will have a son next year, and Sarah, hearing behind a tent wall, laughed at the idea. It says of one of the men,

> And the LORD said unto Abraham, Wherefore did Sarah laugh ...
> Gen 18:13 KJV

The word translated here as "LORD," is the very name of God, the Hebrew here is *Yahweh* יהוה. One of the "men" is literally the LORD our God, and so it is consistently in the rest of the passage. Still, as has been noted, no one can see God and live! It might also be noted that none of this is anything new in either Jewish or Christian theology, and it shows up in various places in the Old Testament, as will be seen. You can read various explanations in various places, *but it is still there.* I am just trying to get you to give these passages their proper weight and to not just "read them away." Later, it plainly says in the chapter that the other two "men" are angels.

> And there came two angels to Sodom at even; and Lot sat in the gate of Sodom: ... Gen 19:1 KJV

There is also more than one account of an "angel" who is treated as the LORD in the Old Testament. When God announces an angel to guide and guard Israel in the wilderness, He says,

> [20] Behold, I send an Angel before thee, to keep thee in the way, and to bring thee into the place which I have prepared. [21] Beware of him, and obey his voice, provoke him not; for he will not pardon your transgressions: for my name *is* in him. Ex 23:20-21 KJV

These things can be called by more than one term, but they are still there, *including* God appearing as a "man." One more example might be good. The wife of a man by the name of Manoah, in the times of the Judges, has an "angel of the LORD" appear to her, Judg 13:3. Later she calls this being "A man of God," Judg 13:6, *ish Ha-Elohim* אִישׁ הָאֱלֹהִים. Then the "man of God" disappeared. Later Manoah prayed for the "man of God" to come back.

> And God hearkened to the voice of Manoah; **and the angel of God came again** unto the woman as she sat in the field: but Manoah her husband was not with her. Judg 13:9 KJV (*bold emphasis added*)

Manoah finally meets the "angel of God" (and remember, there are in our times other angels in rebellion to God, who are not "of God," but this is an "angel of God"). Manoah says to the angel,

> "Are you **the man** who spoke to the woman?"
> Judg 13:11 WEB (*bold emphasis added*).

So the angel appears as a man, which is plain old *ish* אִישׁ, a man. Then we see that

> ... Manoah knew not that he was an angel of the LORD. Judg 13:16 KJV

In other words, he for sure just looked like a man! Then Manoah and his wife offer a sacrifice to the angel of the LORD, just as if he were God, and this "angel of God," **accepts** *the sacrifice, the worship!* There are other accounts also. In Judges 6 it says,

> And there came **an angel of the LORD**, and sat under an oak which was in Ophrah, Judg 6:11 KJV (*bold emphasis added*)

Later this angel speaks to Gideon and it says

> **And the LORD looked upon him, and said,** Go in this thy might, and thou shalt save Israel from the hand of the Midianites: have not I sent thee? Judg 6:14 KJV (*bold emphasis added*)

And so on. If you are going to rule out the LORD our God appearing in human form, you have more to rule out than Jesus Christ in the first century of our age, *if* you believe Scripture. You also have to rule out passage after passage in the Law and the prophets. So it is later that the Lord says that God will come.

The Messiah Rejected and Murdered by Israel

First a messenger will come, calling out in the wilderness,

> ... "Prepare the way of the LORD;
>   Make straight in the desert
>   A highway for our God." Isa 40:3 NKJV

This messenger is to "prepare the way for the **LORD**." That should be clear enough, and as we have seen from the context of the Old Testament, it should not be completely unexpected. So where will this appearance occur? Isaiah tells us,

> ... Say to the cities of Judah, "Behold your God!" Isa 40:9 NKJV

In Judah He will be introduced. Is this some sort of minor appearance? No! "God" vs 9, "the LORD" vs 3, is coming to rule:

> Behold, the Lord GOD shall come with a strong hand,
> > And His arm shall rule for Him;
> > Behold, His reward *is* with Him,
> > And His work before Him. Isa 40:10 NKJV

God Himself is coming to rule? He will be introduced in Judah, and He will come with might, and "His arm shall rule for Him." Is this just some lower angel who is coming? No, remember in Isa 44:24 that the LORD created the heavens all alone, and of this LORD who is coming in Isaiah 40 it says that He is the One,

> [12] Who has measured the waters in the hollow of his hand,
> > Measured heaven with a span
> > And calculated the dust of the earth in a measure?
> > Weighed the mountains in scales
> > And the hills in a balance?
> [13] Who has directed the Spirit of the LORD,
> > Or *as* His counselor has taught Him?
> [14] With whom did He take counsel, and *who* instructed Him,
> > And taught Him in the path of justice?
> > Who taught Him knowledge,
> > And showed Him the way of understanding?
> [15] Behold, the nations *are* as a drop in a bucket,
> > And are counted as the small dust on the scales;
> > Look, He lifts up the isles as a very little thing.
> [16] And Lebanon *is* not sufficient to burn,
> > Nor its beasts sufficient for a burnt offering.
> [17] All nations before Him *are* as nothing,
> > And they are counted by Him less than nothing and worthless.
> [18] To whom then will you liken God? ...
> Isa 40:12-18 NKJV

Clearly, this is the LORD our God *Himself* who is coming. "and all flesh shall see *it* together:" Isa 40:5 KJV, so this is clearly the LORD being actually seen. So if this is God Himself who is coming, to be seen in Judah, to rule by His own power, and to be seen by all flesh, *obviously* He will have to be listened to, and He will *obviously* command whatever He wishes. He then would have to be the new lawgiver whom Moses announced.

"The LORD your God will raise up for you **a Prophet like me** from

your midst, from your brethren. Him you shall hear,"
Deut 18:15 NKJV (*bold emphasis added*)

So this is the God/prophet/Messiah who will save all! A personal savior. "He will bring justice to the nations." Isa 42:1 NASB. He is the cornerstone of all of creation! Then comes more of the story. This cornerstone will be rejected. Even so, He is not rejected by just *anyone*. He is rejected by the builders of God's Holy nation Israel!

> [22] The stone *which* the builders refused is become the head *stone* of the corner. [23] This is the LORD'S doing; it is marvelous in our eyes.
> Psa 118:22-23 KJV

Logically, if "man" is to rule, then you have to even reject God, even if he comes as a man, and particularly if He comes as a "man" who rejects the rule of men. The builders of God's nation do not want this particular "man." And this is from the LORD, for it is "the LORD'S doing" that the unbelieving Jews, the builders, would reject him. They have rejected God's ways, it might even be said, always; and have loved their own ways. Modern Jewish scholar Israel Shahak tells us that the Talmud accepts responsibility for Jesus death.

> "According to the Talmud, Jesus was executed by a proper rabbinical court for idolatry, inciting others to idolatry, and contempt of rabbinical authority. All classical Jewish sources ... are quite happy to take responsibility for it; in the talmudic account the Romans are not even mentioned." *Jewish History, Jewish Religion*, pg 98

So it has worked out that the Jews will not see, not understand this.

> [9] He said, "Go, and tell this people:
> 'Keep on hearing, but do not understand;
> > Keep on seeing, but do not perceive.'
> [10] "Make the heart of this people dull,
> > And their ears heavy,
> > And shut their eyes;
> > Lest they see with their eyes,
> > And hear with their ears,
> > And understand with their heart,
> > And return and be healed." " Isa 6:9-10 NKJV

They have made themselves unworthy of His mercy, so they will not understand when He comes. Then comes the question: How long then will this go on? And the answer? Until the cities of Judah are destroyed, and have no one to live in them.

> Then I said, "Lord, how long?"
> And He answered:
> > "Until the cities are laid waste and without inhabitant,

The houses are without a man,
The land is utterly desolate," Isa 9:11 NKJV

This Messiah will be alienated from His own kin.

> ⁷ Because for thy sake I have borne reproach; shame hath covered my face. ⁸ I am become a stranger unto my brethren, and an alien unto my mother's children. ⁹ For the zeal of thine house hath eaten me up; and the reproaches of them that reproached thee are fallen upon me. Psa 69:7-9 KJV

Thus it is to be that the Jews will trip over their own Messiah.

> ¹⁴ "**He will be as a sanctuary**,
>> But a stone of stumbling and a rock of offense
>> To both the houses of Israel,
>> **As a trap and a snare to the inhabitants of Jerusalem**.
>
> ¹⁵   And many among them shall stumble;
>> **They shall fall and be broken,**
>> **Be snared and taken**." Isa 8:14-15 NKJV (*bold emphasis added*)

Further this Messiah, the Savior of the Jews, the God of the Jews, will be killed by the Jews.

> ¹² Many bulls have surrounded me;
> Strong *bulls* of Bashan have encircled me.
> ¹³ They open wide their mouth at me,
> As a ravening and a roaring lion.
> ¹⁴ I am poured out like water,
> And all my bones are out of joint;
> My heart is like wax;
> It is melted within me.
> ¹⁵ My strength is dried up like a potsherd,
> And my tongue cleaves to my jaws;
> And You lay me in the dust of death.
> ¹⁶ For dogs have surrounded me;
> A band of evildoers has encompassed me;
> **They pierced my hands and my feet**. Psa 22:12-16 NASB

None of this fits the author David, even though he writes in the first person. Bulls of Bashan, men of Israel, are who kill this One. Men vicious like lions, like dogs, who pierce Him. He is "in the dust of death," vs 15. The God who appears, who appears as a man, ... He then dies as a man. Where was He to be pierced, *shanan* שָׁנַן? "They pierced my hands and my feet." Psa 22:16. And the other prophets also bear witness to these things.

> And I will pour **upon the house of David, and upon the inhabitants of Jerusalem,** the spirit of grace and of supplications: **and they shall**

look upon me **whom they have pierced**, and they shall mourn for him, as one mourneth for his only son, and shall be in bitterness for him, as one that is in bitterness for his firstborn.

Zech 12:10 KJV (*emphasis added*)

It is the Jews who rejected Him, who pierced (*daqar* דָּקַר in Zech 12:10) Him, who kill Him, by God's will. So the Jews, fatally, did not listen to their greatest rabbi. Pierced, Isa 53:5. Executed, Isa 53:7, 12. Crushed Isa 53:10. There is more to say from both Isaiah and Zechariah and from all of the prophets. All which is to happen at the hands of a disobedient and obstinate people.

² "I have spread out My hands all day long **to a rebellious people**,
Who walk *in* the way which is not good, **following their own thoughts**,
³ A people **who continually provoke Me to My face,**
Offering sacrifices in gardens and burning incense on bricks;
⁴ Who sit among graves and spend the night in secret places;
Who eat swine's flesh,
And the broth of unclean meat is *in* their pots.
⁵ "Who say, 'Keep to yourself, do not come near me,
For I am holier than you!'
These are smoke in My nostrils,
A fire that burns all the day.
⁶ "Behold, it is written before Me,
I will not keep silent, but I will repay;
I will even repay into their bosom,
⁷ **Both their own iniquities and the iniquities of their fathers**
        together," says the LORD.
"Because they have burned incense on the mountains
And scorned Me on the hills,
Therefore I will measure their former work into their bosom."
Isa 65:2-7 NASB (*bold emphasis added*)

These things will come upon Israel.

¹² He who said to them, "Here is rest, give rest to the weary,"
And, "Here is repose," but they would not listen.
¹³ So the word of the LORD to them will be,
"Order on order, order on order,
Line on line, line on line,
A little here, a little there,"
That they may go and **stumble backward, be broken, snared and taken captive.** Isa 28:12-13 NASB (*bold emphasis added*)

So it *has* happened, line on line.

Unless we understand
the distortions
which have arisen
from rejecting
their own Messiah,
we will not be
prepared for
the changes
which have arisen
among the Jews.

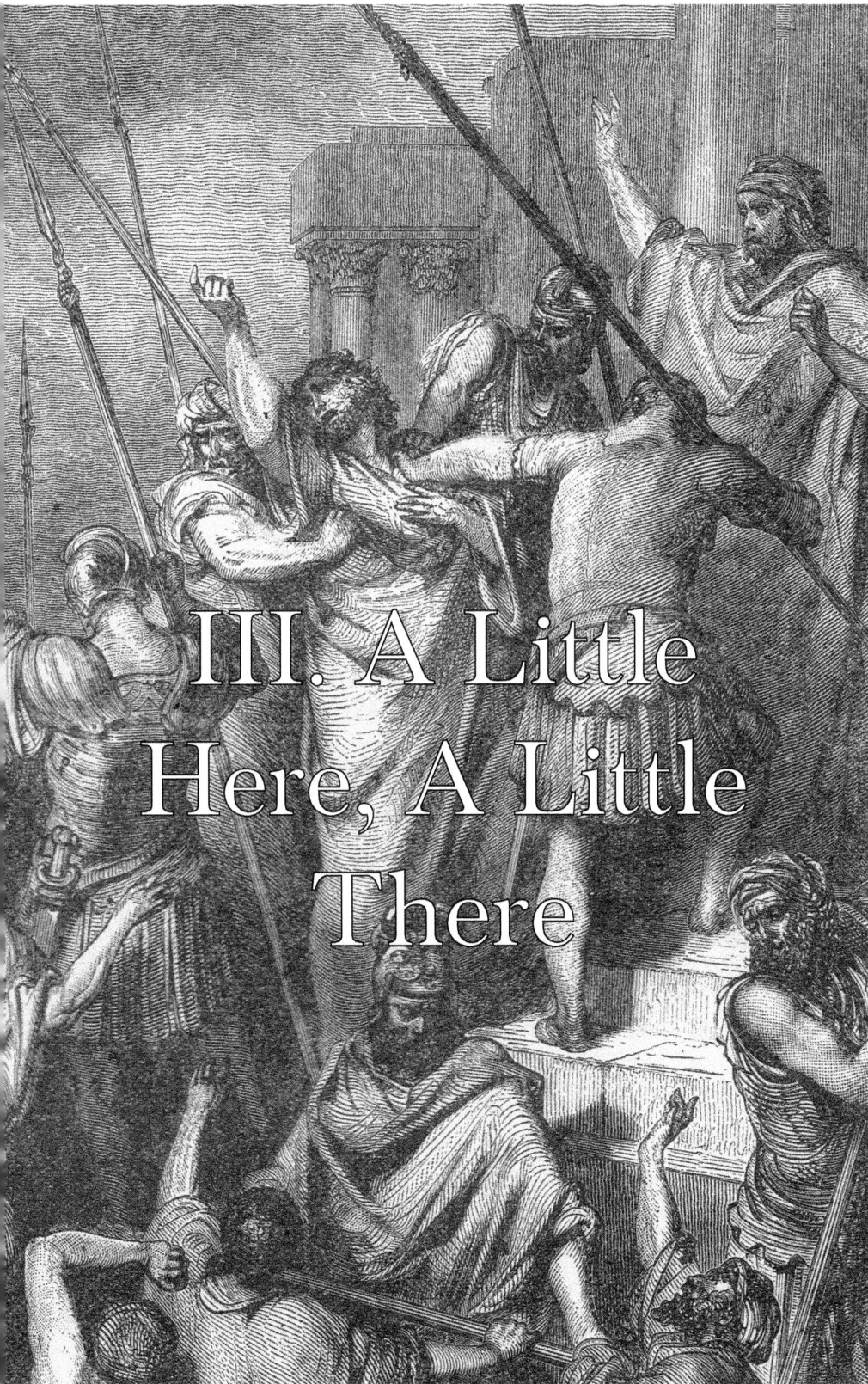

III. A Little Here, A Little There

Therefore shall the word of Yahweh be to them precept on precept, precept on precept; line on line, line on line; here a little, there a little; that they may go, and fall backward, and be broken, and snared, and taken.
Isaiah 28:13 WEB

The Proconsul and the Magician

The "Court Jews" in History.

Telling the story of modern Judaism, it is often hard to know where to start. In this case I am picking an early starting point: the story of Joseph in Egypt in the book of Genesis. Joseph is an alien slave in a foreign land, and he quickly gravitates toward loyal service to those gentiles who are his masters, and throught a s series of circumstances, he soon rises to be the Vice President of Egypt, and the "go to" man for the Pharaoh. He saves Egypt from a tremendous environmental catastrophe.

The Jews down through history, and especially since the first deportation into Babylon, have tried to get key personnel placed near whoever is in power. This has often been described as being a "Court Jew." This has become an art form for them, extending from the Old Testament days, well into today. For a great deal of this, there is no better documentation than Scripture.

We see this in Daniel's service to the Babylonian Empire, which was so exemplary that it was continued in the Persian Empire. See the book of Daniel in Scripture. Although these two examples were involuntary in their origins, the lessons learned from these examples gave many Jews a good impetus to get close to gentile rulers and to *try* to give them good conscientious service. Next, we see Ezra in the Biblical book of Ezra.

> [1] Now after these things, in the reign of Artaxerxes king of Persia, Ezra the son of Seraiah, ... [6] This Ezra went up from Babylon; and he was a ready scribe in the law of Moses, which the LORD God of Israel had given: and the king granted him all his request, according to the hand of the LORD his God upon him. Ezra 7:1, 6 KJV

Ezra proceeded to use his influence, especially in getting a new temple built at Jerusalem. The next we see is Nehemiah, in the Biblical book of Nehemiah. Nehemiah, a godly man, had a very responsible job before the King of Persia. He was responsible for serving the King at meals, and as such was trusted to help protect the king from attempts to poison him.

And it came to pass in the month Nisan, in the twentieth year of

Artaxerxes the king, *that* wine was before him: and I took up the wine, and gave *it* unto the king. ... Neh 2:1 KJV

Nehemiah then used his influence with this gentile king to a obtain a special charter to rebuild his native city Jerusalem and to help his own people. He received his authorization and letters from the king giving him permission to draw from public funds to accomplish the work, and set off to Jerusalem, and to work. He returned to the king's service after completing his mission. These are all sterling examples of how the Jews at their best have operated down through history, **often to the benefit of both** the Jews **and** their gentile masters and there are many such good examples down through history and **even to our present day**.

A Persian king with a cup bearer. From a relief carving.

There have been, and are, women used in these enterprises, so starting more or less in Esther's day there was a covert side to these enterprises, as has already been noted, but often there was plenty of overt work: for instance Poppea as the Jewish mistress and later wife of Nero; and there were the Court Jews.

Professor Heinrich Graetz's multi-volume *History of the Jews*, Philadelphia: Jewish Publication Society of America. 1891-1898, does not use the term "Court Jew" very often, but his history is full of examples of the Court Jews, from ancient times to modern times. He mentions in Volume II the special relationship between the Emperor Caligula, and Agrippa (10 BC - 44 AD). Almost everywhere that he brings up this subject, he mentions gentile envy of Jewish prosperity *throughout history!* This very much included the early centuries. Graetz mentions in connection with ancient Alexandria in Egypt, "burning envy at the prosperous condition of the Judaeans." Graetz *History of the Jews,* Vol 2, pg 180. When speaking of later day Spanish nobles he notes,

> "The impoverished nobles, who possessed nothing more than their swords, were filled with envy of the rich and wise court Jews ; but they were compelled to stifle their feelings." Graetz, Vol 4, pg 76

In fact, I think it is no exaggeration to say that Graetz paints an almost consistent picture of the Jews getting along well with gentile kings and princes and popes (they could help them make money), but only being opposed by the ignorant masses (my terminology, not Graetz's), or "the serpent-like cunning of the clergy, lying concealed but ready to attack the Jews." Vol 4, pg 76. Graetz continually mentions the gentile rulers and popes as trying to protect the Jews, but very often being unable because of widespread opposition to Jewish dominance. He mentions,

> "The court of Vienna invented another means of making Jews contribute to the war. It appointed Jewish capitalists as court Jews, granted them most extensive freedom of trade, freed them from the restrictions to which other Jews were subjected, even from wearing the yellow badge, in a word, afforded them and their families an exceptionally favored position." Graetz, Vol 4, pg 702

The ups and downs of the Jews' relationships with Venice could also be mentioned. They similarly had extraordinary success in Spain, but their successes coupled with their arrogance and hubris often led to big trouble for the Jewish people. These things are also seen in the first and second centuries BC and AD, and in the New Testament.

And What is a Magician?

Then comes the "Court Jew" as a magician/sorcerer, a Jewish magician by the name of Bar-jesus or Elymas, Acts 13:6. He is described in Acts as a magician and as a false prophet (the Greek for magician or sorcerer here is *magos* μάγος, just like in Mtt 2:1, where it speaks of the "magi"). Now "false prophet" we understand: it means one who pretends to speak for God but really does not, and who because he does not really speak for God, and cannot really foretell the future.

What then is a "real" magician? A magician, a "real" magician, is one who tries to use spirits other than the Most High God to carry out his desires. We are instructed to pray only through Jesus Christ to the Most High God. We are warned against dealing with other spirits and told to test the spirits to see if they are of God. Also we are told that any spirit that denies that Jesus is of God and has come in the flesh, is not of God, 1Jn 4:1. Still, how did it come about that many Jews became involved in magic and witchcraft?

Will Durant in his volume *The Age of Louis XIV*, devotes chapter XVI to "The Jewish Enclaves." Durant, who certainly was not hostile toward the Jews, and was very sympathetic to their situation, attributes many of their less savory characteristics to the lowly crafts they were forced to adopt to make a living, and to the Jews being subject to gentile persecution in Medieval and Modern times. In his words,

> "From these occupations, and the humiliations of the ghetto, the poorer Jews developed those habits of dress and speech, those tricks of trade and qualities of mind, that were so distasteful to other peoples and higher ranks." Will Durant, *The Age of Louis XIV*, pg 470

This is a popular view of Jews during the Christian Age. On one hand, notice that this view is generally at variance with the very competent Jewish historian Graetz's view of the Jews as overall being very prosperous during almost the entire Christian age, *and that* inspiring almost continual envy and jealously. On the other hand, what is seen above from Will Durant is among other things, an assessment of how it has appeared to many. Additionally, any serious historian of the Jews has to deal with, and somehow account for, the Jewish *multi-millennia devotion to the occult, witchcraft and magic*, a phenomenon which, as we have seen and will see, cannot be avoided. Likewise Durant attributes this to their persecution and he says that this is what drove them to the occult.

> "The rabbis, who in the middle Ages had been men of courage and wisdom, became in this age devotees of a mysticism that fled from the hell of persecution and penury into a heaven of compensatory dreams. **The Talmud in the Middle Ages had replaced the Bible as the soul of Judaism; now the Cabala replaced the Talmud.**"
> Durant, *The Age of Louis XIV*, pgs 470-471 *(bold emphasis added)*

These are telling admissions: the Bible had been *replaced*, and also he says the Talmud has been *replaced*, in more modern times. These are basic conclusions your author has been led to, but which have not been caught by many, inside or outside of Judaism. The story actually goes back further than even the Middle Ages, as can be seen even in our present texts in Acts. It goes all the way back to the early history of Israel as they were about to enter Canaan. It is a sad story of bad company. "Do not be deceived: 'Bad company corrupts good morals,'" 1Cor 15:33 NASB. That is what the prophet and apostle Paul says. Scripture over and over emphasizes this.

> He that walketh with wise *men* shall be wise: but a companion of fools shall be destroyed. Prov 13:20 KJV

It is a story that began long ago. A story that began with warnings and cautions and advice. The story really begins in the book of Genesis, with talk of a nation that is really going in bad directions: the Amorites. Abraham is told that his descendants will not take over the land of Canaan right away, because the sins of the Amorites were not yet "full" to use the phrase of the King James Version, Gen 15:16. The people of Israel were warned not to let these people continue to live in Palestine because they would make the Israelites sin against the Lord, and entice them to serve their gods, Ex 23:33. They were told why in Deut 7:3-5; that is because it would cause the Lord their God to be angry against them.

We are told over and over in Scripture that the "gods" of these nations were not really "gods." It does **not** *actually* say that they are not "*real*," rather that they are not "gods." Speaking prophetically of what Israel would do, Moses says,

> [16] "They made Him jealous with strange *gods*;
> With abominations they provoked Him to anger.

[17] "They sacrificed to demons who were not God,
To *gods* whom they have not known,
New gods who came lately,
Whom your fathers did not dread. Deut 32:16-17 NASB

What did the Israelites sacrifice to? To "... demons who were not God."
That is the same answer that Paul gives about pagan sacrifices.

> [18] Observe Israel after the flesh: Are not those who eat of the sacrifices
> partakers of the altar? [19] What am I saying then? That an idol is
> anything, or what is offered to idols is anything? [20] Rather, that the
> **things which the Gentiles sacrifice they sacrifice to demons** and not
> to God, and I do not want you to have fellowship with demons. [21] You
> cannot drink the cup of the Lord and the cup of demons; you cannot
> partake of the Lord's table and of the table of demons. [22] Or do we
> provoke the Lord to jealousy? Are we stronger than He?
> 1Cor 10:18-22 NKJV *(bold emphasis added)*

So both gentiles and Jews in sacrificing to other "gods" are actually sacrificing to demons. Are demons real? Are they powerful spiritual beings? The answer in Scripture is yes and yes. They are evidently angels who have sinned against the Lord and have sided with that great angelic rebel Satan. Peter describes angels as those "which are greater in power and might," 2 Pe 2:11 KJV. What then can these powerful <u>creatures</u> do? They can only do as they are *allowed*, to either help man or hurt man. This process can be seen most clearly in Job chapter 1 and 2, and in passages like 1 Kings 22 about the death of Ahab. These demonic angels seem to have plenty of malice toward mankind generally, but, again, can act only as they are *allowed*.

Jesus was in the beginning with God and He was God, *and nothing in heaven or earth, whether material or spiritual, principalities or powers, came into being without Him* (Jn 1:1-3 and Col 1:16). "He is before all things in Him all things hold together," Col 1:17 NASB. From the uniform point of view of Scripture, it makes no sense to petition the help of the lower spiritual powers, whether they are either good or bad. *All* are in the power of God; so seek the LORD, follow Him, petition God Himself. None can help you apart from Him, even in the most prosaic sense.

[1] Unless the LORD builds the house,
They labor in vain who build it;
Unless the LORD guards the city,
The watchman keeps awake in vain.
[2] It is vain for you to rise up early,
To retire late,
To eat the bread of painful labors;
For He gives to His beloved *even in his* sleep. Psa 127:1-2 NASB

Everything in the final analysis depends on God. Departed spirits and Satan himself are helpless before His power. The people of God are supposed to consult the true and living God and not other spirits. The prophet Isaiah accused the Jewish people of these things and wrote,

> [19] And when they say to you, "Seek those who are mediums and wizards, who whisper and mutter," should not a people seek their God? *Should they seek* the dead on behalf of the living? [20] To the law and to the testimony! If they do not speak according to this word, *it is* because *there is* no light in them. Isa 8:19-20 NKJV

It is the old story of being under the influence of those who do not share our values and ideals. However, much of Israel did not heed these prohibitions, as can be seen also in Acts 13. Then over time Israel came to regard help, any help; whether sacred or profane, whether real or imagined, or if only in potential, not in practice; as worth pursuing. So Israel took up the magic practices of the Canaanites. They were warned! They were warned that, "You shall not permit a sorceress to live." Ex 22:18 NKJV. That is how stern Moses' laws were against these practices. It was even promised that the Lord Himself will cut that person off.

> "The person that turns to those who are mediums, and to the wizards, to play the prostitute after them, I will even set my face against that person, and will cut him off from among his people." Lev 20:6 WEB

It **did not** say that they **could not** seek the help from the spirit world, but that God would set His face against those who **did** seek the help of what John calls "other spirits," 1 Jn 4:1. The people of God are not supposed to take up any of the forms of the occult.

> [10] "There shall not be found among you anyone who makes his son or his daughter pass through the fire, one **who uses divination**, one **who practices witchcraft**, or one **who interprets omens**, or **a sorcerer**, [11] or one **who casts a spell, or a medium, or a spiritist**, or **one who calls up the dead**. [12] For whoever does these things is detestable to the LORD; and because of these detestable things the LORD your God will drive them out before you. [13] You shall be blameless before the LORD your God. [14] For those nations, which you shall dispossess, listen to those who practice witchcraft and to diviners, but as for you, **the LORD God has not allowed you *to do* so.**
> Deut 18:10-14 NASB *(bold emphasis added)*

Such practices are "detestable" to God. *It is not a matter of whether in some very limited way it may "work," rather it is that* **"your God has not allowed you to do so."** The Israelites mixed it up with being a prophet like the true prophets of God, and they produced many false prophets, as was discussed earlier, and you can see many such men in the books of Kings, Jeremiah, and Ezekiel, etc. So the Jews took up many of the evil practices of the Canaanites, and it is a strange fact that in an age when the influence of Christ was banishing most demonic worship and service in the world, it is the Jews who covertly kept much of this alive, and who have been a leading conduit for many of these evil practices down to the modern world! Graetz speaking later of the Jewish Kabbalah occultist said the same thing.

> "Then for the first time the Jewish world entered on a "dark age" of its own, with all the appropriate credulity, while only the last traces of such darkness were visible in Europe generally." Graetz, Vol 4, pg 617

As I have shown, that was not "the first time," as Graetz asserts, but that the Jews had continually dabbled in these things down through history. You can see all of this in bits and pieces at different places in history. *Some* Jews (by no means all) were at many times in history practitioners of the vilest parts of these practices. When we think of one who "interprets omens" in the modern world, we think of "reading the stars" or tea leaves, or maybe bumps on your head. In the ancient world, on the other hand, to foresee the future, a favorite was augury, the disemboweling of generally an animal, in order to "read" its intestines, in order to foretell the future. Of course, at times these things took criminal turns. The Roman satirist Juvenal (60-140 AD) commented on the Jewish fortune tellers of his own day.

> "... a palsied Jewess, parking her haybox outside, comes begging in a breathy whisper. She interprets Jerusalem's laws, she's the tree's high priestess, a faithful mediator of heaven on earth. She likewise fills her palm, but more sparingly: Jews will sell you whatever dreams you like for a few small coppers. A young lover for the lady, or a good fat inheritance from some childless millionaire, are predicted (after inspection

Fortune telling by reading the entrails of an animal was common in ancient times. Here is a clay model of a sheep's liver from ancient Babylon, telling the meaning

of a pigeons's steaming lungs) by Eastern fortune-tellers, who'll unravel a chicken's or puppy's innards, sometimes even a child's; the seer can always shop his client."
(From Satire VI), Peter Green's translation of *Juvenal, The Sixteen Satires*, Penguin Books, 2004, pg 51

So she is "the tree's high priestess"? Shades of Genesis? Or shades of what was later the Kabbalistic "tree of life"? Here is a scene which might to some seem to be a Medieval "Christian" "slander," but which is actually from first century AD pagan Rome. It is from a biting satire on what is wrong with Rome of that day, a satire which does not blame the Jews for Rome's problems, nor does it completely exempt them, for their minor part. Sadly, you can run into comments on such things about the Jews throughout history. It has been as the prophet Hosea said.

> [8] "Ephraim has mixed himself among the peoples;
>   Ephraim is a cake unturned.
> [9]   Aliens have devoured his strength,
>   But he does not know *it*;
>   Yes, gray hairs are here and there on him,
>   Yet he does not know *it*. Hos 7:8-9. NKJV

Thus Israel took up many of the wicked practices of the Canaanites, and many of them kept up these things all through the captivity in Assyria and Babylon, through the first century period, and even to this very day. It mentions in Deut 18:10-11 one "who makes his son or his daughter pass through the fire," that is human sacrifice, or "one who uses divination, one who practices witchcraft, or one who interprets omens, or a sorcerer, ... or one who casts a spell," NASB. All of those things involved seeking other spirits, evil spirits. Scripture points out, much of this was not even subdued by the deportations to Assyria and Babylon for their sin, Jer 44:17-25. The connection between the occult and the various streams of Judaism continues to this day. Such can even be seen in other places in the New Testament. Remember earlier that the disciples had run into a magician in Samaria.

> [9] But there was a certain man called Simon, who previously practiced sorcery in the city and astonished the people of Samaria, claiming that he was someone great, [10] to whom they all gave heed, from the least to the greatest, saying, "This man is the great power of God." [11] And they heeded him because he had astonished them with his sorceries for a long time. Acts 8:9-11 NKJV

The Greek word used here for "sorceries," as it is in the New King James Version, is *mageia* μαγεία which is of course related to *magos* or magician. The Jewish link to the occult is something you can see all through history even to modern times. Simon himself was converted to Christ, but not without some lingering attachment to old habits, which Peter sternly warned him to forsake.

Paul and Barnabas in Cyprus.

In Acts 13:2-3 Barnabas and Saul have been separated by the Holy Spirit to do a special work for the Lord. A mission of continuing the spread of the gospel to all of the world. So they are setting sail for Cyprus in Acts 13:4-5. Barnabas, if you know the story, was a Jew who was originally from Cyprus, Acts 4:36. If you remember, when Stephen was murdered and the disciples were scattered, some of the believers went to Cyprus according to Acts 11:19. So Paul and Barnabas set sail for Cyprus, landing at Salamis and preaching in the synagogue there, and went through the whole island, ending up at Paphos. They create enough of a stir on the island that they are brought before the Roman proconsul on the island in Acts 13:6-7.

Sergius Paulus and Elymas.

A Roman proconsul was many things. He was a combination of a State Department diplomat, a judge, and a general. He maintained official diplomatic relations with a country. He ruled over many local matters personally. He acted as a judge or magistrate in many trials. Those guilty of crimes were then often beaten by the official "lictors" who accompanied the proconsul. In time of war, the proconsul drafted and trained local troops to supplement the Roman army, and led them in battle and campaigns. As a group they were tough, intelligent, and able men, who helped maintain order in the empire. Over all, you could say they were good men in the sense of competent government, given the times, and actually much better than most countries in those times.

The mini-hero of our story, the Proconsul is described as "Sergius Paulus, a man of intelligence," NASB. The Jewish magician, in contrast, was having a very negative influence on the Proconsul.

> But Elymas the sorcerer (for so is his name by interpretation) withstood them, seeking to turn aside the proconsul from the faith.
> Acts 13:8 WEB

What was this faith then which Elymas taught? It was certainly not of Moses, else he would not have been a magician. Then Saul faced this corrupt teacher directly.

> [9] But Saul, who was also *known as* Paul, filled with the Holy Spirit, fixed his gaze on him, [10] and said, "You who are full of all deceit and fraud, you son of the devil, you enemy of all righteousness, will you not cease to make crooked the straight ways of the Lord? [11] Now, behold, the hand of the Lord is upon you, and you will be blind and not see the sun for a time." And immediately a mist and a darkness fell upon him, and he went about seeking those who would lead him by the hand.
> Acts 13:9-11 NASB

Sergius Paulus was converted to the Messiah of the Jews, ... but many of the Jews, men and women like the Jewess fortune teller and Elymas included, remained resistant to the call of God's own Holy Spirit, and their own Messiah. Continuously so, it should be added, even to our own times.

Gnosticism and a Lunatic Fringe

There were in the early centuries before Jesus the Christ, some special developments in what modern English would call the occult, that is to say, hidden or semi-secret religion. In ancient terms these would often be called the mystery religions. These religions were called "mysteries," and their teachings (also called "mysteries") were secret, and were things to which you had to be introduced, or taught. Their secrets were not things you could figure out. Someone had to teach you these things. For a fuller discussion of the Mystery Religions, see my earlier volume, *Prophecy Principles*.

As one enters the first and second centuries AD, a major movement in the mystery religions went by the name of what modern scholars often call "Gnosticism." Gnosticism itself is an inexact term, and it is often applied to a wide variety of mystical religious groups of this period. Jewish scholar Gershom G. Scholem puts it this way.

> "'Gnosticism,' ... is a rather loose term. Only a few of the several sects, groups, and tendencies now considered 'Gnostic' were known as such in their time. But this does not preclude the use of this term for the religious movement that proclaimed a mystical esotericism ..." *Jewish Gnosticism, Merkabah Mysticism, and Talmudic Tradition,* New York, The Jewish Theological Seminary of America, 1960, 2012, pg 1

Scholem discusses what he calls Hekhaloth literature (we might call this, perhaps oversimplifying the issues, a literature of the "palaces" of God). Part of his stated purpose was to "... to consider the relationship between the Hekhaloth writings and the talmudic tradition, ... and the elements of Gnostic teaching ..." pg 65. In other words, *did Gnosticism arise out of Judaism?* The title of his book tells the story of the relationship between Jewish Gnosticism and what he calls "Merkabah Mysticism" (loosely, "chariot" mysticism/literature, about what might be called "the chariot of the 'gods'") *and* Talmudic tradition. It has already been shown how Biblical religion from Moses degenerated into a system of authoritative human tradition under the Pharisees, and how these traditions came to be written down and to some extent codified in what is called the Talmud. Then comes another phase. That is latent paganism in Judaism developing into full-blown occult paganism among some of the Jews.

The word Gnostic itself comes from the Greek word for knowledge, *gnosis* γνῶσις. A gnostic then is someone who "knows," that is to say has been initiated into the secrets of whatever religious order is involved, or who at least *thinks* he "knows." Gnosticism, as it is generally known in history, began to develop even before the first century AD, but it is not known by how much. Not all of this "knowledge" is logical, and most of it is not in any way Scriptural, but an overview can be pieced together of some of the key ideas, and how they affected Judaism and Christianity, logical or not. Jewish historian Heinrich Graetz, gives us a succinct look at some of these key teachings in as good a form as any for accuracy and brevity.

> "The Gnostics, or more correctly, the Theosophists, who hovered between Judaism, Christianity and Paganism, and who borrowed their views and forms of thought from these three circles, were drawn also from the adherents of these three religions."
> Graetz, *History of the Jews,* Vol 2, pg 374

If you are investigating the possible Jewish roots of Gnosticism, then comes the embarrassing discussion (at least to Judaism) of the dualism and the pantheism which is rampant in Gnosticism, the occult, and in the mystery religions generally. Jewish scholar Gershom Scholem speaks all around these issues in his works. Overall Scholem is far too reserved to tell us many things in anything like a direct manner. Instead he tends to function as an apologist for the Jewish occult. Graetz, while not dealing directly with origins, speaks frankly of the Gnostic "god" as having a dual nature.

> "The Gnostics pictured to themselves the Divine Being as divided into two principles of a God and a Creator, the one subordinate to the other. God they called Silence or Rest, and depicted him as enthroned in the empyrean heights, without relation to the world. His fundamental attributes were grace, love, mercy. From him proceeded emanations which revealed a portion of his essence ; these emanations were called aeons (worlds)." Graetz, Vol 2, pg 375

Graetz does not say it, but some went further so as to say that there were two grounds of being, two eternal substances (one spiritual and one material), and in essence, two gods. This led some to a treatment of good and evil which Graetz describes in Vol 2, pgs 374-375

> "One sect called themselves Cainites, for no other reason than that its disciples, in defiance of the Biblical narrative, regarded the fratricide Cain as superior to Abel. The Cainites also honored the depraved Sodomites, Esau, in spite of his savagery, and the ambitious Korah. The Ophites and Naasites were filled with similar love of opposition to the Biblical accounts, but they assigned to it a better motive than that of the Cainites. **They took their name from the Greek word Ophis and the Hebrew Nahash (Naas) serpent**, and honored this animal very

highly, **because in the Bible the serpent is considered as the origin of evil**, and, according to the ideas of those times, was looked upon as the symbol of evil, and **as the form taken by Satan**. The Ophites gave thanks to the serpent, by whose means the first human pair were led into disobedience against God, and thus to the recognition of good and evil and of consciousness in general." (*bold emphasis added*)

Most of us in plain terms would call this open manifestations of the worship of Satan. The righteous are counted as wicked, and the wicked are counted as righteous!

The Worship of Evil.

You need to think this out to see the logic in it. All of us can see that there is a terrific battle between good and evil going on in our universe. Scripture supports the totally good Lord our God, Yahweh, the Lord of Hosts (Armies), the Master of Heaven and Earth. If the Lord is the only ground of being, then obviously He will win in the end. Satan, then, is no more than a powerful, but doomed fool, and we have to be fools to follow him. On the other hand, if there are actually *two* grounds of being, if there is in fact an eternal *spiritual* substance and if in fact there is also an eternal (even though, they say, evil) *matter* out of which our universe is formed, *then there are two grounds of existence in our universe. If in* **theory** *these could exist* **independently of each other**, then the winner in this contest is an open bet! So here, for the first time, is presented the possibility of **evil** winning in this universe, and it going on to have an existence completely separate from God! There is more to say here than there is space. For instance, evil matter as a separate and eternal ground of being also speaks of a sort of pantheism (everything is god), and pantheism is all around in the occult, Gnosticism, *and* Jewish Gnosticism. This too is a problem for Scholem, and for all of the occult oriented Jews who want to pretend some sort of allegiance to the Law of Moses. Further, almost all of the commentators on Gnosticism, and on the supposed "evolution of the species," do **not** discuss the **fact** that an "eternal matter" violates the Second Law of Thermodynamics, or entropy. This is the law which in essence says of everything physical that "things run down." And *if* all things run down, then *neither* matter, *nor* anything else which is physical *could* **ever** *be eternal*. **Thus, Gnosticism is** *really* <u>anti-scientific</u>, **not just unscientific!** This is a side point which is almost never discussed. Sorry to inject reality here. It seems to be politically incorrect to point these things out.

Going back to Gnosticism, and following their logic, if you look around, who does it look like is winning the battle between good and evil? If one tests this proposition only after the flesh, then indeed some may conclude that "the evil god" Satan is winning (at least here on earth). Indeed, even Scripture says, "We know that we are of God, and the whole world lies *under the sway of* the wicked one." 1Jn 5:19 NKJV. Suddenly, *if* you believe this anti-scientific foolishness, it becomes an open question whether one should side with the Lord our God or with Satan. Graetz in the quote above is describing Gnostics who are siding with Satan! Their villains are the good men of righteousness in the Bible, and their heroes are the wicked people of Scripture: Cain, the men of Sodom and Gomorrah, the sons of Korah who rebelled against Moses in the book of Numbers, and so on. This would seem to point to parts of the "mystery of lawlessness" of 2Thes 2:7.

Now not all Gnostics took such a position, but here is the key point: **Gnostic theology provided a seemingly "rational" foundation for siding with Satan, a "ground" on which formal Satanism could be erected!** It may take a while for the reader to absorb all of that, but this is one of the key developments. All of this, of course, had some very very negative moral results. Graetz describes it as "the evil Gnostic morality, and ... a dissolute life." Vol 2, pg 377. In Gnostic terminology, what might be called Satan, is described as the Ruler or the Demiurge.

> "Beneath this highest of all beings they set the Creator of the world (Demiurge), whom they also called Ruler. To him they assigned the work of creation; he directed the world, he had delivered the people of Israel, and given them the Law." Graetz, Vol 2, pg 375

So in this system, the creator of the world is the evil "god," and he is the one they call the "true" God of Israel! (See also Scholem, *Jewish Gnosticism* ..., pg 35.)

In Gnostic theory the true God, the spiritual God, was too holy to have anything to do with anything as evil and as flawed as physical matter. So in their theory God emanated a spirit from Himself. This spirit was a good spirit and a powerful spirit, but not quite as good or as powerful as God Himself. This spirit, although a very good spirit, this first emanation did not quite have a full knowledge of God. This spirit then emanated another spirit, even more ignorant of God and more separated from God, and that spirit emanated another spirit ... and on, and on. Finally, a spirit was emanated which was totally ignorant of the true God, and totally evil, in fact a spirit that was evil enough to "create" the physical universe out of evil matter: the god of Israel! *So they said!*

These emanations are pictured by the Gnostics as like the layers of an onion, and is pictured much like the chart on the next page.

It is almost impossible to exaggerate the importance of these key ideas for the development of the Jewish occult and world wide occultism.

So it was natural that somewhere before the appearance of the true Jewish Messiah, Jesus of Nazareth, around 26 or 27 AD, there developed some small, but very important, Satanic splinter groups in Judaism. ***This is NOT explicitly dealt with by most Jewish authors**, occasionally implicitly, but it is there.* It is further to be seen in the main body of Judaism, not only an explicit rejection of their own Messiah, Jesus of Nazareth; but also often a tacit acceptance of a Satanic fringe within Judaism, *within **parts*** of those circles who claimed human tradition as authoritative. Traces of these things are seen in the New Testament, principally written by Jewish prophets of the first century AD. When Jesus was debating with the Pharisees, he said of them,

> [42] Jesus said unto them, If God were your Father, ye would love me: for I proceeded forth and came from God; neither came I of myself, but he sent me. [43] Why do ye not understand my speech? *even* because ye cannot hear my word. [44] Ye are of your father the devil, and the lusts of *your* father ye will do. He was a murderer from the beginning, and abode not in the truth, because there is no truth in him. When he speaketh a lie, he speaketh of his own: for he is a liar, and the father of it.
> Jn 8:42-44 KJV

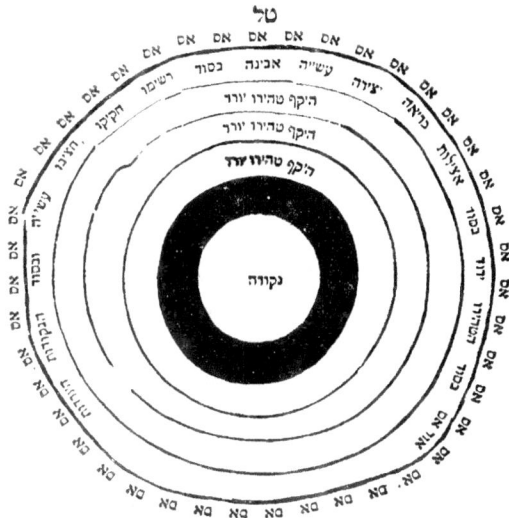

A Hebrew/Gnostic chart of the emanations or spheres preceeding from The Most High God.

There is more than one important observation to make at this point. ***First***, that the occurrence of Satanism is not a phenomenon which is limited to Judaism. The number of true Satanists are minuscule, and they are happily missed in most nations, but they do exist in more than one society, and are hidden in more than one religion, including "Christianity." The worship of the Devil or Satan is something which is seen in varying degrees, and under various names, in a wide range of nations and tribal groups in this world. It is seen in many types of societies, from backward primitive or rural groups, to sophisticated urban groups. There is probably enough documentation to satisfy you in Richard Cavendish's very scholarly, and very disgusting, multi-volume encyclopedia, *Man, Myth, and Magic.* You can perhaps find a copy of it in your local public library, or maybe even in your government school library. Almost always Satanism, because of its very nature in the worship of what is evil, operates in clandestine ways. ***Secondly***, Satanism is never really a partisan national phenomenon. Such groups may at times appear to be useful to national leaders of one group or another, and they may be *willing* to be used at times; but Satanists are implicitly **not** for **any** national group or religion, **including the Jews**. The Satanist, or any worshippers of Evil, are for evil and for Satan, irrespective of who is hurt, especially man. They are implicitly against mankind, and are against *whoever* is in authority or *whatever* is the *status quo*. An English, or German, or American, or Russian, or Israeli intelligence specialist may view an English, or German, or American, or Russian, or Israeli Satanist as "on their side," and trustworthy because they are of the same nation, but this is never really true. This is built into the very nature of the worship of evil. *Thirdly*, Satanism *always* carries with it enormous ethical baggage, including unbelievable filth and degenerative conduct, including rape, pedophilia, incest, murder, and yes, the pagan bugaboo, human sacrifice, cannibalism and much more. These things are part of the package of evil. It can be found in more than one place, and in more than one nation ... including among the Jews.

I have quoted it before, but it is still a good example, British Intelligence's use of English Satanist Aliester Crowley during the period spanning World War I and World War II. Crowley was a degenerate of unbelievable proportions, and was self proclaimed as "the Great Beast." Richard Deacon in his *A History of the British Secret Service*, Taplinger, NY, 1969, discusses the role of Crowley in British Intelligence, and he comments,

> "There has been from time immemorial a strange union between occultism and espionage, probably because occultists tend to go underground and therefore make good agents." pg 311

Crowley's writings are still popular with a certain portion of the occult, and his books can often be seen on sale in major bookstores in the United States.

So what is the point of noting Satanists, or the worshippers of evil, among the Jews? It should be said first that the Jews tend to be concentrated in whatever they do, or as some have phrased it, Jews tend to be "over-represented" in many things. More of this later, but there are proportionally more doctors among the Jews than there are among most gentile groups, and more lawyers, bankers, historians, college professors, and successful businessmen, and so on. Similarly it would seem that there are more Satanists among the Jews than among most groups, but it would seem that it is still very, very small fractional percentages overall. So because of a weird group of coincidences (including the Kabbalah which will be discussed in section IV), both the knowledge of the existence of Satanism is wider among the Jews than among most gentiles, and tacit tolerance of it is wider. (Although I personally would not say that most Jews have knowledge of even the existence of Satanism). Jesus? No! Satan? Yes?

Perhaps it would be well to note the comments of Jesus the Christ through His Jewish prophet John ben Zebedee. Asia Minor has been a hotbed of Judaism and the occult since at least early Christian times. Jesus, through John, addressed a letter to the first century church in Smyrna in what is today Western Turkey. Jesus told them,

> [8] And unto the angel of the church in Smyrna write; These things saith the first and the last, which was dead, and is alive; [9] I know thy works, and tribulation, and poverty, (but thou art rich) and *I know* the blasphemy of them **which say they are Jews, and are not, but are the synagogue of Satan**. Rev 2:8-9 KJV (*bold emphasis added*)

So what point is Jesus is making about these "Jews" who are causing the Christians at Smyrna so much trouble? Two things come to mind. *First,* to the Christians, that they are not really Jews. They are really of the assembly, the synagogue, of Satan! *Secondly,* perhaps to those of historic Judaism, *No,* they are not really Jews. You may think of them as your ally in trying to destroy Christianity, but they are not really your allies. Today they may try to destroy Christians. Tomorrow they may try to destroy Jews. They say they are Jews and are not. They are not *really* Jews. They are Satanists. Men of another religion.

Opposition to all of Mankind.

What then are some of the names for these various emanations or levels of spirits up to God? Sometimes they are spoken of as aeons, perhaps having a relationship to the aeons of times. At other times they are called "spheres" (sometimes even in our Christian song books), reflecting their supposed relationship to God as spheres or layers of reality, like the layers of an onion as has already been mentioned. Sometimes they are called angels or "stars," and there is some sort of relationship between "angels" and "stars" even in Scripture, though there is not time to discuss it here. In first century Greek they were often referred to as *thronoi* θρόνοι, and *kuriotātes* κυριότητες, and *archai* ἀρχαὶ and *exousai* ἐξουσίαι, or in English, as thrones, dominions, and rulers, and authorities. The Jewish apostle Paul tells us that **they are *real*,** and that they were all created by Jesus the Messiah.

> For by him were all things created, that are in heaven, and that are in earth, visible and invisible, whether *they be* thrones, or dominions, or principalities, or powers: **all things were created** by him, and for him: Col 1:16 KJV (*bold and underline emphasis added*)

So these beings **do** exist, and like us are created beings, though far more powerful than men (2Pe 2:11). Also, just like us, they were created *through* Jesus and *for* Jesus the Messiah. There is one more thing though. Since there has been this gigantic revolt in the universe, many of these self-same powers have become the enemies of mankind.

> For we wrestle not against flesh and blood, but against principalities, against powers, against the rulers of the darkness of this world, against

spiritual wickedness in high *places*. Eph 6:12 KJV

Our fight is not really against people, Jew or Gentile, but against these powerful spiritual beings in "the heavenly *places*."

And the Magical Element.

There is also a magical element in Gnosticism. This comes from several lines of teaching, asserting that there is a correspondence of sorts between this material creation and the levels of emanations. In the occult this is summarized in the phrase, "As above, so below." In other words, things cannot change here on earth (the *microcosm)*, unless they also change in heaven (the *macrocosm*), and similarly, things cannot change in heaven unless they also change on earth. It should be pointed out that this teaching is never proved and really cannot be proved. It is just asserted as if it were true. It is just *assumed!*

This has three implications: **First** that if you observe the changes in heaven above, for instance in the stars, then you can tell what will happen on earth: astrology, reading tea leaves, and such things. **Second**, if all things here on earth have to change to fit what is happening in heaven, then you can look at all of the small things here on earth, and tell what is happening or about to happen to *everything* here on earth. So then you can read tea leaves, the bumps on a man's head, the patterns of the clouds, or the entrails of an animal or a man and tell what is going to happen to *you!* This includes every sort of divination or fortune-telling or augury, or whatever. **Third** and last, if you can change the small-world (the *microcosm*) then by doing that you can also change the big-world (the *macrocosm*). *This means man himself can change the universe, and this is called "imitative magic."* So you can hurt your enemy by making an image of him, and sticking pins in the image (a voodoo doll, a microcosm of your opponent, as in the movies), or you can stage a magic play (or a movie, no doubt) in which you defeat or win over your opponent, and so place a curse or a charm on your enemy, and so be able to defeat him in real life. Or possibly you could make a convincing movie about some part of history, and actually change history? Magic! A way to "manipulate" the so-called "gods." *So they say.*

Many Gnostics and other members of the occult, all the way from ancient times to modern, make pretense of possessing great knowledge, and often find admissions of the practice of magic and curses and charms embarrassing to say the least. Actually much so called "magic" is so stupid and low-life and degrading, not to mention often times being wicked in the extreme, that few want to admit to it. Sometimes they want to call it "theurgy," or some other misleading sounding name, just so they can avoid having the subject understood. They try to divide it into "white magic" (magic which is trying to do good, and which supposedly uses "good" spirits), and "black magic" (magic which is trying to do evil, and which uses "evil" spirits). Would you believe, almost no one admits to practicing black magic? If you are talking to someone involved in magic as such, then they are always practicing "white magic." It is always "the other guys" who are practicing "black" magic. Right! You knew that all along didn't you?

At the very highest levels the "magicians" are men like Balaam in the book of Numbers. Balaam, if you remember, was doing things so foolish that he

> ... was rebuked for his iniquity: the dumb ass speaking with man's voice forbad the madness of the prophet. 2Pe 2:16 KJV

It goes downhill from there. There has always been more than a little pretense, sleight-of-hand and plain old "con-artistry" involved in those making pretense to "real" "magic." So what might we be able to see?

First, the evil spirits, including their leader Satan, do actually exist, and are able to act as the Lord God allows them. You can read some examples in the book of Job, chapters one and two.

Secondly, Satan is allowed to reward his servants in such ways as the Lord God may allow. When Satan was tempting the Messiah of the Jews, you can see these things in play.

> ⁵ And the devil, taking him up into an high mountain, shewed unto him all the kingdoms of the world in a moment of time. ⁶ And the devil said unto him, All this power will I give thee, and the glory of them: **for that is delivered unto me; and to whomsoever I will I give it**. ⁷ If thou therefore wilt worship me, all shall be thine. ⁸ And Jesus answered and said unto him, Get thee behind me, Satan: for it is written, Thou shalt worship the Lord thy God, and him only shalt thou serve. Lk 4:5-8 KJV (*bold emphasis added*)

Our Lord does not reprimand these ideas as false. So there is *something* to serving Satan, at some level; and it can be seen that Satan *is* a powerful *creature*, but still a **creature**, not a god. Satan is still subject to the True and Living God's overruling power, as also are you and I. We are *allowed* up to *limits God determines* to decide or to do *whatever* we wish, and God can (and often does) either assist or obstruct us at some point. Is Satan powerful? Yes he is, but on a short leash, so to speak. God is in control, and Satan is *allowed* certain measures of freedom. Satan is allowed enough power to give us a real test, but no more, *unless* God allows it. Paul says.

> No temptation has overtaken you except such as is common to man; but God *is* faithful, who will not **allow** you to be tempted beyond what you are able, but with the temptation will also make the way of escape, that you may be able to bear *it*. 1Cor 10:13 NKJV (*bold emphasis added*)

Thus God promises the faithful that not only is Satan limited in how he can even tempt us, but God sets different limits depending on the strengths and weaknesses of different individuals. *We as human beings are not all powerful,* but we are protected in our LORD. Even so, there are a couple more key areas of Satanic power to discuss.

Thirdly, there is the power of drugs. One of the principal Greek words for witchcraft or sorcery used in the New Testament is *pharmakia* φαρμακεία (for instance Gal 5:20), and this describes the occult use of drugs for "visions" or "magic potions." We get our word pharmacy from this, and witchcraft has always been associated with the immoral use of drugs. A great deal of 1960's "hippie" and "mind expanding" drug taking would fall under this category. If you read their literature, much of it is consciously in the witchcraft category.

Fourthly, and last of all, is the power of hypnosis, with or without drugs. In ancient times this was called charms or spells or incantations. It was never viewed as an innocent activity in Scripture, but as something dangerous and forbidden. The clearest passage is Deuteronomy 18.

> [10] "There shall not be found among you ... [11] ... one who casts a spell, ... [12] For whoever does these things is detestable to the LORD; and because of these detestable things the LORD your God will drive them out before you. [13] You shall be blameless before the LORD your God."
> Deut 18:10-13 NASB

Despite all of the protests of innocence, according to Scripture hypnosis is a dangerous activity which can easily lead us to acting on the foolish evils lurking in our hearts. These are things which normally people have the presence of mind to suppress. You may have noticed, Deuteronomy 18 does not distinguish between drug-assisted spells and those induced through incantations alone. The Establishment news cartels studiously avoid the subject, but it is clear that many of the terrorist acts perpetrated world-wide in our time are from people under hypnotic spells. The spell, the hypnosis, the illusion of a false reality, only has to last long enough for them to press the button or pull the trigger. It appears that they are often programed to self-destruct after killing others. The occult has always possessed considerable expertise in these things, and the knowledge of these things has been put on a more scientific basis in the last hundred years.

Gnosticism is a big subject, and this is only an overview, especially of the Satanic factions involved. Also it must be admitted that much of what has been discussed in this section is so bizarre, so foreign to ordinary thinking and conduct among almost all the peoples of the world, that you may have to think a while about these things, and possibly read this section more than once to see the significance of such ideas among men.

A summary on Gnosticism.

New Testament scholars at times comment on the strange relationship between Judaism and the occult and Gnosticism, and it was not any Medieval development in response to persecution. William Barclay in his book *The Daily Study Bible Series* of commentaries on the New Testament gives us a view of the sort of comments that can be seen from a wide range of scholars. He says, "It is a strange thing that many Jews were sympathetic to Gnosticism." *The Letters to the Philippians, Colossians, and Thessalonians*, Westminster Press, Philadelphia, 1959, pg 120. In his *The Letters to Timothy, Titus and Philemon*, Westminster Press, Philadelphia, 1960, pgs 10-11, Barclay comments,

> "**Sometimes Gnosticism and Judaism joined hands**, and as it were, entered into an unholy alliance. ... It was the claim of certain Jews that it was precisely the Jewish law and the Jewish food regulations which provided that special knowledge and that necessary asceticism; and **so there were times when Judaism and Gnosticism went hand in hand**." (*bold emphasis added*)

These statements are as plain as you can get. More could be added from Barclay and others, but this will do.

Key Point: Magic, witchcraft, sorcery, and divination, *never **really** went away from Israel!*

Jewish scholar Gershom Scholem puts it in other ways. He says that "post-Biblical Judaism" pg 33, brought "mystical reinterpretation of the traditional", *Major Trends in Jewish Mysticism*, pgs 33-34.

> "These theurgical doctrines form a kind of meeting-place for magic and ecstaticism. ... If Merkabah mysticism thus degenerates in some instances into magic pure and simple ..." pg 78

Scholem indeed talks about the "... sheer gibberish of magical abrakadabra ..." in *Jewish Gnosticism* ... pg 76. He speaks of "... the Hekhaloth literature ... its wealth of magical material ..." pg 66. Then he admits these things,

> "seem to suggest strongly an intimate connection between Jewish and Gnostic concepts ..." pg 69

> "... Hekhaloth literature ... strange resemblance to the magical papyri ... I feel the distinction drawn by many scholars today between Gnostic literature proper and the magical papyri is somewhat overstated. ... The theurgic element was not a later addition ... but a basic component ..." pg 75

Quotes like these are as close you get to admissions of Jewish guilt from Gershom Scholem, but these, and others that could be cited, do in fact admit what is unavoidable. These things were not gone in Malachi's time. Among those things which will bring God's judgment are the "sorcerers" in Mal 3:5. So the depths of the occult are not only seen through the denunciations of the prophets. They are also to seen among the Jews of the first century AD, and of the last 2500 years. These same subject-matters will be picked up again in the discussion of the Jewish Kabbalah in section IV, because ancient Gnosticism forms the foundation of what is seen rising later among the Jews.

Not Your Everyday Religious Skills

Almost all of the near eastern peoples had fallen under the cruelty, oppressions, and deportations of the Assyrians and Babylonians; but the Jews emerged with a very distinct identity and outlook. They also emerged with some very unique skill sets: skill sets which gave them a certain unique influence and power. Some of the changes that are seen are normal political reactions to being a conquered people. They do exercise such autonomy and power wielding as they are allowed. They also try to expand that power as far as they think that they may be permitted, without causing a great deal of trouble. For most peoples in the Roman Empire the straining at the leash was minimal, because most had an appreciation of the military prowess of the Romans and of their implacable opposition to rebellion once pressed too far.

Also to be seen are some very strange developments in attitudes and outlook among the Jews. *These developments are not things which are universal* among the Jews, *but* as shall be seen, early on *they became very common*, and they are things which have no part in the Law of Moses and the prophets. As one comes to Acts 6, the Jewish believers in the Messiah of the Jews have formed a coherent group in Jerusalem. They are trying to take care of their own, and to persuade the rest of the nation to received the Anointed One. They were making progress, but the establishment among the Jews, as has already been seen, are interested in other things. There was an outstanding young man among the believers in the Anointed One. His name was Stephen, and it seems he was speaking and acting by the power of the Holy Spirit of God.

> And Stephen, full of faith and power, did great wonders and miracles among the people. Act 6:8 KJV

This new community of believers had been working to care for the poor, as was clearly commanded in the law of Moses, but which had been neglected. When there appeared some holes in their distributions, Stephen was one of the men selected in Acts 6 to more carefully administer to daily needs. Their growth, fidelity to what was right, and their adherence to the principles of the Messiah were difficult to resist or disprove. One synagogue in particular tried to deal with Stephen.

> [8] And Stephen, full of faith and power, did great wonders and signs among the people. [9] Then there arose some from what is called the Synagogue of the Freedmen (Cyrenians, Alexandrians, and those from Cilicia and Asia), disputing with Stephen. [10] And they were not able to resist the wisdom and the Spirit by which he spoke. Act 6:8-10 NKJV

So what does a good church group do when they are not able to refute the truth of God?

> [11] Then they secretly induced men to say, "We have heard him speak blasphemous words against Moses and God." [12] And they stirred up the people, the elders, and the scribes; and they came upon *him*, seized him, and brought *him* to the council. Act 6:11-12 NKJV

They are trying to get those with whom they disagree murdered. Well, let's see? A little perjury will do the job (Ex 20:7). And let's see? A little false witness also (Ex 20:16). They "secretly" induce all of this *against a fellow Jew* to instigate a judicial murder, because they cannot refute the truth of God, which they do not want to accept. What is a "good" man to do against a fellow Jew if he will not keep the false traditions of the fathers? And the "council" in this passage is the Sanhedrin (the Greek is *sunedrion* συνέδριον).

> [13] And set up false witnesses, which said, This man ceaseth not to speak blasphemous words against this holy place, and the law: [14] For we have heard him say, that this Jesus of Nazareth shall destroy this place, and shall change the customs which Moses delivered us.
> Act 6:13-14 KJV

It is easy to see that that the Jews did not hesitate to incite either their Jewish or their gentile rulers to suppress even their *Jewish* adversaries. British General, and Zionist sympathizer, Jan Smuts (1870-1950) gave this characterization of the Jews:

> "They are a bitter, recalcitrant little people like the Boers, impatient of leadership and ruinously quarrelsome among themselves."
> Laqueur, *A History of Zionism*, pg 161

Many of these least endearing characteristics will fade when the Jews at last accept Rabbi Yehoshua as the Messiah He really is. However, one sees that religious disputes between even the Jews themselves often take on a lawless and immoral character, and that is not just in Scripture. I am reminded of a story from Chaim Weizmann's autobiography, *Trial and Error*, Harper and Brothers, NY, 1949. Weizmann was doing what he calls an "agitation" for Zionism in Eastern Europe to try to improve their schools. Certain of the "ultra-orthodox," disagreeing with him, threatened "to denounce me to the police as an atheist, revolutionary, enemy of God and disturber of the peace," pg 26. The judicial murder of Rabbi Yehoshua was *not* an anomaly. The story goes downhill from here, even to this day! And their many successes are in spite of such animosities between factions.

To make his defense, Stephen reviews Jewish history on the subject of fidelity to God's commands, and he summarizes in Act 7:51-53.

> [51] Ye stiffnecked and uncircumcised in heart and ears, ye do always resist the Holy Ghost: as your fathers *did*, so *do* ye. [52] Which of the prophets have not your fathers persecuted? and they have slain them which shewed before of the coming of the Just One; of whom ye have been now the betrayers and murderers: [53] Who have received the law by the disposition of angels, and have not kept *it*. KJV

This is too much for this pretentious body of judges.

> [54] When they heard these things, they were cut to the heart, and they gnashed on him with their teeth. ... [57] Then they cried out with a loud voice, and stopped their ears, and ran upon him with one accord, [58] And cast *him* out of the city, and stoned *him*: and the witnesses laid down their clothes at a young man's feet, whose name was Saul. Act 7:54, 57-58 KJV

So the supreme court of the Jews, the "justices" themselves, carry out the murder of a witness who dares to tell the truth.

Have You Started a Persecution Lately?

It was at this point that Paul received warrants for the arrest of Christians in Damascus. This is all in all not your normal religious setting, and this predates classic Catholicism's suppression of her heretics by many centuries. Thus, early in the development of Christianity, there was a powerful sect within the Jews which advocated following Moses' Law, or perhaps it would be more accurate to say, following the *traditions* of the Jewish "fathers." The Pharisees is our subject. This sect was seen early and was often called "the party of the circumcision," as in Gal 2:12 NASB. To say that they were an active and ruthless group is putting it mildly. They were opposing the baptizing of gentiles, unless they really become Jews, Acts 11:1-3. Herod Antipas murdered the original apostle James in Acts 12:1-3, and the Jewish opponents of Christianity were elated.

Wherever Christianity went, they first tried to persuade the Jews, and only when that failed did they preach to the gentiles, just as at Perga in what is now called Asia Minor or Turkey, Acts 13:46-47. So how did the Jews react to this?

> But when the Jews saw the multitudes, **they were filled with envy**, and spake against those things which were spoken by Paul, contradicting and blaspheming. Acts 13:45 KJV (*bold emphasis added*)

So what did the Jews do? They instigated a persecution.

> But the Jews stirred up the devout and honourable women, and the chief men of the city, and raised persecution against Paul and Barnabas, and expelled them out of their coasts. Acts 13:50 KJV

They do not want to believe, and they perversely do not want *anyone* to believe! So the early **the beginnings of using gentile governments to oppress Christianity whenever possible** can be clearly seen, as it continues to this very day! The disbelieving Jews in Iconium were trying to poison the minds of the gentiles against Christianity in Acts 14:2.

Have You Started a Riot Lately?

The unbelieving Jews followed the preachers from town to town, organizing riots, striving to kill the preachers of the gospel, Act 14:19. Now you might take Acts 14 as an exceptional case of persecution of a then Jewish group by other Jews. But then you can see the behavior of a group of Jews in Thessalonica in Macedonia.

> **But the Jews were jealous**; so they rounded up some bad characters from the marketplace, formed a mob **and started a riot** in the city. They rushed to Jason's house in search of Paul and Silas in order to bring them out to the crowd. Act 17:5 NIV (*bold emphasis added*)

Now it is time to ask *you* the reader a few questions. Do you know, I mean just off hand, do you know how to start a riot? Now it is clear that there are classes which can be taken on this subject. The communists have been in times past very professional in starting and keeping up riots (and it would seem have still retained these, shall they be called, "skills.") It would seem that most large national intelligence agencies at times have classes on the subject of how to start a riot, and use such techniques when they think they will not be found out by their adversaries. I am sure that there are some good instruction books on the subject, but I personally have never seen one. Further, if you think about it, the average person, in the average religious group or church, *would have absolutely no idea about how to go about starting a riot!* I do not think I am exaggerating at all. This is a specialized skill, and from my general historical reading of well directed riots, *most* people would not be adept at this skill. Among other things, it requires such a turn of mind and such a callous lack of compassion about other human beings, that only a few would be good at such a thing. *Have you taken a class on starting riots at your local church lately?*

In contrast, notice that this is a common skill set among the Jews. Almost anywhere that Christianity spreads there seems to be some Jews in the local synagogue who have the time, money, and the skills to start a riot, *almost on demand!* This is not just about the hometown Sanhedrin boys in Jerusalem who arranged a riot to obtain the judicial murder of Rabbi Yehoshua. Those skills are also at hand in Asia Minor and Greece and, seemingly, wherever. The group in Thessalonica also followed the disciples to Berea.

> But when the Jews of Thessalonica had knowledge that the word of God was preached of Paul at Berea, they came thither also, and stirred up the people. Acts 17:13 KJV

These guys seem to be accomplished agitators, and do not seem to need to be at home to be able to start a good riot. Now the Jews were not the only ones with these skills, but they do seem to have them at hand. (The silversmith's union is able to get a good riot up in Acts 19.)

The Jews also seem to be infiltrating any group they do not like, and much of the trouble which early Christianity encountered seemed to be the result of infiltration. Paul wrote,

> And *this occurred* because of false brethren secretly brought in (who came in by stealth to spy out our liberty which we have in Christ Jesus, that they might bring us into bondage), Gal 2:4 NKJV

The Jewish prophet Jude talks about such infiltrators as lawless men,

> For certain people have **crept in unnoticed** who long ago were designated for this condemnation, ungodly people who pervert the grace of our God into sensuality and deny our only Master and Lord, Jesus Christ. Jude 4 ESV *(bold emphasis added)*

Paul in opposition writes of Christians as the true circumcision,

> 2 Beware of the dogs, beware of the evil workers, beware of the false circumcision; 3 for we are the *true* circumcision, who worship in the Spirit of God and glory in Christ Jesus and put no confidence in the flesh, Phil 3:2-3 NASB

In others words, the true circumcision is spiritual, it is of the heart, just as in Deut 10:16, Jer 4:4, and many other passages. It should be remembered that there were also many good Jews in these times. Men like Apollos in Acts 18:24ff. He was refuting Jewish foolishness in Acts 18:28.

In Acts chapter 18 Paul is preaching in Corinth. So some of the Jews made an accusation against Paul in court. They are not willing to live with private acceptance or rejection of Jesus. They want to stop the true Christ. These Jews are not of the same character as the noble Crispus, the leader of the synagogue in Acts 18:8, who came to the Savior. These Jews, just like many of the nations of the world, are truly against Christ ... they are truly anti-Christ. So they use the courts to try to stop the spread of the true religion of Jesus Christ, as they do even today.

> 12 When Gallio was proconsul of Achaia, **the Jews with one accord** rose up against Paul and brought him to the judgment seat, 13 saying, "This fellow persuades men to worship God contrary to the law." Acts 18:12-13 NKJV *(bold emphasis added)*

Gallio was an interesting character in both general history and in the book of Acts. He was the older brother of Seneca the famous Roman man of wisdom and tutor of the Emperor Nero. Later both he, Seneca, and the apostle Paul were all executed by Nero. This incident helps us date these events in the book of Acts. An inscription was found in Corinth that says that Gallio was appointed proconsul for a year in the 26th year of the Emperor Claudius, which would be 51 AD. So that puts this incident in Corinth in the years 51 or 52 AD. You can write that in the margin of your Bible as an anchor to figure out other dates. But Gallio did not want any part of some hair-splitting religious argument that the Jews might want to take to court.

> [14] And when Paul was about to open *his* mouth, Gallio said to the Jews, "If it were a matter of wrongdoing or wicked crimes, O Jews, there would be reason why I should bear with you. [15] But if it is a question of words and names and your own law, look *to it* yourselves; for I do not want to be a judge of such *matters.*" [16] And he drove them from the judgment seat. [17] Then all the Greeks took Sosthenes, the ruler of the synagogue, and *beat* him before the judgment seat. But Gallio took no notice of these things. Act 18:14-17 NKJV

Attention should also be called toward some other things. First, as far as Gallio was concerned, Christianity seemed to be just another Jewish sect. In addition, it is plain that Gallio and other Roman rulers already had experience *with* **Jews** **persecuting** *other* **Jews** *on religious points in* **gentile courts of law!** (Indeed, such can be seen over and over in history through the last 2,000 years. The Jews are a litigious people all through the Christian age, *even against each other.*)

Often the followers of the Christ of the Jews had to just withdraw from the Jews, as in Acts 19:9-10. Then when the Jews were at last able to arraign Paul before gentile courts in Palestine, they made a set-up against him.

> [12] And when it was day, some of the Jews banded together and bound themselves under an oath, saying that they would neither eat nor drink till they had killed Paul. [13] Now there were more than forty who had formed this conspiracy. [14] They came to the chief priests and elders, and said, "We have bound ourselves under a great oath that we will eat nothing until we have killed Paul. [15] Now you, therefore, together with the council, suggest to the commander that he be brought down to you tomorrow, as though you were going to make further inquiries concerning him; but we are ready to kill him before he comes near." Acts 23:12-15 NKJV

Again one can see tenacity, an implacable hatred, and the lawless instincts of which these men are capable, and, *once more*, the complicity of the leaders of the Sanhedrin in attempts at murder. The "church" really *belonged* in the synagogue. The synagogue *should have been* the natural depository of Christ. However,

> [10] He was in the world, and the world was made by him, and the world knew him not. [11] **He came unto his own, and his own received him not.** [12] But as many as received him, to them gave he power to become the sons of God, *even* to them that believe on his name: [13] Which were born, not of blood, nor of the will of the flesh, nor of the will of man, but of God. Jn 1:10-13 KJV (*bold emphasis added*)

Here then is a different skill mix than men usually run into in a religious setting. A different approach, a different intensity, to sectarian disputes. An approach, and a skill set, which continues to this day among some.

The Invisible State: Discipline and Control

At this point comes what many call that "strange survivability" of the Jews. This is what Lucien Wolf described as "the irritating mystery of the persistence of Judaism." (*What is Judaism*, by Lucien Wolf and Claude Montefiore, Living Books, Inc., NY, 1964, pg 9.) There is that strange unified survivability, that unusual adherence to what might otherwise be thought of as outright foolishness: to what can all of this attributed? Well, in part to ... a sword ... a dagger ... a gun, or perhaps is it better described as a *sacari* (the Greek is actually *sikaros* σικάριος) a type of **dagger**, and the word for this dagger became symbolic of assassins as in the "Assassins" of Acts 21:38. The Roman officer asks the Hebrew apostle Paul,

> "Aren't you then the Egyptian, who before these days stirred up to sedition and led out into the wilderness the four thousand men of the Assassins?" WEB

The Greek here is literally "the sikaron" *tōn sikariōn* τῶν σικαρίων. At times "assassins" enforced complicity with Pharisaism with the threat of punishment or even death. This is about,

Jewish Terrorism Against Other Jews.

The truth is that terrorists among the Jews have tended to float to the top. For instance, Menachem Begin, late Prime Minister of Israel, who as head of the Irgun was the leader of the King David Hotel bombing in Jerusalem on July 22, 1946, in which 91 people were killed. Also such things were sometimes not without Sanhedrin sanction, or at least complicity. The Sanhedrin itself, by name (the Greek word is *sunedrion* συνέδριον), is seen in many New Testament passages, although it is often just translated as the "council."

> Then gathered the chief priests and the Pharisees **a council**, and said, What do we? for this man doeth many miracles.
> Jn 11:47 KJV (*bold emphasis added*)

The NIV is a more direct translation here:

> Then the chief priests and the Pharisees called a meeting of the Sanhedrin.

Anyone who opposes their sometimes criminal, or even murderous, and (in the end) suicidal plans, is immediately blackballed. This strident radicalism goes on to this very day. A recurring theme in much Jewish history has been the callousness which Jews often show even toward other Jews, especially "the lesser brethren." This was discussed earlier in the section on the Pharisees.

These are not isolated items from ancient times. The fact is that the Jewish oligarchies have always wanted to *control* the common Jew. So there has always been *the need* for a certain level of separation from the gentiles in order to maintain order and control.

Historian Will Durant called it the "invisible state," as shall be seen later, but it has in truth been so named by many others, including many Jews. The persecution of the religion of the Messiah, of which the Jews have been a major driving force, was three pronged. First, the Sanhedrin directly tried to stop Christianity with imprisonment, force, illegal mobs, and even murder. It also tried to use its political stroke with the Romans. The Jewish supreme council was, as has been seen, complicit with assassination attempts on Paul the apostle in the book of Acts. For them, any knife was good enough to stab an enemy. A Jewish knife or a gentile knife or the knife of an enemy ruler was perfectly acceptable. In this connection you also get some insight into the remarkable adherence of the Jews to Judaism throughout the centuries, and much of it is not pretty. Paul, in his initial holding to zealous Pharisaism was entering the houses of believers and dragging both men and women into prison, Acts 8:3. These things are presented as without trial. Paul told Agrippa about his activities in these things in his trial in Acts 23.

> [9] "Indeed, I myself thought I must do many things contrary to the name of Jesus of Nazareth. [10] This I also did in Jerusalem, and many of the saints I shut up in prison, **having received authority from the chief priests**; and when they were put to death, I cast my vote against *them*. [11] And I punished them often in every synagogue and compelled *them* to blaspheme; and being exceedingly enraged against them, I persecuted *them* **even to foreign cities**."
> Acts 26:9-11 NKJV (*bold emphasis added*)

Many among the Jews themselves understand the fury of this sort of Jewish radicalism better than the gentiles do. The Jews made deals with the Romans (and later with many others) so that they could "administer" their own justice without any "interference" or even any "due process," both in modern terms, and in terms of how a Roman citizen had to be treated. Rabbi Yehoshua warned,

> "But beware of men, for they will hand you over to *the* courts and scourge you in their synagogues;" Mtt 10:17 NASB

So Jesus gives direct evidence of the Jews having "authority" to beat their own, *even in their synagogues*, which it seems they were allowed to do with little interference.

A Jewish Inquisition Deals With Gentile Rulers.

However it goes much further. They evidently had license to act across the boundaries of Roman kingdoms and principalities to legally seize Jews and do with them as they please. It was even to "**foreign cities**" in Act 26:11. Limitations on these powers are seen in other parts of the Roman empire, but it seems to have been exercised without interference in the Middle East. So in the early part of Acts 9 Paul is getting letters from the high priests to the synagogues in Damascus (this would be in Syria itself), authorizing him to bring Jewish Christians bound to Jerusalem. *A Jewish "Inquisition" of sorts*, against their own people. In the case of the Roman empire, we can see from the legal murder of Rabbi Yehoshua that they were *technically* denied the power of capital punishment. Still we also see that they frequently bypass these restrictions. In the case of Stephen in Acts 7, the Sanhedrin acting as a group murders him directly, as a mob, and then extends the persecution in Acts 8, with no gentile interference being recorded. For the gentile rulers in Palestine, this was strictly a Jew versus Jew thing. These are things which are not talked about much in gentile histories, but we do see the footprints of such agreements with various "gentile" rulers in the histories of the last two thousand years. Gibbon for instance talks about after the fall of Jerusalem,

> "The Romans gave a legal sanction to the form of **ecclesiastical police** which was instituted by the vanquished sect. The patriarch, ... was empowered to appoint his subordinate ministers and apostles, to exercise a domestic jurisdiction,"
> *Decline and Fall*, Chapter 16, Part 1, (*emphasis added*)

Jewish scholar Israel Shahak gives more detailed evidence of how this continued in later centuries. He puts it this way,

> "Thus, in the Roman empire of the fourth century AD, in a system created much earlier, all the Jews were in religious matters subject to the Patriarch who had the power to punish them by flogging, by levying fines for religious offenses and by imposing taxes."
> Shahak, Mezinsky, *Jewish Fundamentalism*, pg 3

Shahak refers to Judaism as "A Closed Utopia?" in *Jewish History, Jewish Re-*

ligion, pg 12. He tells us,

> "In many countries—Spain and Poland are notable examples—even capital punishment could be and was inflicted, sometimes using particularly cruel methods such as flogging to death."
> Shahak, *Jewish History, Jewish Religion*, pg 14

Shahak goes on to point out that these things were allowed and even promoted in both "Christian" and Mohammedan countries because of the financial interests which the rulers had at stake, and notes even more severe instances. He tells us, for instance, that Pedro I of Castile gave the Jews in his domain "the right to establish a country-wide inquisition against Jewish religious deviants," pg 60. He quotes Israeli journalist Rami Rosen's November 15, 1996 Israeli *Haaretz* Magazine article, titled "History of Denial,"

> "It includes massacres of Christians [by Jews]; mock repetitions of the crucifixion of Jesus that usually took place on Purim; cruel murders within the family; liquidation of informers, often done for religious reasons by secret rabbinical courts, which issued a sentence of "pursuer" and appointed secret executioners; assassinations of adulterous women in synagogues and/or the cutting of their [the women's] noses by command of the rabbis."
> Shahak, Mezinsky, *Jewish Fundamentalism*, pgs 115-116

For many Jews these have been powerful barriers to escape from Pharisaical tyranny. Still, all of this failed to stop the spread of Christianity. Durant mentions these things, if only in subdued form.

"In the Dispersion **the synagogue had to be both church and government, ...** the Talmud became **the supreme court of an invisible state** stronger even than human hate." (*emphasis added*)
Vol X, *Rousseau and Revolution*, pg 629

Notice Durant's wording. They constituted "an invisible state." However, as you can see, these issues (and really these arrangements) far preceded the "human hate"

Inflicting beatings on the disobedient in a Dutch synagogue, while a worshipper prays in the backgorund. Early 1700's.

of later centuries of which Durant speaks. You can see from what is shown here that this "invisible state" even predates the second destruction of the temple in 70 AD.

And a Jewish court which is "stronger than human hate"? Perhaps Durant should have spoken of a Jewish Inquisition which was as strong as human hate; all against *fellow* Jews who might disagree on an item of purely human tradition.

You can see similar actions in many other situations in Jewish history. As terrible as was the Catholic Inquisition and many of the persecutions of the Jews, it is also clear that at times some Jews called attention to *other Jews,* whom they considered heretics, to the Inquisition of the Catholic church. Now you might call some of this justified, or not, but still *it is clear that Jews have from time to time called down persecution on other Jews by using gentiles.* You can see it first in the New Testament, but it by no means ends there.

These things were for sure an alien influence in Western Europe which had such a great influence from Christianity, even though often in a corrupted and diluted form.

The Third Break: The Jews Reject All Nations

Is this really the Second Break in continuity for the Jews, and was the Third Break the Rejection and Murder of their own Messiah? Perhaps, but if the rejection of all nations was a latent trait in Judaism, with the coming of the Messiah, it now became a dominant trait, and still one of the Jews major breaks from the truths of God.

The Dogs And The Children's Bread.

22 And a Canaanite woman from that region came out and *began* to cry out, saying, "Have mercy on me, Lord, Son of David; my daughter is cruelly demon-possessed." 23 But He did not answer her a word. And His disciples came and implored Him, saying, "Send her away, because she keeps shouting at us." 24 But He answered and said, "I was sent only to the lost sheep of the house of Israel." 25 But she came and *began* to bow down before Him, saying, "Lord, help me!" 26 And He answered and said, "It is not good to take the children's bread and throw it to the dogs." 27 But she said, "Yes, Lord; but even the dogs feed on the crumbs which fall from their masters' table." 28 Then Jesus said to her, "O woman, your faith is great; it shall be done for you as you wish." Mtt 15:22-28 NASB

It is not news to those familiar with Jewish attitudes toward gentiles, that some regard gentiles as dogs, as not quite human. Jesus' comments here reflect the presence of such ideas in His times. This sort of thinking developed some bizarre ideas when you get to issues like adultery and marriage and divorce. Since a gentile woman is really just an animal, then relations between a Jew and a gentile woman is really not adultery ... it is bestiality! So, according to some of these perverted views, the man should be beaten, and the woman should be put to death! *Jewish Religion* ... , pgs 87-88. As you would a dog. She is just an animal! *So some would say!*

The outcome of such views was often a despiteful attitude toward the people of the nations, and a willingness to cheat them without conscience if they could. I mean, if God didn't want them to be fleeced, He would not have made them sheep! Right?

When Rabbi Yehoshua first began His ministry, He constantly insisted that they concentrate on converting the Jews to true repentance. When He sent out His chosen twelve pupils to preach in a limited commission, He gave them special authority, and He told them,

> [5] These twelve Jesus sent forth, and commanded them, saying, Go not into the way of the Gentiles, and into *any* city of the Samaritans enter ye not: [6] But go rather to the lost sheep of the house of Israel.
> Mtt 10:5-6 KJV

Jesus was called a "Rabbi," and that is noted in every gospel except Luke's. When Peter was at the transfiguration on the mountain top, he said, "Rabbi, it is good for us to be here ..." Mk 9:5 KJV. Later, rabbinic standards not withstanding, even John the Baptist was called a Rabbi in his own day, Jn 3:26. "Rabbi" is also used in Jn 4:31, Jn 9:2, and Jn 11:8, but the KJV translates this as "Master," but in the rest of John it translates *hrabbi* ῥαββί, as it actually is in Greek: rabbi. When Judas went to betray Yehoshua, he greeted Him and kissed Him as "Rabbi!" as it is in the most Jewish of our gospels, Matthew and Mark.

There were also overtones of greater ministry yet to come. There was a well to do Roman centurion who asked that his servant be healed. Some of the elders of the Jews sent word to Jesus that he was worthy of aid because he loved Israel and had built their synagogue, Luke 7. In addition, when Rabbi Yehoshua spoke of the kingdom in parables, He clearly said the "the field is the world," Mtt 13:38. It is not just Israel/Judah/Palestine. The field is the world. When He was speaking to a Samaritan woman in Samaria, Yehoshua said,

> [21] ... Woman, believe me, the hour cometh, **when ye shall neither in this mountain, nor yet at Jerusalem, worship the Father**. [22] Ye worship ye know not what: we know what we worship: **for salvation is of the Jews**. [23] But the hour cometh, and now is, when the true worshippers shall worship the Father in spirit and in truth: for the

Father seeketh such to worship him.
Jn 4:21-23 KJV (*bold and underline emphasis added*)

So here Yehoshua clearly indicates to this Samaritan that one day **she**, along with the faithful Jews, will worship the Lord in a new way of the Spirit. The Pharisees, it seems, heard more accurately than many of Yehoshua's own disciples this message of wider circle of reconciliation to the Lord. A message of salvation to the gentiles/nations was a message which scared the Jewish oligarchs, and one which they detested. Such were common Jewish reactions. So when Peter (also called Cephas) was first sent to preach the gospel to some gentiles, it took some doing to get him to overcome his cultural biases, Acts 10. I mean, should you really eat with a "dog"? Even later he retained some of this in-grained superiority to gentiles.

> [11] But when Peter came to Antioch, I resisted him to the face, because he stood condemned [12] For before some people came from James, he ate with the Gentiles. But when they came, he drew back and separated himself, fearing those who were of the circumcision. [13] And the rest of the Jews joined him in his hypocrisy; so that even Barnabas was carried away with their hypocrisy.
> Gal 2:11-13 WEB

Oh, how slowly we change from false cultural norms with which we are often raised, and if we are not on guard, they will quickly reassert themselves. Despite all of that, Yehoshua's ministry was almost exclusively to the Jews. Following His resurrection when He was sending out His disciples to spread the word of life world-wide, even then it was "to all nations, beginning at Jerusalem." As His heralds of the kingdom scattered to bring good news to a dying world, they *"began* to proclaim the word of God in the synagogues of the Jews," Acts 13:5 NASB. They "went into the synagogue on the sabbath day, and sat down," and were then invited to speak, Acts 13:14-15 KJV. This is a recurring pattern in the book of Acts. Then when the Jews were filled with jealousy and blasphemed, they were told,

> ... **It was necessary that the word of God should <u>first</u> have been spoken to you**: but seeing ye put it from you, and judge yourselves unworthy of everlasting life, lo, we turn to the Gentiles.
> Acts 13:46 KJV (*emphasis added*)

*The Jews really **were** to be first.* Instead, they themselves rejected life and prosperity for themselves, ***because** it violated their **cultural** norms.*

What should we make of "the dogs and children's bread"? Jesus seems to be, by these comments, testing both the woman and the listeners in His audience. I think first it should be seen that Rabbi Yehoshua was making the same point that His Father was making in the book of Jonah: that the gentiles too deserved mercy to obtain repentance and life. This is not a strange thing if you really understand your Bible, and the LORD your God. Jonah understood this, and *for this reason* had tried to escape from having to preach to the hated gentile Assyrians. Jonah hated the cruel Assyrian oppressors, and, in true Jewish fashion, was *afraid* the gentiles would repent!

> [1] But it displeased Jonah exceedingly, and he became angry. [2] So he prayed to the LORD, and said, "Ah, LORD, was not this what I said when I was still in my country? Therefore I fled previously to Tarshish; for I know that You *are* a gracious and merciful God, slow to anger and abundant in lovingkindness, One who relents from doing harm.
> Jon 4:1-2 NKJV

To show mercy to vermin? To an Assyrian capital? Like his posterity, Jonah would rather die! Literally! "... please take my life from me, for *it is* better for me to die than to live!" Jon 4:3 NKJV. Death before mercy to a gentile! But as Yahweh was merciful to Nineveh, so the Father gently explains these things to Jonah.

> And should not I spare Nineveh, that great city, wherein are more than sixscore thousand persons that cannot discern between their right hand and their left hand; and also much cattle? Jon 4:11 KJV

Jonah evidently wrote his "word of the LORD", faithfully recording his experiences, his actions, God's actions, what he said, and most important, what God said. **All** souls are mine, the Lord says, Ezek 18:4.

But the Jews were to be first. Rabbi Yehoshua's stance in this story was by no means novel, nor out of place. It was also part of the Law and the prophets at their very core.

The Jews Really ARE Supposed to be First

> O ye seed of Abraham his servant,
> ye children of Jacob his chosen.
> Psa 105:6 KJV

> But I have chosen Jerusalem, that my name might be there;
> and have chosen David to be over my people Israel.
> 2Chron 6:6 KJV

Abram was to walk before the Lord and be blameless. It was to be an everlasting covenant with God to the descendants of Abram and his descendants, Gen 17:1-2, 7.

> For I know him, that he will command his children and his household after him, and they shall keep the way of the LORD, to do justice and judgment; that the LORD may bring upon Abraham that which he hath

spoken of him. Gen 18:19 KJV

The purpose was a blessing. A blessing to all of the earth. "And in thee shall all families of the earth be blessed," Gen 12:3 KJV. So God chose a holy seed. But He still did the choosing. What sort of thing will God bring through Abraham? The looting and oppression of all nations? Stealing the ancestral home of others, just because it is to your advantage and you *can*? Hardly!

> "Your seed will be as the dust of the earth, and you will spread abroad to the west, and to the east, and to the north, and to the south. In you and **in your seed will all the families of the earth be blessed**." Gen 28:14 NASB (*bold emphasis added*)

Why?

> "And because He loved your fathers, therefore He chose their descendants after them; and He brought you out of Egypt with His Presence, with His mighty power," Deut 4:37 NKJV

It is a sentiment which we find expressed over and over.

> For the LORD hath chosen Jacob unto himself, and Israel for his peculiar treasure. Psa 135:4 KJV

Only to Jacob has God shown such mercy.

> 19 He declares His word to Jacob,
>   His statutes and His judgments to Israel.
> 20   He has not dealt thus with any nation;
>   And as for His judgments, they have not known them.
> Praise the LORD! Psa 147:19-20 NKJV

It did and does involve the Davidic line, and the temple mount of Zion in Jerusalem.

> 68 But chose the tribe of Judah,
>   Mount Zion which He loved.
> 69   And He built His sanctuary like the heights,
>   Like the earth which He has established forever.
> 70   He also chose David His servant,
>   And took him from the sheepfolds; Psa 78:68-70 NKJV

It is a promise, but it was *always* a promise with strings attached.

> And in thy seed shall all the nations of the earth be blessed; **because** thou hast obeyed my voice. Gen 22:18 KJV (*bold emphasis added*)

They will be the head and not the tail. Even so, it is not without reference to their conduct.

> 13 And **the LORD shall make thee the head,** and not the tail; and **thou shalt be above only,** and thou shalt not be beneath; ... 14 And **thou**

shalt not go aside from any of the words which I command thee this day, to the right hand, or to the left, **to go after other gods** to serve them. Deut 28:13-14 KJV (*bold emphasis added*)

Preeminence Does Bring Special Scrutiny.

You only have I known of all the families of the earth: therefore I will punish you for all your iniquities. Amos 3:2 KJV

Special position because of the faithfulness of the fathers? Yes! Special responsibility because of the that? Absolutely! Also at some point the special "Servant of the Lord" will bring justice, not just to Israel, but to all the world.

"Behold, My Servant, whom I uphold;
My **chosen** one *in whom* My soul delights.
I have put My Spirit upon Him;
He will bring forth justice **to the nations.**
Isa 42:1 NASB (*bold emphasis added*)

Again it must be asked: is it a blessing to the gentiles to give them oppression? Despotism? Tyranny? Cruelty? Looting? Not by any means! So who is the One, the Special One, who will bring glory to Israel, and justice to the nations? It is the One who is rejected by the nation of Israel.

Thus says the LORD,
      The Redeemer of Israel, their Holy One,
      To Him whom man despises,
      To Him whom the nation abhors,
      To the Servant of rulers:
      "Kings shall see and arise,
      Princes also shall worship,
      Because of the LORD who is faithful,
      The Holy One of Israel;
      And He has chosen You."
Isa 49:7 NKJV (*bold and underline emphasis added*)

Kings will bow to this Suffering Servant of Israel, but "**the** nation", the nation of Israel, will detest Him. So who are the chosen in Israel? It was explicit! *If* you obey *God's* voice *then* you will be God's own possession!

[5] Now therefore, **if ye will obey my voice** indeed, and keep my covenant, **then ye shall be a peculiar treasure unto me** above all people: for all the earth is mine: [6] And ye shall be unto me a kingdom of priests, and an holy nation. ... Ex 19:5-6 KJV (*bold emphasis added*)

A kingdom of priests? A *holy* nation? That is many things, but it is not the Jews of the last thirty-five hundred years. So how did the LORD react?

> **And the LORD rejected all the descendants of Israel,** afflicted them, and delivered them into the hand of plunderers, until He had cast them from His sight. 2Kgs 17:20 NKJV (*bold and underline emphasis added*)

What blessing did Yehoshua bring when He came?

> Unto you **first** God, having raised up his Son Jesus, **sent him to bless you,** in turning away every one of you from his iniquities.
> Acts 3:26 KJV (*bold emphasis added*)

Yehoshua *came* to bring the Jews *first* out of their sins, so that they could be properly blessed. Many of the Jews did repent and turn, and they received the blessings of the New Covenant. These things will bring thanks forever from the nations.

> Therefore I will give thanks to You among the nations, O LORD,
> And I will sing praises to Your name. Psa 18:49 NASB

So the preaching to the nations, the gentiles, began.

> When they heard these things, they held their peace, and glorified God, saying, Then hath God also to the Gentiles granted repentance unto life. Acts 11:18 KJV

But that was a novel concept to the first century AD Jewish audience. It should not have been, but it was. Were they not to love the alien as themselves, Lev 19:34? That is not close to the traditional approach of treating the gentiles as animals, or touching gentiles as causing uncleanness? The gentiles could have life? Who would have thought it listening to the traditions of the elders? All of this incredulity was among the early *New* Covenant Jews, that they were to show mercy to all. It was thus salvation to all, as many as our Lord will call.

> Even us, whom he hath called, not of the Jews only, but also of the Gentiles? Rom 9:24 KJV

So there is no distinction. The Lord is the God of all. We (Jew and Gentile together) are all one in Christ, Gal 3:28.

> For there is no difference between the Jew and the Greek: for the same Lord over all is rich unto all that call upon him. Rom 10:12 KJV

The racists, whether Southern white land barons, German Nazis, or Jewish radicals ... are put down. The LORD is the Lord of all.

> [9] Tribulation and anguish, upon every soul of man that doeth evil, of the Jew first, and also of the Gentile; [10] But glory, honour, and peace, to every man that worketh good, to the Jew first, and also to the Gentile: Rom 2:9-10 KJV

But Who is REALLY a "Jew"?

There is a real question, constantly debated among the Jews, *because* they are often not sure who they really are. It has seemed to me at times that every Jew on earth has written a book on "what is a Jew," and that one could spend the rest of his life on just this question. Scripture has something to say about it, and the previous Scriptures quoted on the subject are the real answer.

God is good to Israel. That is what Asaph says in one of my favorite psalms. But who is Israel? Originally it was the physical descendants of Jacob, whose name was changed to Israel, the man who had wrestled with both God and man and prevailed, Gen 32:24-28. So who is the *real* Israel? The psalmist Asaph gives the answer in Psa 73:1. **True Israel** is the pure in heart.

> Truly God is good to Israel, even to such as are of a clean heart. KJV

Then to make sure that we do not miss the point, the inspired psalmist Asaph goes on to say that he was *almost* no longer part of Israel.

> 2 But as for me, my feet were almost gone; my steps had well nigh slipped. 3 For I was envious at the foolish, *when* I saw the prosperity of the wicked. Psa 73:2-3 KJV

Then comes another part of the Biblical evidence. Jew is also used of those faithful to God in the highest spiritual sense. Finally Pilate asks Yehoshua if He is the King of the Jews, He says *"It is as* you say," Mtt 27:11 NKJV, or to put it in colloquial English, "You said it." Paul says,

> But he *is* a Jew, which is one inwardly; and circumcision *is that* of the heart, in the spirit, *and* not in the letter; whose praise *is* not of men, but of God. Rom 2:29 KJV

And of course, Jesus says to the Samaritan woman,

> Ye worship ye know not what: we know what we worship: **for salvation is of the Jews**. Jn 4:22 KJV (*bold emphasis added*)

So *not all* who are physical children are really Jacob's children, else Asaph could not have otherwise nearly slipped from that standing! Otherwise Esau could not be excluded from the promise.

> 6 But it is not as though the word of God has come to nothing. For they are not all Israel, that are of Israel. 7 Neither, because they are Abraham's seed, are they all children. But, "In Isaac will your seed be called." Rom 9:6-7 NASB

No, it is the children of promise who are blessed.

> 8 That is, They which are the children of the flesh, these *are* not the children of God: but the children of the promise are counted for the seed. 9 For this *is* the word of promise, At this time will I come, and Sara shall have a son. Rom 9:8-9 KJV

So it is NOT physical descent which counts, else the descendants of Ishmael and Esau would also be part of the promise. *Instead, it is a spiritual thing, even from the first.* The Law says the same. Circumcision was the sign of the covenant made with Abraham, Gen 17:11. Not long after it was explained that the true circumcision was of the heart. Where then did God's hostility arise against Israel in the desert?

> [41] And *that* **I also have walked contrary unto them**, and have brought them into the land of their enemies; if then **their uncircumcised hearts be humbled, and they then accept of the punishment of their iniquity**: [42] **Then will I remember my covenant with Jacob**, and also my covenant with Isaac, and also my covenant with Abraham will I remember; **and I will remember the land**.
> Lev 26:41-42 KJV (*Bold emphasis added*)

So what is the real solution?

> **Circumcise** therefore **the foreskin of your heart**, and be no more stiffnecked. Deut 10:16 KJV

There is the core of the matter. Instead, what were the Jews of the first century AD like? They were just like their fathers.

> "*You* stiff-necked and uncircumcised in heart and ears! You always resist the Holy Spirit; as your fathers *did*, so *do* you." Acts 7:51 NKJV

What more authority do you want? And what better commentary is there on what is yet to come? Under that single name of "Jew" have come many of the *very best* men of the last two thousand years, and many of the worst.

> O ye seed of Israel his servant, ye children of Jacob, his chosen ones 1Chron 16:13 KJV

Thus comes the curse which has not yet left physical Israel.

The Messiah, the Gentiles, and the Jewish Reaction

Many realized the Messiah was to save "the world," Jn 4:42, Lk 2:32, etc. Likewise, the prophets testify to this. The Lord speaking through the mouth of Isaiah tells us of the Messiah

> "I am the LORD, I have called You in righteousness,
> I will also hold You by the hand and watch over You,
> And I will appoint You as a covenant to the people,
> **As a light to the nations**, Isa 42:6 NASB (*bold emphasis added*)

The Messiah is not just a light to Israel. He will also be a *light* to the nations, the *goyim* גּוֹיִם. Not bondage and exploitation, but to bring them freedom.

To open the blind eyes, to bring out the prisoners from the prison, *and* them that sit in darkness out of the prison house. Isa 42:7 KJV

The Messiah is too great to be limited to saving physical Israel.

He says, "It is too small a thing that You should be My Servant
To raise up the tribes of Jacob and to restore the preserved ones of Israel;
I will also make You **a light of the nations**
So that My salvation may reach to the end of the earth." Isa 49:6 NASB

Then follows that verse which says that the Messiah will be abhorred, not by the nation**S**, but by the singular nation, *the nation* of Israel.

Thus says the LORD, the Redeemer of Israel and its Holy One,
To the despised One,
To the One abhorred by **the** nation ... Isa 49:7 NASB (*emphasis added*)

The Jewish Mob and the Unthinkable Union

There was some conflict between many of the Jews and the early Christians. The apostles in Jerusalem have talked to Paul about these things in Acts 21:21. It was at that time decided that Paul would pay the expenses of some men who were making a vow in the temple, Acts 21:23-24, 26.

Then trouble started when some Jews from the Roman province of Asia saw Paul. The time of vows was just about over, Acts 21:27. Now it was a law that men of the nations could not go into the main temple area, the *hieros* ἱερό ς. Some of the notices forbidding gentiles to enter the temple area upon pain of death, have been discovered in modern times. Also these men had previously seen Paul with a young gentile named Trophimus, Acts 21:29. If you remember, Trophimus had been mentioned earlier in Act 20:4 as one of those accompanying Paul on his missionary journeys. He is mentioned one more time in Scriptures as being involved in the work of Christ. Look carefully at the trouble makers! This is the work of religious trouble makers who care nothing for the truth. They were doing very little thinking, and a whole lot of "supposing." Even so a major riot was quickly stirred up, Act 21:30.

Finally, the police (Roman sol-

One of the original inscriptions from Herod's temple in Jerusalem, forbidding gentiles to

diers) came to his defense, and to find out what was going on, Acts 21:31-33.
The crowd was shouting many different things, so the centurion started to take
Paul to the barracks for questioning, which would have been the fortress Anto-
nio, Acts 21:34. They halted at the stairs, Acts 21:35-39; and Paul received permission to speak to the crowd, Acts 21:40. Would you want to reason with a
mob that had just been trying to beat you up and kill you?

Hear my defense, Paul says,

> [1] Men, brethren, and fathers, hear ye my defence *which I make* now
> unto you. [2] (And when they heard that he spake in the Hebrew tongue
> to them, they kept the more silence: ...) Acts 22:1-2 KJV

"Hebrew tongue" or "dialect" is in Greek *Hebradi dialectō* ʽεβραΐδι
διαλέκτῳ.

I am a Jew of Tarsus, and trained under Gamaliel, Paul says in Acts 22:3.
Gamaliel was an important rabbi and is also known from secular history. He
was of the Pharisees of the school of Hillel (evidently he was Hillel's grandson).
He was the equivalent of a 'doctor of the law', a Ph.D. He was so highly regarded that he was not just called rabbi or teacher, but he was 'rabban' or 'our
teacher'. He was known by the title "the glory of the law." Mishnah 9. 15 says,
"Since Rabban Gamaliel the Elder died there has been no more reverence for
the Law, and purity and abstinence died out at the same time." In Acts 5,
Gamaliel gave some of the wisest advice that the Jews received from their own
Sanhedrin. He counseled caution, and not jumping to persecute someone. In
truth, that is what most rational people would have said to do. However, Paul
himself had persecuted Christians.

> [4] And I persecuted this way unto the death, binding and delivering into
> prisons both men and women. [5] As also the high priest doth bear me
> witness ... : from whom also I received letters unto the brethren, and
> went to Damascus, to bring them which were there bound unto Jeru-
> salem, for to be punished. Acts 22:4-5 KJV

Then Paul described Yehoshua speaking from heaven to him.

> [6] And it came to pass, that, as I made my journey, and was come nigh
> unto Damascus about noon, suddenly there shone from heaven a great
> light round about me. [7] And I fell unto the ground, and heard a voice
> saying unto me, Saul, Saul, why persecutest thou me? [8] And I
> answered, Who art thou, Lord? And he said unto me, I am Jesus of
> Nazareth, whom thou persecutest. [9] And they that were with me saw
> indeed the light, and were afraid; but they heard not the voice of him
> that spake to me. Acts 22:6-9 KJV

Notice the mob is still quiet at this point. Being blinded by the light from
heaven as he was going to Damascus, Acts 22:10-11. "Who knows?" the mob
evidently must have thought. Maybe Jesus *did* speak to this man from heaven.

The Jews listened patiently *until* Paul mentioned the gentiles.

> "Then He said to me, "Depart, for I will send you far from here to the Gentiles.' " Acts 22:21 NKJV

Jesus as a prophet? This was okay. An angel or the Lord Himself speaking to Paul from heaven? Well, perhaps it really happened. **But salvation for the gentiles, the hated *goyim* of the world?** This they could not stand.

> They listened to him until he said that; then they lifted up their voice, and said, "Rid the earth of this fellow, for he isn't fit to live!"
> Act 22:22 WEB

Mercy to the gentiles? Life and glory for the gentiles? Unthinkable! They may out of self-interest treat a gentile fairly, but there is nothing in this distorted world view to compel fair treatment. Even in those formally abandoning the Jewish religion, the same patterns and associations are often still seen.

What is the root of this alienation? A false religious cult among the Jews. It has been **a cult of hatred, hostility, and grasping covetousness toward *all* gentiles**. *This is a cult that is _foreign to Moses' Law_, and the _prophets_, and the _New Covenant_ of the true Messiah of the Jews, Rabbi Yehoshua.* Stripped of its cover, when all but the most superficial traces of Judaism are removed, all that is left is a completely unprincipled pursuit of the riches and pleasures of this world. **This may be worldly success, but it is also worldly trouble and has nothing to do with *either* the Law of Moses or Christianity.**

Opposition to Christianity

The Scriptures do not speak of all opposition to Christianity as coming from the Jews, but it does speak of the Jews (both in the Old Testament and the New Testament) as primary antagonists to the rule first of God and then of the Messiah, which is indeed what has happened.

Even the Old Testament gives abundant proof of the Messiah's divinity, and more than one Jew has been convinced of it down through history. This is not about just the New Testament, nor about false conversions or "assimilations" or by the sword of later days. Even militant Jewish historians admit the sincerity of many of the Jewish conversions to Christianity.

Also Jesus clearly hit the Jewish expectations of exploiting the Gentiles. He did not give a system whereby the Jews would conquer the world with a sword of steel or bronze, drenching all the gentile nations with their own blood, opening the way for pitiless exploitation by the Jews, and the enslavement of all other peoples to the Jews. Instead, the preaching of Jesus Christ brought a system whereby the shlemiels, the stupid goyim, are invited to become part of Israel! Outrageous! Outlandish! Unthinkable!

Even so, this is clearly part of the gospel, even in the Old Testament, as has been repeatedly shown. It *is* good news (which is what "gospel" means) to the *world*. It is implicit from the first, for "in thee shall all the families of the earth be blessed," Gen 12.3. "The field is the world," Mtt 13:38. "And other sheep I have, which are not of this fold," Jn 10:16 KJV. "The promise is unto ... all who are far off," Acts 2:39 KJV. In the gospel, those nations which were once "excluded from the the the commonwealth of Israel, and strangers to the covenants of promises," Jesus now reconciles "them both in one body to God through the cross." "So then you are no longer strangers and aliens, but you are fellow citizens with the saints, and are of God's household," Eph 2:12, 16, 19 NASB.

> [27] For **as many of you as have been baptized** into Christ **have put on Christ**. [28] There is neither Jew nor Greek, there is neither bond nor free, there is neither male nor female: **for ye are all one in Christ Jesus**. [29] And if ye *be* Christ's, **then are ye Abraham's seed, and heirs according to the promise**. Gal 3:27-29 KJV *(emphasis added)*

It was foreshadowed in the prophets more than one way, for instance in the cleansing of the Aramaean general Naaman in 2 Kings 5. Remember, the promise was not that the Jews would exploit the nations and drench them in blood, but rather that in Abraham, "all the families of the earth will be blessed," Gen 12:3. The rabbis of Pharisaism had badly misinterpreted Old Testament prophecy.

The basic point that is being been made is that the problems which the Jews of the Christian age have pre-date Christianity by quite a bit. The most important issues are:

(1.) Their tendency to live by man-made rules other than Scripture, yet still try to call it Moses' religion.

(2.) The bitterness and animosity they so often harbor toward other men, especially toward the gentiles, *but often even toward each other*. Nothing could have been more striking to the Jews than Jesus' picture in Luke 10 of a heretic Samaritan, a gentile, who in normal human compassion helped an injured Jew, when his own had stood aside, and refused to be concerned.

(3.) Their talent for political "trouble making," shall it be called? It is something at which they have been good, but that has often brought great trouble on their own heads.

For a fact, the concept of accepting the gentiles, the nations, as "brothers," was extremely alien to the Jewish mindset. The gentiles, literally the "nations," (the Hebrew word is *goyim* גּוֹיִם, and the Greek word is *ethnōn* ἐθνῶν, a plural form of *ethnos* ἔθνος) were not, and often are not, really considered equal to the Jews. In 21st century American news-cartel terms, this would be called by most a "racist" view of others.

So the Jews viewed Jesus as an obstacle to *their vision* (not God's) of a universal exploitation of the nations by the Jews. They only thought in terms of badly misused passages like Psa 58:10, where it says,

> The righteous shall rejoice when he sees the vengeance;
> He shall wash his feet in the blood of the wicked, NKJV

So Jesus came to be regarded by the Jewish leadership as someone who would in fact *prevent* their dream of Jewish exploitation and plunder, an attitude which has literally continued *among some* to this very day.

Jesus also touched on the trafficking with other spirits. This was an undercurrent in first century Judaism, but a very real and powerful one, and one that over time would be dominant in their outlook, habits, and directions. The full explanation of these teachings in Christianity was given by the apostles after the resurrection, but it is implicit in everything Jesus taught about Himself. He is the One and only One through whom everyone in heaven and on earth must go, *or* go on to suffer punishment for their own sins. Of course, if accepted, this renders all of the Jewish pursuit of the control of "other spirits" to be profane and immoral and foolish. Many missed this point, but it seems the unbelieving Jewish leadership did not miss the point. This will be covered in further detail in the next section on the Kabbalah and other spirits.

So many Jews did and do, try to sidetrack the Gospel. First, it begins with cautious interviews and probing questions in the Galilean's "press conferences." Then it becomes bitter when it becomes clear that He will not turn a blind eye to their outrageous exploitation of others, including "the lesser brethren." Worse, He will not agree to them putting human traditions above the Word of God. Then they set traps to destroy Him in the public eye, or to bring the wrath of the gentile rulers down on Him. All to no avail! You can read the entire conflict from multiple eye witness sources in the Gospels. Finally, they give up trying to trap Him in public. He turns every question against them. He is given a hero's welcome as He enters Jerusalem in Luke chapter 19. He has to stop and weep over Jerusalem.

> ... "If you had known, even you, especially in this your day, the things *that make* for your peace! But now they are hidden from your eyes."
> Lk 19:42 NKJV

The Jews then became organizers of the persecution of the true religion of the Jews. Should we murder an itinerate rabbi who preaches love and humility and service to God and to man? Such is small change to those focused on worldly power. So they considered the matter in a closed door meeting. The word used for the "council" in Jn 11:47 is *sunedrion* συνέδριον, literally the "Sanhedrin."

> [47] ... convened a council, and were saying, "What are we doing? For this man is performing many signs. [48] If we let Him *go on* like this, all men will believe in Him, and the Romans will come and take away both our

place and our nation." [49] But one of them, Caiaphas, who was high priest that year, said to them, "You know nothing at all, [50] nor do you take into account that it is expedient for you that one man die for the people, and that the whole nation not perish." [51] Now he did not say this on his own initiative, but being high priest that year, he prophesied that **Jesus was going to die for the nation**, [52] and **not for the nation only**, but in order **that He might also gather together into one the children of God who are scattered abroad**. [53] So from that day on they planned together to kill Him.
Jn 11:47-53 NASB (*bold emphasis added*)

At first they think they have won. *They* realized, even though His disciples seemingly did not, that Jesus prophesied that He would rise from the dead. They tried to prevent that ... and failed. But now their opposition is sealed by murder. Repent? Unthinkable, at least now. They pay off the soldiers and fix it with the Roman rulers so the soldiers are not put to death. They think once again they have won and have kept thinking it for two thousand years. *But there were too many witnesses, both to His life, and His death, and His resurrection.*

In the movie *Fiddler on the Roof*, there are entertaining reviews of the plight of many Jews in Russia in the late eighteen-hundreds and the early nineteen-hundreds. It emphasizes the traditions of historical Judaism, while perhaps even blaming God for their plight and questioning God's justice and judgments, even in terms that can be clearly called blasphemous by orthodox believers, both Jewish and Christian. In one particular scene, where the hero sings "If I were a rich man," toward the end of the song he says, "We have the disease ..." (which indeed they do), "but what we need now is the cure!" Indeed they do. But they were specifically offered the cure ... and they specifically rejected it ... to hold on to what one Jewish writer described as "the futile way of life inherited from your forefathers," 1Pe 1:18.

So we see a rabbi of no particular importance in the Judean power structures ... murdered by the Jewish leaders for the supposed good of the Jews. Rabbi Yehoshua is intolerable. Lying and oppressive traditions, witchcraft and other gods we can abide, but a humble rabbi who is to be wrongfully executed as a criminal? No problem! Right? They are, indeed, always rejecting the Holy Spirit, Acts 7:51

The idea that government should have nothing to do with religion is foreign to Scripture. The Jews know this. They are not opposed to a religious state. Modern Israel is in a real sense a religious state, although not technically so. The Jews are opposed to their own Messiah. They are opposed to Christianity. It is Jesus their own Messiah that they have hated and do hate, so they hinder acknowledgment of the Christ in gentile governments as much as they can. As Isaiah said, the Jews were stumbling over the rock of safety.

[13] Sanctify the LORD of hosts himself; and *let* him *be* your fear, and *let*

him *be* your dread. [14] And he shall be for a sanctuary; **but** for **a stone of stumbling and for a rock of offence to both the houses of Israel**, for a gin and for a snare to the inhabitants of Jerusalem. [15] **And many among them shall stumble, and fall, and be broken**, and **be snared, and be taken**. Isa 8:13-15 KJV (*bold emphasis added*)

This pattern of opposing and trying to undermine *anything* contrary to *their* plans continued. Paul, as a former Pharisee, writes of Judaic infiltration of Christianity in Gal 2:3-5.

[3] Yet not even Titus who *was* with me, being a Greek, was compelled to be circumcised. [4] And *this occurred* because of false brethren secretly brought in (who came in by stealth to spy out our liberty which we have in Christ Jesus, that they might bring us into bondage), [5] to whom we did not yield submission even for an hour, ... NKJV

Jews using the gentile courts to suppress Christianity, or even other Jews whom they happen to dislike, has already been demonstrated. Paul summarized this reactionary and subversive influence of the Jews in a letter to the Thessalonians.

[14] ... the Jews, [15] Who both killed the Lord Jesus, and their own prophets, and have persecuted us; **and they please not God, and are contrary to all men**: [16] Forbidding us to speak to the Gentiles that they might be saved, to fill up their sins alway: for the wrath is come upon them to the uttermost. 1Thes 2:14-16 KJV (*bold emphasis added*)

The Jewish opposition to the LORD of Glory was not new. Nevertheless, the Master did receive His kingdom; **it will fill this present world**, and **He will return to reward His servants** and to punish those who hate Him.

Reject Your Own Christ And Accept What?

If we will not listen to the truth, we must listen to lies! That is just the way it is.

I am come in my Father's name, and ye receive me not: if another shall come in his own name, him ye will receive. Jn 5:43 KJV

They readily and consistently reject the humble prophet from Galilee when he comes announcing Himself as the Messiah and speaking words of peace and mercy from the heart. However, when the charlatans from the occult come proclaiming themselves as the Messiah, they often find a ready audience among the Jews. The Jewish historian Graetz is witness to a great deal of this, and so is the Jewish historian Josephus. Rabbi Yehoshua was right! So Jewish leader Rabbi Akiba and many other Jews, while opposing of Jesus of Nazareth, accepted Bar Kokhba as messiah, in the early second century.

Of course, that was an abortive revolt, a false christ, one among many, resulting in the Jews losing the right to even *live* in Jerusalem. They do not have a problem with someone claiming to be the Christ. A fraud which might meet worldly success standards is perfectly acceptable. But a religion of justice and mercy and freedom to all, including the gentiles? Unthinkable.

They rejected the concept of *Elo-him* אֱלֹהִים, the plural form of the word "God," and plurality in one God, as in Genesis 1. So they went about setting up their own trinity of gods, as shall be soon demonstrated. They rejected as absurd the concept of God coming as a man, so some among them set about creating their own God-man.

And there are other strands of thought in Judaism which should be noted.

An Affinity for Plato

Perhaps I should have emphasized Neo-Platonism in this subtitle, and it is there. There has been among the Jews a strange affinity for Plato, Platonism, and Neoplatonism, and it is not all good. This is strange for several reasons. First, it seems that the model of Plato's *Republic* is not what moderns would call a republic at all. The model is the Spartan militaristic and communal state. In Plato, the ultimate in good government is the communal state or to be stated more plainly in modern terms: a communist state. Most do not associate "militaristic" with communism, but it was associated with ancient Sparta *and was with* modern communism in Russia and Eastern Europe. And there is no clearer model for Nazism than Plato.

Before even getting to "militaristic," there are other problems. The Law of Moses was by no means a law for a communal society. There was private property. It is the underlying premise of "You shall not steal," Ex 20:15. Moses' Law was so emphatic about private property that it was immoral to even *want* what your neighbor had.

> Thou shalt not **covet** thy neighbour's house, thou shalt not **covet** thy neighbour's wife, nor his manservant, nor his maidservant, nor his ox, nor his ass, nor any thing that is thy neighbour's.
> Ex 20:17 KJV (*bold emphasis added*)

Marriages are notoriously loose in communal societies, but the command is "Thou shalt not commit adultery." Ex 20:14. Family values are key in God's plans in both the Old Covenant and the New Covenant. You do not leave your mama and your daddy to cleave to your commune. Rather,

> Therefore shall a man leave his father and his mother, and shall cleave unto his wife: **and they shall become one flesh.**
> Gen 2:24 KJV (*bold emphasis added*)

Scripture actually asserts that these are *not* things which are optional extras, but instead they are spoken of as things built into our biology, which indeed they are. Unnatural unions, for instance homosexuality, are to be considered as threats to the society overall, and those involved are indeed to be put to death.

> If a man lies with a male as he lies with a woman, both of them have committed an abomination. They shall surely be put to death. Their blood *shall be* upon them. Lev 20:13 NKJV

But this is Moses' Law! It is only an issue *if* you have any *supposed* fidelity to Moses' Law. In contrast, in Plato's Republic, men and women were on a more equal basis, with state ownership of everything and everyone. And the leadership? It was to be a select group of homosexuals who were just a cut above everyone else, and who would tell everyone else what they could or could not do. You could really say it was a totalitarian anti-family state. This philosophy has been a very popular picture of "good" government to Liberals, both in the past and now. The Liberals mouth glowing tributes to "democracy" and "freedom," but deep down they despise the common man, whom the LORD our God loves, and they support the totalitarian state.

How did it come about that Plato came to have so much influence among the Jews? I am not sure I know all of the answers, but some factors can be seen.

First, Plato has quite a bit to do with the occult. (Occult means hidden religion including witchcraft, magic, and that sector known as the "mystery religions" as has been discussed previously, and is discussed in more detail in my earlier work, *Prophecy Principles*.) Actually it was natural for Platonism to develop into the more clearly occult-like Neoplatonism. If the occult is considered as being a mostly hidden iceberg, then Plato is the visible tip of the iceberg. The scholars and the advocates strenuously object to the occult associations, but they are there. In that context Plato outlines the perfect government for which these cults should, and for the most part do, aim. (Was this really part of the "subversion" for which Socrates was actually executed? That is only a question, you understand.)

In this way Jewish involvement in the occult was one lead-in to Plato. The essentials are all there: the spheres, the demonic spirits, the "other world" of spiritual beings which is especially part of Jewish Gnosticism.

Perhaps also there are other factors. Evidently a Spartan (Lacedemonian) king of the second century BC contacted the Jews and *claimed the Spartans were descendants*

Plato

of Abraham! Here is what Josephus tells us.

> "... Onias, died [about this time], and left the high priesthood to his son Simon. [225] And when he was dead Onias, his son, succeeded him in that dignity. To him it was that Areus, king of the Lacedemonians, sent an embassage, with an epistle; the copy whereof here follows: [226] AREUS, KING OF THE LACEDEMONIANS, TO ONIAS, SENDETH GREETING. "We have met with a certain writing, whereby we have discovered that both the Jews and the Lacedemonians are of one stock, and are derived from the kindred of Abraham. ..."
> Josephus, *Antiquities*, 12.4.10, 224-226

Is this another piece of the puzzle? Perhaps. Plato was possibly a more benign influence in the Jewish philosopher Philo. At any rate, when the Jews started being involved in revolutionary activity, that activity often began to take on a communal character, and a Platonic character. Before the term "communists" and "socialist" became popular, one political term often used in the West was the "Levelers." They want to put all people on the same level.

Jewish scholar Israel Shahak in *Jewish History, Jewish Religion*, notes that,

> "Using the concepts of Platonism ... based on 'Jewish ideology' should not seem strange. It was noticed by several scholars. ... Moses Hadas, who claimed that the foundations of 'classical Judaism' ... as it was established in the talmudic sages, are based on Platonic influences and especially on the image of Sparta as it appears in Plato. ... the Platonic political system, adopted by Judaism as early as the Maccabean period (142-63 BC) ... There can be no better definition of 'classical Judaism' and of the ways in which the rabbis manipulated it than this Platonic definition." pgs 12-13

Thus, according to these scholars (including Shahak), what they call 'classical Judaism' was **no longer *really* Biblical**, but was *really* **Platonic, as early as the second century BC!** You may remember, that is exactly what Rabbi Yehoshua said, that the religion of the Jews was no longer Biblical.

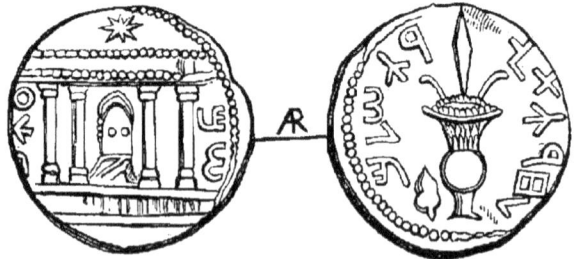

A coin issued by war-like Jewish false messiah Bar Kokhba, of the early second century AD. Unlike Jesus, he was supported by much of the Jewish establishment. "Bar Kokhba" literally meant "son of a star." His star is seen shining over the Jerusalem temple on the front. (He was also called "Bar Kosiba," son of a liar.) He was captured and executed, and this revolt resulted in a ban on any Jews living in Jerusalem, a ban which lasted many centuries.

[45] Do not think that I will accuse you to the Father: there is one that accuseth you, even Moses, in whom

ye trust. [46] For had ye believed Moses, ye would have believed me: for he wrote of me. [47] But if ye believe not his writings, how shall ye believe my words? Jn 5:45-47 KJV

Then when the Jews started committing their "secret traditions" into writing in the Kabbalah (which will be addressed in the next major section), those writings proved to be very much influenced by Platonism and Neoplatonism. Here is the way the *Atlas of Jewish History* puts it:

"In Italy the encounter between the Kabbalah and the Renaissance led to its infusion with strong neoplatonic element." pg 144

That is for sure a true statement from these Jewish historian's point of view, but in reality, as has been shown, what might be now called "Neoplatonic influence" in the Jewish occult, clearly predates formal Neoplatonism. It was also clearly predated much of Gnosticism and its branches.

Meddling With Revolutions

Mohammedanism as a Grand Design?

Then comes another strange part of the story and it seems that Mohammedanism should be discussed, at least briefly. Its significance for Christianity was huge. Christianity seemed dominant in the West after the conversion of the Roman empire to Christianity. For a while, this dominance had no serious rivals. The rise of Mohammedanism was a major game changer. It became a replacement, and a challenger, and to some extent, a conquerer of Christianity.

The Mohammedans conquered the Middle East, and their holdings at their height stretched all the way from Greece and the Balkans in the East to Spain in the West. They came very close to being able to conquer Europe in its entirety. Even when the decline of Mohammedanism began, it was still a fierce and daunting adversary to Christianity.

Then there were some interesting things about Mohammedanism. You can see these things discussed many places, but I have chosen to reference Will Durant's fourth volume in his "The Story of Civilization," series, *The Age of Faith,* Simon and Schuster, NY, 1950. There are several reasons for using him as the base here. Although he is very cold toward Christianity in general, he is good in some other respects. He gives an amazingly balanced picture of Catholicism pgs 75-78 (and the rest of the chapter), except he begrudges its otherworldliness. But for instance, Durant will say that Christianity was "sullied with superstition and cruelty" but he would never say such of paganism, much less of Mohammedanism or Judaism. He is basically sympathetic to *both* Mohammedanism and to Judaism. Book III of this volume is a very Jewish view of Judaism. This space (75 pages out of 1100 pages) I would say is *fully* justified, but not by what Durant tells us. He does not really account for the Jews successes, or for the hatred accorded them, and leaves much out. But he is also very readable. Durant was a liberal icon a couple of generations back, and I think we can detect in Durant some of the present day Liberal infatuation with Mohammedanism. Last but not least, to the general reading public, he is very accessible, and he notes some very interesting things about Mohammedanism.

Durant acknowledges that "Allah" was a pre-Moslem tribal idol (pg 161), and then more or less drops the subject. He says of Mohammed that "His basic ideas ... seem Jewish in proximate origin, even in form and dress." pg 184. He goes on to say that Mohammed put no trust in the form of either the Old Testament or the New Testament (pg 184), so the influence was not really Biblical. He does say that the "Koran is modeled on that of the Hebrew prophets" (pg 184), which seems at first glance to be a contradiction, but he does clarify this.

> "The teachings of the Koran about angels, the resurrection, and heaven **follow the Talmud rather than the Old Testament. Stories that make up a fourth of the Koran can be traced to haggadic (illustrative) elements in the Talmud**."
> Durant, *The Age of Faith*, pg 185 (*bold emphasis added*)

His account of Mohammedanism includes many phrases like, "as in Judaism" (pg 167), "the Judaism of the Koran" (pg 349), and "Divorce ... as by the Talmud" (pg 181). Durant notes that Mohammed "uses Jewish ideas" and makes Allah equal to Yahweh (pg 184). Durant notes things like the "same frequent phrase in the Talmud," "recalls the rabbinical use," etc., pg 184

Durant also notes that Mohammed took a Jewish wife (pg 170), that the Arab calendar is like the Jewish calendar (pg 171), that "In the Koran, as in the Talmud, law and morals are one ..." (pg 179), and that "As in Judaism, celibacy was considered sinful." (pg 181).

When Durant speaks of the development of government in Mohammedanism, he notes among other things, that "**by strange but repeated coincidence** these useful traditions echoed ... still more the Mishna and Gemara of the Jews." p 226 (*bold emphasis added*).

Durant also notes what could be construed as Jewish occult influences in the Arab world, when he says, "The theology, as in nearly all Moslem thinkers, is Gnostic and NeoPlatonic ..." (pg 254). Durant discusses the belief in magic among the Mohammedans, and notes "Here at the end, as in its beginning, Arabic philosophy was Aristotle Neoplatonized," pg 337. Durant notes on page 138 that the roots of the Mohammedan mystics, the Sufi, are Neo-Platonic. And speaking of Gnostic influence, although the prophet accepted Jesus as a prophet, he maintained that Jesus did not really die on the cross (pgs 184, 186), a central position taken by many Gnostics.

Durant notes the early Jewish acceptance of Mohammed at Medina, pg 166. What then was the general Jewish reaction? He notes that Mohammed formed a concordant with the Jews, pg 169. The Jews, Durant notes, welcomed the Arabs as liberators, and the Mohammedans tended to protect what we would call the "Christian 'heresies,'" pg 218. Many of the details are lost in Western histories, but Durant notes later that the Jews aided the Mohammedan conquest of Spain, pg 299.

All that Durant says on these things has not been covered. Durant was a sophisticated and observant researcher and historian, with a good eye for noticing significant facts and events and persons, and he is not so arrogant as to think his observations do not need documentation. Obviously, there were other influences in the rise of such a major world religion. Christianity also was a factor, but a significantly lesser one, and no doubt some of the common ground between the Mohammedanism and the Jews is due to common traditions. It is not noted by Durant, but the Jews and the Mohammedans have shared a mutual animosity toward Christianity.

All of this is an incredible tally of "accidental" influence, to say the least, in what became the greatest anti-Christian force in the world for well over a thousand years. Christianity was suppressed in that area of the world where it first flourished: the Middle East, North Africa, and Asia Minor. Christianity was "allowed," but it was no longer a public religion. No new church facilities could be built, and all attempts to convert others were outlawed and suppressed. All of which, overall seemed to "work." The success of the Mohammedans in suppressing Christianity where, for instance, the pagan Romans and many others had failed, has been widely noted in books like *The Decline of Eastern Christianity under Islam: From Jihad to Dhimmitude*, by Bat Ye'or, 1996, Associated University Presses, NJ.

Rabbi Louis Finkelstein in his *The Pharisees,The Sociological Background of the Their Faith*" Vol I, 1940, page x, succinctly puts it this way,

> "The energies which **Pharisaism** called out of the Arab Peninsula, brought new life to this ancient country and made it once again the center of world thought, commerce, and even government."
> (*bold emphasis added*)

In other words, he attributes the successes of Mohammedanism to the influence of Pharisaism.

The reaction of the Jews to these things has been sort of a love-hate relationship over the centuries. In the early swirls of conquest, sometimes *both* Christianity and Judaism were suppressed. Much is made of many European countries requiring special clothing or badges of Jews, but the Mohammedan rulers were at times requiring such of both Christians and Jews. It appeared for a while that Mohammedanism would progress unified and almost unhindered, but then splits occurred within the sect, and the Shia/Sunni split provided the avenues for limiting both their reach and their grasp.

In our present time, the Jews and the Mohammedans are at odds, but it has not always been that way. Although Christianity suffered and declined in the Mohammedan world, the Jews in the East overall seem to have held their own or even increased their influence. You do not have to read very far into modern accounts about "Islam," to find it asserted that the Mohammedan world was very much more tolerant of Judaism than was the "Christian" "world" (if I may be allowed such a misnomer). When the Mohammedans invaded Spain, *The Historical Atlas of the Jewish People*, General Editor Eli Barnavi, Schocken Books, NY, 1992, informs us that

> "... the Jews welcomed the Muslims as saviors. ... Moreover, they actively collaborated with invaders who rewarded them by leaving the defense of certain conquered cities to Jewish garrisons." pg 81

And while Durant sidesteps the issue of who really financed the Arab conquests, *The Historical Atlas of the Jewish People* speaks of a "Judeo-Arabic culture", and says,

> "... Bagdad ... Jewish bankers who soon formed an affiliation with the courts of high Arab officials and potentates. By financing their military campaigns and luxurious lifestyles, these bankers became indispensable to the Muslim rulers, and in return were allowed to farm taxes." pg 82

Thus, strange as it may seem to us today, many Jews of the past thirteen hundred or so years have often preferred the familiarity and security of the Middle East over the West, and when things went wrong in the West, scurried back to the safety of Turkey or North Africa!

Crypto-Jews and Their Hosts

There are many examples in history of crypto-Jews, and Jewish subversion of their hosts, which are easy to investigate. For instance, the back and forth relationship of the Jews with the Republic of Venice: often being kicked out, and often returning in deals made for the "advantage" of both parties. Will Durant in his volume, *The Age of Faith*, Simon and Schuster, NY, 1950, documents that the Jews had aided the Moslems in their conquest of Spain, pg 299. Durant is hardly anti-Jewish. Naturally, this ties in very closely with the later standoff between the Spanish and the Jews, which will be looked at later. *A Historical Atlas of the Jewish People*, pg 78, notes the same, and ties it to the Jew's later problems in Spain and Portugal.

"711: [AD, nf] Muslim conquest of Spain. According to Lucas de Tuy (13th century), the Jews delivered Toledo into the hands of the invaders. The accusation of "treason" during the Muslim invasion will be raised often against the Jews and *conversos* in the 15th century."

Jewish historian Cecil Roth in his book on the *Marranos*, tells us "other Marranos were believed to maintain an extensive espionage service in the Peninsula." pg 285; and mentions that some of the Jews in Spain acted as intelligence sources for the Turks, pg 205. So there was indeed treachery among some Jews against Spain. Other Jews later tried to engineer a Dutch takeover of Brazil, pg 285; and failed it might be added. Then some of the refugees of the failure to conquer Brazil, went to "New Amsterdam" (New York City), pg 293, which was then mainly Dutch.

The revolutionary inclinations of many Eastern European Jews almost everywhere stirred up the hackles of the scores of small national groups. Despite this, the Jewish radicals' reach was often further than their grasp. They had a persistent tendency to take politically suicidal positions, and then treat all Jews who did not want to line up and slit their own throats, as traitors, and sometimes as also being "anti-Semites."

From William Tyndale on, protests against false religious practices tended to take on revolutionary overtones, even almost taking on the form of religious cults. These fissures were clearly exploited as such by the "mystery of lawlessness," and the international commercial powers.

The Jews have long seemed to nurture in their midst some of the greatest masters of revolution, mob violence, and intrigue, even from ancient times. So we have a situation where the Jews, to satisfy their desire for advancement, to seek that dominance over the nations which they had assured themselves they had the right to seek, and to exploit the stupid gentiles, whom they had assured themselves they had they right to exploit; time and again made themselves the mortal enemies of the societies which were their hosts.

> *The truth is that the Jews have been adept at making enemies of their friends, and alienating those who would help and nurture them.*

Some of these things are so well documented that even Jewish historians do not bother to deny them. Others are well enough documented that these same historians, without acknowledging the truths of the matter, merely note that the Jews were accused of these things. For instance, in the Persian invasion of Palestine in 613-614 AD,

"As the Persian armies were advancing, the Jewish communities were rising in revolt against local Byzantine rulers and hailing the Persians as liberators. ...

"Later Christian sources, however, accused the community of collaboration with the invaders ..." *A Historical Atlas of the Jewish People*, pg 77

Or from Graetz in his *History of the Jews*,

"Whenever a party in Christendom opposes itself to the ruling church,
it assumes a tinge of the Old Testament, not to say Jewish, spirit."
Vol 4, pg 222 (*bold emphasis added*)

And again from Graetz,

"Catholics accused Jews of secretly supplying the Hussites with money
and arms;" Vol 4, pg 222.

Of course, when things reach this state, they tend to swiftly go down hill.
Will Durant points out that the libertine Pope Alexander VI was possibly Jewish, and that he was called "the Marrano Pope," *The Renaissance*, Simon &
Schuster, NY 1953, pg 411. The attempt is being made here to only quote
sources that are very pro-Jewish, but such things pop up in history almost continuously during the Christian age, and all across the map.

Jewish Successes in Spain as "Marranos."

In opposition to the occasional infiltration of an adversary, the Jews of
Spain began a mass, false, "full-conversion" to Catholicism—Marranos as they
came to be known. (The term "marrano," although widely used today even by
the Jews themselves, *is* a Spanish word for a "pig, or hog," *Oxford Spanish
Dictionary*, 2008, 2012.) It seems this is the first time the Jews came to completely realize the full power of crypto-Judaism. Graetz also speaks of these
things.

"Under the guise of Spanish or Portuguese merchants, they founded
large communities in Bordeaux, Amsterdam, London, and in various
parts of Italy. From their step-fatherland they brought with them a
higher culture and an aristocratic demeanor. Consequently they did
not suffer from the contempt with which other Jews were treated in
political and social circles. In fact, the Jews of Marrano descent looked
down upon their co-religionists as gypsies, on account of their external
deterioration." Graetz, *History of the Jews,* Vol 5, pg 729

A phenomenon which Graetz repeatedly documents is the favor the kings
of the nations gave toward the Jews.

"Pucci straightforwardly said to the Portuguese ambassador, "The king
of Portugal, like the king of Spain, is more attracted by the Marranos'
wealth than concerned about the orthodoxy of their creed;""
History of the Jews , Vol 4, pg 505

The Jews always tried to wiggle their way to the top, and once there were often careless about stepping on others. There are, of course, many other factors. *A Historical Atlas of the Jewish People*, pg 148, speaks in some carefully worded language about the Marannos.

> "... marranism. Communities of Jews who had been forcibly converted ... were naturally more inclined to accept the **antinomian tendencies** ..." (*bold emphasis added*)

So these things heightened lawless tendencies among these Jews.

The Spanish, over time, came to realize the Jews were not only good money makers, and an economic asset to their kingdom, but also that the Jews represented a powerful subversive threat to the religious foundations of their kingdom, and a powerful potential "fifth-column" in case of war. Only a summary can be given here. An era of forced conversions to Catholicism began in Spain in 1391. But by the late 1400's it was clear that the policy of forced conversions was a failure and had created an even greater danger to the nation. The "New Christians" were not really Catholics at all, but still very much Jews, and still very opposed to Christianity, which to their minds was represented by Catholicism.

There is no better source here for the average English reader, than Jewish historian Cecil Roth's *A History of the Marranos*. It is a good reference on the subject of the Jewish Marranos. Roth gives an impressively impartial history of the Marranos. He is definitely at his best here. According to Roth, "The classical land of crypto-Judaism, however, is Spain." pg 7. Here, thanks in part to Jewish boldness, and in part to the Inquisition, it can be seen most clearly how it worked, and its potential. All of these lessons had been clearly absorbed in Judaism by the time of the "Enlightenment."

At first, the Spanish thought they had won and that their Jewish problem was solved. But such a large ethnic group, opposed and hostile to their "host," and working in concert to undermine their host, soon had very different results. The Marranos "... were Jews in all but name, and Christians in nothing but form." Roth, *The Marranos*, Shocken Books, NY, 1974, fourth edition, pg 20

> "They all but dominated Spanish life. The wealthier amongst them intermarried with the highest nobility of the land, few impoverished counts of hidalgos being able to resist the lure of their gold. Within a couple of generations, there was barely a single aristocratic family in Aragon, from the royal house downwards, which was free from the "taint" of Jewish blood." Roth, *The Marranos* pg 21

Several pages of documentation follows. In the south they were near one-third of the population, *The Marranos*, pg 27. The 1480 supreme courts of Cortez and Aragon "were presided over by persons of Jewish extraction." pg 21. They became the bishops and cardinals of the church, and were able to continually root out any gentile competition for high office, *even in their own country!*

"Indeed, there was hardly a single office of importance at either court, especially in the financial administration, which was not occupied by the descendants of some converted Jews, or by members of families closely allied with them." Roth, *The Marranos*, pg 25

The discussion can go on in many directions. Many have speculated that Christopher Columbus was actually a Jew. Will Durant discusses the possibility. Cecil Roth rejects this idea, but in reviewing the inconclusive historical data, actually makes a very good case for Columbus being Jewish (*Personalities And Events In Jewish History,* 1953, The Jewish Publication Society of America, 1953, pgs 192-211). Remember that often crypto-Jews were operating in circumstances in which discovery might mean their death, so every effort was made to completely conceal their Jewish identity.

In Portugal, "Their wealth was enormous." "They almost monopolized commerce." "The export trade of Portugal, especially, was very largely in Marrano hands."*The Marranos*, pg 76. "Meanwhile, the conversos spent money lavishly at Rome to induce the papal Curia to take a merciful view of their plight." pg 82. Pertinent quotes from Cecil Roth alone could go on for pages and pages. By the mid 1400's it was clear that "conversions" had made the problems of Jewish dominance worse instead of better,.

These problems come up over and over in the history of the last 2,000 years. Where does the loyalty of this country-less nation really lie? Or as some have phrased it,

"the painful question of "dual allegiance,"" *A Historical Atlas of the Jewish People*, Eli Barnavi, Shocken Books, NY, 1992, pg 36.

Then Came the Inquisition

In the sorry mess which followed, the Inquisition was set up in 1478, to ferret out this very real underground threat to their faith and to their nation. It was given very broad powers in what was considered a national emergency. Jewish historian Josepf Kastein interestingly comments,

"It cannot be denied that as a political fight it was justified and consistent." *History and Destiny of the Jews*, Garden City Publishing Company, NY, 1936, pg 229

*The Inquisition **did** save the nation and the Spanish world for Catholicism. As Roth points out, **many** of the Jews in Spain, just like the Incas and the Aztecs, did convert to Catholicism under pressure, and disappeared into the Spanish people, **even to this day!*** Roth comments that the Inquisition was so efficiently catching the Jews that the burnings actually fell off, *The Marranos*, pg 277, and etc. Later events, though, proved many had just gone further underground, pgs 281ff, etc. In 1492, after years of great Jewish influence through the ruling aristocracy in

Spain, followed by a period of crypto-Jewish success, the Marranos, the Jews, were at last expelled from Spain in a very harsh manner. Cecil Roth in *Personalities And Events In Jewish History,* pg 192, says it was "with every circumstance of cruelty." The problems though did go on for a considerable period of time. In *A Historical Atlas of the Jewish People*, it is noted that those false Catholics who escaped Spain, the "Conversos" as they call them,

> "... were not completely free from molestation ... In France they had to maintain some semblance of Catholicism for more than two centuries, but their Jewishness was an open secret. ... Judaism ... was reduced to a private ceremonial practice ..." pg 132

Roth also carefully documents the generally harmful effects of such an underground existence on the faithful practice of a religion, and how among those Jews genuinely converting to Catholicism (and he clearly notes that many did), some retained some knowledge of their Jewish customs and roots with pride. Others retained some of their Jewish customs, but had completely lost any knowledge of its origins. He clearly shows that there are plenty of both in Spain, to this day. The numbers and influence of the Jews in Spain, and their frequent assimilation into gentile families in Spain even *before* the era of forced conversions, have made many speculate that *most* modern Spaniards have at least some Jewish blood in their veins.

The Jews have frequently shared both the advantages and liabilities of clever scheming. They have *often* helped both sides and hurt both sides in many conflicts, all in fishing for their own advantage. The short term advantages were often great, but it almost always finally came to light, and the long term effect, as with the Jewish Marranos of Spain who went under cover, was often even deeper seated suspicion and hostility.

In conclusion, the Inquisition was a completely ruthless intelligence agency for the Spanish to sort their way through a very real and a very serious national security problem. Roth carefully points out that forced conversion was never a part of true Christianity. Here is another case of the reaction against religious and political subversion producing results as bad as the disease. What can we call the forced "conversions," and the Inquisition against the Jews, but ghastly. As I read these terrible accounts of the 15th and 16th century AD, I could not help but think of Moses' writing of the curses which would fall upon the Jews if they remained unfaithful, Deuteronomy chapters 27 and 28. Over time of course, unregulated, unbridled, power such as the Inquisition wielded became a threat to all, and was eventually shut down.

The Jews have down through history, acted as though it was shameful that they "had to" convert to Christianity to be "accepted." On the other hand, many people, both Jew and gentile, hold to their own beliefs in spite of rejection by ruling elites, and never consider a false conversion just to gain money or position. Honest gentiles from more than one faith suffer each day for these things, without feeling the "need" for a false conversion.

Truly the behavior of the Marranos against both the Spanish people and each other, and the behavior of the Inquisition toward both the Spanish people and the Marranos, are blights on both of these sects. One can only cry for the meanness and hardness of heart of both sides.

Have two millennia of clever scheming and infiltration really brought the Jews peace? Money? Yes. Power? Yes. But peace? The only answer that can be given if one takes the broad view, even of the Jews among themselves, is: NO!

Running if you have to? Yes! Faking another religion to survive? No! At least that is not a strategy counseled in Scripture. Once again, Scripture never advocates concealing our religion for "survival," in either the Old Testament or the New Testament! Perhaps that is the most telling Biblical commentary on these things.

As with many
cultures and religions,
it is not just a single thing
which may warp
and perhaps even ruin
what is good.
It is quite often a nest
of related ideas
which work to
distort us
and turn us aside.

IV. The Fourth Break: The Kabbalah and Other Spirits

> They have provoked Me to jealousy by *what* is not God;
>   They have moved Me to anger by their foolish idols.
>   But I will provoke them to jealousy by *those who are* not a
>   nation;
>   I will move them to anger by a foolish nation. Deut 32:21 NKJV

The source of most modern witchcraft, magic, occult teaching, and secret societies is the Jewish Kabbalah. Like many of the words in the hidden "sciences," if we may be pardoned the term "science," the word Kabbalah is spelled many different ways, such as: Cabbala, Cabbalah, Cabala, Qabala, Qabalah, Kabala, Kabbala, or Kabalah, and heaven knows you may see a new variation tomorrow. They love to play word games.

The First Cause and the Emanations

One of the keys to the Jewish Kabbalah of the 12th and 13th centuries AD Spain, is that it actually springs from ancient Gnosticism. Some quotes from Jewish scholar Gershom Scholem will suffice.

> "the central ideas, as well as many details, go back as far as the first and second centuries." Gershom Scholem, *Kabbalah*, New American Library, NY, 1978, pg 15

In other places he comments that the doctrine showed,

> "Remnants of a clearly Gnostic terminology and symbolism are preserved ..." Scholem, *Kabbalah*, pg 43

> "The Kabbala ... was the offspring of ... an older ... and essentially Gnostical tradition ... and ... Jewish Neoplatonism."
> Gershom Scholem, *Major Trends in Jewish Mysticism*, pg 175

> "Existing alongside these Platonic definitions is the theosophic conception of the *Sefirot* as forces of the divine essence or nature,"
> Scholem, *Kabbalah*, pg 100

The Sefirot as part "of the divine essence," but Jesus could *not* be such?

> "the speculative Kabbalah moved between two great heritages, the Bible and talmudic Judaism on the one hand and Greek philosophy in its different forms on the other." Scholem, *Kabbalah*, pg 88

Such observations could be multiplied many times over, from many different scholars, but these should suffice. Some think that Gnosticism sprang from what many call ancient "Merkabah" mysticism. Merkaba is from the Hebrew word for chariot, *merkava* מֶרְכָּבָה. The studies of Elijah being taken to heaven in a fiery chariot in 2 Kings 2, and the visions of God seen by Ezekiel in for instance Ezekiel 1, led to intense speculation about "the chariots of God," or of "the gods," and how men might ascend "the heavenly spheres" to meet with God Himself.

> "Merkabah terminology is found in a hymn-fragment in the Dead Sea Scrolls, where the angels praise "the image of the Throne of the Chariot" (Strugnell). ... the emotional and ecstatic contemplation of the Merkaba experienced as an ascent of the heavens, namely "descent to the Merkabah," though entering pardes ("paradise")."
> Scholem, *Kabbalah*, pg 13

In the period from the first century BC to the second century AD these things seemed to have morphed into what can be generally called "Gnosticism." Scholem says this "may be termed "Jewish and rabbinic Gnosticism."" *Kabbalah*, pg 13. There were many variations in what is *now* called Gnosticism, but the general principles are refuted in the New Testament, especially the letters of Paul to the Colossians and Ephesians, and to Timothy; and in the Gospel of John, and the letters of John. Scholem shows that some of this was already brewing in Judaism.

> "it is known from Josephus that the Essenes possessed literature which was both magical and angelological in content. ... They possessed the original Book of Enoch, both Hebrew and Aramaic ..."
> Scholem, *Kabbalah*, pg 10

Put in a straightforward way, Gnosticism had at a minimum two gods. **First** they had the ultimate God, the First Cause of everything, or the *Ein-Sof* ("the Infinite"). However in their theory this ultimate God is very remote and detached. Also, as was mentioned earlier, they were inclined to have two eternal grounds of being: one spiritual and one material. The spiritual was all good and all pure spirit, but matter, though implicitly eternal also, was severely flawed and evil. The problem then was how could a completely good and pure spiritual God form *anything* out of something as evil and flawed as matter. So what was the solution? The First Cause "emanated" a spirit from Himself who was overall pretty good, but not quite as good or quite as powerful as the First Cause. Then this spirit emanated a spirit that was not quite as powerful or as good as he was. Then that spirit emanated another spirit, and that another, and so on, until at last a spirit came into being who was totally evil, totally wicked, who was, in fact, so wicked and evil that it was able to form our present universe out of flawed and wicked matter. So *they* say. **Secondly** this totally evil being was then the creator "god" of this present world. Many scholars like to argue endlessly about this point or that point, but Jewish historian Heinrich Graetz in his 19th century *History of the Jews*, gives some very succinct summaries without trying to quibble to the advantage of this or that modern day occult sect, or scholarly position. This is how Graetz summarized all of this:

"Beneath this highest of all beings they set the Creator of the world (Demiurge), whom they also called Ruler. To him they assigned the work of creation; he directed the world, he had delivered the people of Israel, and given them the Law."
Heinrich Graetz, *History of the Jews*, Vol 2, pg 375

So the evil "god" was actually the creator of the world. ("Samael" or "Simyael" are names used for Satan "the blind god," Scholem, *Kabbalah,* pg 385, 386.) Under so-called "Christian—Gnosticism" then, the "god" of the Old Testament was Satan, and the God of the New Testament was then the spiritual First Cause. There are shades of these ideas in much so called "Christian" theology even to this day. Sometimes the "God" of the Old Testament is implicity viewed as being evil, and the God of the New Testament is viewed as good. *So Gnosticism, has harmfully influenced many "Christian" ideas and perspectives age long.* So in this system the "good guys" of the Old Testament were those who opposed the evil god of the Old Testament: Cain, the men of Sodom and Gomorrah, Balaam, Jezebel, and so on. The "bad guys" of the Old Testament were then Able, Abraham, David, and so on! I cannot help but think of what Isaiah said.

> [20] Woe unto them that call evil good, and good evil; that put darkness for light, and light for darkness; that put bitter for sweet, and sweet for bitter! [21] Woe unto *them that are* wise in their own eyes, and prudent in their own sight! Isa 5:20-21 KJV

More than one observation should be made here. *First* is that since matter was implicitly eternal, some sort of **evolution** became **a theological and a political necessity**. (And, yes, the occult is about politics.) Matter is eternal and is only "formed" into our present creation, so all of this mandates evolution of some sort. Evolution of the species has gaping holes in its so-called "evidence," all of which is well known, but is systematically covered up by the media cartels, and the "educational" establishment. Despite the evidence, evolution is a political necessity for a Gnostic/occult political world system. What then is this? Pure "political science."

Second, there are variations in different gnostic systems as to how many emanations there were between the First Cause and our present universe. The default answer is that there were a series of ten emanations as in the diagram on the next page. (Also compare the differing diagram on page 101)

Third is that the emanations in total represent the celestial chariot which we need to ascend in order to get to the true God. "The chariot of the gods." Scholem summarizes it this way,

> "Emanation in its totality is the "Celestial Chariot" and individual components are "parts of the Chariot" ..." Scholem, *Kabbalah*, pg 111

There are also variations in the theories of the emanations among occult groups. On one hand many treated the emanations as if they were just extensions of God Himself.

> "**According to this view, the Sefirot do not constitute "intermediary beings" but are God Himself.** "The Emanation is the Divinity," ... **The main part of the Zohar also tends largely toward this opinion** ... "He is They, and They are He""" (Zohar, 3:11b, 70a)"
> Scholem, *Kabbalah*, pg 101 (*emphasis added*)

> "The Sefirot emanate from Ein-Sof in succession ... they do not thereby leave the divine domain."
> Scholem, *Kabbalah*, pg 102

So in these views the emanations ARE God, and *there is* both *good and evil* in God! So there is also more than one "being" ("emanation") in the one

The ten emanations pictured according their relationships, as the so called "tree of life." This also is a common way of presenting the Sefirot.

God. Think of the Kabbalistic views of "god" in the *Star Wars* series of movies, in which there is a "dark side" of "the force." In fact, in this interpretation, one of these "emanations" is evil enough to form our present material universe out of evil matter! On the other hand, often times,

> "Sefirot are seen not as the essence of God but only as vessels of tools ... developed to the extreme where the Sefirot, being intermediaries, pray to God Himself ..." Scholem, *Kabbalah*, pg 101-102

Take your pick of evil nonsense which has *nothing* to do with Scripture! Scripture, both Old Testament and New Testament refutes such nonsense.

> Every good gift and every perfect gift is from above, and cometh down from the Father of lights, with whom is no variableness, neither shadow of turning. Jas 1:17 KJV

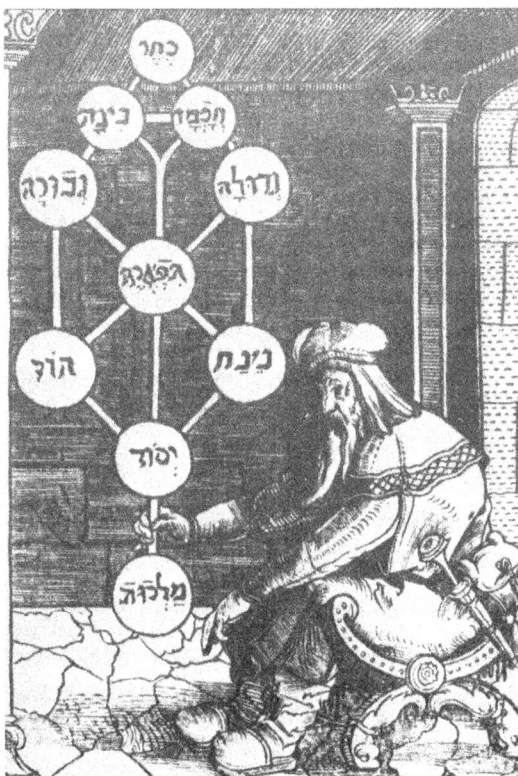

Or from the prophet David

> [4] For You *are* not a God who takes pleasure in wickedness,
>   Nor shall evil dwell with You.
> [5]   The boastful shall not stand in Your sight;
>   You hate all workers of iniquity.
> [6]   You shall destroy those who speak falsehood;
>   The LORD abhors the bloodthirsty and deceitful man.
>
> Psa 5:4-6 NKJV

The emanations are also called "aeons" or "spheres," and were often associated with angels and stars and the planets of our solar system. Scholem comments that "the tendency to portray them as Gnostic aeons did not entirely disappear." *Kabbalah*, pg 100. In New Testament times they were often called by the occultists "thrones, or dominions, or principalities, or powers" (as in the KJV in Col 1:16). Paul the apostle indicates these spiritual powers *are real*, and were *all* created **by** Jesus, and *for* Jesus.

> [16] For by him were all things created, that are in heaven, and that are in earth, visible and invisible, whether they be thrones, or dominions, or principalities, or powers: all things were created by him, and for him: [17] And he is before all things, and by him all things consist. Col 1:16-17 KJV

To summarize what Scripture teaches about these "principalities or powers," (or as they are called in the NASB "thrones or dominions or rulers or authorities") These powers, these created beings, like men were originally created "very good," Gen 1:31. Again, just like many men, they have revolted against God. These powers then have become what mankind is fighting against in our spiritual struggles.

> **For our struggle is not against flesh and blood**, but against the rulers, against the powers, against the world forces of this darkness, against the spiritual *forces* of wickedness in the heavenly *places*.
> Eph 6:12 NASB (*bold emphasis added*)

The Greek words for these evil spiritual beings are the same in Col 1:16 and Eph 6:12, and also these are the same words which are used for these powers in much of first and second century AD Gnostic literature. *Remember!* Scripture does not maintain that there is nothing to all of these Satanic powers. Only that,

> For these nations, that you shall dispossess, listen to those who practice sorcery, and to diviners; but as for you, **Yahweh your God has not allowed you so to do**. Deut 18:14 WEB (*emphasis added*)

Some things are clear: the teachings about the Sefirot are false. In so far as there is *any* reality behind them, these are angelic powers which have gone bad, or as they are commonly called: demons. To put all of this another way: the spiritual powers which the Kabbalists seek to control and use or abuse, or *worship*, are the Satanic powers of wickedness who are the inflexible enemies of mankind. Most of the Kabbalists do not acknowledge all of this. Some Jewish researchers at times candidly admit the truth.

> "According to the cabbala, the universe is ruled not by one god but by several deities, of various characters and influences, emanated by a dim, distant First Cause."
> Israel Shahak, *Jewish History, Jewish Religion*, pg 33

That is as plain a statement about the Kabbalah as you will find.

So what we see in the Kabbalah is what we see down through all of history: the Jewish nation as ever unfaithful to the Lord their God, and in hot pursuit of the favor (or the control) of other "gods" and spirits.

These early Gnostics basically formed groups of "mystery religions," as is discussed in more detail in the chapter "Some Age Long Mysteries," in my first book, *Prophecy Principles*. These theories were at first only orally transmitted from generation to generation, only to be revealed to certain "superior" persons who were worthy to know these things. Then in the 12th and 13th centuries some groups of Spanish Jews claimed to be writing down these traditions in what is now called the Kabbalah. Of one of those writers, the Jewish historian Heinrich Graetz comments,

> "It is not to be doubted that Elisha ben Abuya was well acquainted with Gnostic literature, as also with Grecian songs, and with the writings of the Minæans. It is also certain that **he knew of the fundamental doctrine of the Gnostics, which represented God as a dual being**, and that, **like the Gnostics, he despised the Jewish Law**. He is also said to have adopted practically the evil Gnostic morality, and to have given himself up to a dissolute life."
> *History of the* Jews, Vol 2, pg 377 *(emphasis added)*

And so have many Jews of such a bent, down through the centuries.

Gematria as a Key

These Kabbalists often maintained that the Scripture gives the ultimate truth in these matters, but that it was only through Gematria. *The New Oxford American Dictionary* defines Gematria as,

> "a Kabbalistic method of interpreting the Hebrew scriptures by computing the numerical value of words, based on those of their constituent letters."

In both Hebrew and Greek the letters of the alphabet *also* have numeric values (they did not have separate characters for numbers as we have today), and so these letters also functioned as numbers. (Much like our "Roman numerals.")

Thus words also have numeric values, and the numeric values can be calculated in more than one way. According to the Kabbalah the "real" truth of the
Bible was in the calculation of the numeric values of the words. The plain sense
of the words was only for children and never gave the "higher truths" that one
really needed. I remember seeing many years ago, advertised in a Jewish cata-
log, some Jewish "Bible commentary" software. I thought, well, uh-h-h-h, I
might as well try it out and see what I can learn. Imagine my surprise when I
discovered that this "commentary" "helped me" by enabling me to quickly run
through all the ways that the numeric values of words could be calculated! By
these methods then, the Kabbalists.

> "... substituted for a refined religious belief, fantastic and even blas-
> phemous chimeras. The intellectual degradation of the Jews in the fol-
> lowing centuries is to a large extent their work. They led astray both
> their own times and posterity through designed or unintentional im-
> position, **and the injuries which they inflicted on Judaism are felt
> even at the present day**."
> Graetz, *The History of the Jews*, Vol 4, pg 3 (*bold emphasis added*)

Graetz is writing in the late 1800's.

> "It is almost impossible to give an idea of the abuse which the Zohar,
> or Moses de Leon, practices in the interpretation of Holy Writ, and
> how he twists the sense of the words." Graetz, Vol 4, pg 15-16

> "Thus **the secret lore** of Moses de Leon naturally **has free play to
> pervert everything and anything**, and give it the seal of sublimity,
> and in this manner to promulgate a false doctrine, not only absurd,
> sometimes even blasphemous and immoral."
> Graetz, Vol 4, pg 15 (*bold emphasis added*)

That Great Forgery: The Kabbalah

The secret or hidden arts (and that is what the word "occult" means, "hidden") have always dealt with knowledge that has been kept secret or hidden.
Often the Kabbalah was considered hidden because it was knowledge which
was considered too sacred to be revealed to the great mass of what they
considered detestable people. (There is going on here, no little intellectual snobbishness!) Sometimes these things were kept secret because it would make its
practitioners look foolish to the great majority of people, or would be reprehensible to society at large. Finally, it is no secret that some of these things were
kept secret because they involved criminal activities, sometimes of the most
grotesque nature. So these are a wide range of reasons and motives for secrecy.
Regardless of motive, most of the theory and practice of the occult was kept
secret and only orally transmitted from extreme antiquity. How far back is this

"extreme antiquity"? The Encyclopedia Britannica 2010, says under "Kabbala" that,

> "The earliest roots of Kabbala are traced to Merkava mysticism. It began to flourish in Palestine in the 1st century AD ..."

It goes back at least this far, and the occult practitioners frequently claim it goes even further back, some claiming all the way to Adam! Only it was always forbidden to write it down. (Sacredness? Stupidity? Criminality? You name it!)

However this ancient secret tradition supposedly began to be written down in medieval Spain in the 12th century AD. It is a large collection of works. Most people involved only read and study bits and pieces or sections of it. However, almost all modern occult doctrine, witchcraft, magic, astrology, other forms of "foreseeing" (divining) the future, the "New Age," and most of the secret societies, have their roots in the Jewish Kabbalah.

One of the authors of the Kabbalah, Moses de Leon, hit upon the strategy of writing down these gnostic theories and selling them as if they had been written by some distinguished Jew of ancient times. He created a forgery which has been successful beyond anyone's wildest dreams. Graetz comments that the only real question,

> "... about Moses ben Shem Tob de Leon (born in Leon about 1250, died in Arevalo, 1305) is only whether he was a selfish or a pious impostor." Graetz, *History of the* Jews, Vol 4, pg 11

Now truth is part of the criteria for recognizing a revelation from God. It is easy to see this in the Law of Moses, Deut 18:22, and many other passages. The Hebrew prophets of the first century also agreed with this. The half-brother of Rabbi Yehoshua says of these charlatans,

> [12] These are spots in your feasts of charity, when they feast with you, feeding themselves without fear: clouds *they are* without water, carried about of winds; trees whose fruit withereth, without fruit, twice dead, plucked up by the roots; [13] Raging waves of the sea, foaming out their own shame; wandering stars, to whom is reserved the blackness of darkness for ever. Jude 12-13 KJV

Nevertheless, at this point comes another staggering thing about the Kabbalah. *Almost everyone* acknowledges that the Kabbalah is a fraud, a fictitious book. The most adoring advocates of the Kabbalah will almost *immediately* acknowledge that it is a fraud, and *then* ... act as if *it does not matter a whit!* This is really incredible if you think about it. For most people if you could really *prove* that the Koran or the Bible was a fraud, you immediately lose your audience for sincere study. Somehow though, with the occultists, the fact that a book is fake is no reason to avoid studying it, as if this acknowledged forgery somehow contains the greatest of eternal truths. However, this is what you see, almost consistently, across the board, from the beginning, even down to our times! The main book is the Zohar (*zohar* זֹהַר meaning shining, or brightness as in Ezek 8:2, Dan 12:3.) Only for a very short time was it *ever* accepted as a genuine.

> "There were, of course, Kabbalists who doubted that the Zohar had originated with Simon bar Jochai and his school, but none the less did they pay homage to the book as to a pure source for Kabbalistic theories." Graetz, *The History of the* Jews Vol 4, pg 20

So though a fraud, evidently these works did seem to reflect the mish-mash of secret oral tradition on which some really pagan Jews had been subsisting for over a twelve hundred years. So Graetz says,

> "If the Zohar did not bring the Kabbalists anything essentially new, it exhibited to them what they did know in so peculiar a form and language, that they were wonderstruck. Everything in it is contrived for effect, for illusion, and for fascination." *History of the Jews*, Vol 4, pg 21

Then when Moses de Leon died, they

> "... discovered the simple truth from Moses de Leon's wife and daughter. Moses de Leon had never possessed the original copy."

> "His wife frankly related that she had often asked her husband why he published the productions of his own intellect under a strange name, and that he had answered that the Zohar would not, under his own name, have brought him any money, but assigned to Simon bar Yochai it had been a lucrative source of income." Graetz, Vol 4, pg 20, 21.

Even so, some Jews beside Graetz treat all of this as something of an embarassment in reference works. Everyone speaks of the complexity of the work. Richard Cavendish in *The Black Arts*, Capricorn Books, NY, 1967, comments,

> "The Cabala is often mystifyingly obscure and is so complicated that almost anything said about it is bound to be oversimplified." pg 81.

Cavendish, like most, also acknowledges that most of this teaching reaches back to ancient Gnosticism.

> "Many of the basic ideas of the Cabala are also found in Gnosticism ... about the time of Christ." Cavendish, *The Black Arts*, pg 82

However, at least some of the problem goes back to the *original* occult doctrine **often** being **contradictory** and **inconsistent**. Graetz summarizes some of the issues this way.

> "It is not positively certain whether the Zohar is to be regarded as a running commentary to the Pentateuch, as a theosophic manual, or as a collection of Kabbalistic sermons. **And its contents are just as curious, confused and chaotic as its form and external dress.**"
> Graetz, *History of the Jews*, Vol 5, pg 14 (*emphasis added*)

Gershom Scholem also comments,

> "it is impossible to speak of single system," Scholem, *Kabbalah*, pg 13

In other words, a great deal of this **is _contradictory material_**, which in part accounts for the contradictory explanations that you read of the Kabbalah and the Zohar. The occultists, especially those at the top, do not like to admit this because they generally make serious pretense to great knowledge.

> "not a single system ... but a multiplicity of approaches, widely separated from each other **and sometimes completely contradictory**." Scholem, *Kabbalah,* pg 87 (*emphasis added*)

> "... their **tendency toward neoplatonism. Jewish version of neoplatonic theories** of the Logos and the Divine Will, of emanation and of the soul ..." Scholem, *Kabbalah*, pg 44 (*emphasis added*)

> "**Platonic and Gnostic tendencies are interwoven in them**." Scholem, *Kabbalah*, pg 47 (*bold emphasis added*)

> "the influence of asceticism", Scholem, *Kabbalah*, pg 44

The late Jewish scholar Gershom Scholem has been for all intents and purposes the world's leading authority on the Kabbalah for the last one hundred years, so he must be dealt with as a commentator in more detail. A section "About the Author" from page 495 of his work *Kabbalah*, tells us,

> "Gershom Scholem is one of the towering figures in modern Jewish scholarship. He left Germany in 1923 and joined the Hebrew University, Jerusalem, first as librarian and eventually as Professor of Mysticism and Kabbalah. His combination of painstaking analysis, penetrating philosophical insight and profound historical understanding has added new perspectives to Jewish Studies. Since 1968 Professor Scholem has been president of the Israel Academy of Sciences and Humanities:"

Here are some blurbs from the back cover of his book *Kabbalah*.

> "Gershom Scholem is without challenge the greatest living authority on kabbalah" -*St. Louis Post-Dispatch*

> "Concise and dependable information on practically any aspect of Kabbalism."- *Library Journal*

> "The clearest possible exposition and interpretation of a subject that will never cease to fascinate" -*Kansas City Star*

Of Scholem and his writings on the occult, Jewish scholar Israel Shahak writes,

> "Sholem, Professor Gershon: 1897-1982, founder of the modern study of Cabbala; wrote many authoritative books on Jewish mysticism."

Shahak, *Jewish Fundamentalism*, pg xiv

So most, if they want to speak of the Kabbalah authoritatively, quote from Scholem. Even so, some cautions need to be made. Unfortunately Scholem seems to have had an agenda of protecting Judaism's reputation, though this is really hard to do with the Kabbalah. At times his agenda seems to include distancing the Kabbalah from both Gnosticism and pantheism, both of which are heretical even to Talmudic Judaism, and both of which (despite all the double talk by both Scholem and those he quotes) are impossible to avoid. He does a better job dealing with pantheism, but cannot really eliminate that either. In the end he clearly has to acknowledge the Gnostic heritage of the Kabbalah. The result of Scholem's **unspoken apologetic stance** is that *his sections on doctrine are dense and, like the original, full of contradictions.* You can read Scholem's sections on basic ideas, and come out not really having much of a grasp of "the basic ideas." Scholem does deal with all of the major items of Kabbalistic doctrine, however, the average reader of his book *Kabbalah* would never guess the centrality of the doctrine "As above, so below," and the "macrocosm" and the "microcosm," although they are clearly the key points in witchcraft and magic and a host of other occult "sciences" arising out of the Kabbalah. *So almost any reasonable inference made by the reader can be proven from Scholem and also can be denied from Scholem* (much as it is with the original texts). This is done all while carefully quoting from all of the important sources! In a way this is much like an encyclopedia article which is intended to always tell the truth, but never really give any understanding of the topic. It almost seems you would need some sort of "key" from Scholem (a secret one?) to profitably read and draw conclusions.

So Jewish scholar Israel Shahak, while recognizing Scholem's place in Kabbalah scholarship, put it this way,

> "The great authorities, such as Gershom Scholem, **have lent their authority to a system of deceptions in the 'sensitive' areas**, the more popular ones being the most dishonest and misleading."
> *Jewish History, Jewish Religion*, pg 16 (*emphasis added*)

Or again from Shahak and Mezvinsky in *Jewish Fundamentalism in Israel*, Pluto Press, 1999.

> "Actually, Scholem refrained from mentioning that many Jewish opponents of Cabbala, ... expressed more sharply their opposition to the predominant Lurianic form **on the ground that it denied monotheism. Since then, scholars** who have written in English about Judaism, including Scholem himself in later books, **have not**, with few exceptions, **questioned whether Judaism in all its forms and all times was monotheistic and/or whether many pious Jews were believers in monotheism**." pg 163 (*bold and underline emphasis added*)

In other words, the clear Jewish drift from the historic monotheism to what is really rank paganism was not really dealt with.

The average reader who really wants a candid working view or ethical view of the Kabbalah would do better to look at Richard Cavendish's *The Black Arts*. Cavendish is scholarly, candid, straight forward, and does not have an "orthodox" religious or ethnic agenda to protect. Is this text wicked and evil? Well, here is what it says, Cavendish seems to say, and does not weigh you down with scholarly obscurantism. Some of the evidence which he accepts as historical is shocking at times, but to some extent this true of all historians who deal with "out of the ordinary" subject matter. Cavendish's multi-volume occult encyclopedia *Man, Myth and Magic, The Illustrated Encyclopedia of Mythology, Religion and the Unknown*, Editor Richard Cavendish, Marshall Cavendish, NY, Reference Edition, 1983, 12 Volumes, is considered a must have source in many libraries across the country. Despite its frequently distasteful, or even pornographic subject matter, it even shows up in some high school libraries! Although it can be useful for serious research on the occult, it should be said that *Man, Myth and Magic* is not for the faint of heart nor the spiritually or emotionally immature. If you smell an open sewer, why investigate in detail, or dive to the bottom of it to see what is really there? Foolish! You may never come up.

On the plus side, Scholem quotes from many sources not available to most gentile scholars (as also does Graetz), including sources that "have not been printed, notably the commentary of Moses Cordovero", *Kabbalah*, pg 238 (which Scholem quotes continually). Scholem's analysis of the forged character of the Zohar is clearly without equal, clearly demonstrating the large number of grammatical, geographical, and linguistic errors inherent in these forgeries.

However, if Scholem ever really lets his hair down and plainly tells the truth about Kabbalism, it does not seem to have been in English. So what we have is a typical piece of public occult work, where if you are so rash as to draw some conclusion from what is said, and that conclusion is somehow inconvenient to the occultists, then they will immediately say, "Oh, you are just misunderstanding." Then if you go off in the only other way it can *also* be interpreted, and that *likewise* is inconvenient to acknowledge, then again you will be told, "Oh, you just have not seen the higher truth involved here," or "the translations really don't do justice to the text here," and so on.

Then comes whoever *you* just talked to about this bizarre mess called the Kabbalah. *You* are lucky! The man *you* just met has recently discovered the true key to understanding the Kabbalah! (So they say!) The others you have listened to? They are good men, they just lack depth. How fortunate *you* have talked to "the one" who *truly* understands! The others you have talked to or read are essentially treated as well meaning fools.

> "And thus there came into the world a book, the book Zohar (brilliancy), which for many centuries was held by Jews as a heavenly revel-

ation, and was and partly is even now regarded by Christians as an old tradition. **But seldom has so notorious a forgery so thoroughly succeeded.**" Graetz, *History of the Jews*, Vol 4, pg 12 (*bold emphasis added*)

"So a new text-book of religion **was by stealth introduced** into Judaism. **It placed the Kabbala**, which a century before had been unknown, **on the same level as the Bible and the Talmud, and to a certain extent on a still higher level.**"
Graetz, Vol 4, pg 22 (*bold emphasis added*)

Some of the rabbis did object to this foolishness. Graetz mentions for instance Elias del Medigo,

"He had the courage openly to express his opinion that the Kabbala is rooted in an intellectual swamp, that no trace of this doctrine is to be found in the Talmud, that the recognized authorities of ancient Judaism knew nothing of it, and that its supposed sacred and ancient groundwork, the Zohar, was by no means the work of the celebrated Simon bar Yochai, but the production of a forger. **In short, he considered the Kabbala to be made up of the <u>rags and tatters</u> of the neo-Platonic school**." Graetz, Vol 4, pg 292 (*emphasis added*)

"Mental Effeminacy and Childish Enthusiasm"

This is what Jewish historian Heinrich Graetz calls the Kabbalah:

"mental effeminacy and childish enthusiasm for the pseudo-doctrine of the Kabbala." *History of the Jews*, Vol 4, pg 292

Then another factor comes into play in the occult and the Kabbalah. An inclination toward fornication and adultery, and a tendency to focus on various types of "sex magic." Raphael Patai in *The Hebrew Goddess*, Third Enlarged Edition, Wayne State University Press, Detroit, 1990, speaks of orgies, "sexual license" "sexual rioting", and "Ritual license" pg 85, 86. Patai informs us that, "Satan, in the shape of the serpent, had intercourse with Eve who thereupon bore Cain and Able. Thus sexuality became the original sin." pg 98. He talks about, "the Zohar ... with its penchant for sexualizing the entire spiritual world" pg 125; and talks about "the persistent sexual imagery of the Kabbala," pg 279. Most are not so candid about such things.

Gershom Scholem puts it this way,

"also in the striking use of sexual imagery is a particular characteristic of the Zohar and Lurianic Kabbalah. ... Many kabbalists did their utmost to minimize the impact of this symbolism ..." *Kabbalah*, pg 110

In "The Influence of the Kabbalah on Judaism" pg 190ff, Scholem says,

> **"Mystical and demonic motifs became particularly intertwined in the area of sexual life and practices ..."**
> *Kabbalah*, pg 195, (*emphasis added*).

On the other hand, Scholem declares,

> "Only in the writings and poetry of the Kabbalist of Safed is there an obviously strong erotic overtone." *Kabbalah*, pg 160

So which part of Scholem do you wish to believe?

Demons, Plato, and the Kabbalah

Under "Demonology in Kabbalah" pp 320-326, Scholem lightly touches on these significant issues. He mentions that demons are viewed as mortal and that by their beliefs demons are produced by sexual intercourse with humans, and they need humans, pg 321ff. So, Scholem cites that,

> "Devils born out of nightly pollutions are called "the stripes of the children of men" (II Sam. 7:14; see Zohar 1:54b)" pg 323.

Additionally Scholem points out that, **"Belief in demons remained ... down to the present**." Kabbalah, pg 326 (*emphasis added*). The reader does not have to go far to document these ideas in our present day, especially among Jews and crypto-Jews in our movie and entertainment industry. There is a major Jewish influence in our modern movie and entertainment industry. A great number of these people are into the Kabbalah and the occult. As a group they are by no means experts (but then again, who is, and is acknowledged by all?), but their dominant views are Kabbalistic. This influence is seen over and over in our movies and entertainment. The media cartels often slyly comment on this or that actor or actress or director in emotional turmoil as "dealing with their demons," or "dealing with their childhood demons," or "dealing with their mid-West demons" or Jersey or California demons, and so on. The media comments are made so that one might assume that they are just speaking metaphorically. However to these benighted individuals who have dabbled in demonic activities to boost their careers, these are terrifyingly destructive conflicts. (See Deuteronomy 18 as has been repeatedly quoted.) They have forgotten the admonition to them that because of these detestable activities, "Yahweh your God ..." will destroy nations which practice these things, and that "Yahweh your God has not allowed you so to do." Deut 18:12-14 WEB.

In a real way this is just a continuation of a pagan view of the demonic as the "real" secret of success in this life. In a listing of spirits the Greeks would speak first of gods, then lesser divinities and demons, then "heroes" (living men and glorified men) and finally ordinary men. As in Plato's *Laws* 4.717b, "as also in assigning to the former gods the things superior, the opposites of these. Next after these gods the wise man will offer worship to the daemons, and after the daemons to the heroes. After these will come private shrines legally dedicated to ancestral deities;" *Plato*, Perseus 2.0 edition, Yale University Press, 2000, New Haven & London.

Sometimes the words "demons" and "gods" would be used interchangeably, and sometimes demons would be listed as lower beings, as is the practice with Christians. In Plato's *Symposium* it says all the demonic (*daimonion* δαιμόνιον) "is between divine ..." (*theou* θεου, meaning literally those things which are of God) "and mortal." It speaks of "great spirits." This almost sounds like early American Indians talking, but in the Greek it is literally "great demons" *daimōn mega* δαῖμων μἐγα, and then goes on to discuss their role as intermediate beings. They are said to convey to men "all divination and priestcraft concerning sacrifice and ritual, and incantation, and all soothsaying and sorcery." *These are almost exactly the same claims made by the New Agers, and other Kabbalah oriented groups*, and you can see them channeling such "spirits"/demons, on television. This same passage in Plato calls erotic love (the Greek word *eros*, spelled *eros* ἔρος or *erōs* ἔρως in Greek) one of these great demons (*daimon mgea* δαῖμων μἐγα). It calls one wise in such things literally "a demonic man" (*daimonion anār* δαιμόνιον ἀνῆρ) 202d-203a (Perseus 2.0 edition, Yale University Press, calls it a "spiritual man"). Greek religion is a good example, as seen here, how their religion, *the Kabbalah, Platonism, modern paganism and the New Age* **are literally inseparable from the demonic!**

Socrates of old believed that what made him wiser than other men was that he had a demon. These sorts of facts embarrass classical scholars to no end, so they often like to spell it different, like "daimon," or "daemon" or call it "genius", "god", "gods", or "guides" (as in New Age theology), one's lot, or fortune, or destiny, or a controlling "force" (as in "the force" in the Star Wars movies), or almost anything, and pretend that it has nothing to do with Biblical demons.

You can read widely in many English translations of the Greek Classics and look in vain for a plain translation of the Greek word for "demon." However, demons are

Socrates

very much there. Recently I even ran into someone who wanted to say that Socrates "daimon" was his conscience. Liddell and Scott's *Greek-English Lexicon*, Oxford At the Clarendon Press, 1889, is sort of the "unabridged dictionary" of Classical Greek, but alas, this does not show up in its authoritative 1700 plus pages. (Your minister may have an abridged computer version of Liddell and Scott published by Harvard and the Public Broadcasting System which you can search.) The regular words in Greek for conscience are *suneidāsis* συνείδησις

(as in the New Testament), and also the Classical Greek word *sunesis* σύνεσις. Further, it does not fit the context in Plato at all, as was showed above from *Laws* 4.717b, and as you can demonstrate the same from many other passages. Anyway, nice try. One more quote might be in order, from *Plutarch's Lives*.

> "... I do not know but we shall be compelled to accept that most extraordinary doctrine of the oldest times, that mean and malignant spirits [literally "demons" *daimonia* δαιμόνια, nf], in envy of good men and opposition to their noble deeds, try to confound and terrify them, causing their virtue to rock and totter, in order that they may not continue erect and inviolate in the path of honor and so attain a better portion after death than the spirits themselves."
>
> *Plutarch's Lives*, Vol VI, with an English Translation by Bernadotte Perrin, G. P. Putnam's Sons, NY, 1918, pgs 4-5, Dion II:3

That is not far from the view of demons in Scripture, and all in all is not a bad description of the spiritual warfare of the devil and his angels against men, but something for which paganism offers no solution.

The plain fact is that Socratic/Platonic "wisdom" is self-confessedly demonic, and this is the fountainhead of all Western philosophy. Plato's Republic is the master blueprint for Communism, Nazism, cultic communes both East and West, and the lesser forms of Socialism and totalitarian-fascism used in what many call the "good" western governments. Plutarch plainly called this contact with the spirit world "demonic evil" *daimona ponāron* δαίμονα πονηρον Dion II:2, which classical scholar Bernadotte Perrin translates as "evil genius" in the Loeb-Harvard series. All of this is pertinent to a discussion of Judaism because of its Platonic and Neoplatonic inclinations.

Some biblical scholars like *McClintock and Strong's Cyclopedia* spell it "daemon." They point out that both the Bible and pagan writers use the words *daemon* and *daemonion*, interchangeably, and that Plato derives the word from damon, which means "knowing," "in allusion to the superior intelligence and consequent efficiency ascribed to daemons;" (from the article "Daemon").

Many ancient or even current examples could be cited. The brilliant eighteenth century poet and scientist Johann Wolfgang von Goethe, believed that he had a demon and that it was the reason for his achievements in literature and science. He said he had to obey his "demon" (Angelloz, *Goethe*, pg 141). In fact Goethe thought that all of the world's greatest men had demonic influence, and he wrote, "The greater a man is the more he is influenced by demons ..." (Angelloz, *Goethe*, pg 238).

Did Goethe actually have demon "possession"? I cannot say. Still, his literature is clearly filled with overtones that are "religious," but not really Christian. The Encyclopedia Britannica says he had "wisdom often termed Olympian" (i.e. pagan religious), and calls some of his poetry "magical" (Encyclopedia

Britannica, Inc. © 1994-2001). He had been a member of a devil worshipping secret society the Illuminati (although he later renounced this group), and his most famous work, *Faust*, is an epic poem about a professor who sells his soul to the devil.

You should also remember that part of our so-called "scientific" "psychology" came from the occult. An example is Carl Jung, one of the "fathers" of modern psychology. His father was a Lutheran minister, but he rejected Christianity, entered the occult, had his own "familiar spirit" named "Philemon", and engaged in speaking to the dead (called necromancy in the King James Version, see Deut 18:11). When discussing these things we are dealing with the tip of the iceberg. Modern Psychology and Psychiatry, like Hollywood, is riddled from top to bottom with occult teaching about man and his "psyche" (literally his soul *psuchā* ψυχῆ). All of which makes the modern trend to abandon Biblical counseling for "psychology" ironic.

A full discussion of prominent moderns who openly claim demonic help would take more space than I have here. Goethe and Jung are the tip of the iceberg, and it ranges from men such as have been mentioned, to occult weirdoes and mental patients. However, for each brilliant "success" "the process" of Satanism produces, there are hundreds or thousands of gruesome ruins that never see even worldly success. For 99% of the people involved it destroys both body and soul and gives almost nothing in return. The occult world of the lodge, and the coven, and witchcraft, and the "New Age," grooves on "other spirits," and actively seeks what a Christian would call "demonic help." Sometimes it is called mediums, channeling, or seances in current entertainment and literature. You can see this clearly on many television shows, and much current fiction.

What the Greeks or the Bible calls demons, Germanic, Scandinavian and Celtic paganism often called "fairies" or "elves" or "leprechauns," or "dwarfs," etc., and a great deal of this has carried over into the English speaking world, in part to disguise its roots. The brothers Jacob Ludwig Carl Grimm and Wilhelm Carl Grimm, of the *Grimm's Fairy Tales* fame, were Jewish Kabbalists. It has often been associated with ventriloquism and with those who had other "personalities" speaking through them.

For those in modern England and America, it escapes notice that for most of the last two thousand years "fairy tales" were considered "occult" in origin, and were not considered to be proper stories for children. It was not until the 19th century that fairly tales came to be considered "good reading." Of course, Hollywood has been a leader in making them "kiddie fare," and if you will look at most of the "G" or "General Audience" rated films for children, *many* of them have occult overtones. If you look carefully, misunderstood "dragons" are also a favorite theme in the children's cartoon world.

Many, like the Jewish philosopher Philo, have pointed out the word demon is often used by the pagans to designate what Christians would call angels. The devil and his demons are also called in the New Testament "the devil and his angels," Mtt 25:41.

It is a very negative picture in the New Testament. Demons are described as unclean spirits, shall they be called "filthy spirits," Lk 8:29-30. They are called principalities and powers in Eph 6:12, and other passages. These spirits believe in God and they fear God, in fact they even tremble in fear about God (Jas 2:19), and they recognize Jesus as the Son of God, as seen in passages like Mtt 8:29 and others. In the book of Revelation it pictures the worship of the gods of the nations as the worship of demons, in passages like Rev 9:20.

At this point comes a special "female" spirit with "whom" (?) the Kabbalists are entranced.

The Shekinah and The "Female" Side of "god."

First lets look at the Shekinah, the supposed presence of the Lord our God. This is really a continuation of the previous discussion under "How Long Did Asherah Worship Go On?" (pg. 62.)

The Hebrew roots are *shakan* שָׁכַן or *shaken* שָׁכֵן meaning *to settle down, live, abide, dwell.* This in turn brings us to *Shekanyah* or *Shekanyahu* שְׁכַנְיָהוּ, or the Septuagint Greek *sechenia* Σεχενια, which has the sense of speaking of God dwelling or having His presence in a certain place, as to say "Yah has taken up His abode." The *Hebrew Aramaic Lexicon of the Old Testament* (HALOT) takes it in the sense of "Yahweh has taken up residence."

Eaton's Bible Dictionary, M.G. Easton M.A., D.D., Illustrated Bible Dictionary, Third Edition, Thomas Nelson, 1897, says,

> "Shechinah itself is a Chaldee word meaning resting-place, **not found in Scripture,** but used by the later Jews to designate the visible symbol of God's presence in the tabernacle, and afterwards in Solomon's temple. When the Lord led Israel out of Egypt, he went before them "in a pillar of a cloud." This was the symbol of his presence with his people. For references made to it during the wilderness wanderings, see Ex. 14:20; 40:34-38; Lev. 9:23, 24; Num. 14:10; 16:19, 42. It is probable that after the entrance into Canaan this glory-cloud settled in the tabernacle upon the ark of the covenant in the most holy place. We have, however, no special reference to it till the consecration of the temple by Solomon, when it filled the whole house with its glory, so that the priests could not stand to minister (1 Kings 8:10-13; 2 Chr. 5:13, 14; 7:1-3). Probably it remained in the first temple in the holy of holies as the symbol of Jehovah's presence so long as that temple stood. It afterwards disappeared. (See CLOUD.)" (*bold emphasis added*)

As far as a Biblical summary of the concept, something along this line is as good as you will see. In the Gospel of John it says,

> No man hath seen God at any time; the only begotten Son, which is in the bosom of the Father, he hath declared *him*. Jn 1:18 KJV

Later in the same Gospel Jesus relates

> ... "Have I been with you so long, and yet you have not known Me, Philip? He who has seen Me has seen the Father; so how can you say, 'Show us the Father'?" Jn 14:9 NKJV

So it is said of Jesus,

> [6] Who, being in the form of God, thought it not robbery to be equal with God: [7] But made himself of no reputation, and took upon him the form of a servant, and was made in the likeness of men: Phil 2:6-7 KJV

So it is possible to have a visible and touchable reality of God's presence, though of course, classical Judaism strenuously objected to Jesus' claims in these things. In spite of this, in the Kabbalah, the presence of God, **the Shekinah took on a whole new meaning**. It became a being, **a separate being, a** *feminine* **being or person**, who is sometimes viewed as being part of God, sometimes viewed as an "emanation" from God, and sometimes viewed as a co-regent with God, that is to say, a *goddess*. **You can pick what you want to quote in the Jewish occult.**

> "... it later becomes hypostasis distinguished from God, a distinction first appears in the late Midrash to Proverbs (Mid. Prov 47a: "the Shekhinah stood before the Holy One, blessed be He, and said to Him."" Scholem, *Kabbalah*, pg 31

> "there arose another original concept—the identification of the Shekhinah with keneset Yisrael (the community of Israel). In this obviously Gnostic typology ... into the Gnostic concept of the Shekhinah or "the daughter" ..." Scholem, *Kabbalah*, pg 31-32

In this analysis both Scholem and Patai are in agreement. On one hand, even among the Jews, the Shekinah is viewed as nothing more than "God's Spirit" in some Jewish literature (for instance, in a casual mention in *The War Within, Israel's Ultra-Orthodox Threat to Democracy and the Nation*, Yuval Elizur and Lawrence Malkin, pg 32). Others protest such simplistic identifications and go far beyond anything in Scripture, as for instance in Scholem's discussion in *Major Trends in Jewish Mysticism*,

> "What was previously undifferentiated in the divine wisdom exists in the womb of the Binah, the "supernal mother" ..." pg 219

> "... here the stream of divine life takes its course and flows through all the Sefiroth, and through all hidden reality, until at last it falls into the "great sea" of Shekhinah **in which God unfolds His totality.**"

pg 220 (*emphasis added*)

So the so-called "Trinity" is reprehensible, but the Shekinah (it is spelled both ways), the mother earth/Asherah figure (?) as being the one in whom "God unfolds His totality"? No problem. Right?

One of the early Kabbalists, Moses Cordovero (1522-1570) spoke of the sex act as a sacred action, Patai, *The Hebrew Goddess*, pg 206-207. Then arrives the issue of sexual intercourse with the great female spirit, the "Shekinah," the supposed presence of God. Scholem avoids most of this, but per Patia in *The Hebrew Goddess*, Jacob has sex with the goddess but only after he died, pg 141, but Moses while still in the flesh. Scholem comments in some detail on these things in *Major Trends in Jewish Mysticism*, pg 226-227. In typical style Scholem goes on to comment that **"Dimly we perceive behind this mystical image the male and female gods of antiquity,** anathema as they were to the pious Kabbalist." pg 227 (*bold emphasis added*). He really must mean the not very pious Kabbalist. He points out that "... the Zohar makes prominent use of phallic symbolism" and again he comments that this is "not a minor psychological problem considering the author's strict devotion to the most pious conception of Jewish life and belief." pg 228.

So when Graetz and many other Jews protest all of this obscene foolishness and call the Kabbalah a "book of lies," Scholem says,

> "Charges of this kind simply misconstrue both the morality and the tendency of the Zohar, and are hardly relevant even to the literary form of presentation ..." *Major Trends*, pg 228

Oh! Does all of this sound stupid, or adolescent, or even infantile? (Which, it must be said, is *another* reason for keeping all of this secret.) In that case Scholem assures us, you are tending to "misconstrue" both the morality and the form of the Zohar! Right! Don't you see? To his credit Scholem does point out that all of this development of the doctrine of the Shekinah is *completely outside of both the Bible and the Talmud*.

> "In all the numerous references to the Shekhinah in the Talmud and the Midrashim ... there is no hint that it represents a feminine element in God." *Major Trends* ..., pg 229

Scholem admits that this is a major stumbling block to accepting the Kabbalah, **and argues that the Kabbalah's _dominance_ among the Jews despite this pornographic foolishness is a tribute to the Kabbalah's strength.** He even finally admits the pagan character of these doctrines.

> "... **idea originally belonged to the sphere of pagan mythology.**" [An understatement, *nf. emphasis added*] "In the Gnostic speculations on the male and female aeons, i.e. divine potencies, which constitute the world of the pleroma, the 'fullness' of God ..." Scholem, *Major Trends* ..., pg 230.

Perhaps you noticed, these last few quotes are within a few pages of each other in Scholem. **The bottom line: paganism never really left the ancient Jews, *even to this day*.** Then Scholem admits the centrality of these doctrines to the Kabbalah.

> "In the symbolic world of the Zohar, this new conception of the Shekhinah as the symbol of "eternal womanhood," occupies a place of immense importance and appears under an endless variety of names and images ... The union of God and the Shekhinah constitutes the true unity of God, which lies beyond the diversity of His various aspects, Yihud as the Kabbalists call it." *Major Trends,* pg 230

So he does finally say it. There is much more of this foolishness to discuss, and we have not even touched on Lilith, the great female night demon (or "goddess," you pick) with whom God supposedly goes to bed when the Shekinah is not available (!), but this will do, so the reader can sense the direction of these doctrines. Clearly these are shades of Asherah, and Astarte, and Isis, *et al*, even as Raphael Patai openly admits.

On and on you can read of the endless sexual reveries of these sex obsessed occultists, these majestic scholars who like sex hungry teenage boys are focused on every detail of sexual intercourse that can be imagined. They are well described by Rabbi Yehoshua's half brother Jude as "filthy dreamers," Jude 8 KJV. "... but what they know as naturally as brute beasts, in those things they corrupt themselves." Jude 10 KJV. It is way past time to call this foolishness to account even within Judaism, and indeed it will be. Graetz, though an unbelieving rationalist, is not far from the mark in many of his comments about the Kabbalah.

A Tendency Toward Magic and Spells

Everyone likes to dodge it, but it is a fact that the Kabbalah has led to widespread witchcraft and magic. So you begin to get subtle quotes like this from Scholem.

> "A theurgic **tendency** also appears ..." Scholem, *Kabbalah*, pg 48 (*bold emphasis added*)

"Theurgic"! Here is an evasive pseudonym for the low-life activities of trying to cast a spell so that you make lots of money, make an enemy have a fatal accident, have success at this or that, or seduce Mrs. so-and-so. If you even begin to look at Neoplatonism, some of the earliest apologies you will meet are for the "theurgic" elements which abound. It is all so embarrassing to these pretenders to high level spirituality. Of course we are assured that the real "masters" in these things never stooped to such low-life activities. Oh, yeah! Right! Sure! But it is indeed part of the Kabbalah and its philosophical fronts such as Neoplatonism. **If you look around, the middle ground between witchcraft-**

magic and rationalism in modern America is the "positive thinking" occult propaganda which is all around us. Still, these obscurantists never like to call it what it is, but, if they are scholarly at all, they have to at least admit its presence.

> **"the growth of the magical element** and the tendency to preserve the theurgic traditions." Scholem, *Kabbalah*, pg 56 (*emphasis added*)

That is about as close as it gets in Scholem, for him to admit the vile black magic practices which go along with the Kabbalah. Then the question comes, "Who said anything about "black" magic?" The answer of course is *really **no one!*** Whoever you are talking to who is involved in theses things has ***never*** been involved in such evil things, and ***never*** would be! *Oh, no, no, no!* You see *it is always **the other guys*** who are involved in "black" magic. If they admit to *anything* it is nothing more than so called "white magic," that is to say "good" magic using "good" spirits. It should be remembered what the Law of Moses says about magic and witchcraft.

> [10] "There shall not be found among you anyone who makes his son or his daughter pass through the fire, one who uses divination, **one who practices witchcraft, or one who interprets omens, or a sorcerer,** [11] **or one who casts a spell, or a medium, or a spiritist, or one who calls up the dead**. [12] "For whoever does these things is **detestable to the LORD**; and because of these detestable things the LORD your God will drive them out before you. Deut 18:10-12 NASB (*bold emphasis added*)

So what is the key point to be made here from Deuteronomy 18? It is that Scripture does not distinguish between so called "black" or "white" magic. As far as Scripture is concerned it is ***all*** "black," that is to say, it is ***all*** evil. Graetz writes of the Kabbalistic revival among Palestinian Jews of the 1500's.

> "Once again, as in the early days of Christianity, Galilee, especially the district of Safet, became the scene of a host of evil spirits, of people possessed with devils, which challenged mystic exorcism, and revealed profound mysteries; and it is impossible to say whether the possessed appeared in consequence of the exorcisers, or the latter of the former. It was a period of Kabbalistic mania, coincident with **profligacy and moral degradation,** and its victims despised not only the sciences, but even the Talmud with its exhortations to sobriety. Then for the first time the Jewish world entered on a "dark age" of its own, with all the appropriate credulity, while only the last traces of such darkness were visible in Europe generally."
> Graetz, *History of the Jews*, Vol 4 pg 617 (*bold emphasis added*)

> "The earliest stratum of the *heikhalot* **strongly emphasizes this magical side** ..." Scholem, *Kabbalah*, pg 15 (*bold emphasis added*)

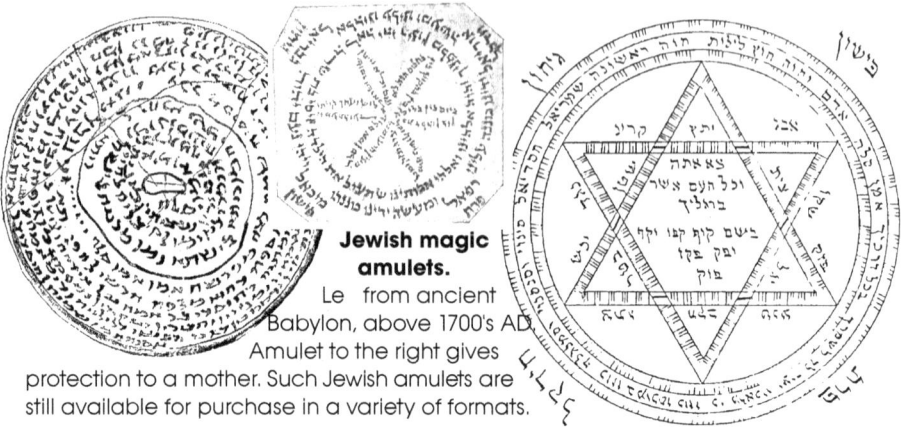

Jewish magic amulets.
Le from ancient Babylon, above 1700's AD. Amulet to the right gives protection to a mother. Such Jewish amulets are still available for purchase in a variety of formats.

There is though one last point that should be made, one which is clearly not emphasized by Scholem, but which is very significant. The main New Testament word for witchcraft or sorcery is the Greek word *pharmakeia* φαρμακεία, and, yes, that is where we get our modern word pharmacy. The occult has always been associated with use of drugs for "magical effects," and "casting spells" (hypnosis), healing, or yes, even poisoning. Over the years the occultists developed quite a repertoire in the use of drugs, and that is part of the overall story. Then comes the masterpiece of foolishness.

Then Man Saves God?

In these theories the Shekinah becomes associated with the Jews of the Old Testament, as has been pointed out.

> "The union of God and the Shekhinah constitutes the true unity of God, which lies beyond the diversity of His various aspects, *Yihud* as the Kabbalists call it." Scholem, *Major Trends in Jewish Mysticism*, pg 230

But the Shekinah ends up being exiled when Israel is exiled, *and becomes separated from the First Cause,* the Great God our Father ... *so they say!* This is

> "... what the Kabbalists call "the exile of the Shekhinah."" *Major Trends ...*, pg 232

So how can the Shekinah be restored as the consort, the companion, may we say "the wife," of God the Father?

> "In the present unredeemed and broken state of the world this fissure which prevents the continuous union of God and the Shekhinah **is somehow healed or mended by the religious acts of Israel**: Torah, *mitswoth* and prayer." Scholem, *Major Trends ...*, pg 233 (*emphasis added*)

Blasphemy of the highest sort! **So instead of Israel needing God** and being healed by God, they propose a man centered universe in which **God needs man**, and is healed and restored to his bride by godless men!

"Everything that is done by the individual or the community in the mundane sphere is magically reflected in the upper region, i.e. the higher reality which shines through the acts of man."
Scholem, *Major Trends ...*, pg 233

That is to say, man saves God, NOT God who saves man! This subject will come up again later, but these teachings are not without their effects on doctrine and practice and politics. For *IF* it is man who saves ... and *not* God ... then it is **up to man to act** ... not waiting for God! The patience of Psalm 27, et al? It is forgotten. Like Satanism itself, it is the Scriptures in reverse.

There is much more to tell about the Kabbalah. Many books could be written showing how anti-Biblical, unscientific or even anti-scientific and foolish are just the publicly available materials on the Kabbalah (and you can bet that the most damaging testimonies are NOT publicly available). There are stories of the "spiritual masters" ascending the spheres to God Himself, and on and on and on. Hopefully this is sufficient to show the reader a little of the true character of these teachings. Never will this foolishness look worse than on the final day of judgment which is swiftly coming upon us.

A Messiah Machine

Then comes another implicit characteristic of the Kabbalah and the occult forces it unleashes. It is messianic in character. It rejects Jesus of Nazareth as Messiah, and despises Him beyond words, but it intends to offer its own messiah. Who is this messiah? Well, uh, it might, uh, accidentally be *themselves!* (Which, it must be said, goes right along with 1Jn 4:2-3.)

It might be neat to document all of the false messiahs the Kabbalah has spawned, but that would take more than one volume in itself. Gershom Scholem in *Kabbalah* put it this way:

"... messianism became part of the very core of Kabbalah. ... Now it became combined with messianic and apocalyptic trends which laid greater stress on man's journey toward redemption ...", pg 68

A few examples will show the character of how these things developed, time after time. Graetz writes of Abraham Abulafia:

"Abulafia proceeded to the island of Sicily, and in Messina he met with a favorable reception, gaining six adherents. Here he finally proclaimed that he was not only a prophet but the Messiah, and set forth his claims in writing (November, 1284)."
Graetz, *History of the Jews,* Vol 4, pg 7

Or again, of another Kabbalist,

> "Avila pursued his course, and fixed the last day of the fourth month
> (1295) as the beginning of the Messianic redemption."
> Graetz, Vol 4, pg 9

Graetz even comments that some Jews left Judaism and went over to Christianity as a result of these ludicrous failures. Then there was Isaac Abrabanel.

> "According to his reckoning, the advent of the Messiah must of necessity be in the year 1503, 5263 years after the creation of the world, and the end would come with the fall of Rome, about twenty-eight years later." Graetz, Vol 4, pg 482

There were a series of prophecies which seemed to validate his claims, and even some popes were taken in (Graetz, Vol 4, pg 505), but in the end the "messiah" failed. Graetz sarcastically comments on such as this.

> "No science affords more certainty as to the Godhead of Christ than Kabbala and magic! Even Pope Sixtus IV (1471–1484) was by this means so strongly attracted to the Kabbala that he was eager to procure Latin translations of Kabbalistic writings for the benefit of the Catholic faith." Graetz, Vol 4, pg 292

So these things came into our modern world, with television, and the movies, and elves, and dwarfs, and fairies, and acted out "documentary" pseudo-history often being the modern salesmen for the ideas of the Kabbalah.

Isaac Luria's Kabbalism

Now we come to one of the most significant men for the development of the Kabbalah: Isaac Luria Ashkenazi, the "Ari" (1534-72). Graetz admits that traditional Talmudic Pharisaism (which is what it is), left the heart seeking something more satisfying.

> "The dry study of the Talmud, which filled the mind with voluminous learning, unfruitful hairsplitting, and mere formulas, yet failed to satisfy the wants of the heart," Graetz. *History of the Jews*, Vol 4, pg 618

Luria, a Palestinian rabbi, focused on some of the latent traits of the occult, and what he thought were some solutions to the Jewish dilemmas. Graetz says that he basically created a new Kabbalah. It is clear that the occultist had by now absorbed many elements from Christianity, so much so that it appeared that they approved of some sort of trinity. Graetz comments,

> "The Kabbalists had gone so far in their imitation of Catholicism that they had adopted auricular confession and the adoration of martyrs."
> Vol 4, pg 623

Graetz says that it was due to Luria that the Zohar came to be viewed by many Jews (and in our own day by many gentiles also) as being on the same

plane as Scripture (Vol 4, pg 625). If you have the opportunity to visit a synagogue today, and if they are selling any books or charts, probably among them
will be kabbalistic materials. Luria believed he held the keys to prophecy, the
coming of the Messiah, and the saving of the world, and that,

> "he possessed the soul of the Messiah of the branch of Joseph, and that
> he had a Messianic mission." Graetz, Vol 4, pg 622

He was in fact a medium or a channeler of various spirits, and a necroman-
cer (he consulted the dead). Of course all of these activities were forbidden in
the commandments from Yahweh given at Mount Sinai, Deut 18:9-12, etc. So in
seeking solutions for the Jewish dilemmas, Luria, along with many others, was
still going back to many of the sources of their problems, and the bitter fruits of
these things were not long waiting. Scholem says of him,

> "Here we are dealing with an extreme case of Gnostic reaction in the
> Kabbalah ... The Gnostic reaction ... reached its highest point in Luria ...
>
> "... they gave the Kabbalah a completely new appearance. ... The
> Gnostic character of these ideas **which constitute a new mythology in
> Judaism**, cannot be doubted." *Kabbalah*, pp 74-75

I cannot help but think of Paul's warning to Titus, to not be "paying
attention to Jewish fables and commandments of men who turn away from the
truth." (Titus 1:14 NASB). At any rate Graetz and Scholem credit Luria with
something new in the Kabbalah, but Scholem goes on to show that these things
were not really new in the occult: they go all the way back to ancient Gnosticism. Graetz says,

> "His delusion was that the Messianic period would commence at the
> beginning of the second half of the second period of a thousand years
> since the destruction of the Temple, i. e., in 1568."
> Graetz, Vol 4, pg 624

So we are looking once again at messianic fantasies. In fact, this was really
even from the first of the Kabbalah. Moses de Leon's *Zohar* (probably the single
most important book of what we call the Kabbalah) sets the date for the Messiah to appear as 1268 AD (Scholem, *Kabbalah*, pg 232). He said that Moses will
appear and herald the final appearance of the Messiah. The period of transition
will end in 1312 AD.

In Jewish messianism there are some powerful combinations of playacting,
conjuring, spells/hypnosis, and just old fashioned slight of hand and ventriloquism, all of which have been a part of such things from time immemorial.
Scholem, seeming to speak as an adept, says of Luria that much of this cannot
be understood, only experienced, *Kabbalah*, pg 74. Scholem then goes on to
notice,

> "The messianic element is far more noticeable here than in other kab-

balistic systems ... Such tensions finally broke in the Shabbatean messianic movement," pg 75

Or as Scholem put it in another place,

"... Lurianism had created a climate favorable to the release of Messianic energies ..." *Kabbalah*, pg 246

After the Ari's, Luria's, untimely (or timely?) death, a certain Vital Calabrese became a key leader, and soon let it be know that indeed he was the true Messiah. So it goes on and on. Graetz says that all of these things had terrible effects on Judaism, and in fact *Lurianic Kabbalism became the leading element in Jewish occultism, **even to this day.***

"The harm that the Kabbalistic doctrines of Lurya caused in Jewish circles is inexpressible. Judaism became surrounded with so thick a husk of mysticism, **that it has not even yet succeeded in entirely freeing itself**, and showing its true kernel." Graetz, Vol 4 pg 625.

"The parasitic Kabbala choked the whole religious life of the Jews. **Almost all rabbis and leaders of the Jewish community ... were ensnared** by the Kabbala." Graetz, Vol 5, pg 52 (*bold emphasis added*)

Graetz is writing in the late 19th century, and died in 1891. Even today, many Kabbalistic Jews still fault Graetz for his opposition to this foolishness. All of this also set the stage for the most important Jewish false messiah of modern times.

Shabbetai Sevi

Scholem spells his name "Shabbetai Zevi" in his book *Kabbalah*, and spells his name "Sabbatai Sevi" in his book *Sabbatai Sevi, The Mystical Messiah*. The variant spelling in the quotes which follow depend on the original texts. He says the Shabbatean Movement was,

"the largest and most momentous messianic movement in Jewish history subsequent to the destruction of the Temple and the Bar Kokhba Revolt." Scholem, *Kabbalah*, pg 244

In the same context Scholem notes that **the lead up to Sevi was the Kabbalah coming to a "dominant position in Jewish life**." pg 244 (*emphasis added*). There is a great deal of literature about Sevi. Graetz and Scholem both wrote of him in more than one place. Scholem has a fully annotated study of him (*Sabbatai Sevi, The Mystical Messiah, 1626-1676*, Gershom Scholem, Princeton University Press, 1973, Princeton, NJ, which is 1,000 pages long, hereafter referred to as "*... The Mystical Messiah*"). He represents an interesting study in both Judaism and the Jewish occult, and the extremes they can reach. And there were and are other currents in Judaism. Scholem quotes the illustrious Maimonides about "apocalyptic" things:

> "One should make it a rule not to occupy oneself with legends and midrashim on the subject ... as they are conducive neither to the fear nor the love of God ..." "the beliefs of the rabble"
> Scholem, ... *The Mystical Messiah*, pp 13, 14

But the Kabbalah had indeed become a pervasive influence in Judaism.

Sevi was a Sephardic rabbi, evidently born in Smyrna in 1626 and died in 1676. Kabbalistic prophecies were pointing to 1666 as the key year of the messiah. (And yes! The occult does have a love affair with the imperfect number six, and try to use that number continually as an omen of good luck. You can even see it in our movies in our own day.) Scholem says that Sevi was a "manic-depressive," *Kabbalah*, pg 246; and when he was in depression he went off to himself. I do not know when "messiah committees" (to coin a phrase) came to be regarded as necessary. Clearly the more effective of the modern political messiahs have had committees surrounding them, protecting them, and helping them, covering for the normal mistakes which mortal's make, but which cannot be allowed to be known. The groups surrounding many political "messiahs" are good modern examples that are easy to study. The decision was made early that these guys had to be made to look good, *no matter what!* This is bound to be grating service to endure, but it seems to be standard operating procedure now for any "wannabe" messiah, whether religious or secular.

For Sevi, if there was a full committee (and there may have been), the head of that committee was Rabbi Nathan of Gaza. He announced he was the Elijah of the messiah. He is the one who pushed and prodded the laid back Sevi into making a public stand. Scholem tells us Nathan "fell into a trance and announced" Sevi's messiahship, *Kabbalah*, pg 250. The amount of promotional work Nathan did was phenomenal. Sevi became the talk of both the "Christian" world, the Jewish world, and the Mohammedan world. It is beyond the scope of this book to analyze the hows and whys of this "happening," but it was clearly astonishing. Graetz makes many pertinent observations,

> "Sarah, his [Sevi's] wife, who by her loose conduct worked on the passions of the male population. The bonds of chastity, drawn much tighter among Eastern Jews than in Europe, were broken."
> Graetz, *History of the Jews*, Vol 5, pg 135

Another member of the committee looks to have been Samuel Primo.

> "Samuel Primo, in the name of his divinity, directed a circular to the whole of Israel in semi-official form:
> **The first-begotten Son of God, Sabbatai Zevi, Messiah and Redeemer of the people of Israel,** to all the sons of Israel, Peace!"
> Graetz, Vol 5, pg 143 (*bold emphasis added*)

Notice that accepting humble Jesus of Nazareth as "the only begotten of

God" has been repulsive to the Jews, accepting Sevi as "The first-begotten Son of God"? Well, that seems to have been alright! Jesus said this had to happen, Jn 5:43.

> "Forged letters and docu-ments were the order of the day; conscientiousness and uprightness had utterly dis-appeared. Thus the mist of false belief grew thicker and thicker, and one was no longer able to get at the truth." Graetz, Vol 5, pg 151

At his height Sevi was headed to Constantinople to put "the Great Turk's" crown on his own head, liter-ally, as if it were magic. Jews in vari-ous places were quitting their jobs and waiting for the messiah to lead them to Jerusalem. There were

Sabbetai Sevi or Zevi, a spectacular Jewish false messiah of the 1600's. This is thought to be an authentic image.

parties and demonstrations all over the Western world, and large bets were be-ing placed in Holland as to how soon Sevi would be crowned.

Some of the rabbis were naturally suspicious and attempted to warn both the Jews and the Mohammedan authorities, but they were shouted down in the enthusiasm, or even had to run and hide. Some gentiles were even caught up in the excitement. Scholem tells us that, "Commerce came to a standstill every-where," *Kabbalah*, pg 261. **Sevi signed things "firstborn son God," "your father Israel,"** "the bridegroom of the Torah," **"I am the Lord your God Shabbetai Zevi."** Scholem, *Kabbalah*, pg 262. (And it must be once again pointed out, that *if these sorts of things are acceptable from a kabbalistic point of view,* which they were, *then these same ideas render null and void the traditional Jewish objections to Jesus of Nazareth as the very Son of God.*) But of course it had to be that, "I am come in my Father's name, and ye receive me not: if another shall come in his own name, him ye will receive." Jn 5:43 KJV.

Several authors emphasize the antinomian streak in Sevi and his teachings, and there are both hints, and clear evidence of sexual excesses among Sevi and his followers. Sevi proclaimed himself as "He who permits the forbidden." Scholem, *Kabbalah,* pg 258. Scholars, rabbi, rich people, poor people, all were caught up in the mania, pg 252-253. Scholem says it was "a strange mixture of solemn dignity and unrestrained license" pg 254

The Turks were used to revolts and very sensibly did not want to make a martyr out of Sevi. Their handling of Sevi was very astute. They had him arrested, kept in special confinement, allowed his followers to visit and support him, and had him brought before the Ottoman Sultan Mehmed IV. The Sultan among others things, visited at length with Sevi over some period of time, listening to him talk and obviously trying to evaluate him. Rabbi Nathan meanwhile was still back in Palestine during all of this.

Then a decision was made: Sevi would have to convert to Mohammedanism or be executed. There is much more to the details, but then, **the "messiah" decided to ...** *convert to Islam!* To the Turks he denied he had ever made any claims that he was the messiah!

You can only imagine the consternation which this caused. Sevi remained in prison, but still had very relaxed visitation rules so that his adherents could visit. There were even reports of sexual license during imprisonment, Scholem, *Kabbalah*, pg 268. Finally he was deported to Albania. He still had a great deal of freedom but he was no longer sought as a messiah by most, and he died in Albania. Nathan of Gaza immediately started defending Sevi's actions and began a small cult which continued to follow Sevi. Scholem tells us of Nathan,

> "On Shabbetai Zevi's orders he went to Rome for the performance of a secret magic ritual destined to hasten the fall of the representative of Christendom." *Kabbalah*, pg 267

Nathan said that Sevi was still the messiah, and portrayed the defection as some sort of secret grand strategy for the conquest of the world. When Sevi died Nathan said that he had ascended to some sort of higher plane, and that he expected him to come back in 1706 AD. The sect which now arose was called Shabbateans or the Doenmem. His loyal followers, like their master, also converted to Mohammedanism. In public they were Mohammedans, but in private they were still some sort of Jews. Would it be valid to call them crypto-Jews? Maybe, or maybe not. Scholem says,

Rabbi Nathan of Gaza, one of the main organizers and promoters of false Messiah Sabbatai Zevi. The Kabbalah has in fact proved to be some sort of "messiah machine," always seeking to put forth new candidates to be the savior of the world.

"essentially, **it represented an antirabbinic revolt in Judaism**."
Scholem, *Kabbalah*, pg 278 (*emphasis added*)

So here is another of the seeds of defection from the Halacha, the traditional law brought by the Pharisees. Remember, Jesus commented that there are some in the occult, "which say they are Jews, and are not," Rev 2:9 KJV.

"Some towns in Podolia and Pakotia were full of Talmudists who, in Sabbatian fashion, scoffed at the Talmud, rejected the law of Judaism, and, **under the mask of ascetic discipline, lived impure lives**."
Graetz, *History of the Jews*, Vol 5, pg 272 (*bold emphasis added*)

It was gradually driven completely underground because of its lawless character. Some Hasidim in Poland "contained strong element of Shabbateanism" according to Scholem, and

"... there is evidence that not a few of the most influential moral preachers and authors of moral literature of a radical bent were secret Shabbateans of the moderate and hasidic wing."
Scholem, *Kabbalah*, pg 278

The "hasidic wing" of Sabbatenaism? Graetz writes that Sabbatians were,

"... anathemas of the rabbis. They had only forced the Sabbatians to disguise themselves better, and to counterfeit death; but they flourished secretly, and their following increased."
Graetz, *History of the Jews*, Vol 5, pg 272

"Among these Salonica Sabbatians, then, shameless profligacy, even incest, were openly practiced so their enemies declared."
Graetz, Vol 5, pg 210

Modern "Salonica" is the ancient city of "Thessalonica." Graetz goes on to say,

"There are still in Salonica descendants of the sect of Sabbatai-Querido-Berachya, who observe a mixture of Kabbalistic and Turkish usages." Graetz,Vol 5 pg 211

"Recently the sultan granted the Donmah, now said to number 4,000 members, the free exercise of their religion." Graetz, Vol 5, pg 211

Graetz also writes of others, for instance of David Oppenheim, chief rabbi of Prague.

"Now and then he allowed the erroneous doctrine of the Salonica Sabbatians to crop out, viz., that sin can be overcome only by a superabundance of sinfulness," Graetz, Vol 5, pg 217-218

All of which is not far from the accusations made against the Apostle Paul,

And *why* not *say*, "Let us do evil that good may come"?—as we are slanderously reported and as some affirm that we say. Their condemnation is just. Rom 3:8 NKJV

So none of these things are really new. They have all been part of the Jewish occult since at least the first century AD. Then there came a lawless young man by the name of,

Jacob Frank: The Original "Big Brother"?

Jacob Frank (1726-1791), born in Poland, was a continuation and a development of the Shabbatean movement. Many Jews of Thessalonica (modern Salonica) have been continuously into the occult since ancient times, and it seems that Jacob was initiated into the Shabbateans here. He began preaching the revelations which he received, and called his followers "Frankists" after himself. At some point *he also converted to Mohammedanism.* Graetz says that Jacob,

> "was one of the worst, most subtle, and most deceitful rascals of the eighteenth century." *History of the Jews*, Vol 5, pg 272

> [Jacob] "taught his disciples to acquire riches for themselves, even by fraudulent and dishonest means. Deceit was nothing more than skillful artifice. **Their chief task was to undermine rabbinical Judaism, and to oppose and annihilate the Talmud**." Vol 5, pg 274

Also their objective was clearly to obtain political power, wherever and however it could be secured. As with many other Shabbateans, Jacob and his group were soon accused of ritual orgies, and a Polish congress of rabbis petitioned the authorities to burn the Frankists at the stake. This caused a previously secret sect to be put in the light of day.

The Frankists responded by saying that their only holy book was the *Zohar*, which they said did not contradict the doctrine of the trinity, and said that they rejected the Talmud. The local bishop took them under his protection, and the Catholic church tried to use them for publicity purposes. A series of debates followed between the Frankists and the Jewish rabbis on the subject of the Talmud. (This was indeed a "Jews" versus "Frankists" battle. Compare again Jesus' words in Rev 2:9) The Frankists proved themselves to be able scholars, and the Jews were reluctant to defend the Talmud straightforwardly lest they offend the authorities. (The anti-Christian and anti-gentile sections of the Talmud would have been very hard to handle in a public debate.) The Frankists more or less won the debates, and at last the Frankists "converted" to Christianity! To Jacob Frank changing formal religions was a small and insignificant matter.

Graetz says plainly that it was the Kabbalah itself which laid the groundwork for these developments.

"It was the Kabbala that had kindled the torches for the funeral

pile of the Talmud." Vol 5, pg 282 (*bold emphasis added*)

In other words, Graetz is saying it was the Kabbalah which led the Jews to abandon the Talmud. This in turn was part of what led to the Fifth Break in Judaism, which will be discussed later.

There is extensive literature on Jacob Frank and the Frankists, just as there is with Sevi. He called himself the "Good God," **"the Big Brother,"** and "the Great Brother." He also called himself, "He who stands before God," and taught a doctrine of a sort of "purification by transgression"!

Like so many "messiahs" before and after him, he overplayed his hand. He kept demanding that a section of land be turned over to him, and over time the Catholics became wary of Jacob. Accusations of heresy were made against him again, and he was tried and convicted, and barely escaped being burned at the stake. Finally imprisoned, his influence over his followers did not diminish.

After 13 years he was released by a Russian general during a Russian invasion of Poland. He moved first to Austria and then to Germany, finally living as a wealthy nobleman, "the Baron of Offenbach." Where Frank got his money was always a mystery (Scholem, *Kabbalah*, pg 303). However, many Frankists were well educated and wealthy, Scholem, *Kabbalah*, pg 300, etc. So as with many traditional "mystery religions," they tended to be a cult of the elite.

> "Some of the Hoenig family remained Frankist Jews even after their elevation to the nobility ..." Scholem, *Kabbalah*, pg 304

> "In Warsaw in the 1830's most of the lawyers were descendants of Frankists, many of whom were also businessmen, writers, and musicians." Scholem, *Kabbalah*, pg 308

Scholem lists other connections in Prague (pg 306), and he notes a group migrated to the USA in 1848-1849 (pg 307). After Frank's death they "... began to combine revolutionary mystical kabbalistic ideas with the rationalistic view of the Enlightenment," and reached high positions in government. (pg 304.) He says that links between the Shabbateans and Russian authorities may be from 1765, and that there were also secret links to Shabbateans in Germany (pg 302).

One can also run into bits and pieces of information here and there "off the grid" about the Frankists. Revolutionary activities seemed to follow the group, and some speak darkly of the influence of so called "Frankist lodges" on revolutionary activities. Depending on who you talk to, some Frankist were involved in the French Revolution. Other Frankists supposedly saw Napoleon as a potential messiah. (As a side light, British war propaganda during the Napoleonic Wars sometimes spoke of Napoleon as the anti-christ, and some of this lingers on in some older English language commentaries still in print on the book of Revelation.)

When the Revolution of 1848 failed, one extended Frankist clan/family decided to emigrate to the United States in 1849, first to Indiana, then in 1851 to the Louisville, Kentucky area. They were the Brandeis family, *Louis D. Brandeis, A Life*, Melvin I. Urofsky, Shocken Books, NY, 2009, pgs 4-6. One of their descendants, Louis Brandeis (1856-1941), became a leading social reformer, a leader of Zionism in America, a Justice of the U. S. Supreme Court, 1916-1939, and a major influence on how law is practiced in America today.

Scholem says that several Frankists were involved in the "Young Turks" revolution in 1908, and he says that three of them served as ministers in the revolutionary Turkish government, (*Kabbalah*, pg 330-331). With thorough searching the reader will turn up other links.

Scholem also says that groups of Frankists and Shabbateans survived until well into the 20th century, "breaking up only in the mid-20 century ..." (*Kabbalah*, pg 284), however he does not really tell us how he knows this. He says that following the Greco-Turkish War, the group was forced to leave Salonika (modern Thessalonica) in the population exchanges, pg 330-331. Then he tells us, almost in opposition to this,

> "the original framework of the Konyosos sect survived, and as late as 1970 many families still belonged to this organization." Scholem, *Kabbalah*, pg 331 [this edition was © 1974, so this note would imply the Frankists are still current, nf]

Also he says that few Frankists have any interest in migrating to Israel.

Then when David Luhrssen (University of Wisconsin) wrote the history of the German occult sect "Thule Society" (which was instrumental in developing Nazism) in *Hammer of the Gods, the Thule Society and the birth of Nazism*, Potomac Books, Washington, D.C., 2012, one of the key figures was Rudolf Freiherr von Sebottendorff. Luhrssen says he was a "central figure," and part

Jacob Frank. Was he in fact the original "big brother"?

of the trail of evidence leads to the Salonika Jews, pg 50-51!

This is about a small but significant religio-political cult, and all of this dangerous foolishness continues unabated to this very day.

Of the Sabbatai Zevi episode what can be said except: shameful, stupid. But no more shameful than many of the present things which are not acknowledged, and no more stupid than some of the things to come.

It is not publicly discussed, but some in the occult seem to have given up on reproducing Bible prophecy in their false messiah. It is too complicated. It cannot be done by men or by angels. Many have now become satisfied with a king of their earthly kingdom which saves the world, their saving people, and whoever becomes this "king," becomes the Messiah, *ipso facto*. The messiah in this perspective, does not save the world. Rather the messianic people save the world, and their king becomes the Messiah of the Messianic kingdom. Rather like Stryder in the kabbalistic *Lord of the Rings* series.

In our own day most of the false prophecies of the imminent start of the millennium on earth come the from mouths of shills, or crypto-Jews, with Judaism and the Kabbalah standing further in the background, so as to not be tainted by the ridiculous failures.

Even so, for every "would-be" messiah you can read about, there are probably dozens whom no one notices, and they include both Jews and gentiles. As a former resident of Alaska I cannot help but remember the "Bare Foots," as they were called, in Homer, Alaska in the 1960's and 70's. If you really want to get some perspective on false messiahs, try Jason Boyett, *Pocket Guide to the Apocalypse, The Official Field Manual of the End of the World*, Relevant Books, Orlando, FL, 2005, 161 pages. Boyett's satirical approach proposes to document the many false-christs, especially of the last thousand years. He does give an impression of continual false messiahs, almost seeming to be a new one every year. He does mention Sevi. He misses Abraham Abulafia, Avila, Isaac Abrabane, and Luria, and probably many others. There are so many it is hard to catch all of them. Now Jesus said "**many** shall come in My name, saying, I am the Christ," Mtt 24:5. Boyett, in contrast, seems to say that if there have been this many false-christs, then Jesus must have been wrong! You be the judge!

So if you start reading of the haredim in Israel of today, you will soon run into the devout and brilliant rabbi so-and-so, who has assembled quite a following. Rabbi so-and-so says the signs are indicating the messiah is very near, and then Wha-lah! The messiah is revealed, and it is ... who would guess ... rabbi so-and-so himself! So the stories go on and on, and falter, and die, and are buried.

Does it need to be mentioned that some so called "Messianic Jews" whom you might hear on radio broadcasts are Kabbalists. Some, by and large, will not straight forwardly acknowledge the true Christ of the Jews: Rabbi Yehoshua, Jesus of Nazareth.

The Kabbalah is at its roots messianic in character, in fact it can almost be described as a "messiah machine." It does not really mind a god/man in the flesh. *It merely objects to Jesus of Nazareth as that God/man.* You could say that all of this began with the Kabbalah of the 12th and 13th centuries, but actually you can see all of this already in full bloom in Josephus histories of the Jews of the first centuries BC and AD, and in the events leading up to the disastrous Bar Khockba revolt of the early 2nd century AD.

The Effect of the Kabbalah on the Jews

"Jewish mysticism transformed Jewish beliefs without changing, except for a few details, Jewish observance. Between 1550 and 1750, the great majority of Jews in western Europe accepted the Cabbala and its set of beliefs. ... **Mysticism is still accepted by and constitutes a vital part of Jewish fundamentalism**, being especially important in the messianic variety."
Shahak, Mezvindky, *Jewish Fundamentalism*, pg 4 (*bold emphasis added*)

It should also be noted that this is the classic way the "mystery religions" change the content of a target religion into "what should have been intended," without altering the outward form. *So ancient Pharisaism itself has become a victim of mystery religion infiltration.* In historical perspective, this is a process which has for the most part been completed in much of Judaism, and is still in progress in much of Western Christianity. Some of the effects I think can be succinctly described.

The Success of Dark Illusions

Graetz eloquently summarizes the effects and points to the historical roots.

"The empty Kabbala could not fail to arouse enthusiasm in empty heads. **With the Zoharist mystics, as with the Essenes, the expectation of the Messiah was the center of their system.**"
Graetz, *History of the Jews*, Vol 4 pg 482

So Graetz is saying that producing an effective false-christ of world proportions has always been at the center of the occult systems.

"... belief in the kingdom of Satan, in evil spirits and ghosts."
Graetz, Vol 4, pg 22

"Zohar sowed the seeds of unclean desires, and later on produced a sect that laid aside all regard for decency." Graetz, Vol 4, pg 22-23

This, it might be added, is particularly true of the Jewish Hollywood and media set.

"quibbling interpretations of Holy Writ, adopted by the Kabbalists and others infected with this mannerism, perverted the verses and words of the Holy Book, and made the Bible the wrestling-ground of the most curious, insane notions. The Zohar even contains utterances which seem favorable to the Christian dogma of the Trinity of the Godhead."
Graetz, Vol 4 pg 23

"the Fathers and Princes of the church believed firmly that the Kabbala contained the mysteries of Christianity. ... Kabbala was to rise out of the ruins of the Talmud." Graetz, Vol 4, pg 583

"Thus the Talmud was burnt, and the Zohar spared ..."
Graetz, Vol 4 pg 584

So this is a progression in which first the words of men replace the words of God (Pharisaism), and then is finally written up as the Talmud, and it in essence supersedes Scripture. Now what is seen is the occult and seeking other spirits superseding the Talmud and soon of the Halacha, in all but form.

"During the last three decades of the sixteenth century the Kabbala gained sole mastery in Palestine, conjured up apparitions, and encouraged orgies of mysticism." Graetz, Vol 4 pg 617

A few quotes from *Kabbalah*, by Gershom Scholem, will be sufficient, although it can easily be documented from many other sources.

"As early as the 13th century there began a tendency to interpret the halakhah in kabbalistic terms ..." pg 191

"From the 17th century onward, kabbalistic motifs entered the everyday prayer book and inspired special liturgies ..." pg 193

"Many kabbalistic concepts were absorbed at the level of folk beliefs, such as ... the demonology of the later Kabbalah." pg 194

So how influential was the Kabbala? Almost everything in Judaism turned on it. Even to this day.

"The penetration of kabbalistic customs and beliefs, **which left no corner of Jewish life untouched ... Mystical and demonic motifs became particularly intertwined in the area of sexual life and practices ...**" Scholem, K*abbalah,* pg 195 (*bold emphasis added*)

"**from** 1500 to 1800 (at the most conservative estimate) **the Kabbalah was widely considered to be the *true* Jewish theology** ... In the course of this period an open polemical attack on the Kabbalah was practically unheard of ..."
Scholem, *Kabbalah,* pg 190 (*bold emphasis added*)

So there has been in Judaism a continual susceptibility to religious conmen, as long as they contained no taint of Christianity. This susceptibility is widespread among the Jews, even among many who consider themselves secular, or even "atheists." It goes under the heading of kabbalistic lore. Few of them are really experts on the Kabbalah, although much of their lives are guided by Kabbalistic principles. Many times they disdain any formal practice of any religion, or perhaps are to some extent "anti-religious." Despite all of that they often treat kabbalistic lore as some sort of "science" which is beyond needing to be proved. Were hapless gentiles caught up in such insanity from some "Christian" source, it would be the subject of endless exposés and even ridicule on television and in the movies. But because the source is kabbalistic, the news and entertainment cartels gives these delusions full cover. If they deal with them at all, it is only in tones of respect and awe.

It was discussed earlier about what Scripture says of those who say they are Jews, but are not really Jews, but are really of the synagogue of Satan, Rev 2:9.

> "From these traditions came the zoharic theory of the *sitra ahar* (the "other side")," Scholem, *Kabbalah*, pg 55.

But clearly this is NOT speaking of "the other side" of the True and Living God in whom there is no variation or shadow of turning, Jas 1:17. Still, the worship of evil among some is clearly spoken of, even by Scholem.

> "According to the "Gnostics" of Castile ... there also exists a complete hierarchy of the "emanation of the left," which is the power of uncleanliness that is active in creation." Scholem, *Kabbalah*, pg 123

> "three dark emanations" Scholem, *Kabbalah*, pg 123

> "According to the Zohar there is a spark of holiness even in the domain of **"the other side,"** ..."
> Scholem, *Kabbalah*, pg 125 (*emphasis added*)

The most visible examples of this is in groups such as the Frankists, for whom doing any wrong or criminal act, or carrying out any deception or hypocrisy is insignificant. Scholem speaks of

> "the antinomian tendencies (which belittled the value of the Commandments)" *Kabbalah*, pg 22

It was a synagogue of Satan, an irrational, anarchistic, wing of "Judaism," which became a perennial negative influence in Judaism. They maintained their flirting with other spirits and with paganism, even when most of the Western world has severed their links with other "gods."

All of these heresies are (at their roots) really anti-Jewish. Anti-Jewish both in the sense of the true Judaism of Moses' Law, and also anti-Jewish in the sense of the Old Testament denomination of rabbinical Pharisaism. It is a terrible and sad heritage the Jews have embraced, in order to avoid listening to Moses and the prophets of old. In truth it may be said of many Jews of the last two thousand years, when dabbling in the occult/Kabbala, they have often not realized what foul seed, what lethal demonic forces, they have partaken of until it was too late for them to withdraw.

Let me emphasize what was previously said. Many nationalities have used such groups when it was convenient. The English, the Germans, the Russians, the Americans, to name a few, have used such groups when they thought it was in their interests. But these groups are not really pro-English, pro-German, pro-Russian, or pro-American. These are men who have been completely turned to

... "the Dark Side," to Satan himself, by seduction, or by decision, and by no little duress. Despite any ethnic roots, or any cover or any rhetoric, **neither are they *really* Jewish either**. The sooner the Jews wake up to these realities, the better. They are betraying both the true Messiah of the Jews, *and* the Jewish people, *and* themselves.

However, it is still there.

A Passionate Quest for Knowledge of All Sorts

As the occult Gnostics of old sought to know about everything so they could master everything, so the Jews in following the occult have been very systematically following every trace of knowledge or so called knowledge, and have branched out on incredibly wide fronts. These attitudes and orientations have even driven Jews not involved in the occult into wide ranging investigations of a broad spectrum of topics. Wherever the frontiers of knowledge are, from the sublime to the ridiculous, there you will find some Jews, usually as masters of whatever "art" is involved. *There have been many good things to come from this*, such as in science, and they are good at passing things along to each other. Despite their continual conflicts with each other, their abilities to critique themselves in worldly matters are astonishing, and their mentoring systems are without parallel for such a large group, despite their problems.

This has had many good effects for the Jews in worldly terms. While current gentile "scholarship" tends to concentrate on what the latest generation has decided, the Jews tend to search everything, both old and new, and thus are inclined have a continual advantage. They have also become masters of many good and worthwhile pursuits. They are many of the great men of our world in science, literature, politics, medicine, religion, and you name it (and I am not even speaking here of any of the many crypto-Jews, many of whom also are well known).

In science the effects have been some of the most telling. The occult dabbling in drugs/alchemy/chemistry lead many Jews to become leaders in medical and industrial fields, and forming part of the basis of our modern drug industry, with both its good points and bad points.

Much of theoretical physics has had something of a kabbalistic touch since at least the late nineteenth century. But whether some of this results in long term scientific progress ... the jury is still out.

The Jews are many of the leaders of the great movements of our world, though still preferring to remain unnoticed. Look around! They are the ultimate "men of this world." However it is only of this world that they are masters; not of the next world which their prophets have all promised from Samuel forward. They have not listened to other Hebrew voices which would have warned them.

[15] Do not love the world nor the things in the world. If anyone loves the world, the love of the Father is not in him. [16] For all that is in the world, the lust of the flesh and the lust of the eyes and the boastful pride of life, is not from the Father, but is from the world. [17] The world is passing away, and *also* its lusts; but the one who does the will of God lives forever. 1 Jn 2:15-17

Their occult dabbling not withstanding, they have not passed the gates of death, or secured redemption, which is only available in their Christ whom they have rejected. On the other hand, their passion for mastery in *all areas*, means that they have always had their masters of the dark side.

And the Political Influence

Now you might try to tell me that this Kabbalah stuff is just a few kooks, but look around at regular bookstores and occult bookstores and off beat shops. It has never been just a few off beat "kooks" that are involved, and that is the way it has been down through history. Just like with Ronald Reagan and other government leaders of our own times, just like in fictional movies like "Raiders of the Lost Ark," the magicians and astrologers have often gotten the ear of otherwise intelligent rulers in an attempt to manipulate them with these teachings. Then comes the other side of these things. When you have groups that are reliable in keeping secrets they soon become ready tools for political intrigue, and that is the way it has been since ancient times. So our dictionary says **the definition of "cabal" in English is "a secret political clique or faction: a cabal of dissidents."** *"Magic" and the occult have always been involved in politics and war down through history.* So the use of occult arts to influence rulers is something that can be seen throughout history, and stories like you see in Acts 13 with the Jewish magician at the ruler's side, are seen all through the Christian age! Raiders of the Dark Arts, both Jew and Gentile, still ride. So the Kabbalists came to have a tendency to become an evil influence in all of their various hosts.

> Woe to them! For they have gone in the way of Cain, have run greedily in the error of Balaam for profit, and perished in the rebellion of Korah. Jude 11 NKJV

So To What Has Israel Been Faithful?

The Jews have not been faithful to *anything:* Not to God, not Moses Law (even in a legalistic sense), not even to the traditions of the fathers or to the Talmud, or to "rabbinic" Judaism. Not really to anything or anyone except the god of this world. Often not even each other.

Jewish scholars Israel Shahak and Norton Mezvinsky make note of the continuation of the occult into our own times, even among the so called "secular" Jews, in *Jewish Fundamentalism in Israel*, Pluto Press, Ann Arbor, Michigan, 1999. They refer to the Israeli "right" or "the right and religious parties" as being "Israel B."

> **"Members of Israel B, following some historic Jewish customs, believe in magic and witchcraft; they often practice it themselves or follow directives supposedly derived from it by rabbis and cabbalists**. (Books in Hebrew detailing instructions for spells and witchcraft recipes have been best sellers in Israel for many years.) Individuals who are reputed to achieve success by use of magic frequently obtain political power in Israel."
>
> Shahak, Mezinksy, *Jewish Fundamentalism* ..., pg 156 (*emphasis added*)

They refer to Israeli author Tom Segev, who is well known in both Hebrew and English. His book *Elvis in Jerusalem, Post Zionism and the Americanization of Israel*, Metropolitan Books, Henry Holt and Company, New York, 2002, is a good short read on modern Israel and the influence of American culture on modern Israel.

> "Tom Segev, a columnist for "*Haaretz*" and one of Israel's best known authors, wrote that the use of magic by Jews was nothing new in Judaism. In his March 26, 1999, Hebrew-language *Haaretz* article, Segev transcribed a magical recipe found in a book, composed in talmudic times (AD 200-500) but still popular in the Diaspora in the eighteenth century." *Jewish Fundamentalism in Israel*, pg 157

And to cause a judge to release the guilty?

> ""Slaughter a lion cub with a copper knife. Gather its blood; tear out its heart and put the blood into it. Then, write the names of angels on the cub's face, and wipe the names with three year-old wine. Mix the wine with the blood. Next, take three heaps of perfume (names omitted). After purifying yourself, stand before the planet Venus at night with the perfume and the blood, which must be put on fire." ... Segev reported that the **Israeli scientists participating in this Congress believed magic to be "an inseparable part of Judaism**—used in past intrigues involving rabbis.""
>
> *Jewish Fundamentalism in Israel*, pg 157 (*bold emphasis added*)

I think it is no exaggeration to say that no other religious group approaches the insanity involved in the Kabbalistic radicals of the Jews. If these were American Christian groups, they would be the subject of constant investigative reporting and media derision, but since this is occult religion and anti-christian, the establishment media cartels by and large blithely ignore it. All of this is just a formula for disaster, and it is steadily working (Deut 32:35). Also it should be noted that many secular Jews, just as in many of Shahak's quotes, implicitly view the whole thing as something of an embarrassment, and ignore these things as far as possible.

The truth is that mere human effort, or the assistance of other spirits, is inadequate to give us life and prosperity. It is in the end sterile and demeaning, and without the ability to keep us from sinking ever deeper into our wrongs. Rabbi Yehoshua predicted all of this in the first century. Listen to his words.

> [43] "When an unclean spirit goes out of a man, he goes through dry places, seeking rest, and finds none. [44] Then he says, "I will return to my house from which I came.' And when he comes, he finds *it* empty, swept, and put in order. [45] Then he goes and takes with him seven other spirits more wicked than himself, and they enter and dwell there; and the last *state* of that man is worse than the first. So shall it also be with this wicked generation." Mtt 12:43-45 NKJV

A curse remains on the people of physical Israel, even to this day. The full results can only be avoided by repentance and turning to the Messiah: Rabbi Yehoshua of Nazareth.

> [12] He who said to them, "Here is rest, give rest to the weary,"
> And, "Here is repose," but they would not listen.
> [13] So the word of the LORD to them will be,
> "Order on order, order on order,
> Line on line, line on line,
> A little here, a little there,"
> That they may go and stumble backward, be broken, snared and taken captive.
> Isa 28:12-13 NASB

If we do not recognize
these religious turns
among the Jews,
we will not understand
the directions
they have taken,
and the things
which have happened,
and what both
Jew and Gentile
need to do.

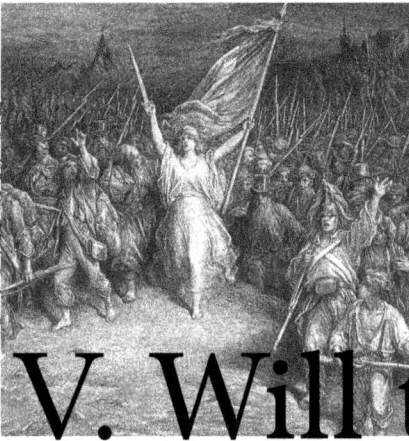

V. Will the Real Super Race Please Stand Up!

... In due time their foot will slip;
For the day of their calamity is near,
And the impending things are hastening upon them.' Deut 32:35 NASB

The Bogus "Semitic Race"

"You shall answer and say before the LORD your God, 'My father was a wandering Aramean, and he went down to Egypt and sojourned there, few in number; but there he became a great, mighty and populous nation.'" Deut 26:5 NASB

The KJV translates this "A Syrian ready to perish was my father," speaking of Abraham, the forefather of the Jews.

Semite noun

a member of any of the peoples who speak or spoke a Semitic language, including in particular the Jews and Arabs.
ORIGIN from modern Latin *Semita*, via late Latin from Greek *Sēm* *'Shem,'* son of Noah in the Bible, from whom these people were traditionally supposed to be descended.
New Oxford American Dictionary

Semitic ... adjective

1 relating to or denoting a family of languages that includes Hebrew, Arabic, and Aramaic and certain ancient languages such as Phoenician and Akkadian, constituting the main subgroup of the Afro-Asiatic family.
2 of or relating to the peoples who speak these languages, esp. Hebrew and Arabic.
New Oxford American Dictionary

The Dictionary is correct. (Don't laugh. They aren't always. Just compare different dictionaries.) The terms Semite/Semitic are really linguistic terms, language terms, *not* racial terms. Surprised? On the next page is a chart of the general development of Semitic languages, which followed Shem's descendants being separated linguistically following God's confusion of our languages.

A close examination of the historical data with the genealogical data available from the book of Genesis reveals that the linguistic lines and genealogical lines did some crossing very early in history. As Jewish writer Walter Laqueur

The Main Groups of Semitic Languages

```
                          |
    Western                          Eastern
       |                             Akkadian
       |
       |                          _____|_____
       |                          |            |
       |                       Assyrian     Babylonian
       |
  Northwest Group_____Southwest Group
       |                          _____|_____
       |                          |                    |
       |                     Ethiopic (Ge'ez)        Arabic
       |                     (Tigre, other dialects)
     __|_____
     |            |                    |              |
  Ugaritic  Canaanite/Phoenician     Hebrew        Aramaic
     _____|
     |                                        |
  Western Aramaic                        Eastern Aramaic
  (Judeo-Palestinian,                    (Judeo/Babylonian
  Biblical, Samaritan dialects)          Syriac, other dialects)
```

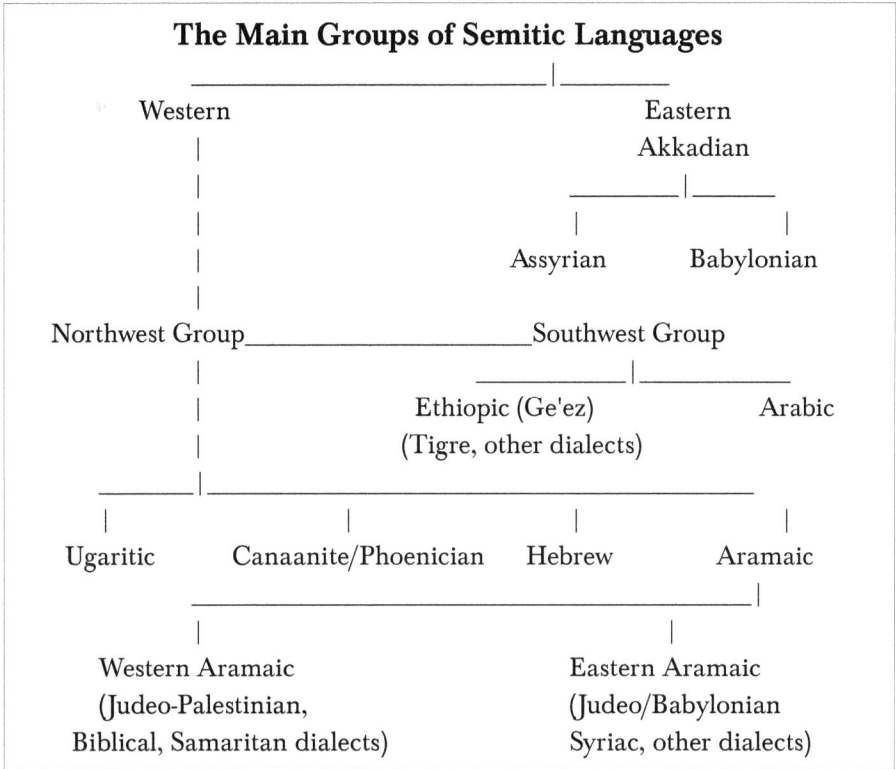

puts it, "the Jews were ... children of Israel, related to the Arabs," *A History of Zionism*, pg 45.

This might be a good time to look at some of the writings of Lucien Wolf (1857-1930). *The New Standard Jewish Encyclopedia*, Doubleday & Company, NY, 1977, Fifth Edition, dismisses Wolf as an "English historian, journalist and Jewish public worker." But even that article indicates he was more than that. He was in effect an unofficial ambassador for the Jews (this was before the nation of Israel was established), and was recognized as such. The encyclopedia article mentions "he became Secretary of the Joint Foreign Committee of the Board of Deputies of British Jews," to the Paris Peace Conference in 1919, and was "partly responsible" for a treaty about the treatment of minorities. He was a regular at the League of Nations. An interesting study of Wolf as a diplomat is *War, Jews, and the New Europe, The Diplomacy of Lucien Wolf 1914-1919*, by Mark Levene, Oxford University Press, 1992. He was against Zionism, as *many* Jews *were* and *are*. So Wolf is often treated as an idiot by the Zionists and the dominant Zionist media. Nonetheless, Wolf was a long way from an idiot. He was an urbane and sophisticated advocate for the Jews, wherever he could be of service, and he had many telling points to make. His refutation of the widely debated *Protocols of the Learned Elders of Zion*, is still the standard text on the subject. The Jews, once again acting as a "nation within a nation," had more than one such man. Another was Nahum Sokolow, and another was the spectacularly successful Chaim Weizmann, and others have shown up here and there in various nations down through history.

The interest here is Wolf's analysis of the nature of the Jews. This is taken from his article "The Zionist Peril" in *The Jewish Quarterly Review*, Vol XVII, Macmillan And Co., NY, 1905. Wolf makes some interesting assessments of the Jews as a race.

> "Nevertheless the balance of evidence is against the separate race theory. So far as the Bible can guide us, it distinctly shows that the Jews were of Aryan origin, ..." pg 8

Regrettably, we need to stop right there before continuing with Wolf's quote. He is here reciting evidence which is widely quoted about the Jews, and that is widely misunderstood by all around, including many of the Jews. In fact a large section of the modern Jews are called Ashkenazi. Some say that as much as 85% of the modern Jews are Ashkenazi, and that the other 15% are Sephardic or Spanish Jews. The Ashkenazi are named after Ashkenaz, a great-grandson of Noah, the son of Gomer, who was the son of Japheth, Gen 10:1-2. Wolf is basically right, Ashkenaz would be considered an "Aryan," but *this evidence really points to **many modern Jews as having A GREAT DEAL of gentile parentage.*** In fact, much of Judaism uses the term "Ashkenazi" to mean German (See *The New Joys of Yiddish*, Leo Rosten, pg 18). *The rest of the story is that **this is the wrong Biblical ancestry for a Semite!*** Because you see, Semites as such are descendants of another son of Noah, Shem, Gen 10:1, 21-31. As the word is used today (except as a propaganda word), Semite is mainly a linguistic term, as has been pointed out. The Palestinians, the Syrians, the Egyptians and the Arabs, are all truly Semites. Incredibly, perhaps reflecting the racial biases of the English people of his time, Wolf is here claiming to not really being a Semite, but an Aryan!

Now Lucien Wolf was as bad as many other Jewish writers at throwing around the term "anti-Semite" for anyone who opposed him. On page 10 of this same article Wolf protests, "The modern Jew, even in the most grotesque caricature which the anti-Semites draws of him, bears but little resemblance to his Western Asiatic ancestors."

New Oxford American Dictionary tells the same story.

Jew ... noun
> a member of the people and cultural community whose traditional religion is Judaism and who trace their origins through the ancient Hebrew people of Israel to Abraham.

So the correct term would be "anti-Jewish," not "anti-Semite," which as you can see, is an ***ignorant* misnomer** used as a **cheap propaganda smear word**, against anyone who would disagree with the Jews, or oppose *any* of their plans. Sometimes this smear word is even used against Jews. The Egyptians are Semites. The Libyans and Syrians are Semites. The Saudis are Semites. As Lucien Wolf so carefully points out, many (perhaps most) modern Jews are not really Semites. The closest many ever come to really being "Semitic" would be in learning Hebrew or Arabic, just as you and I as gentiles might learn it. It is easy to see that at best, this is nothing like a homogenous descent of the Jews. Even so, the law of Moses expects others to join Israel and gives regulations for these things (for instance, circumcision in Ex 12:48, etc.). Jewish historian Cecil Roth categorically states there is no Jew today who does not have proselyte blood in his veins. You can easily see why he might say this. But to return to Wolf's analysis of the Jews as a "race."

> "... and that Anthropologically they were in a state of flux until after the return from Babylon, when Ezra and the High Priest organized Judaism. What happened to them then has happened to every organized religious community in the world since. A centripetal anthropological movement set in. **In this way what is called "the Jewish race" was formed. But strictly speaking it is not a race. It is merely a religious community of great antiquity**, ..."
> *The Zionist Peril*, in *The Jewish Quarterly Review*, Vol XVII, Macmillan And Co., NY, 1905, pg 8, (*bold emphasis added*)

I think this statement, of the Jews as a "race" in a secondary sense, can basically be accepted. I think this is what Jesus meant in Mtt 24:34, that the Jewish "generation"/"race" will not pass away before His Second Coming, which is clearly described in Mtt 24:29-31. This is discussed in detail with the other Matthew 24 issues in *Prophecy Principles*. One of the definitions of "race" in the *New Oxford American Dictionary* is,

> • a group of people sharing the same culture, history, language, etc.; an ethnic group: *we Scots were a bloodthirsty race then.*

Personally I do not think the addition of many gentile elements into the seed of Abraham side-track the main issues, any more than the addition of proselytes in Mosaic or Davidic times. You can see this analysis is many places, and from many points of view. Take for instance the words of Israeli diplomat and scholar Abban Eban.

> "Judaism is the Jewish *religion*, those who are born Jews are Jewish people, Israel today is the Jewish *state*–but what constitutes the Jewish *race?* ... But ... the labeling of the Jews as a race (a practice now discredited by anthropology) ..."
> *Heritage: Civilization and the Jews*, Abban Eban, Summit Books, NY, 1984, pg 297 (*emphasis Ebban's*)

There you have it. Anthropologically, there is no such thing as the Jewish race. To be anti-Arab is to be anti-Semitic. To be anti-Syrian is to be anti-Semitic. Beyond this, even Scripture speaks of the Jews as being of gentile parentage.

> And say, Thus saith the Lord GOD unto Jerusalem; Thy birth and thy nativity *is* of the land of Canaan; thy father *was* an Amorite, and thy mother an Hittite. Ezek 16:3 KJV

A Historical Atlas of the Jewish People credits "Wilhelm Marrs, the German political agitator," with inventing the term "antisemitism" in the very late year of 1873, pg 186.

But the practice of the Jews segregating themselves from all other nations (the *goyim* גּוֹיִם in Hebrew, that is to say, the nations) goes way back in history, and at least in part the Judaic practices go back to Moses' Law. Actually, the command there was not to *intermarry* with the *Canaanites*. The Canaanites had been involved in many accursed practices of a sexual, a religious, and a criminal nature. At the time Abram had been promised Canaan for his descendants, the Canaanites were already involved in many of these great sins, but they were not *yet* so evil as to be displaced. So Abram was told,

> [15] And thou shalt go to thy fathers in peace; thou shalt be buried in a good old age. [16] But in the fourth generation they shall come hither again: for the iniquity of the Amorites *is* not yet full. Gen 15:15-16 KJV

Even so, for some in Abram's time, their sins were full, for while Abram was still alive both Sodom and Gomorrah were destroyed. The Amorites' sins included some of the grossest forms of idolatry, which included human sacrifices, ritual fornication, and many evil practices.

Irrational Anti-Jewish Hatred and Malice?

Is there such a thing? Obviously so in some places. Perhaps not as much as many might think. In the case of the Jews, it has just been shown that the correct term would be "anti-Jewish," and not "anti-Semite."

Hatred is among the arts of a propagandist, to prepare us to viciously oppose ALL of some certain nation, group, or religion. These are ways to turn an otherwise sensible man into a homicidal maniac of a soldier, who will kill on sight any, say, Japanese, or Chinese, or ... you name it. Obviously there was much of this in Nazi Germany. Jewish historian Charles Higham in *Trading With the Enemy, The Nazi-American Money Plot* 1933-1949, Barnes and Noble, NY, 1983, 1995, points outs that there was much of this in *parts* of the very powerful Western Establishment (Higham slyly calls them "The Fraternity"). The implication of his work is that much of this probably continues in this powerful group, but covertly so in our own day. So the Jews do have some very powerful "enemies," and in high places of worldly power and influence.

Such foolishness has no place in any sensible personal outlook. We should be immediately suspicious of anyone who tries to get us to automatically hate and despise everyone automatically of any certain group. Inflammatory propaganda is seldom a good documentary source.

Who Then Should We Oppose, and What Should We Support?

Paul told us what we should do.

> [14] That we *henceforth* be no more children, tossed to and fro, and carried about with every wind of doctrine, by the sleight of men, *and* cunning craftiness, whereby they lie in wait to deceive; [15] But speaking the truth in love, may grow up into him in all things, which is the head, *even* Christ: Eph 4:14-15 KJV (*bold emphasis added*)

This is clearly what the Jewish Messiah taught. Lastly, it should be asked,

Perhaps there is another side to irrational hatred and malice?

What about irrational malice and hatred toward anyone who criticizes Jews, or who might say absolutely *anything* about Jews in any way, that might be considered unflattering or negative? Are only gentiles to be put in the glaring light of criticism? Are Jews *alone* to be immune from ALL criticism, and ANY negative comments? Might that also be a factor, and once a again a cover for plans that are far less than worthy?

What about irrational anti-gentile malice and hatred? Might that also be a factor? Might that also be a cover for greed and despicable treatment of others?

Separations, Isolations, and Bigotries

By the time Israel reached Canaan, the Canaanites were clearly beyond reform. So God had decided to destroy them as a people. The dangers to Israel of the Canaanites remaining in the land were great. Here are the commands:

> [1] When Yahweh your God shall bring you into the land ... [2] and when Yahweh your God shall deliver them up before you, ... **then you shall utterly destroy them**: you shall make no covenant with them, nor show mercy to them; [3] neither shall you make marriages with them; ... [4] For he will turn away your son from following me, that they may serve other gods: so will the anger of Yahweh be kindled against you, and he will destroy you quickly. ... [16] You shall consume all the peoples who Yahweh your God shall deliver to you; your eye shall not pity them: neither shall you serve their gods; **for that will be a snare to you.**

Deut 7:1-4, 16 WEB (*bold emphasis added*)

These were destructive religions and cultures, and Israel was to have nothing to do with them. Their sins were those which bring destruction on a nation (yes, even to this day), and which were outlawed in Moses' Law. So there was to be no covenant with them, no intermarriage. These nations were to be totally destroyed. So it was within Israel,

> He that sacrificeth unto *any* god, save unto the LORD only, he shall be utterly destroyed. Ex 22:20 KJV

So then it was to be with the Canaanites as seen in Deut 7:2 above, or even with a city within Israel as seen in Deut 13:12-15. But it was supposed to be different with other peoples. So Deuteronomy 7 was **not** the ultimate instructions for gentiles or for warfare.

> [10] "When you approach a city to fight against it, you shall offer it terms of peace. [11] If it agrees to make peace with you and opens to you, then all the people who are found in it shall become your forced labor and shall serve you. ... [15] **Thus you shall do to all the cities that are very far from you, which are not of the cities of these nations nearby.** [16] Only in the cities of these peoples that the LORD your God is giving you as an inheritance, you shall not leave alive anything that breathes." Deut 20:10-11, 15-16 NASB (*bold emphasis added*)

So pay attention: *the rules which applied to the degenerate Canaanites did* **not** *apply to* **all** *men, not to all of the nations, not to all of the goyim!* To illustrate how the issues lay, in Numbers 12 we are told that Moses in the wilderness married a "Cushite" (Ethiopian) woman, presumably black, for which Miriam and Aaron faulted him, and God justified him.

There were other issues of course. For example, the Israelites were held by law to certain food restrictions. This would place some restraints on dealings with other nations. On the other hand, many nations have variations in dietary rules for themselves. Some do not eat meat, certain types of meat, or will not eat sushi, or this or that. Some people *cannot* or should not eat sugar or peanut butter or whatever. One can be run into such differences everyday, but these are not in themselves insurmountable barriers to enjoying a meal together. The considerate and conscientious host and the considerate and conscientious guest, deal with such issues everyday. So yes, these were to some extent barriers, but not insuperable barriers.

There were yet other barriers. For instance, a Jew was not to lend to another Jew at interest, but could lend to someone of another nation and charge interest. More is made of this than should be. As a matter of fact, most of us loan things to relatives or our own nationals on different terms than we would loan to just anyone else in the world. In Moses' Law that closeness of kinship was to extend to their entire nation. If you think about it, that too need not signify an impossible barrier to treating others right. In fact, in Moses' Law it was commanded,

> [15] One ordinance *shall be both* for you of the congregation, and also for the stranger that sojourneth *with you*, an ordinance for ever in your generations: as ye *are*, so shall the stranger be before the LORD. [16] One law and one manner shall be for you, and for the stranger that sojourneth with you. Num 15:15-16 KJV

Or again,

> [16] Circumcise therefore the foreskin of your heart, and be no more stiffnecked. [17] For **the LORD your God** ... regardeth not persons, nor taketh reward: [18] He **doth execute the judgment of the fatherless and widow, and loveth the stranger, in giving him food and raiment.** [19] **Love ye therefore the stranger:** for ye were strangers in the land of Egypt. Deut 10:16-19 KJV (*bold emphasis added*)

Traditions of the Fathers and the Gentiles.

Here is another of the places where the Old Testament denomination of Judaism parted from the Law of Moses. In their *traditions* they reduced the gentiles, the *goyim*, literally "the nations," all of them, to some sort of subhuman species. To eat with them, even to touch them, became a forbidden thing. Also **contrary to the Law of Moses**, it was acceptable to take advantage of these subhumans. After all, were not God's chosen people to inherit the entire earth? Thus when Rabbi Yehoshua spoke of a brother who has wronged you, He said first to try to talk to him, and then take along one or more witnesses, and then,

> "f he refuses to listen to them, tell it to the assembly. If he refuses to hear the assembly also, let him be to you as a Gentile or a tax collector." Mtt 18:17 WEB

Yehoshua's comments are reflecting that the Jews had nothing to do with the gentiles. But from ancient times, it was reflected in the Law and the prophets that the blessings of the Messiah were to extend to all of the earth. What did the Lord tell Abram?

> and in thee shall all families of the earth be blessed. Gen 12:3 KJV

Or again when Isaiah spoke of the Messianic reign, he says,

> [2] And it shall come to pass in the last days, *that* the mountain of the LORD'S house shall be established in the top of the mountains, and shall be exalted above the hills; **and all nations shall flow unto it.** [3] And many people shall go and say, **Come ye, and let us go up to the mountain of the LORD**, to the house of the God of Jacob; **and he will teach us of his ways**, and we will walk in his paths: for out of Zion

shall go forth the law, and the word of the LORD from Jerusalem.
Isa 2:2-3 KJV (*bold emphasis added*)

So all nations were to learn the ways of the descendants of Abraham.

Having said that, Pharisaical/Talmudic Judaism is a long way from all of this. Also the culture or sub-culture in which we are raised, though it be wrong or even evil, can often be a difficult thing to overcome. So we see the struggles of the apostle Peter, as he was trying to overcome these Judaic (not Mosaic) misconceptions in which he had been raised. They in fact mirror the struggles of many Jews down through the ages in learning to practice the truth. First, when Peter was speaking the Word of the Lord from Mount Zion by the Holy Spirit, and he preached the first sermon to the newly formed church, he spoke the truth.

> For the promise is unto you, and to your children, and to **all that are afar off**, *even* as many as the Lord our God shall call.
> Act 2:39 KJV (*bold and underlined emphasis added*)

His words said that this salvation was for ALL, and indeed it was, as Isaiah and all of the prophets pointed out. But when it came time to actually bring that salvation to the gentiles, the Lord practically had to beat Peter over the head to get him to do it. Peter fell into a trance,

> [11] He saw heaven opened and a certain container descending to him, like a great sheet let down by four corners on the earth [12] in which were all kinds of four-footed animals of the earth, wild animals, reptiles, and birds of the sky. [13] A voice came to him, "Rise, Peter, kill and eat!" [14] But Peter said, "Not so, Lord; for I have never eaten anything that is common or unclean." Acts 10:11-14 WEB

Those "crawling creatures" in the NASB are *herpeton* ἑρπετόν, literally reptiles, which are totally forbidden in the Law of Moses. But the Lord told Peter,

> A voice came to him again the second time, "What God has cleansed, you must not call unclean." Acts 10:15 WEB (*bold emphasis added*)

Peter was at a loss for what this meant, and then he was led by a series of events to the house of a Roman centurion by the name of Cornelius,

> *A* devout *man*, and one that feared God with all his house, which gave much alms to the people, and prayed to God alway. Acts 10:2 KJV

Peter is told to go there "without misgivings." Then Peter declared the conclusion of the matter.

²⁸ And he said unto them, Ye know how that it is an unlawful thing for a man that is a Jew to keep company, or come unto one of another nation; but God hath shewed me that I should not call any man common or unclean. ...

³⁴ Then Peter opened his mouth, and said, Of a truth I perceive that God is no respecter of persons: ³⁵ But in every nation he that feareth him, and worketh righteousness, is accepted with him.

Acts 10:28, 34-35 KJV

Thus began that which was the most hateful of all to that Old Testament sect called Judaism, the preaching of the gospel of the Messiah to the gentiles, to the nations of the world. They preferred their traditions of harshness to the good news of mercy to all which was, as has been shown, forecast all along in the Old Testament. But that was not the end of Peter's struggles. The tug of culture and tradition still had a hold on this man, though by inspiration he spoke the truth more than once. So you can see in Paul's letter to the Galatians in chapter two, a fine piece of Jewish hypocrisy in Peter.

¹¹ But when Peter was come to Antioch, I withstood him to the face, because he was to be blamed. ¹² For before that certain came from James, he did eat with the Gentiles: but when they were come, he withdrew and separated himself, fearing them which were of the circumcision. Gal 2:11-12 KJV

Knowing the truth, but fearing the Jews, Peter succumbed to the temptation to treat the *goyim* as unworthy and unclean! Without a doubt he was neither the first Jew nor the last one to give in to such pressure to treat gentiles as second class citizens, even to this day.

The Kabbalah and a Cosmic Superiority.

Americans are really good at congratulating themselves on how wonderful they are, but the Jews are even better at this. In Isaac Luria's Kabbala, the dominant form of kabbalistic thinking in our modern age, the good part of the human race comes from the Jews, and the evil part (who would have guessed) came from the gentiles. As Graetz summarized Kabbalistic views:

"From the most evil part of the soul material emanates the heathen world; the people of Israel, on the other hand, come from the good part." Graetz, *History of the Jews*, Vol 4, pg 620

"It is the concrete destiny of the human race, and of the Jew as the principal bearer of this mission ... to overcome this polarization from within the human condition created by the first sin.

"... Judah Halevi's metaphor ... of Israel constituting the heart of the nations was taken over by the author of Zohar and the kabbalists of

Genoa, who spoke of the Jewish people as being "the heart of the cosmic tree"" Scholem, *Kabbalah,* pg 154

There are many other Jewish sources that can be used to document these things, but one that is readily available to most Western readers is *Jewish Fundamentalism in Israel,* Israel Shahak and Norton Mezvinsky, Pluto Press, Ann Arbor, Michigan, 2004, and Shahak's *Jewish History, Jewish Religion, The Weight of Three Thousand Years,* Pluto Press, Sterling Virginia, 2002. The following quotes about Jewish scholar Israel Shahak are from the back cover of *Jewish History, Jewish Religion.* Shahak is said to be:

> "... an outstanding scholar, with remarkable insight and depth of knowledge. His work is informed and penetrating, a contribution of great value." [Jewish scholar] Noam Chomsky

> "The future of the Palestinian people would have looked much brighter if there had been more Israelis like Shahak ... An outstanding personality." *The Jerusalem Times*

> "Shahak is the latest—if not the last—of the great prophets." Gore Vidal

> "Shahak is a very brave man who should be honored for his services to humanity ... One of the most remarkable individuals in the contemporary Middle East." Edward Said

Shahak was brought up in the Warsaw Ghetto and was a survivor of the Bergen-Belsen concentration camp. His documentation of many of the values of Judaism is both scholarly and extensive. He documents that the general nature of Judaism is not really Biblical (which by the way is exactly the point Rabbi Yehoshua was making during His ministry). The rabbis feel the Bible is not authoritative unless interpreted "by talmudic literature," etc., *Jewish Fundamentalism,* pg 5. So Shahak correctly points out, and as was said here earlier, that "Judaism," i.e. Pharisaism, did not exist during what he calls "the Biblical period," (that is, prior to 586 BC), pg 2.

Of the anti-gentile attitudes of the Jews which Shahak documents, most of it is just more documentation of what Graetz and Scholem really had no choice but to admit.

> "The essence of Haredi thought is the notion of an abyss separating the Jews from the Gentiles."
> Shahak, Mezvinsky, *Jewish Fundamentalism,* pg 15

> "The anti-Gentile feeling is strongest among the most religious Jews but exists as well in this secular milieu."
> *Jewish Fundamentalism,* pg 98

The Original Kook?

Shahak tells us of leading Rabbi Avriham Yitzak Kook, the elder, (1865-1935), the Chief Rabbi of Palestine 1920-1935, who was thought by his followers to be inspired.

> "... Rabbi Kook, the Elder, the revered father of the messianic tendency of Jewish fundamentalism ... said "The difference between a Jewish soul and souls of non-Jews—all of them in all different levels—is greater and deeper than the difference between a human soul and the souls of cattle.""" *Jewish Fundamentalism*, 2004, "Preface to the New Edition," pg xix

So there is a greater difference between a Jew and a Gentile than there is between a man and a cow! His teaching was based on the the Lurianic Kabbalah which was discussed earlier and which taught that the entire world was created for the Jews. You can see that he was no marginalized fundamentalist radical. He was the Chief Rabbi of Palestine. Kook rejoiced in the death of millions of soldiers in World War I because he thought this indicated salvation was approaching for the Jews, and that the Messiah would be coming soon, *Jewish Fundamentalism*, 2004, pg xx. Clearly though, Kook is *not* speaking of Jesus of Nazareth, though this is often missed by Protestants who rejoice in the so-called "messianic Jews." (It was noted in *Prophecy Principles* that the Irish poet and occultist William Butler Yeats *also* thought the chaos following World War I would produce the beast of Revelation.) Kook seems to be identifying the State of Israel as the real kingdom of heaven on earth.

Jewish History, Jewish Religion
The Weight of Three Thousand Years

Israel Shahak

forewords by **Gore Vidal** and **Edward Said**
with a new introduction by **Norton Mezvinsky**

"A trail-blazing, double taboo-breaking piece of dynamite.
Middle East International"

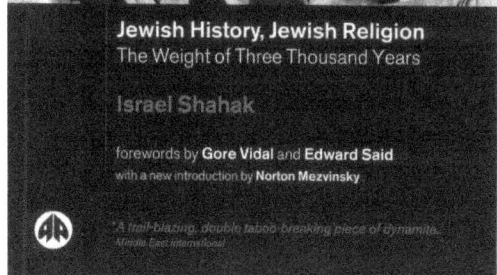

Jewish scholar Israel Shahak's *Jewish History, Jewish Religion*, is a good source for a beginning overview of Judaism in our modern world.

Shahak, in more than one of his works, compares Kook and people like him with the worst forms of Nazism, and Western European Arianism. Also Shahak and Mezvinsky admit,

> "As Jews, we understand that our own grandparents or great-grandparents probably believed in at least some of the views described in our book." *Jewish Fundamentalism* 2004, pg xx

There are two key points to make. The first is that none of this is new. This mindset was very much in place in the first century with the Pharisees and Sadducees. It was part of the culture from which Jews like the Apostles Peter, John and Paul had come. In the early centuries of the Christian age these views developed and spread in the Babylonian Talmud. The second is that a sense of superiority is not the whole story. Shahak quotes one Rabbi Aviner noting that the nations are bound by "codes of justice and righteousness," however "**such laws do not apply to Jews**." *Jewish Fundamentalism*, pg 71, *(bold emphasis added)*. Shahak speaks of the Halacha (from the Hebrew *halach* הָלַךְ, which means the walk or the way), which is the sum of the laws and traditions and customs of the sect called "Judaism"/the Pharisees, and the implications are astounding.

> "The Halacha permits Jews to rob non-Jews in those locales wherein Jews are stronger than non-Jews. The Halacha prohibits Jews from robbing non-Jews in those locales wherein the non-Jews are stronger. Gush Emunim dispenses with such traditional precautions by claiming that Jews, at least those in Israel and the Occupied Territories, are already living in the beginning of the messianic age. ... Gush Emunim rabbis have continually reiterated that Jews who killed Arabs should not be punished." *Jewish Fundamentalism*, pg 71

Allow me to point out, they are not talking about killing in warfare, but of private murders. So there is in addition *a smug sense of lawlessness among some*, that while its immediate roots are Kabbalistic, the historical roots go all the way back to Post-Babylonian-Exile Judaism. Rabbi Yehoshua documented how the Jews felt they had no obligation to help their poor aged parents, *if* they had first made sort of a "living will" of their property to the temple or the synagogue. I mean, after all, you cannot take what belongs to God and give it to your aged mom? Right? Well, that is what some of their traditions said, Mtt 15:5-9. And an oath to do something, or to tell the truth? There are all sorts of lawless but "acceptable" ways around your oaths, if you just do it right. Rabbi Yehoshua reprimanded them for these things in Matthew 23. None of this is of course just in ancient attitudes. Jewish historian Graetz noted in the 19th century, "How little value Christians attach to the oath of a Jew!" *History of the Jews*, Vol 5, pg 316. So there has been a certain sort of lawlessness in parts of Judaism going all the way back to ancient times, as has been shown, although much of the immediate modern roots go to the Kabbalah, and the modern occult groups in Judaism. Shahak then goes on to emphasize that these groups have had a profound influence on Israeli policies and notes that,

> "Ben Zion Katz explained convincingly that the above doctrines be-

came part of Hassidism." *Jewish Fundamentalism*, pg 58

These attitudes apply to most of the varieties of ultra-conservative sects of modern Judaism, but perhaps a special note on Hassidism is in line. There was a reaction against the so called "Enlightenment" among the Jews. The result, starting in the 17th century was the Hassidism, or as Jewish historian Graetz called it, "The new Chassidism." Most of the modern ultra-conservative cults in Judaism have Hassidic roots.

> "There arose in Poland **a new Essenism, with forms similar to those of the ancient cult,** with ablutions and baths, white garments, miraculous cures, and prophetic visions. Like the old movement, it originated in ultra-piety, but soon turned against its own parent, ...
>
> "... the adherents of which announced the grossest superstition to be the fundamental principle of Judaism, and formed an order of wonder-seeking confederates."
>
> Graetz, *History of the Jews,* Vol 5, pgs 374-375 (*emphasis added*)

So Graetz is relating these phenomena to the ancient Essences, and goes on to call this "Kabbalistic mysticism." In other words, **although these movements hide behind a veneer of Scripture, they are really occultist, Kabbalists, often of the rankest sort.** *If* it is accurate *at all* to call them "conservatives," then **what they have really "conserved" is the witchcraft and magic doctrines from ancient times which resulted in the first destruction of the Jewish nation in 586 BC!** Some of the fruits of this can be seen in the quotes from their modern day followers. Shahak explains the values of many Kabbalistic Jews.

> "Two contrary types of soul exist, a non-Jewish soul comes from three satanic spheres, while the Jewish soul stems from holiness."
>
> *Jewish Fundamentalism,* pg 60

In time these sorts of teachings produce calloused attitudes and have major effects on both ethics and actions. Since there was no shame to them in deceiving gentiles, the temptation to lie and then excuse themselves was often simply too great to resist. Jews at every level of society often fell prey to these vices, enough so that Jews often became the perennial con artists of note in the societies where they lived. This often added to the suspicions under which the Jews lived, much to the detriment of those Jews who tried to live in honor and integrity with the gentiles, and who refused to be involved in cheap, short-sighted, tricks. Sadly, I must add, although much of this has gone away among Jews in America, not all of it has.

Shahak speaks in some detail of the massacre of 29 Arabs (including children) and the wounding of others by medical Doctor Baruch Goldstein in 1994. Goldstein, while in the Israeli Army, had refused to treat Arabs (even those in the Israeli Army) and was never punished. Posters appeared in Israel praising Goldstein and protesting why he had not killed more Arabs. Of course, such lethal foolishness would never be tolerated in America of the 21st century. What then was Goldstein's defense? *The traditions of the Jews: the Halacha!* Shahak says that Goldstein illustrates the influence of the Jewish Fundamentalist in Israel. When radical Gush Emunim Rabbi Levinger was asked about these things, he answered: "I am sorry not only about dead Arabs but also about dead flies." *Jewish Fundamentalism*, pg 100.

There is far more here that is worthwhile to quote, but it all runs along the same lines. Shahak treats these false ideas as coming from the Kabbalah (Shahak spells it "Cabala"). That is the case, but, in its fundamentals, the Kabbalah merely continued the Jewish teachings about the intrinsic superiority of the Jews and of their right to take anything they want from the gentiles. Often they were only limited by practical matters, as whether they might get caught, or whether there might be a backlash. (And often there was.) Shahak's comment is that, "Lubovitch and other ideologies could prove to be calamitous." *Jewish Fundamentalism*, pg 62. That could turn out to be a great understatement. The Kabbalah then views Jewish superiority as something that is built into the nature of the universe, and which really cannot even be changed by conversion. **Thus the true power of the Kabbalah is *only* for the Jews** (per this point of view), though some may in condescension pass on parts of this teaching to some of the "better" gentiles. This is a point which is often missed by many gentile Kabbalists. For moderns these attitudes are easier to document by the Kabbalah, though it will not show in normal Kabbalistic literature in the bookstores. Shahak and others have noted that most of the sensitive passages in the Talmud and other Hebrew literature *have been eliminated in English translations* so as to avoid trouble with gentiles. So for the serious researcher it is often necessary to go back to the Hebrew and Yiddish sources.

Even Jewish Hostility to Jews.

It should also be recognized that some of this goes all the way down to Jews against Jews, with some groups feeling themselves much superior to others. Shahak notes that the Jews always felt they had an obligation to murder what they felt were apostate Jews. This can be seen in the New Testament in Paul's persecution of Christians, and also in the attempt to assassinate Paul in Acts chapter 23. Shahak tells us that Maimonides in his commentaries repeated the duty to kill such, and said these rules applied to all, *Jewish Fundamentalism*, pg 140. In Tsarist Russia many of the "ultra-orthodox" (often called the Hassidsor, or Chassidsor) were very zealous in putting to death secular Jews. Hundreds were drowned, *Jewish Fundamentalism*, pg 146-147. *In fact some of the radical rabbis think the Holocaust was only just punishment for many secular Jews!* Shahak documents these attitudes (*Jewish Fundamentalism*, pg 31), and they are easily documented by nearly every study of modern Jewish fundamentalism. Compare for instance Aviezer Ravitsky's *Messianism, Zionism, and*

Jewish Religious Radicalism, The University of Chicago Press, Chicago, 1996.

Finally, in the late 1800's Jewish autonomy in Eastern Europe was abolished, and the Jews too were put under Austrian, Prussian, and Russian law. Shahak says that as bad as that was, it was still probably better than the law of the rabbis. **In fact, until the late 1800's Jewish riots against other Jews may have exceeded gentile "pogroms," and indeed had many of the same characteristics,** *Jewish Fundamentalism*, pgs 132, 133.

Shahak states categorically that the Israeli government bribed the Iraqi government to seize Jewish property and strip the Jews of citizenship in order to get Iraqi Jews to migrate to Israel, *Jewish Fundamentalism*, pg 47. There are similar accusations from different points of view about the Zionists, who were mainly secular Jews. (Most Americans are *not* aware that most Jews *never were* Zionists.) So Elizur and Malkin in *The War Within, Israel's Ultra-Orthodox Threat to Democracy and the Nation*, tells about Israeli ultra-orthodox protesters carrying signs, one of which read, "THE ZIONIST WANTED THE HOLOCAUST," and another said, "IF HITLER HAD NOT EXISTED, THE ZIONISTS WOULD HAVE INVENTED HIM", pg 23. Indeed, you can find such accusations coming from several directions *within* Judaism.

I remember seeing an interview on American television a few years back with an Israeli school teacher who was wrestling with the way some African Jews were being marginalized in Israel. She was protesting, "Who are we? Who really are we?" That for sure is the key question.

Hostile and Demeaning Attitudes Toward Women.

There is not enough space to deal with all of the weird ideas that are involved in the Kabbalah and among the ultra-orthodox, but among the most demeaning are some of the attitudes towards women.

"The Haredim repeatedly refer to Jewish women, engaged in politics, as witches, bitches or demons." *Jewish Fundamentalism*, pg 37.

It is not just the Arabs, but the Israelis also have restrictions on women driving. "Women are forbidden to drive buses or taxis. They can drive private cars only if no males apart from those in their own families, or other women, are passengers. These and many other rules are followed in Haredi neighborhoods." *Jewish Fundamentalism*, pg 38. From an ultra-orthodox point of view, a man should never walk between two dogs, two pigs, or two women! That is literally taught to young males among some of the ultra-conservative Jewish sects of today in Israel. All of which has nothing to do with either the Old Testament or the New Testament. It only has to do with empty human traditions and occult theories. You can read of these things many places, including in *Jewish Fundamentalism*, pg 37-38, etc. In "Discrimination Against Women" in Israel in *The War Within*, Elizur and Malkin tell of a situation where the women literally have to ride "at the back of the bus," pgs 162-164. The authors call these and other things, "shameful practices of forced separation."

The issues of military service for all has not even been touched. The government support of ultra-orthodox men to become life-long students of the Talmud, who never have to work to support themselves or their families, and are supported by the state, and until very recently have been completely exempt from any sort of military service. *A Jewish tendency to want to avoid military service throughout history, has come back to haunt the modern state of Israel!*

So there is no real "Judeo-Christian Ethic."

Shahak says this hatred of gentiles is not really new and views it as coming from the Kabbalah. Despite that, as has been shown, these things go further back than the 12th and 13th century writing of the Kabbalah. It was pointed out in the section on "The Jewish Mob and the Unthinkable Union," that what was really unthinkable to the Jews was any union, any real equality, any fellowship, with anyone as low as a gentile, and so it has continued to some extent even to our own day. Then when you work out these principles in something like medicine, the outcomes sound like something out of a book about the Nazi concentration camp doctors.

> "The Halacha dictates that a pious Jewish doctor may treat Gentiles when his refusal to do so might be reported to the authorities and cause him or other Jews unpleasantness." *Jewish Fundamentalism*, pg 100

When Shahak speaks of the "dictates" of the Halacha, he is really showing that these things are deeper than the 12th century Kabbalah.

> "The terms "human beings" and "others" in the Halacha refer solely to Jews." *Jewish Fundamentalism*, pg 103

Shahak repeatedly points out that these things tend to be falsified in English language treatments, sometimes just by omission, but also at times by outright lying about the truth of these matters. Also, he repeatedly points out that **the truth can be readily documented in Hebrew**, *Jewish Fundamentalism*, pg 150, etc.

Thus the very insanities in early Pharisaism which Rabbi Yehoshua protested against, have come to haunt modern Israel. The bearded sages of Judaism which are seen on television, who are supposedly extremely devoted to the Law of Moses, are really devoted to kabbalistic doctrines which have very little to do with Scripture. And the secular? Shahak (who died in 2001) estimated that 25-30% of Israelis are secular, 50-55% are traditional, and 20% are "religious" (these are his terms), *Jewish Fundamentalism*, pg 7. To the side of all this is that the Kabbalah is still a pervasive influence in all of Judaism, among even the so-called "secular." For instance, the American media has talked about the Kabbalah's influence among Jewish actors, actresses, producers and directors, but clearly one would call almost all of this group "secular." Among the secular, the Kabbalah is often viewed as some sort of "higher view" of "natural law," or even as a higher view of what is really "science." So you have the incredible situation where there are many who pride themselves on being "secular" or even "anti-religious," but who cling in faith to Kabbalistic ideas, **yet who do not call their Kabbalism "religious."** This does not include all secular Jews, but such ideas are wide-spread. If you are a Jew and are reading this, you need to think out what you are seeing around you, and the ideas you are seeing expressed.

There you have the core of the claims of mainline of Judaism for the past two thousand or more years, **and the unseen culprit behind much of what is called "anti-semitism."** You cannot nurse such feelings of superiority toward others without it generating attitudes and actions which over time come to be noticed by others. Most Americans are too separated from Judaism for these things to be easily spotted, but clearly the Arabs are too close to the situation not to see these terrible attitudes for themselves.

Who then are the "whistle blowers" against the Jews? They are mainly of the Jews! Surprise! Surprise! Do you want to read the most damning condemnations of Jewish attitudes and strategies? No need to go to some "despicable" "anti-Semite" who couldn't document his way out of a wet paper bag! The most profound condemnations of the foolishness of the Jews can be fully documented from the Jews themselves, indeed, from both sides of the aisle! You can start with the condemnations of the Jewish prophets and the Old Testament, continue with the condemnations of the Jewish prophets of the New Testament (and yes, they were for the most part Jewish, as much or more than any man who has ever lived), go on to the "secular" Jews, and close with the rabbis and the Kabbalists themselves! Paul said he was, "circumcised the eighth day, of the nation of Israel, of the tribe of Benjamin, a Hebrew of Hebrews; as to the Law, a Pharisee;" Phil 3:5.

The Fifth Break: The Halacha Begins to Fade

Putting the word of man before the Word of God was the *First Break*, the preparatory break. That led directly to the *Second Break*, the fatal rejection of their own Messiah. No longer a green tree (Lk 23:31), Israel then in time entered the *Third Break*, the rejection of all nations and peoples. This was followed by the *Fourth Break*, which formalized the seeking of other spirits in the Kabbalah. Now comes the *Fifth Break*, to sever their relations with both the Word of God *and* the man-made commentaries and man-made traditions which supposedly "explained" God's Word. It was a break from the Halacha, the walk, the way. The Halacha pretended to be Scriptural, but it really superseded God's Word, it took precedence over God's Word. It was the first logical step away from God, in a man-based orientation. However to gain superiority in their dealings with gentiles, the Jews first *allowed* many to escape the Halacha. Then tasting the sweet fruits of victory over the gentiles, and the freedom from this man-made prison, more and more *wanted* to escape Pharisaism permanently. So another major break in continuity began for the Jews.

Penetrations, Separations, Limitations.

Jeremiah's advice to the Jews was to,

> 'Seek the welfare of the city where I have sent you into exile, and pray to the LORD on its behalf; for in its welfare you will have welfare.'
> Jer 29:7 NASB

Often, though, they did not do that. The Jews, all through history, have tended to complain about what they view as the gentiles irrational rejection of the Jews on equal terms. They will endlessly regale you with stories (and books) of how they have been irrationally treated as evil. *True enough, some terrible things have been done to some Jews who have done no wrong.* Even so, not *all* of this distancing between Jews and Gentiles has been the work of the nations. Take for instance the subject of military service.

The Jews were not part of any certain place, with the resulting obligations and ties, except Jerusalem, where they could not go. So they became part of every place, a truly international people, with no particular roots.

It was natural then that there was among the Jews a serious aversion to serving in the military of any of the nations, even in ancient times. Sabbath issues were always brought up, and the common worship of pagan gods among pagan troops. In this way, hatred of such service became so severe that many rulers since ancient times have excused them from military service, and this aversion has continued down to our present day. There have been many good and noble exceptions all through history, but avoiding military service was often the pattern and was another block and barrier to the acceptance of the Jews. The Jews wanted the protection which troops could provide, but did not want to pay their dues, do their part. This provided another source of antagonism. This can be seen even in the twentieth century. An easy to see example is in Chaim Weizmann's problems with the Russian Jews in England. Weizmann was trying to get the British to guarantee a national home for the Jews in Palestine and was meeting with considerable success. The British were hurting for troops, but Weizmann had a terrible time getting Russian Jew refugees in England to volunteer for service even in the Middle East! This is documented at length in *Chaim Weizmann, The Making of a Statesman*, by Jehuda Reinharz, Oxford University Press, NY, London, 1993, pgs 176ff, etc. So the Jews would frequently claim full allegiance to a nation in which they happened to dwell, but would with all artfulness decline to defend those peoples to whom they claimed faithfulness. There have been exceptions of course. Many Jews served in the Allied armed forces during World War II, and these things are well documented in places like *A Historical Atlas of the Jewish People.* You can also see it other times and places. Rabbi Leo E. Turitz and Evelyn Turitz in their *Jews in Early Mississippi*, University Press of Mississippi, Jackson, Mississippi, 1995, commented on Jews in the South during the American Civil War.

> "In their former European lands of oppression Jews actually sought to avoid conscription by any means; yet here in the South they fought willingly and with zest." pg xxi

They go on to mention notable examples. Even so, the odds are good, if you have Jewish friends in the United States of today, that they and their sons have avoided military service, so far as possible, even in the wars which they think America should have fought, and in which the state of Israel has been the major benefactor. (Iraq and Afghanistan have definitely not *benefited* from these wars of the early twenty-first century! Nor has the United States, with the exception of the Military-Industrial Complex.) In many Jewish eyes, dying for some gentile country to which they claim allegiance is in general terms something for the golems, the stupid goyim, to do. Much of this slowly began to change in the 19th century, as Jewish leaders realized that to get the penetration into society which they desired, they must also accept even the most extreme of risks, even that of death in a goyim war.

Thus the Jews often complain that no nation would accept them. Instead, many a nation would and *has* accepted the Jews, *but the Jews would not, could not, accept the nations!* They were *better* than the nations. They figured these dumb clucks were just for plucking. So after a while, when the initially sympathetic nations saw how they were truly regarded, rage and indignation arose, and the animosity was mutual.

Then came unintended consequences: discrimination became a liability. The Jews discovered they could achieve much more power, if they *are not* recognized as a separate group with extraordinary privileges. The Marranos proved beyond question the leverage to be gained by not being such a distinct and separate group. So the spirit of the Marranos became a dominating spirit in Judaism. But to have this power, the rabbis had to risk losing their tight-fisted control of ordinary Jews. It was and is, in part, a great contest between the spirit of the Marranos and the spirit of Pharisaical Judaism. The spirit of the Marranos won in the great "illumination," the great "Enlightenment" as many called it. All of this being true, there were still other factors working to destroy what is really Pharisaism, and some of these things had been working for a long time in Judaism.

Quite often the Jews have been unwilling to admit that the reason for many of their civil disabilities was the result of some behaving like predatory foreigners instead of as loving friends and neighbors. Their often-observed willingness to mercilessly fleece the goyim, almost always ended up being noticed and marked and left that characteristic bad taste in the mouth of others. It must be said, *many*, perhaps *most,* among the Jews have *all along* dealt with their gentile acquaintances in a fair and honest manner, but also often bore the repercussions of the bad behavior of parts of the Jewish community. Clearly *not all of this* has been an issue of gentile stupidity and ignorance. There has been enough fault to go around.

The most modern forms of all of this are well represented by the modern Kooks, father and son rabbis. They are the twentieth and twenty-first century face of what has for 2200 years been an issue: a Jewish hostility and contempt toward **all** gentiles. ***This is the root and branch of the Jew versus Gentile conflict.*** It is a sad story. Many have sought to be the friends of the Jews or to convert them to less hostile ways. Really though, this can only be changed by Rabbi Yehoshua, their great prophet ... when He is ready.

Venice and the Ghetto?

One of the big mysteries to many people, including many Jews, is the ghetto. What sort of malicious hatred was it that caused the gentiles to so hate the Jews, so despise them, that they would not even allow them to live among the gentiles! I mean, we can understand disliking someone, but to despise them to such an extent that it requires total isolation? Where did this start? Venice is the answer.

With all of their problems in various places, including with the Catholic church, the Jews seemed overall to get along very well with the papacy. Historian Will Durant in his volume *The Age of Faith* paints a picture of some popes who were very tolerant of the Jews. Similarly, Jewish historian Graetz repeatedly points out that the popes, like many princes and kings of the times, were always in need of money. So as long as the Jews had money, which because of their trading and their banking they generally had, and so long as they were willing to spread some of it around, the Jews were welcome, and even accorded a measure of protection. Graetz speaks of Duarte de Paz, a Maranno himself. (Should he be called an ambassador for the Marranos? Or a lobbyist? Or just an "influence peddler"?)

> "His clients, the Marranos, kept him well supplied with money, which, for good or evil, was almighty at the pope's court."
> *History of the* Jews, Vol 4, pg 513

For a while, the Popes even suspended the Spanish Inquisition, and Graetz even speaks of,

> "... the old school of worldly-minded, diplomatic, by no means bigoted,

princes of the church." Vol 4, pg 515

Graetz speaks especially of Paul III who was particularly favorable toward the Jews, and notes that he had a personal Jewish physician "who dedicated some of his works to him," Vol 4, pg 515. Unfortunately for the Marranos, the money ran out before the palms to be greased ran out. Even so, as has been noted, this area of the Mediterranean never had the scale of disasters, as say, Spain, Poland, or Germany for the Jews.

Venice though was a different place. Venice was all about putting together cartels/monopolies and raking off "millions," to put it in the American vernacular. Personal feelings? Morality? Venice made an outward show of Christianity, but, at the end of the day, money, not morals, mattered to the Venetian oligarchy. Historian Will Durant notes that sometimes the Venetians sold even *Christian* slaves to the Mohammedans, *The Age of Faith*, pg 454.

> ""We are Venetians, after that we are Christians." ... Venetian merchants sold arms and slaves, and sometimes military intelligence, to Moslems at war with Christians." Durant, *The Age of* Faith, pg 711

Both the Jews and the Mohammedans could freely come and go in Venice. So how did all of this come about? The Jews could obviously prosper in such a non-Christian environment, and they did. The ghetto and its name came from Venice, where the Jews were first officially set apart. For a detailed treatment from a Jewish point of view, see Jewish historian Cecil Roth, *Personalities and Events in Jewish History*, Philadelphia, Jewish Publication Society, 1953, which has a chapter on the ghetto, pgs 226-236. The Jews there "controlled a great part of the maritime trade of Venice—particularly that with the Levant, which owed its prosperity to them," *Personalities*, pg 240. So also even the mighty Turks owed their "prosperity to them." Of the Jewish "ghetto" of Venice and their bankers, Roth writes,

> "The variety of pledges which Venetian Jews accumulated in their hands in the course of business was bewildering. All the treasures of palaces along the Grand Canal ... sometimes succumbed to the magnet of the Ghetto." *Personalities*, pg 240-241

But in such a cutthroat environment Venice was also very zealous of money *for herself*. Sharp deals which cut against Venice were often dealt with very severely. Venice had secrecy laws for trade whose penalties reached all the way to capital punishment. Durant, *The Renaissance*, pg 313.

So the Jews also had a many ups and downs with the Venetians. At times the Jews were banned from the city, but later things were patched up and they were all back in business together. But *no one* really talks about the reason for the ghetto. Although it is unspoken, it is plain. The rabbis were still in control of the Jewish population, and their discipline was strict and severe, as has been shown. So when a Jew attempted to escape from this Pharisaical tyranny, the

Jews had deals in place with many gentile rulers to discipline and punish their own. In this way the gentiles generally stood aside when such things were to be done. It might be merely pursuit and discipline: perhaps fines, or penance, or even cutting off a nose or an ear, literally. Sometimes, however, it meant the murder of the errant brother by assassins, as was noted and is clearly documented in the New Testament in the trial of Paul in Jerusalem. Obviously, at this point the Jews often (but not always) had to clear their dealings with the ruling gentile authorities. But there were other things which were also noticed. The rabbis did not pursue *everyone* who left Judaism! Curious! Then the authorities began to look at the situation more closely.

On one hand, most can sympathize with someone trying to escape the rabbinical tyranny they were under. Here was the equivalent of a multi-volume encyclopedia of nit-picking rules that everyone had to follow (the Talmud). Some of it was convenient if you wanted to sin, and there was *always* a way to sin while observing the letter (but not the spirit) of the laws and traditions. Some of it was near laughable, but it was no laughing matter. Some of it might be considered insane in almost any other context, but mostly it was just ridiculously burdensome, and without any real point as far as the Law of Moses itself was actually concerned, as Rabbi Yehoshua repeatedly pointed out.

For instance, you are not supposed to work on the sabbath day. That is Moses' Law. What does that mean? The rabbis had an answer. There were thirty-nine classes of actions which were forbidden, including for instance, bearing a burden. What is a burden? The answer: it is picking two dried figs, or more, on the sabbath day. Or take one which weighs on Judaism to this day. There is the command,

> "You shall not boil a young goat in its mother's milk." Ex 34:26b

So we have another command *of which I have no doubt*, "Yes, for our sake it was written" (1Cor 9:10); to teach us principles of justice and righteousness and equity, but which would seldom be encountered in real life, either then or now. On the other hand, the rabbis would argue, how do you know whether the cream you are about to put in the sauce for the meat, did not the come from cow who bore the calf you are eating? Thus we enter a hairsplitting rabbinical field day with the conclusion (supposedly based on Ex 34:26 above) that one must *never* eat meat or milk products together! Are there cheeseburgers for instance, in the worldly Valhalla of the orthodox Jews? No, is the answer, and this is the foundation of the dual kitchens (one side for milk products and the other side for meat products) of kosher Jews, to this day. And so it goes, on and on and on and on into absurdity. Many Jews *did and do* want to escape all of this *human* foolishness, which is not really from Moses' Law, but from human traditions. The Jews and the Jewish historians do not really want to admit the real numbers of the losses.

Still the problem persists: the rabbis pursued some of the errant tenaciously, viciously, you might even say rabidly. Others ... well they seemed to just let them go. Why? Perhaps some of that also is understandable. Here is some shlemiel about whom *no one* cares. We just do not have the time or money to chase him. Good riddance! Let the gentiles have him. But others might even be noteworthy, like Esther in the book of Esther for instance, who also are not pursued. Why? Then the gentile authorities noticed some other things about the Jews. The Jews had considerable skill in infiltrating their enemies, and, on occasion, undermining them. These things have been widely known for literally millennia. Some, like Haman in the book of Esther, have found out the hard way. Others though have noticed these skills, honed over centuries. So the ex-Pharisee Paul the apostle noted,

> And *this occurred* because of false brethren secretly brought in (who came in by stealth to spy out our liberty which we have in Christ Jesus, that they might bring us into bondage), Gal 2:4 NKJV

As a former Pharisee, who had acted under orders to imprison and put to death those who varied from the halacha, Paul knew well the strategies they employed. So Paul states categorically that the Jewish high-command had infiltrated Christianity early with the purpose of drawing it back into Pharisaism. Others, all along, have also noticed such things, and it was not just about religious disputes, but quite often it was clearly about political infiltration and scheming.

So what to do? No doubt many a gentile prince looked with dismay on these machinations and carefully listened to his native intelligence advisors. On one hand, he may have wanted to protect (to the extent he could) some poor Jewish soul just wanting to escape all of this deadly foolishness, just out of a sense of justice and human decency. On the other hand, he *had* made deals with the Jews, and he was *supposed* to deliver the errant to the rabbis. Furthermore, his kingdom *did* need the trade which the Jews brought, which he could not easily replace. Then beyond this, the Jews had materially added to his own treasury! What then to do?

And What was Venice's Answer?

Isolate them! Yes, we need their trade, their skills, and their connections. No, we cannot risk political or religious infiltration. Isolate them! Let the Jews live and trade here but keep them apart and well identified to block as much as possible their incredible skills in infiltration. And the well meaning who just want to escape this religio-political-merchant tyranny? They said in effect, "To hell with them. We are in this for money and cannot afford the risk. *We*, anyway, will not help them escape!" So the ghetto was first born in Venice. Over time this solution appealed to more and more dominions. And oh yes, did we mention? **This was also acceptable to the rabbis.** *It made escape from their grasp even harder for the average Jews.* Yes, acceptable. All around! For centuries.

The fact of the voluntary nature of much of this is documented from time to time in various sources. Chaim Weizmann spoke of the old Yishuv in Palestine in the early 1900's as living "immured behind the walls of a ... ghetto **of their own making**, and stronger than any which an enemy could have erected ..." *Trial and Error*, pg 229 (*emphasis added*). The same could be said of many of the Hasidim in modern Israel. Again in a picture closer to our modern world, he speaks of modern Italian Jews (early 1920's), as living peaceably, partially assimilated and some 15,000 (out of 50,000) in "a **voluntary ghetto** in Rome," pg 286 (*emphasis added*).

It is a testament to the ingenuity of men, that so many Jews, despite such tremendous barriers, still managed to escape. Some of the numbers will be discussed later, but clearly many could and did escape.

Lessons Learned from the Marranos

Two things then made some very deep impressions on Judaism. Somewhere in the late 1700's the Jews in Europe came to see how awesome was the power to be gained by the Jews if they infiltrated the West *en masse*, rather than in part, as had been the practice. The Marranos had moved on to other countries.

> "Under the guise of Spanish or Portuguese merchants, they founded large communities in Bordeaux, Amsterdam, London, and in various parts of Italy. From their step-fatherland they brought with them a higher culture and an aristocratic demeanor. Consequently they did not suffer from the contempt with which other Jews were treated in political and social circles. In fact, the Jews of Marrano descent looked down upon their co-religionists as gypsies, on account of their external deterioration." Graetz, *History of the Jews*, Vol 5, pg 729

Did they meet with some rejection? Yes? How did they respond?

> "Christian society refused to recognize them as Germans, and, therefore, they desired to show, by stripping off their original garb, that they were Germans, naught but Germans, and kept up only a distant connection with Judaism." Graetz, Vol 5, pg 628

The history of the Marranos was the irrefutable tell-tale evidence of how much was to be gained, and in most countries it would not involve the risks which the Marranos sustained in Spain and Portugal. This clearly involved breaking bonds of traditional Pharisaic/Talmudic/Rabbinic barriers to assimilating with the gentiles. It also meant loosening the strangle-hold of the orthodox rabbis on the great body of the Jewish people. The debate was fierce, as it always is among the Jews, but the decision was made and began to be implemented by around 1800. Some say the changes followed the outline of the pronouncements of the so-called "Great Sanhedrin" invoked by Napoleon

Bonaparte, February 9 to March 9, 1807. Jewish historian Cecil Roth points out that when the Nazis started trying to sort all of this out, they viewed all Jewish conversions to Christianity as false if they had occurred *after* 1800 (Cecil Roth, *Personalities And Events In Jewish History*, pg 49). The "Enlightenment" among the Jews won and received acceptance even by many of the rabbis and carried with it the start of mass Jewish assimilation into gentile societies. *This is a story that has had both **good and evil** effects for **both** Jews and **gentiles**, a story that is by no means over.

The second lesson which the Jews learned from the Marranos' experience was of a more fearsome nature. It was the awesome power to break up enemies and to enforce compliance with authority of a totally ruthless and immoral terrorist weapon like the Inquisition. Both of these things made deep impressions on the Jewish psyche.

Despite a great deal of Jewish propaganda to the contrary, the malice of others has not been the undoing of the Jews, nor has it been their mistakes which have so often caused hostility. Rather, it has often been their successes which have been their nemesis.

Moses Mendelssohn and the Great Coup.

Because of top-down controls, just as we see in the New Testament and reflecting the Jewish establishment's conflict with Rabbi Yehoshua and his followers, the Jews have often been a negative force in the world, a force of accelerated decay in both their "friends" and their foes. But it does not have to be that way. Gentile historian Will Durant also speaks of the desire of many Jews to free themselves from these compulsions based solely on human traditions. He tells us that,

> "Now at the height of his fame and influence Mendelssohn persuaded Marcus Herz to translate into German that Vindication of the Jews which Manasseh ben Israel had addressed to the English people in 1656. To the translation he added a preface on "The Salvation of the Jews" (1782), in which he pleaded with the rabbis to abandon their right of excommunication." *Rousseau and Revolution*, pg 640

So the battle was joined with Moses Mendelssohn (1728-1786) almost unwillingly, almost unwittingly it would seem, in the lead.

Many things had happened. Jewish historian Heinrich Graetz does acknowledge that all of the Talmudic hair-splitting "had sharpened their intelligence," *History of the Jews*, Vol 5, pg 335. But he also points out that "The air of the Ghettos was impregnated with Kabbala." pg 236. Last then but not least, Graetz noticed that,

> "Rabbinical and Kabbalistic expositors had so distorted the simple biblical sense of the words, that everything was found in it except the

actual contents." Vol 5, pg 328

Jewish writer Walter Laqueur points out (1972) that even many liberal Jews thought the Jews *needed* the ghetto to survive, *A History of Zionism*, pg 7.

So although there were many things which were negative in the Jewish situation and education, some exceptional things had happened in their development. There are many good things to say about Mendelssohn and his influence on the Jews. Graetz obviously admires him and devotes considerable space to talking about these events. There is much to say, and a great deal of it has to do with good things which developed. Jewish leader Lucien Wolf, whom we quoted earlier, gives this account.

> "A hundred years ago a new hope dawned in Jewry. Its objective was indicated by the famous treatise "Über die bürgerliche Verbesserung der Juden," written at the instance of Moses Mendelssohn by Christian Wilhelm Dohm. Its means were illustrated by Mendelssohn himself in his still more famous translation of the Bible into classical German. These two works pointed the way to the new life. They virtually bade the Jews accept their dispersion as, humanly speaking, an irrevocable fact, and to give the only possible logical effect to it by demanding political rights and social incorporation at the hands of the nations among whom the inscrutable accidents of history had distributed them. At the same time **they recognized that the success of emancipation largely depended on the Jews themselves**, and ... that **the new departure** established itself almost without the consciousness of a wrench." (*The Jewish Quarterly Review*, Vol XVII, Macmillan And Co., NY, 1905, pgs 4-5. (*bold emphasis added*)

I called this "The Fifth Break." **Wolf calls it "the new departure."** Wolf described the change this way in a letter of August 31, 1916, to James Rothschild.

> "... the plan of political and social assimilation as accepted by the Jewish people over a hundred years ago, has a record of splendid achievement to its credit." Jehuda Reinharz, *Chaim Weizmann ...* , Oxford University Press, NY, 1993, pg 101

Rabbi Louis Finklestein in his *The Pharisees, The Sociological Background of Their Faith*" Vol I, 1938, says more simply that Mendelssohn was "the creator of a renewed synthesis between traditional Judaism and the learning of the West." pg xxii. To summarize,

> "The **beginning of the outward liberation of the Jews from the cruel bondage of thousands of years** was also connected with Mendelssohn's name, and like his activity for their internal freedom was unconscious, without violence or calculation." Graetz, *History of the Jews*, Vol 5, pg 336 (*bold emphasis added*)

What then was Pharisaical-Talmudic-Rabbinic Judaism? According to Graetz it was **"... the cruel bondage of thousands of years ..."** On Mendelssohn's part much of this effect "was unconscious" but nevertheless dramatic. What then are the points which I am making? They are four.

One is that here is **a real break in the tyrannical control of the rabbis over the Jews overall, and their ability to discipline and control with and for the Halacha**, a control which has been continuous since pre-Christian times, as has been documented. There were additional factors, including the weakening of Poland as the then center of Talmudic Judaism, in part because of the partitioning of Poland by the Russians in the late 1700's.

Two, all to the side of Mendelssohn, as far as I can tell, this also opened the way for a massive double-edged "assimilation" of the Jews into gentile culture and society, especially in the West.

Three, the initial net effect was to visibly loosen the adherence of Western Jews to Halacha. The *first* break was from the Word of God to let the words and the traditions of men rule. The result was the Halacha, a mixture of God's laws, men's traditions, and men's words. *Next* was rejecting and murdering their own Messiah. *Then* came the rejection of all gentiles, and *then* began the formalizing of the pursuit of other spirits with the Kabbalah. *Now* there is a break from this Halacha, this body of human traditions.

Four, the end results of assimilation and the the abandonment of the Halacha are still being sorted out in our own time, over two centuries later, *especially* in the land of Israel itself. For an early 21st century view of the status of these struggles within the modern state of Israel, and a resurgence of Talmudism, see *The War Within, Israel's Ultra-Orthodox Threat to Democracy and the Nation*, Elizur, and Malkin. Also see the works of Israel Shahak.

Jewish author Walter Laqueur calls assimilation, "self-surrender for the sake of a higher, trans-historical goal," *A History of Zionism*, pg 37. Laqueur and others do not say it outright, but obliquely acknowledge that much of the purpose of assimilation was political.

There is also another factor in Jewish "assimilation." This is a point which is missed by many gentile observers, that Jewish ancestry is only counted through the mother. What? Only through whom? Yes, you heard right, only through the mother.

This is quite contrary to most gentile thinking. The tendency is to count "real" descendants as only through the father. In this thinking, it is only the male line that counts. If you are a descendant of some person through the male line, *then* we tend to count descent as "real." Not everyone does this, but that is the common in many places.

But that is not the way it is with the Jews. So when Israeli journalist Tom Segev in *Elvis in Jerusalem* (Metropolitan Books, Henry Holt, NY, 2002), is speaking of who is legally a Jew in Israel today, he says that the court decisions in Israel have been made that "Jewish affiliation is awarded **only to people with Jewish mothers**, or those who have been converted to Judaism by an Orthodox rabbinical court." pg 89 (*bold emphasis added*). Strange to many of us of the nations, no doubt, but this is in line with the Halacha of many centuries.

Then come some additional questions. How did this come about? The explanations I have heard go along this line: The key to really being Jewish is being raised by a Jewish mom. It is the mothers who do most of the actual raising of the children, and that is what counts. True, you may have a Jewish father, but he is away at work. He often has little influence on the raising of the children, but if you have a Jewish mom, *that* is what really makes you a Jew. Or to think differently about it, it is the seed of woman (Gen 3:15) that counts in this case.

But so what? What does all of this mean for the subject under discussion, in our case of crypto-Jews and assimilation? This means that our subject may have what seems a perfectly Jewish name, a name like for instance: Goldberg, or Goldfarb, or Bronstein or whatever, but he may not *really* be Jewish at all. It is not his last name that counts (although that might indeed be an indicator). *Rather, does he have a Jewish mother?*

Then comes the final point. Where intermarriage is involved, the one who is *really* Jewish may have a name like Smith, or Jones, Carpenter or whatever, *but may really be Jewish* or a crypto-jew, an unrecognized Jew. His dad may be a gentile, but if his mother (or his grandmother on his mother's side) was Jewish, then he or she is actually counted as Jewish!

So by this standard, any descendants of the Persian King Xerxes by his Jewish wife Esther? They would be Jewish by these standards!

Then one can see things like "Irish-Catholic" presidential candidate John Kerry. In 2003 the *Boston Globe* ran a lengthy piece in which they suddenly found out that Kerry had Jewish ancestry through his mother's side! Wha-Lah! John Kerry is really Jewish, not a gentile! The article would have meant little to most gentiles, but to the broad Jewish readership in the north east this would emphatically mean that Kerry is Jewish, which Kerry's political advisors wished to make known!

Which brings up another point: that assimilation and crypto-Judaism has gone so far in the United States and many other places that *many Jews* do not recognize all of the crypto-Jews around them. So if a crypto-Jew like John Kerry is running for president, even the Jews might need to have him pointed out to them as Jewish! Similar things have happened concerning other contemporary leaders like Hillary Clinton, Howard Dean, General Wesley Clark, Joseph Liberman, and many others. These sorts of things are going on all the time, but most do not notice. Part of the standard for outing yourself as "really" Jewish seems to be whether they are sure that any gentile intelligence agencies concerned already know these things.

So some of this indeed means really deep cover.

How Deep, How Far Back, and How Loyal?

Then one comes to another issue in sending covert representatives into alien societies, that of maintaining resources and integrity undercover. It should be admitted that these are difficult issues.

Here is the key issue: if a person is good at infiltrating a foreign society, it is generally because they have come to appreciate the good facets of that society. In fact, if an infiltrator is *unable* to appreciate what is good about a foreign society, then *he probably* will not be able to successfully carry out his or her role in that society. If the whole society being infiltrated is implicitly distasteful to the infiltrator, he or she will probably not have the stomach to carry out their role of being assimilated, and will perhaps be *fatally* compromised. As a side point, generally speaking there are almost always some positive sides to even the most corrupt societies, and that is why those societies continue to stand before the Lord our God.

As a curious point then, good operatives, because they are able to appreciate what is good about their target group, they often become better citizens of that group *than the natives!* They have none of the qualms of the natives about systematically applying these good characteristics to everything in that society or group. Also generally speaking, the Jews have an excellent record of being *able* to become one with other societies. Jewish writers often note that in Germany the Jews became 110% German, in the United States they became 110% American, or in England 110% English. *The agents **often** look better than the actual natives do!*

However, if the successful infiltrator *does appreciate* what is good about a target society, there is a special danger: that the infiltrator appreciates the foreign society so much, *that he or she decides to change sides!* **They decide to change their allegiance to that society in which they initially were only trying to hide!** It is as if they come to say, "Wait a minute! Why am trying to undermine such good people? I love these people. Why would I want to hurt them?"

This is a common problem faced by intelligence agencies the world over in placing agents in foreign societies. If their agents are really good at what they do, then they have a greater likelihood of "going over to the other side," or as it is sometimes put, as "going native." As Napoleon sarcastically put it, "The spy is a natural traitor."

Sometimes these things happen on a small scale, and other times such things can even happen *en masse!* Perhaps, T. E. Lawrence (of "Lawrence of Arabia" fame), and the love he came to have for Arab society, and his disillusionment at their being mistreated in the finale of World War I, is a good example of these things. So there is more than one issue involved in Jewish success in gentile lands.

Also uncommented on by almost all, both Jew and Gentile, has been the historic Jewish ability to both hide and move great amounts of money, enough money at times to rescue kings and princes and nations! Such things are easier in our modern world, than even in the recent historical past. It has indeed often been massive amounts of money. Graetz tells the story of the Jews loaning William III the money for his take-over of the English crown. It was to be an easy, bloodless, revolution. But even bloodless revolutions require large amounts of money. William III offered to sign a note. The Jewish money lender Baron de Gras declined.

> "Isaac (Antonio) Suasso, created Baron Alvernes de Gras by Charles II, of Spain, was able to advance to William III, for his semi-adventurous expedition to London to obtain the English crown, two million florins without interest, with the simple words, "If you are fortunate, you will repay them to me; if not, I am willing to lose them.""
> Graetz, Vol 5, pg 205

This ability to accumulate and then secure such large amounts of money has alone been no small feat. Kings could accumulate great amounts of money, and they had armies and fortifications to defend their winnings, but they also had to support and maintain those fortifications and armies. This is about huge amounts of money from trade and exchanges, money for which all sorts of rascals would gladly torture or kill, and which the Jews were able to disperse and hide, and still bring to bear at the proper times for trade or rescue. There have been plenty of losses from accidents or war or extortion, as is seen from time to time in history. More than one bandit and more than one European prince has held a wealthy Jew for ransom, even as in our own times. Still, their ability to maintain and move such wealth in hostile environments is a tribute to their abilities in clandestine environments. This, in turn, is related to the entire subject of the crypto-Jews.

Sometimes insights into some of these things come from unlikely sources. In our case from the book *The Bible in Spain, OR, THE JOURNEYS, ADVENTURES, AND IMPRISONMENTS OF AN ENGLISHMAN IN AN ATTEMPT TO CIRCULATE THE SCRIPTURES IN THE PENINSULA,* by George Borrow, John Murray, London, 1923.

The first edition of this book was in 1842. In the Preface (written Nov. 26, 1842), the author, George Borrow tells of being sent to Spain by "the Bible Society" to be "distributing the Scripture." He was evidently a "Jewish Protestant" (?), but that is only by implication. He speaks of "others who wrought good service in the Gospel cause." He speaks of editing "the Spanish New Testament at Madrid." He obviously loves Spain and attributes her faults during the 15th to 18th centuries to Catholicism. Mr. Borrow writes in the style of an adventure travelogue.

Jewish   historian   Cecil   Roth   in   his   *A*   *History of the Marranos*, which has been referred to earlier, speaks disparagingly of Borrow as "an imaginative purveyor of the Bible in Spain," and of "the exuberant fancy of the author," pgs 358-359. I would conclude that Roth knows that the author is of Jewish descent, but that by implication. Finally, Roth says, "There is perhaps more in it than was at one time thought; and it is worth while to cite it at length; —" and then goes on to quote about 3 pages worth of what is a 6 page description in the original. Obviously Roth's reluctant conclusion is that the passage is authentic. The following includes parts Roth quotes, and parts which he does *not* quote. Earlier Cecil Roth was quoted to the point that there were *many* **genuine** conversions of the Jews to Catholicism during the period of the Spanish Inquisition. But George Borrow tells in detail of a meeting *in 1835* with a Marrano while traveling in Spain. The word "Marrano" though never occurs in the passage, nor does the word "Jew" or "Jewish." It is all by implication, and one can only wonder at what some readers must have thought of the passage under consideration.

Now the Spanish Inquisition was established in 1478. The Jews were formally cast out of Spain in 1492 (the same year that Jewish [?] explorer Christopher Columbus discovered America), and the Inquisition ferociously sought out and ground up crypto-Jews into the middle 1660's. Roth says that by this time "crypto-Judaism had been almost completely suppressed." *Marranos*, pg 283. This story in contrast is almost two-hundred years later, two-hundred years *after* they were "completely suppressed."

There was some interaction between Borrow and the Marrano, and then the crypto-Jewish man said, "Are you then *one of us?*" Then at the last of their visit the Marrano says, "**Let us, therefore, pass the day together in communion, like brothers,** and then proceed on our separate journeys." Borrow, pgs 155, 161 (*emphasis added*).

The Spanish Marrano in the passage is a polygamist. He actually has two wives but passes off one of them as sort of a concubine, or you might say, a mistress, "my *amiga*, for appearance sake." In the story which continues, his being a crypto-Jew is sort of an open secret. He and his family and those associated with him pretend to be faithful Catholics, and he and his family pretend to be poor, but the astute in the community know better. The picture painted here is of a rich Marrano family living discretely among Catholic neighbors, with both his real identity and his wealth being at least suspected by some, and their money being surreptitiously used as needed to secure their safety.

> "*Myself.*—Are you known for what you are? Do the authorities molest you ?

> "*Abarbenel*—People of course suspect me to be what I am; but as I conform outwardly in most respects to their ways, they do not interfere with me. True it is that sometimes, when I enter the church to hear the

mass, they glare at me over the left shoulder, as much as to say "What do you here?" And sometimes they cross themselves as I pass by; but as they go no further, I do not trouble myself on that account. With respect to the authorities, they are not bad friends of mine. Many of the higher class have borrowed money from me on usury, so that I have them to a certain extent in my power; and as for the low *alguazils* and *corchetes*, they would do anything to oblige me, in consideration of a few dollars which I occasionally give them; so that matters upon the whole go on remarkably well." pgs 158-159

Then in the tradition of the Pharisees or the synagogue of Satan, he says,

"The truth is, that our family has always known how to guide itself wonderfully. **I may say there is much of the wisdom of the snake amongst us.** We have always possessed friends ; and with respect to enemies, **it is by no means safe to meddle with us,** for it is **a rule of our house never to forgive an injury, and to spare neither trouble nor expense in bringing ruin and destruction upon the heads of our evil-doers."** pg 159 (*bold emphasis added*)

He goes on to tell how he had some, who decided to mess with him, thrown into prison and to die there. There is really no religious head for them in the country, but there are certain "holy families" and holy men. Then he speaks of certain Marranos as *still* infiltrating the clergy.

"*Myself.*–What you say surprises me. Have you reason to suppose that many of you are to be found amongst the priesthood?

"*Abarbenel*–Not to suppose, but to know it There are many such as I amongst the priesthood, and not amongst the inferior priesthood either; some of the most learned and famed of them in Spain have been of us, or of our blood at least, and many of them at this day think as I do. There is one particular festival of the year at which four dignified ecclesiastics are sure to visit me; and then, when all is made close and secure, and the fitting ceremonies have been gone through, they sit down upon the floor and curse." pg 160

In the account given by Borrow, the crypto-Jews are mainly hiding in small groups in small towns, with any domestic servants also being Jews and often finally marrying into the families. And the money? Oh yes, the money? What were some of the ways of securing it? How was it hidden and maintained? The Marrano in George Borrow's book does ply a trade, but only half-heartedly. He is wealthy enough that he does not have to work.

"*Myself.*–You say you are wealthy. In what does your wealth consist?

"*Abarbenel*–In gold and silver, and stones of price; for I have inherited all the hoards of my forefathers. The greater part is buried underground; indeed, I have never examined the tenth part of it. I have coins of silver and gold older than the times of Ferdinand the Accursed and Jezebel; I have also large sums employed in usury. We keep ourselves close, however, and pretend to be poor, miserably so; but on certain occasions, at our festivals, when our gates are barred, and our savage dogs are let loose in the court, we eat our food off services such as the Queen of Spain cannot boast of, and wash our feet in ewers of silver, fashioned and wrought before the Americas were discovered, though our garments are at all times coarse, and our food for the most part of the plainest description." pgs 157-158

Astonishingly this is nearly two hundred years *after* the Inquisition had won, and had rooted "*all*" of the Jews out of Spain! Wow! Jewish historian Cecil Roth is similarly impressed and goes on to say,

> "In spite of these **and similar revelations**, nothing reached the outside world which made it appear that any trace of the Marranos had survived beyond the first decades of the nineteenth century, at the latest." *Marranos*, pg 361 (*bold emphasis added*)

Also Roth well documents how difficult it is to maintain religious fidelity under such conditions, and how much of "proper" doctrine and ritual become severely degraded.

For comparison, look at European powers, both friends and foes, who have had the opportunity to continuously infiltrate the United States since the early days in the late 1700's, and still have the need to send fresh crops of agents. You do not need to be in FBI counterintelligence to see these things in America today. You just need to read the papers, or maybe even to just look around, depending on where you are.

If you are making comparisons, there are actually very few comparisons to Jewish survival "undercover," or as Jewish authors often put it, as "crypto-Jews." "Human intelligence" (HUMINT, as the intelligence world puts it) is about the information which humans can directly collect, as opposed to, for instance, electronic intelligence, etc. In the area of human intelligence, depth of coverage means everything. That is to say, how far back were you able to infiltrate this society or group, and are your agents still trustworthy? Is it further back than any of the members of the target group can remember? In the area of "human intelligence," *no one* can match the depth of the Jews.

So if you were trying to gauge the degree of "assimilation" of Jews into gentile America, what would you say? What can you say? My personal estimate is that half or more of the Jews of Europe and America are so called "crypto-Jews," that is to say, they are not *readily* recognized as Jews. So if you take at face value Silbiger's figure that 2% of the population of the United States is Jewish, this estimate would mean that there is another 2% of Jews who are, to some degree or another, "under cover" or crypto-Jews.

What then would be the nature of these crypto-Jews? I think it would include all sorts, from the lily-white innocent, to the miscreant. Some of these would be children of a Jewish mother and a Gentile father, children who really favor their mother's religion. Some would be those who do not advertise their Jewishness. Many (but not all) of these would readily admit such if it came up, and so on. Some would be those who are drifting away from Judaism and would like to forget their Jewish ancestry, but are an unknown value in a crunch. There are many in this class as will be seen later. Many of these may even be unknown in the giant databases of our world. Silbiger writes,

> "Indeed, even today many Jewish people would rather reserve the subject of their success ... Older Jewish Americans, in particular, **have downplayed** their success **and their Judaism** in an effort to avoid unwanted attention and possible trouble."
> Silbiger, *The Jewish Phenomenon*, pg 3 (*bold emphasis added*)

Silbiger goes on to say that when someone requested anonymity he tried to respect that request. In these ways it is easy to see that for some Jews there is still awareness that all of this success could blowup in their faces. Many know of some of the outlandish revolutionary plans of *some* Jews and some gentiles.

At some point though, you obviously come to those who are seriously undercover for some purpose or another. Perhaps a beautiful young Esther who is being groomed by her cousin to infiltrate the harem of a king?

Neither Impotent, nor Omnipotent

I think it is clear from an unbiased view of Jewish history, that not all Jews have been involved in nefarious schemes to exploit or tyrannize others. There are glimpses of these things from time to time in their own accounts. There have always been strong measures of Jewish opposition to foolish Jewish maneuvers to oppress all gentiles. You can see it all through history. Sensible Jews often try to bring to reason the irrationally rebellious, especially those of "the other side," that is to say, the synagogue of Satan. No doubt many good men among them have all along cursed and fumed as they watched multiple schemes, short range smart, and long range ludicrous, clever and foolish, unfolding to bring tragedy upon their own people. Often there are few indications of Jewish influence, but at other times it is hard to miss the influence. For instance, with ...

The Puritans and Jewish Influence.

Graetz paints a glowing portrait of Puritan warriors in his *History of the Jews*, Vol 5, pg 26. The Puritans were chaffing at their restrictions during the same period of time when the Marranos were leaving Spain and Portugal. As with many groups all through history, many of the Puritans wished for freedom and power and influence which they did not have. One of the missing ingredients was money. Most English accounts of the Puritan revolution speak vaguely of London or Dutch financiers of the Puritan revolution. Most accounts treat these things as being of no consequence, but the truth is that in all of these things, wars and revolutions in particular, *a great deal* of money is required, and also clearly, the Puritans got the financing which they needed, while the Royalists in great measure did not. So as the revolution progressed, Graetz notices that "public life and religious thought assumed Jewish coloring." Some were explicitly looking for the millennium. Several quotes from Graetz *History of Jews*, might be pertinent.

> "But other Puritans were so absorbed in the Old Testament that the New Testament was of no importance. Especially the visionaries in Cromwell's army and among the members of Parliament, who were hoping for the Fifth Monarchy, or the reign of the saints, assigned to the Jewish people a glorious position in the expected millennium." Graetz, *History of the Jews*, Vol 5, pg 27

> "One author proposed the seventh day as the day of rest, and in a work showed the holiness of this day, and the duty of the English people to honor it. This was in the beginning of 1649." Vol 5, pg 28

> "But the Israelite spirit among the Puritans, especially among the Levelers, or ultra-republicans, was not suppressed by these means. Many wished the government to declare the Torah the code for England." Vol 5, pg 28

> "The partiality of Cromwell's officers for the old Jewish system is shown by the serious proposition that the Council of State should consist of seventy members, after the number of the Jewish synhedrion. In Parliament sat General Harrison, a Baptist, who, with his party, wished to see the Mosaic law introduced into England." Vol 5, pg 34

Graetz does not use the term "crypto-Jew," but he does say,

> "Some secret Jews from Spain and Portugal were already domiciled in London, among them being the rich and respected Fernandez Carvajal." Vol 5, pg 38

Graetz credits Cromwell with trying to win the Jews over "to Christianity by friendly treatment." Vol 5, pg 43.

Rabbi Louis Finklestein in his *The Pharisees, The Sociological Background of the Their Faith"* Vol I, says that, "The Puritans did not of course recognize themselves as successors to the Pharisees; nor would they have wished ..." such. Then he goes on and credits Thomas Huxley with recognizing "the evidence for the kinship between Puritanism and Pharisaism," and says that research since that time has confirmed Huxley's "intuition," pg xvii. Finkelstein credits both John Bunyan and John Milton as having "a large admixture of Pharisaism," pg xviii. I am obviously in the minority here, but when I look closely at the personal life of key revolutionary John Milton, what I see is more of an intellectual occultist, than either a Christian *or* a Pharisee, but that is just my view. Further, I sure do not see Pharisaism in John Bunyan. I am letting Finkelstein make his own points. Then Finkelstein does say of Milton that,

> **His paradoxical sympathy for** the rebel, as personified in **Satan and his cohorts,** and for authority as hypostasized in God, which helps to make Paradise *Lost* so moving an epic, **was characteristic of the original Pharisaism.** Vol I, pg xviii (*bold emphasis added*)

Well! Who would have thought an expert on the nature of Pharisaism and of Judaism would have made a point like that! But there it is! Finkelstein himself notes that Milton "immersed himself deeply not only in the Hebrew scriptures, but in rabbinic tradition as well," pg xix

Historian Will Durant also points out some of these things. One of the radical wings of the Puritan Revolution was the "Levelers" (we would today call them communists, i.e., they wanted to put all people on the same level). Durant says some of them "called themselves Jews," and that

> "... somehow Jehovah the God of Hosts fitted better their needs than the Prince of Peace described in the New Testament."
> Will and Ariel Durant, *The Age of Louis XIV*, pg 461

Notice that Durant's comment reflects the gnostic view that the God of the Old Testament is different from the God of the New Testament! Which means that this sophisticated historian really understands neither testament!

I am not of Puritan ilk (by birth or by decision), but to give Finkelstein some of the credit he is seeking for Pharisaism, I would have to admit that many of the good things that have made America great, have been due at least in part to our Puritan heritage in America. The really difficult thing is *to learn from* the Old Covenant (meaning the writings of the Mosaic Covenant, *NOT* from human tradition) while clinging to the New Covenant for our statutes. For a fact, the Puritans did absorb more of Pharisaism than they should have; but to also give them proper credit, they did try to use "all scripture" for "training in righteousness" (2Tim 3:16), as indeed we all should. Again, we in America have profited from the Puritan attempts. For a fuller discussion of the issues of putting the Old and New Testaments in perspective, see the section, "A Lamp in a Dark Place," in *Prophecy Principles.*

Regardless of your point of view, from ancient times straight through today, the Jews have a tendency to be involved in revolutions, wherever they happen, and whether they are instrumental in starting them or not. These are things in which they have skills and experience not really to be matched by any other group.

Heinrich Graetz, the Jewish Historian.

Heinrich Graetz (1817-1891), born in Prussia (now Poland) as Tzvi Hirsh Graetz, was a notable Jewish scholar, and to him both Jews and gentiles owe a debt for his now classic six volume *History of the Jews.* He had an early Jewish Ph.D. from the University of Jena, and may still have had a greater secular perspective on Judaism than any scholar to date. His doctoral dissertation was on Judaism and Gnosticism. He was literally in the middle of the great clash of ideas going on in Judaism, which is still bearing fruit. Chaim Weizmann in 1949 noted "the great Jewish archives have been plundered or destroyed," *Trial and Error*, pg 356. In Graetz almost unique position, he had access to libraries and documentation of which some are no longer available. Clearly, rabbis allowed him access to histories and documentation to which no gentile scholar would be given access, and few or none today have the span of access which he had in his day. When I think of the tons of absolute hair-splitting nonsense which he waded through to give just treatment of this or that Jewish quarrel, or this crisis or that, I can only tip my hat to such a fine and patient scholar. Did he make mistakes? Oh yes. Everyone does. But he was open-minded enough, and impartial enough, to offend a little bit of everyone, *even to this day!* (Jewish Kabbalists typically cannot stand him for his no-nonsense treatment of Kabbalistic "absurdities.")

Graetz though was hardly an unbiased historian. He was, as should be expected, partisan for Judaism. He had many of the same blind spots to their own prophets as the Jews of Old Testament times had. Graetz dutifully defends Judaism where he can, and admits what he must. To his credit, much that is just plain foolishness among the Jews, he identifies as such. He sometimes avoids the truth when he can, but much of what he does admit about the Jews is worth noting.

In one sense, he is the epitome of the

Jewish historian Heirich Graetz

rootless modern Jew, for he really believes neither Scripture, nor the authority of rabbinical human tradition, nor the demonic kabbalistic nonsense. He has the glory and the limitations of rational human knowledge, and all of its ultimate fruitlessness as is pointed out in 1 Corinthians chapters 1 and 2.

Graetz praises to no end the sophistries by which the brilliant Mendelssohn denied the Talmudic roots of modern Judaism, but, alas, they are still there. Graetz would like to maintain that Judaism/Pharisaism can be maintained separately from the foolishness of what he might call Talmudism, and he never really faces the fact that it cannot. The inconvenient truth is that if you just follow Moses and the prophets, instead of following rabbinic traditions, it leads to the One and Only Savior of the world: Rabbi Yehoshua of Nazareth. What Rabbi Finkelstein clearly sees, Graetz never really recognizes: that modern "Judaism" is in its essentials Pharisaism, which is not really Moses Law. This it has always been. The spirit of the ancient Pharisee remains intact through all of the morphing, and ups and downs, and through all of its various forms, including its dabbling with Belzebul. **That is the core of the Jewish problem:** *a human stand on human reason, apart from the Word of God,* with all pretense and outward form of righteousness, and only a veneer of Scripture.

The Polish Massacres.

So for much of Judaism, just like for many of the Pharisees and Sadducees of old, Moses and the prophets also became, not something to believe, but a facade behind which to hide what one really believes. Even so, the culturally bred temptation to deal with gentiles in a rapacious ways was often too much to resist. This is about a hubris, a lofty arrogance and disdain, which defies normal compassion. The Jews may and do at times picture true human love and compassion, *but they **often** did not practice it **either toward each other,** or toward gentiles.*

The overreach of the Polish Jews in the 1600's may well be a type of the hole which the Jews are digging for themselves in modern day Israel. The Jews were as always successful entrepreneurs, and in Eastern Europe were, over time, able to work their way into a cozy relationship with Polish royalty. The Jews, because of their international trade, could provide money which the indigenous population could not match. So the Jews became a special privileged class of both financiers, advisors, and business managers, and

> "... were able, to a certain extent, to form an independent state within the Polish state." Graetz, Vol 4, pgs 641-642

Such things happened over and over, did they not? The Polish Jews then fell into a trade which they had successfully plied since pre-christian times: tax farming. It has similarly earned them much animosity, both in the early centuries of our age, and later in Poland and other places. Jewish historian Josephus writes at some length about some of the successful Jewish tax farmers of Greek and Roman times, and as has been pointed out, almost all of the key things you need to learn about the Jews you can learn from Scripture. Yehoshua's apostle Matthew was a contract tax collector, a tax farmer.

> As Jesus passed on from there, He saw a man named Matthew sitting at the tax office. And He said to him, "Follow Me." So he arose and followed Him. Mtt 9:9 NKJV

And the gospels mention a rich chief tax collector.

> [2] Now behold, *there was* a man named Zacchaeus who was a chief tax collector, and he was rich. [3] And he sought to see who Jesus was, but could not because of the crowd, for he was of short stature.
> Lk 19:2-3 NKJV

It was even in New Testament times a lucrative but often morally ambiguous way to make a living, and tax collectors were often spoken of in the same breath with "extortioners, unjust, adulterers," Lk 18:11 KJV. Now it happened in Poland that the Jews in Graetz words, "formed a state within a state," and

> "Three noble houses, the Koniecpolski, Vishnioviecki, and Potocki, had control of colonization in the Ukraine and Little Russia, and they transferred to their Jewish business agents the farming of the oppressive imposts falling on the Cossacks. ... That there might be no evasion, the Jewish revenue farmers had the keys of the Greek churches, and when the clergyman wished to perform a baptism or a marriage, he was obliged to ask them for the key." Graetz, Vol 5, pg 3

Other things developed, but the central thing was that,

> "With fatal blindness Polish Jews offered the nobility and the Jesuits a helping hand in oppressing the Zaporogian Cossacks in the Ukraine and Little Russia. ... the Jews settled in the district expected to enrich themselves and play the lord over these pariahs. They advised the possessors of the Cossack colonies how most completely to humiliate, oppress, torment, and ill-use, them; they usurped the office of judges over them, and vexed them in their ecclesiastical affairs." Graetz, Vol 5, pg 6

Then Graetz speaks with candor which many Jews cannot forgive.

> **"No wonder that the enslaved Cossacks hated the Jews**, with whom their relations were closest, almost more than their noble and clerical foes. **The Jews were not without warning what would be their lot, if these embittered enemies once got the upper hand."**
> Graetz, Vol 5, pg 6 (*bold emphasis added*)

Such oppression was bound not to last, and revolt finally came, headed by a Cossack by the name of Bogdan Chmielnicki.

"A Jew, Zachariah Sabilenki, had played him a trick, by which he was robbed of his wife and property. Another had betrayed him when he had come to an understanding with the Tartars. Besides injuries which his race had sustained from Jewish tax farmers in the Ukraine, he, therefore, had personal wrongs to avenge. His remark to the Cossacks, The Poles have delivered us as slaves to the cursed breed of Jews, was enough to excite them." Graetz, Vol 5, pg 7

The Polish massacres came in the 1600's, and, going back to injustices such as these, there is much anti-Jewish feeling in Poland even to this day.

Revolutions, Power Grabs, and Anarchy

The Jewish role in the French Revolution is scarcely noted any more. Even so, of the French Revolution Jewish historian Graetz speaks very favorably. He points out that the Jews received special exemption from persecution:

"The attack upon a belief in God, when the two blaspheming deputies, Chaumette and Hebert, succeeded in inducing the convention (November, 1793–May, 1794) to set up the religion of Reason, had likewise no effect upon the Jews. The intense hostility and anger felt to religion and the Divinity were directed only against Catholicism, or Christianity, by whose servants mankind had ever been degraded, who themselves had sacrificed myriads of victims, and during the Revolution had fomented a civil war." Graetz, Vol 5, pg 450

Moses Hess and an Earthly Zion.

As we come to the early 19th century, we also come to the beginnings of some of the pivotal movements of the 20th century. In a relatively short period of time there were laid the foundations for modern Socialism, Marxism, Communism, Zionism, and Anarchism.

A key person in some of these things was a young Jewish socialist by the name of Moses Hess. Socialism was the rage and was developing a decidedly Hegelian bent. (The Platonic roots of much Jewish thinking has already been pointed out.) It was Moses Hess who converted Frederick Engels and Karl Marx to communism and to dialectical materialism, *A Historical Atlas of the Jewish People*, p196. It may have been Hess who first called religion the "opiate of the people." Hess was one of many who were involved in the revolutions of 1848, and he had to flee when those revolutions failed. Hess also laid some of the foundations of later developed Zionism, especially in his pivotal book *Rome and Jerusalem* (1862).

There was a burning desire for some sort of Platonic "utopia," and one of the key questions was how this was to be achieved. Marx and those who followed him soon focused on a "dictatorship of the proletariat" as the way to bulldoze away the old order to make way for the New Order. What then was to be the center of the New Order? Were Zion and Zionism to be the center and focus of the new order? A secular Zion in Jerusalem below? Well some thought so, including it appears Moses Hess. If then this world saving messianic kingdom of the Jews, this Zion on earth, was indeed to be established and save the earth ... would not the ruler of the messianic kingdom be the messiah? Many both inside and outside of Zionism have so reasoned.

The aim of Hess's socialism was to "chase God from heaven." One of his main subjects in his book (1862) is the "messianic reign," and how to achieve it. Hess in fact said,

> "... the "Kingdom of Heaven," and "the world to come," are identical with the Messianic age, the rebirth of the Jewish nation."
> Moses Hess, *Rome and Jerusalem*, Bloch Publishing Co., NY, 1918, pg 52

But Moses Hess is not speaking of "God," whom he seems to despise, but rather of a human "Kingdom of Heaven." And the king then, the messiah of this human "messianic kingdom"? *Any* Jew could fill the bill.

> "Every Jew has within him the potentiality of a Messiah and every Jewess that of a *Mater dolorosa*." *Rome and Jerusalem*, pg 45

In this way, it does not matter who ends up being the ruler of this human "Kingdom of Heaven," he will *ipso facto* become the "messiah." Hess is advocating a secular Zion, a socialist Zion, to save the world, and then appointing the "messiah." Actually such ideas may not be anything recent. According to Jewish historian Josef Kastein, it was Rabbi Akiba who by his "authority" "appointed" Bar Kokhba as the **messiah** to lead the massive Roman Empire wide Jewish revolts during the early 2nd century AD. (From, *History and Destiny of the Jews*, Garden City Publishing Co, Inc., Garden City, New York, 1936, pgs 193-**194**. Kastein here is a translation from German, and uses different spellings of the names.[1]) Akiba was a leading rabbi of his time, and was and is honored. He was what some call a "mystic," that is, really an occultist. Both Bar Kokhba and Rabbi Akiba died in these revolts.

Moses Hess continues.

> "Scientists and Socialists should work hand in hand for the last liberation of humanity, for the emancipation of all forms of labor from speculation." *Rome and Jerusalem*, pg 222

---

[1] The cover of Kasteins' book quotes the Berlin *Vossische Zeitung* as saying, "This book was written with daimonic inspiration ..." And "Destiny"? It is another inconclusive evolutionary view of the Jews, ending by saying "no definite course can be marked out ..." then vaguely calling on his evolutionary "God" to continue to guide them, pg

"The Messianic era is the present age, which began to germinate with the teachings of Spinoza, and finally came into historical existence with the great French Revolution. **With the French Revolution**, there **began the regeneration** of those nations which had acquired their national historical religion only through the influence of Judaism." Moses Hess, *Rome and Jerusalem*, pg 138

Clearly Hess views the anti-Christian French Revolution having had "the influence of Judaism," and as *beginning* the regeneration of the nations. He advocates a classic socialist style revolution, after the form of the atheistic French revolution, which was to bring on the utopia and the "messianic" reign and a rule from Zion of whatever Jew happens to end up as the Messiah. Also notice that *none of this is very far from Kabbalistic thinking, thinking in which **man becomes god, and "saves" himself and the world**,* and ... oh yes, ... who also saves God (!!??).

Even so, was a "dictatorship of the proletariat" the best way to rid the world of the gentile governments and to pave the way for this earthly utopia centered in earthly Jerusalem? Anyway, how could you trust this so-called benign "dictatorship of the proletariat" to melt away at the end? So argued anarchists like Russian-American Jewess Emma Goldman and others. From this came the anarchistic terrorists of the late 19th century and early 20th century, on to the American cousin of Libertarianism, which would have government sort of whither away, while all of us perhaps live out the Satanic motto of lawlessness: "Do what you will"?

So Hess laid some of the intellectual foundations of communism and Zionism and anarchism. Lastly then, it should be pointed out that these were **not** "secret" plans. Instead these were, in fact, very publicly laid plans. Hess's book, for instance, is freely available as of this writing, even in English translation on the Internet.

A Secular Zion, A Worldly 'Savior,' From A False Bible?

Let us stop for just a minute to note that the Zionist movement of the 19th and 20th centuries was mainly a secular movement, with mainly secular ideology, support, and financing. True enough, there were some religious Zionists among them, and they served well and at the right time fought well. But the movement was from the first of secular origin and character.

These men, starting with Moses Hess for instance, did not believe in the God of the Bible, neither of the Old Testament or the New Testament, and rejected not only the Talmudic Halacha of Jewish teachings and traditions, but also the very Word of God itself. These were men who would immediately satirize any belief in a Biblical account of creation, or the Exodus and God coming down on Mount Sinai, or the powerful actions of God in history. Clearly these men did not want any sort of return to an "orthodox" rabbinic tyranny.

A Historical Atlas of the Jewish People says the secular Jews "had to engineer their own emancipation," pg 198. Ah! Pure Kabbalistic, Talmudic, unbelief. God is slow so we must act! H-m-m-m-m-m-m! Oh how far that is from Psalm 27:14's "Wait on the LORD"!

In the words of Laqueur, *A History of Zionism*, "It is impossible to exaggerate the impact of Russian socialism on the Zionist Labor movement," pgs 270-271. They wanted "a nation for the Jews, not a Jewish state." In their early communes they wanted to "'liquidate the family as a social unit, recognizing it only as expression of erotic life'." pg 299. But alas, the necessity of God's plans is even written into our genes!

Much of this is probably a surprise to most Americans listening to the news cartels of the last one hundred years. Of course, the Zionists had trouble getting large numbers of Jews to buy into this foolishness. If you realize these things, it is unsurprising that there was and is much formal opposition to these secular Zionistic ideas, even among the Jews, even to this day, even in the nation of Israel in Palestine. So Vienna's chief rabbi in Herzog's time argued outright that "Zionism was incompatible with Judaism," Laqueur, pg 96.

Even so, these predominantly unbelieving Jews who reject Scripture, want *us* (the nations, the goyim) to believe that *God* is the One who gave them all of this land *forever*. They want us to believe that they have a right to drive off and kill the Arabs and Palestinians, and that once their secular nation has "saved" the world, the ruler of this secular "messianic" kingdom will be the messiah? Oh!

Marx and the Revolutionaries.

Karl Marx is also an interesting figure of Jewish descent. (A crypto-Jew? A Frankist Jew? Or someone of "the other side" as Gershom Scholem calls them. Or just an apostate Jew?) There is a body of evidence which may indicate that Karl Marx was a conscious Satanist. You may have run into such evidence from various sources. One easy-to-reference source for Americans is Richard Wurmbrand's *Marx and Satan*, Living Sacrifice Book Company, Bartlesville, OK, 1986. Wurmbrand, a protestant minister who was tortured by the Communists, carefully documents his case, but as his book shows, it is easier to document these things in Europe, this being in the main a European historical issue. He makes it clear that,

> "I do not claim to have provided indisputable proof that Marx was a member of a sect of devil-worshipers, but I believe that there are sufficient leads to imply this strongly. There are certainly enough leads to

suggest Satanic influence upon his life and teaching, while conceding that there are gaps in the evidence ..." pg 113

I think that is a fair minded summary of the available evidence. Wurmbrand and others begin by showing Marx being influenced by what even his father viewed as demonic activity, beginning in his adolescence.

Several points should be made here. Including that this follows in the directions suggested by Jacob Frank and his followers in their tendency to follow "the dark side" or "the other side" or "left hand path," as they called it. Remember our earlier discussion of *The Kabbalah and Other Spirits*, and especially our discussion of Shabbetai Sevi and Jacob Frank. From a Satanic point of view, Marx's pitting himself against and hating all "gods," is reminiscent of the ultimate "man of lawlessness" who is coming as,

> [3] ... the son of destruction, [4] who opposes and exalts himself above every so-called god or object of worship, ... 2Thes 2:3-4 NASB

From that perspective the alignment of Communism against all religion and all gods certainly makes sense as preparation for an *earthly* utopian messiah, *i.e.* a bulldozer clearing old structures for new construction. In contrast Graetz does not consider the revolutions of 1848 as any threat to the established social order. Rather,

> "Unexpectedly the hour of freedom for the European Jews dawned with the revolutions of February and March (1848) ... An intoxicating desire for liberty came over the nations of Europe, more over-powering and marvelous even than the movement in 1830. With imperious demands the people confronted their princes and rulers."
> Graetz, Vol 5, pgs 696-697

I was reading an account of the early 1900's seating of the Communists in Russia with the help of Western financiers, and one opponent called them "Anarcho-Communists." That is not far from the mark. Creating anarchy as a precursor to new and different structures. A handful of men do the scheming and harvest the rewards of duplicity. The great body of the Jews often do not participate, but are habitually silent regarding what they know. But when the fraud is revealed, again and again it has been the Jews as whole who do the suffering.

They do not like to admit it, but even Jewish historians sometimes obliquely acknowledge the Jewish leadership role in many of the bloodiest revolutions of the modern world. In *A Historical Atlas of the Jewish People*, the authors talk about the Communist revolt in Russia and speak of "the disproportionately large presence of Jews in revolutionary movements," pg 196. In a country in which Jews are small minority, at the first conference of Soviet Writers in 1934, 20% were Jewish, pg 215. On page 214 they say that 25% of the Bolshevik **leaders** were Jewish. (Of course, figures like these typically do not account for crypto-Jews unless they were very well known as such, for instance Trotsky. Jewish authors generally try to avoid revealing crypto-Jews unless they are sure such identifications cannot be avoided.) Also, at the Moscow show trials of 1936-1938, many of the victims were Jewish. Walter Laqueur in his *A History of Zionism*, says that "in view of the fact that Jews were conspicuous in the Russian revolutionary movement, allied efforts to win over Russian Jewry did not come as a surprise," pg 202. In this category would definitely be Winston Churchill, as shall be discussed next. Although these things are widely known, they are very seldom emphasized. Clearly this is about a significant influence from the Jews. So there tends to be a level of general complicity among many Jews with undercover operations, even if the schemes themselves are stupid, and even if they may not basically be favoring this or that scheme. Laqueur speaks repeatedly about Jewish revolutionary leadership and speaks of supplying "the revolutionary parties with leaders and lieutenants," pg 109. That is a fair statement of the public influence of the Jews in these matters, as was widely known all over Europe.

ILLUSTRATED SUNDAY HERALD, FEBRUARY 9, 1920.

ZIONISM versus BOLSHEVISM.

A STRUGGLE FOR THE SOUL OF THE JEWISH PEOPLE.

By the Rt. Hon. WINSTON S. CHURCHILL.

Winston Churchill gave a good summary of what was generally known among the well informed, and in intelligence circles in Europe by the early 1920's. It was in a famous article in the *Illustrated Sunday Herald* of February 9, 1920, pg 5 (see the picture above). Key parts of this article are widely quoted, including by Pat Buchanan in *Churchill, Hitler, and the Unnecessary War*, pgs 401-402. Churchill said,

> "The conflict between good and evil which proceeds unceasingly in the breast of man nowhere reaches such an intensity as in the Jewish race. ... We owe the Jews in the Christian revelation for a system of ethics which even if it were separated from the supernatural, would be incomparably the most precious possession of mankind ... And it may well be that this same astounding race may at the present time be in the actual process of producing another system of morals and philosophy, as

malevolent as Christianity was benevolent ...

"There is no need to exaggerate the part played in the creation of Bolshevism and in the actual bringing about of the Russian Revolution by those international and for the most part atheistical Jews. It is certainly a very great one; it probably outweighs all others. The majority of the leading figures are Jews. Moreover, the principal inspiration and driving power comes from Jewish leaders. ...

"This movement among the Jews is not new. From the days of Spartacus-Weishaupt to those of Karl Marx, and down to Trotsky (Russia), Bela Kun (Hungary), Rosa Luxembourg (Germany), and Emma Goldman (United States), this world-wide conspiracy for **the overthrow of civilization and for the reconstitution of society on the basis of arrested development**, of envious malevolence, and impossible equality, has been steadily growing. ... and now ... have gripped the Russian people by the hair of their heads and have become practically the undisputed master of that enormous empire." (*bold emphasis added*)

Such things might be hidden in the far reaches of the world, but Europe was too close to these things for the truth to not be widely known, and known it was. Not mentioned by most who quote only parts of the Churchill's article was that he was opposing the revolutionary side of Judaism, and working to avoid its influence in England, while he was supporting the Zionist wing of Judaism and praising it as wholesome and constructive. Such candor is not appreciated in the halls of power, and the article was later an embarrassment to Churchill.

Gentile Holocausts.

What then was the outcome of these communist-style revolutions? Although the liberals in Western Europe and America do not like to talk about it, the result was a series of monstrous gentile holocausts which covered about one-third of our world. Many do not realize it, but part of the communist revolutionary strategy was to simply murder everyone in a nation who might provide leadership against the revolution. This would mean to murder all teachers, lawyers, businessmen, intellectuals ... anyone who was educated and could think rationally and sensibly, and who could thus lead any opposition to the revolution. The strategy was to thus leave a power vacuum in which only the communist leadership would survive. So the strategy was implicitly genocidal, to implement radical turns of direction among large groups of people.

So anywhere communism gained control, the general result was a slaughter of about one-third of the population over about a twenty year period following the revolution. The figures vary, depending on your source, and how they calculate the figures, but the numbers for the total death toll for the communist's revolutions of the twentieth century *start at* around 100 million, and go up from there. In fact even *before* World War II had started, the communists in Russia alone had murdered "between 17 and 22 million." Yale history professor John L. Gaddis in *We Now Know: Rethinking Cold War History*, Oxford University Press, NY, 1997, pg 8, calls these figures as "now agreed in both Russia and the West ... — substantially more than twice the number of Hitler's victims in the Holocaust." "We Now Know" he says, but really these things were well-known even in the 1920's and 30's, even though the news cartels in America and Europe tried (and try) their best to suppress this information. There was a series of Gentile Holocausts of gigantic proportions.

One ex-Communist and ex-Soviet secret agent, courier, and later senior editor for *Time* magazine, Whittaker Chambers, described the Communists' way of dealing with dissent in this way.

> "What Communist has not heard those screams? They come from husbands torn forever from their wives in midnight arrests. They come, muffled, from execution cellars of the secret police, from the torture chambers of the Lubianka, from all the citadels of terror now stretching from Berlin to Canton. They come from freight cars loaded with men, women, children, the enemies of the Communist State, locked in, packed in, left on remote sidings to freeze to death at night in the Russian winter. They come from minds driven mad by the horrors of mass starvation ordered and enforced as policy of the Communist State. They come from the starved skeletons, worked to death, or flogged to death (as an example to others) in the freezing filth of sub-arctic labor camps." Whittaker Chambers, *Witness*, Random House, NY, 1952, pg 14

That is still not a bad one-paragraph synopsis of Alexander Solzhenitsyn's first person accounts in his three volume *The Gulag Archipelago*, which was not published until some 21 years later. It is ironic that the international news cartels still treat it as impolite to remind people of these monstrous crimes of Communism. I cannot help but think of one of the characterizations of the the the Christian age in the book of Revelation.

> [7] When He opened the fourth seal, I heard the voice of the fourth living creature saying, "Come and see." [8] So I looked, and behold, a pale horse. And the name of him who sat on it was Death, and Hades followed with him. And power was given to them over a fourth of the earth, to kill with sword, with hunger, with death, and by the beasts of the earth. Rev 6:7-8 NKJV

You may or may not like this part of a characterization of the last two-thousand years of history, but in many ways it is accurate, not just of ancient or medieval times, but also, as is seen here, of much of modern history. And there has been no discussion the holocaust of 60 million completely innocent babies murdered in the United States since 1973, just to serve the currently favored gods of convenience and pleasure.

What could be more vile than the Nazi concentration camps and extermination programs for the Jews and other opposition. Still in many cases the butchery by the Communists was far more degrading and horrific, and widespread. Genocidal holocausts are terrible things, whether they are Jewish holocausts or gentile holocausts. Even so, *Hitler literally killed his millions,* **and the communists killed their tens of millions.** None of this is trivial. *None* of this was right or good. But the outlines of these things were made known by escapees to Western Europe. Both the fact of these exterminations and of the Jewish leadership in these things was well known in Hungary, and Czechoslovakia and Poland, and, oh yes, ... did we mention Germany? Germany barely escaped Communist revolutions in the years right after World War I, and suffered bloody times even during their first brush with communism.

The Jews are big on citing the group guilt of others for the sins of a few, as a curse against the group which should not be easily dismissed. These sorts of ideas are also sometimes reflected in Scripture, as in the story of Aachen in Joshua chapter 7. In truth such things are repeated over and over in history. For instance when an entire nation suffers defeat because of the treachery of a single turncoat, or for the sins of a single foolish leader. Or when an innocent child suffers for the drunkenness of another. Such things are built into the nature of sin, and are part of the reason sin is so reprehensible. In truth we can never just sin for ourselves. But it is not just the gentiles who often bear responsibility for the sins of a minority. It is the Jews also.

If you have any close Jewish friends, or if perhaps you have spent some time studying in modern Israel, you have probably noted many families may have a son or daughter who was involved as an activist in one revolution or another, or this or that extremely radical political movement, with no sense of disgrace or dishonor on the part of the family. In modern Jewish history, twice elected Israeli Prime Minister Menachem Begin began his career as the leader of the terrorist Irgun organization, which was responsible for the infamous terrorist bombing of the King David Hotel in Israel. It happened on Monday, July 22, 1946, in which 91 people were killed and 46 were injured, most of them innocent members of the staff of the hotel, or lower level clerks and secretaries. Begin himself led the massacre of 254 Arabs in the village of Deir Yassin in association with the Lehi group. Also twice elected Israeli Prime Minister Yitzak Shamir was a terrorist leader associated with the Lehi terrorist group (also called the Stern gang). The Stern gang, in addition to many sabotage bombings, carried out 42 assassinations. Shamir was involved in the murder of UN mediator Count Folke Bernadotte. (Count Bernadotte, by the way, was personally instrumental in saving 20,000 Jews from Hitler's concentration camps.) Not surprisingly, at one time there were "Wanted" posters for Shamir as a terrorist. All of this is in the public record, and readily available in English.

Perhaps a good example of how these things have worked down through the Christian Age is to look at Chaim Weizmann's account of his upbringing. Weizmann was a Zionist, and a principal in negotiating the Balfour Declaration and in the establishment of the nation of Israel. He also was Israel's first President. The student visitors to his home during his teenage years in Pinsk included "Zionists, assimilationists, Socialists, anarchists, every variety of revolutionary." They argued and debated and intellectually fought each other in the Weizmann home, his mother saying, "They've got to be fed ... or they won't have the strength to shout." She would bury "our" revolutionary pamphlets in the garden, and when the police raids would come, mom would seek to cover for the students. Weizmann's mom was philosophical about all of this. "Whatever happens, I shall be well off. If Shemuel [the revolutionary son] is right, we shall be happy in Russia; and if Chaim [myself] is right, then I shall go to live in Palestine." Chaim Weizmann, *Trial and Error*, Harper and Brothers, NY, 1949, pgs 12-13. Weizmann also mentions in his biography that Schemuel lived with him for a while in Manchester, England; attended the 6th Zionist's Congress and was for accepting Britain's offer of Uganda to the Jews. Weizmann then does not mention him again. Schemuel returned to Russia as a Bolshevik revolutionary and was in 1936 executed as a traitor by Stalin. Had he indeed turned into a counter-revolutionary to Stalin? I am sure it hurt, but Weizmann does not address the issues. For sure "the revolution devours its children." You can multiply such stories of the Jews over and over by simply reading publicly available histories and biographies. One could argue that both brothers were right, although the experiment in Israel has been more stable. Also it should be pointed out that these have been common patterns of Jewish life since at least the second century BC, indeed even before that. Here is how some of the opponents of the Jews described them in the fifth century BC.

> [11] This is the copy of the letter that they sent to Artaxerxes the king: Your servants the men beyond the River, and so forth. [12] Be it known to the king, that the Jews who came up from you are come to us to Jerusalem; they are building the rebellious and the bad city, and have finished the walls, and repaired the foundations. ... [15] that search may be made in the book of the records of your fathers: so shall you find in the book of the records, and know that this city is a rebellious city, and hurtful to kings and provinces, and that they have moved sedition within the same of old time; for which cause was this city laid waste.
> Ezra 4:11-12, 15 WEB

If you take an overview of Josephus' histories from the times of the Maccabees through the end of the first century AD, they are rife with continual tumults and revolutions, which reflected a continual breeding of radicals of the most extreme sorts in many Jewish families. All of which in the end proved to be their undoing. Naturally when any nation finds itself in the crosshairs of a takeover or a revolution, then it starts to take more severe methods towards those who would overthrow them ... or they soon find themselves overthrown ... and dead. And when Rabbi Yehoshua chose His inner circle of followers, one of them included a member of one of the larger radical Jewish religio-political-revolutionary groups. I am talking about Simon the Zealot, Mk 10:4.

Later when Weizmann was trying to integrate revolutionary refugees from Russia and Eastern Europe into Israel, he commented in a letter to Herbert Samuel,

> "how we are to transform these *farouches* embittered souls into productive human beings I don't quite see yet." Reinharz, pg 276

The Stern Gang, the Kabbalah, and Revolution.

The so-called "Stern Gang" (Lehi) is also a good case study in order to see the wild nature of some Jewish revolutionary activity. They were evidently a "black-ops" group (illegal operations) spun off by the Jewish authorities in Palestine from the Irgun Jewish terrorist group. At that time much was unclear. The Jewish authorities evidently felt they had to test all of their options. After Israel became a state, they formally disbanded Lehi. Then early the next year (1949) they issued a general amnesty to Lehi members. In 1980, Israel started a new military decoration, the Lehi ribbon, an "award for activity in the struggle for the establishment of Israel." All of which of course points to Lehi being part of embryonic Israel's pre-state operations, something that they might need to be able to deny if it did not work out, and parts of it did not work out.

The early history of Lehi is the strangest to us today. It was known that Hitler wanted to get rid of the Jews of Europe, but the decision to murder all Jews was not yet known. (In fact, Pat Buchanan in *Churchill, Hitler, and The Unnecessary War* documents that the decision for the Holocaust was actually not made until the Wannsee Conference in early 1942, well after the start of the invasion of Russia in the spring of 1941, pgs 310-311. It was then "not a cause of the war but an awful consequence of the war," pg 311.) Historian Thomas Fleming makes a similar point in *The New Dealers' War*, Basic Books, NY, 2001, pgs, 259-260. Lehi tried to negotiate with the Germans to get the Jews whom Hitler did not want in Germany as immigrants for the soon to form Israeli state. The British were not allowing any more Jewish immigration to Palestine. Lehi wanted to make a deal with the Germans to continue this immigration. Lehi then would oppose the British in Palestine (which they did), and aid Germany in the conquest of the Middle East. Some say that they even wanted to make Israel into a fascist state under Germany.

To put all of this into 1940 perspective, it should be remembered that many of the early immigrants to Israel were socialists/Zionists, an off shoot of Platonic thinking among the Jews, which was shown to be part of unbelieving Judaism's thinking since pre-Christian times. Their ideal was a communist style state with a philosopher king (a messiah?) as its head. This is part of why the kibbutz farming communes were promoted in the early settlement of Palestine by the Jews in modern times. And the fascists? They also were Platonic socialists. In fact Mussolini was an international hero among the socialists of continental Europe, England, and America in the late 1920's and early 1930's. Mussolini was interviewed as a clever and far-sighted national hero by the leading liberal magazines, and newspapers (Jonah Goldberg, *Liberal Fascism*, THE SECRET HISTORY OF THE AMERICAN LEFT *from MUSSOLINI to the POLITICS OF CHANGE*, Broadway Books, N.Y., 2009, pg 29). Goldberg even points out that "Jews were overrepresented in the Italian Fascist movement from its founding in 1919 until they were kicked out in 1938." pg 26. And Nazi's? Well they were just *"national socialists"* instead of *"international socialists"* like the Communists. Hitler was supposed to fit the mold of the enlightened philosopher-king, and so he seemed to many Germans!

So Lehi tried, and actually contacted the German government, and tried to negotiate with the Germans for the release of Europe's Jews, but got nowhere. In retrospect it is easy to see they would not succeed, but it was by no means so clear in 1940. And there were other Jewish negotiations with the Nazis which were more successful, as is documented by Edwin Black's *The Transfer Agreement, The Dramatic Story of the Pact Between the Third Reich and Jewish Palestine*, Dialog Press, Washington, DC, 1983, 1999, 2001, 2009.

So who was called upon to lead Lehi? A bright intellectual Jew by the name of Avraham Stern in 1940. Stern studied Hebrew and the Greek and Roman classics at Hebrew University and was one of their top students. He served first in the Haganah and later as an officer in the terrorist Irgun organization. Some interesting side lights come up on Stern in a *Wall Street Journal* book review by Hillel Halkin, December 20-21, 2014, pg C6.

> "Stern was a charismatic and driven leader who foolishly believed that Zionism could work with the Axis powers against the British Colonial rulers of Palestine ...

> "Stern was an odd breed, a nonbelieving religious messianist. He rejected the Jewish God in whose faith he had been raised because this God was letting the Jews of Europe be annihilated."

A "**a nonbelieving religious messianist**"? Who rejected God because He failed? That is *almost* a contradiction in terms. Clearly he believed in something. He did "believe" that God existed and that God had failed [in His duty?] to take care of the Jews. Halkin also calls it "the largely secular Stern gang," but there is nothing secular about what we see here in Stern. It has been pointed out that many present day Jews are "secularists," but religiously believe in Kabbalistic thinking as some sort of higher level "science." Also Halkin calls this thinking as, "also as a form of political lunacy that would reappear in a new guise long after the group's demise."

Halkin seemingly is speaking of the messianic Jews of today. What then was the strategy? The article speaks of Stern's

"... belief in what is known in Jewish tradition as "forcing the end," **making God take action by setting in motion eschatological events that He cannot take back.**" (*bold emphasis added*)

They are going to "**make**" God take action? Is this some sort of "magic"? So what is this all about? You see Stern was another "secular" Kabbalist, and this is all Kabbalistic doctrine about how "man" needs to save God and save the world. You may remember when this work first talked about the Kabbalah and "The First Cause and the Emanations," pg 148. It was said that the Kabbalists viewed the True and Only God as very remote, and only the lower emanations as being "active" in our present world. So it was necessary in their thinking that "man saves God," as was shown in the section about the Kabbalah.

Halkin does not even mention the occult or the Kabbalah, but that is the unidentified subject in this book review. So,

"Stern imagined the Jewish people not only taking up arms in conquest of its ancient homeland **but compelling God to be the zealous warrior-deity of the Bible once again.**" (*emphasis added*)

So what were these unholy warriors to do? Murders, assassinations, bombings, the massacre of Arabs, and even the accidental killing of some Jews. The normal fare of terrorists. So they could compel God to do ... what?

This is only an isolated sampler, but at the center of Jewish revolutionary activity is the Kabbalah/Gnosticism and *twisted views* of *God* and *our world*, and *of the Jews*. So twisted as to justify the heinous things they do.

Does God sometimes stand back to let us see what will happen? Indeed He does at times. Of Israel Isaiah writes,

And when ye spread forth your hands, I will hide mine eyes from you: yea, when ye make many prayers, I will not hear: your hands are full of blood. Isa 1:15 KJV

Does God act? Will he act in behalf of his people?

For since the beginning of the world
    Men have not heard nor perceived by the ear,
    Nor has the eye seen any God besides You,
    Who acts for the one who <u>waits</u> for Him.
Isa 64:4 NKJV (*emphasis added*)

Yes, God does act, and will act, and it happens all the time, though often men do not notice or perceive it. (And this is not about the issue of so-called "miracles.") Where then is the defect? In a bitter and hasty people who will not "wait for Him." They have chosen their own plan instead of God's. So they end up bearing the fruits of their own plans, as we gentiles also often do.

> "They have corrupted themselves;
>> They are not His children,
>> Because of their blemish:
>> A perverse and crooked generation." Deut 32:5 NKJV

God said it. Moses said it. Rabbi Yehoshua said it. It is true.

Avraham Stern was killed in a British police raid in 1942.

Opposition to Jewish Revolutionary Activities.

Earlier I quoted from *A Historical Atlas* and from Will Durant. Gentile historians tread lightly on the subject of Jews and revolution for fear of a Jewish backlash. The Jews do not want these things to be widely known. Sometimes various historians do obliquely deal with the subject of Jewish revolutionaries.

At times the adversaries of the Jews have said, "Enough! We just want to be rid of you." But not often. Most men and nations love money too much. So the Jews have frequently been able to insinuate themselves into the highest levels of power in society, after society, after society. This is about continual careers of great skill and ability, which have been repeatedly marred by reaching just a little too far. Of ability and foresight being undermined by arrogance and the despising of others. In our times this is especially about the Arabs, but really Jewish disdain applies to all men, all of the gentiles. It just tends to show up at different times and in different ways.

No doubt *the Jews have been* **at times** *the* **innocent scapegoats,**
but by no means as constantly as they would argue!

Even so, they have continually had the gall to cry foul when anyone dared to oppose them. *Any* trouble with others is *always* someone else's fault in their eyes. The result being the "persecution" of the Jewish "race," "anti-Semitism" as they call it. Sometimes the Jewish infiltration of others is approvingly noted, even if the authors recognize it as wrong.

> "These talented but sinful Jewish women did Judaism a service by becoming Christians." Graetz, Vol 5, pg 425

> "The Jewish world is greatly indebted to its two apostate sons, Borne and Heine. They did not indeed destroy all German anti-Jewish feeling, but they at least subdued it. ... Young Germany, which originated the present state of culture, and created the Year of Liberation, 1848, is the offspring of these two Jewish fathers. ...
> **This Messianic time, when it arrives, will have been prepared by two Jews, who were fulfilling their national mission."**

Graetz, Vol 5, pg 556 (*bold emphasis added*)

That is about as close as you will get in general Jewish literature to admissions of complicity or leadership in some of these world shaking events.

Revolutions and their organization and their expenses are normally things which are *not* in the view of the great body of people. It was pointed out under the heading "Have You Started a Riot Lately?" pgs 111-114, that these things have always required money and training and organizing. So what do these sorts of things cost? Every once in a while the public gets a chance to see. For instance, if you have a small, relatively peaceful, community of say 20,000, what does it really cost to start a good series of riots? According to the *Washington Times* a total of over $33 million dollars was provided in one year to leftist groups to organize riots in Ferguson, Missouri in 2014. (And these figures *only* include partial figures for 2014.) These figures included busing in leaders and agitators and rioters from all over the nation. These figures do not include the considerable expenses of the Federal government or of the national media cartels in providing cover for those stirring up the trouble. According to the *Washington Times* of January 14, 2015,

> "There's a solitary man at the financial center of the Ferguson protest movement ... it's liberal billionaire George Soros ..."

It might should be added that it was liberal *Jewish* billionaire George Soros who was at the financial center. A couple of things should be noted. First, there is still a taste among *some* Jews for riots and revolution, although by no means among all. Second, of course, would be to note how staggeringly expensive such things are, especially if you extrapolate these figures to include the scope of a full revolution in a modern Western nation. Most people are not aware of these things or their tremendous costs.

Soros also is a very interesting figure. His birth name was György Schwarts. He is from a Hungarian Jewish family that managed to escape the Holocaust by assimilation. Soros himself for a while took the name "Sandor Kiss," and even to some extent cooperated with the Nazis. Soros as a boy even delivered notices to other Hungarian Jewish families to report for deportation to concentration camps. On one hand, he can be quoted as rejecting the Jewish faith and is part of that section of Judaism which has advocated many policies which are clearly anti-Israeli. Many have noted what some have called his "predatory financial maneuvers," which are well known and widely publicized in the international financial media. For example, he accepted a $2.9 million dollar fine from the French for insider trading. Before the London School of Economics he has stated his purpose is to "puncture the bubble of American supremacy." *The Shadow Party. How George Soros, Hillary Clinton and the Sixties Radicals Seized Control of the Democratic Party,* David Horowitz and Richard Poe, Thomas Nelson, Inc., Nashville, 2006, pp. 67, 78-81, 83, 97. Soros seems to be functioning as a lightning rod for financial interests (not all Jewish) with a taste for revolution. And one more thing. All of this fits the pattern of Moses Hess' destructive phase of world revolution, with the much more difficult constructive phase coming from another direction. Truly, Soros' "Open Society" has no real answers for what to build; only for what "needs" to be destroyed.

So the cabals (from the word Kabbalah) still exist. None of the revolutionary activities of 1789, 1848, and 1917 have gone away. They have merely put on newer clothes, slightly changed their banners and phraseology, and acquired new office space, to prepare for a new round of would-be messiahs. All of these things are still current history. Again, *this is not talking about secret things, but only about things which are not widely known or acknowledged.*

In city after city, and country after country, the Jews gain good position and respect and great wealth, by good service and loyal and faithful advice, and mature and sensible operations, as also Joseph did in Egypt, and Daniel, Ezra and Nehemiah in Babylon and Persia. In city after city and country after country, they also then earned the wrath of the authorities, and the irrational hatred of the mob by foolish schemes against the "stupid goyim" rulers or people, schemes which were of course soon found out, and which no media influence could paper over, and which were in truth contrary to all manners and morals and good business sense, *and* Moses *and* the Prophets *and* Rabbi Yehoshua. Very often, significant portions of the Jews simply have not had the good sense to act with honor in personal dealings. So finally there always came a time to pay for these sins, as it comes for all of us. Sins which were also contrary to the Law of Moses, which they had rejected, but not contrary to their corrupt traditions. Ten thousand volumes of coverup stories will not eliminate these basic truths, which in the end must be faced.

Rabbi Joseph Telushkin in his book *Jewish Humor: What the Best Jewish Jokes Say About Jews*, (William Morrow and Co., Inc., NY, 1992) tells a story of Jews and revolution. Leon Trotsky was a crypto-Jew, pretending to be a Russian during the Communist Revolution in Russia. There were many such. His real name, as is widely known, was Lev Davidovich Bronstein, and he along with many other crypto-Jews formed most of what might be called "the officer corps" of the revolution in Russia. The story goes that the chief rabbi of Moscow approached Trotsky for protection of the Jews from persecution. Trotsky rebuffed him saying, why come to me? "I am not a Jew." The rabbi replied, "That's the tragedy. It's the Trotsky's who make the revolutions, and it's the Bronsteins who pay the price." pgs 126-127.

Such has been the case for much of the last two thousand years. **Notice that** Trotsky was *not **primarily*** a Jew, but ***primarily*** a revolutionary. Again, *much of Jewish revolutionary activity is against Moses' Law and traditional Judaism, and the Jews. That is the sober truth many Jews choose to ignore.*

Owning the Media?

There is in fact often a defense of Jewish influence in some surprising places. Mearsheimer, and Walt in their book *The Israel Lobby and U.S. Foreign Policy*, are protesting excessive Israeli influence over U. S. foreign policy, principally coordinated through AIPAC, the American Israel Public Affairs Committee. They do as objective and dispassionate presentation of the evidence as they can, citing both the pros and the cons, and make a good case for this being "undue" influence, even to the point of trying to push the United States into wars which benefit neither America nor the Mohammedans, but which were at least intended to benefit modern Israel. Even so, they point out that,

> "There is no question that some Jewish Americans, such as Martin Peretz and Mortimer Zuckerman, use their positions in the media to advance their views on Israel and the Middle East. **This behavior is legitimate and unsurprising**, as all elites tend to use their privileged positions to advance their various interests."
> pg 169 (*bold emphasis added*)

They go on to point out the Jewish monitoring and attempting to influence the reporting of the news concerning Israel as *proof* that the Jews do NOT control the media.

> "It is therefore wrong—and objectionable—to argue that Jews or pro-Israel forces "control" the media and what they say about Israel. In fact, the reason that the lobby works so hard to monitor and influence what the main-stream media says about Israel is precisely that the lobby does not control them." pg 169

Once again: the Jews are *neither* omnipotent nor impotent.

If we do not understand the directions many
Jews have taken, we will not understand
the severity of the reactions which
will eventually come, or what
the Jews, or ourselves,
need to do.

VI. "As *It Was*
Against
Your Fathers"
1Sam 12:15

But if ye will not obey the voice of the LORD, but rebel against the commandment of the LORD, then shall the hand of the LORD be against you, *as it was* against your fathers. 1Sam 12:15 KJV

[21] And she named the child Ichabod, saying, The glory is departed from Israel: because the ark of God was taken, and because of her father in law and her husband. [22] And she said, The glory is departed from Israel: for the ark of God is taken. 1Sam. 4:21-22 KJV

Then the glory of the LORD departed from the threshold of the temple and stood over the cherubim. Ezek 10:18 NKJV

This section is chiefly prophecy. Not my prophecies, but the Lord's.

Success and Stress: He Who Digs a Pit.

[15] He made a pit, and digged it, and is fallen into the ditch which he made. [16] His mischief shall return upon his own head, and his violent dealing shall come down upon his own pate. Psa 7:15-16 KJV

So freed from the Ghetto, freed from recognition as Jews; the Jews pursued excellence and position in literally *every* field. Every art, every science, every engineering skill was to be learned to the ultimate. In this quest for excellence, the Jews, though they often could not get along with each other, supported each other for prominence and sorted out their issues mainly in private. *It was and is still a game of "beat the gentiles,"* **only the gentiles did not know it!** They indicated they were assimilating. They were essentially taken at their word. In reality it was just like the Marranos ... but without the risks they took in Spain. The results have been phenomenal.

The Jews were not long in attaining outstanding successes in the West. It was not just that they were being successful, but that, much as in Spain, they were becoming a dominant influence all over the West. Often we in America think of this as just a British or American thing, but it was much wider than this. Take for instance Germany. Jewish writer Walter Laqueur in *A History of Zionism*, MFJ Books, NY, 1972, speaks of the German Jews. He points out that the Jews had an early advantage in banking. In 1807 there were more Jewish than gentile banks in Berlin, and in Bavaria during this period, "80 percent of the state loans of the Bavarian government ... were provided by Jewish bankers." pg 6.

> "In Berlin they constituted in 1905 less than 5 per cent of the population but provided 30 per cent of the municipal tax revenue; in Frankfurt on Main 63 per cent of all Jews had in 1900 an income of more

than 3,000 marks; only 25 per cent of the Protestants and no more than 16 per cent of the Catholics reached that level." pg 25

"Out of a hundred Christian boys in Germany only three went to a gymnasium, the grammar school which was the stepping stone to the university, but twenty-six out of a hundred Jewish boys went to these schools. ... In Prussia after the First World War every fourth lawyer and every sixth physician was a Jew; in the big centers such as Berlin and Vienna the percentage was higher still." pg 26

Laqueur is obviously proud of these accomplishments. He goes on to speak of "a galaxy of chemists and physicists, mathematicians and physicians, who inscribed their names in golden letters in the annals of science." pg 26. That is, if anything, an understatement.

We tend to think of Germany as backward in these things, and having "anti-Semitic" tendencies, but Laqueur points out, "There was less antisemitism there than in France or Austria, not to mention eastern Europe," pg 156. In many ways Germany was more open than England at the same time, pgs 156-157, etc. For instance, Jews could not attend English universities until 1870, pg 25. Laqueur says of Zionism, "The seat of the movement was after all in Germany"; and the London *Times* viewed Zionism as "merely a tool of the German Foreign Ministry," pg 143. There are similar things across West Europe and America, and similar stories can be told in Britain and America and elsewhere.

A Historical Atlas of the Jewish People points out that in 1881-82 in Berlin, Jews accounted for 11-12% of the doctors, and 8-9% of the reporters. In 1900 in Austria 16.2% of Jews were in the professions or government administration, pg 165.

In Edwin Black's *The Transfer Agreement, The Dramatic Story of the Pact Between the Third Reich and Jewish Palestine*, Dialog Press, Washington, DC, 2009, Black points out that when Hitler took over in 1933, 75% of attorneys in Berlin were Jewish (and close to these figures in doctors), pg 58. "Ninety per cent of the world's fur industry was in Jewish hands ..." pg 131. One source spoke of "the Jewish share of the wine trade" as 80%, pg 265. Also Black repeatedly points out that most Jews were Germans first and Jews second, and very much wanted to stay in Germany (pages 167, 175, 177, etc.).

Such quotes from Jewish sources could go on and on. But particularly in Germany it was felt that the Germans had done as much as anyone to advance the Jews and to be able to claim them as allies. There had been pogroms in Russia, but not in Germany. Jewish units with Jewish officers, served in the German army in both 1870 and in World War I. According to Black, in World War I 100,000 Jews served in the German armed services, 80,000 in the trenches, and 12,000 were killed, pg 168. [Which means that probably another 24,000+ were wounded, nf.]

When the Zionists started negotiating with various nations for help in establishing a national homeland, there were negotiations with the German government, as well as with the Turks and the British. The *Historical Atlas of the Jewish People* notes that when World War I came the Germans encouraged Jewish revolt against the Russians and promised "full equal rights to the Jews in any territory conquered by the Germans." On the Russian side "the Jews were suspected of collaboration with the Germans, and 600,000 of them were banished from the front," pg 210. There are similar stories from a variety of sources, for instance in Mark Levene's *War, the Jews, and the New Europe, the Diplomacy of Lucien Wolf, 1914-1919*, Oxford University Press, 1992. Technically, the Zionists were supposed to be neutral. In reality there was a tendency for German-Jews to be pro-German, and Lucien Wolf spent much of his time denying pro-German actions by Eastern European Jews. He was trying to get both sides to act with the utmost of neutrality to avoid postwar repercussions. The German High Command often returned Russian Jews captured on the Eastern front back to Russia as revolutionaries to work for the overthrow of the Tsar. As is well-known, the German High Command helped smuggle Lenin from Switzerland, across Germany, into Russia in a sealed railway car, for the purpose of knocking Russia out of World War I (which was done).

On the other side, the Zionists in England, under the leadership of Chaim Weismann, soon became very pro-British. At a time when Britain was being overwhelmed by the adversities of World War I, they agreed in the Balfour Declaration to support the Jews in seeking a national homeland in Palestine. So the British then opened another front in the Middle East to add to the responsibilities of the nation. Then for the Zionists, as Laqueur put it in *A History of Zionism*, the "aim was to induce America to join the war against the central powers as soon as possible" (pg 180), and the British were obviously expecting Zionist help in the new war winning strategy. *A Historical Atlas of the Jewish People* calls the Balfour agreement "a typical piece of wartime calculation," pgs 198-199. Weizmann biographer Jehudah Reinharz, goes to great length to deny any "deal," and speaks of what he calls "the myth of Jewish power and influence in the United States and Russia," but does say,

> "From the point of view of the British policy makers, the Balfour Declaration was a last-minute bid to tip the scales of war in their favor." Reinharz, *Chaim Weizmann, The Making of a Statesman*, pg 212

Weizmann assured the British "of world-wide Jewish support or potential support ..." Reinharz, pg 211. Such veiled statements are about as close to the truth as you can get in most places.

Israeli writer Tom Segev is more explicit, and summarized British leaders World War I views on the Jews. The British "admired ... despised ... and above all feared" the Jews. "They believed the Jews controlled the world." *One Palestine Complete, Jews and Arabs Under the British Mandate*, Tom Segev, (translated from the Hebrew by Haim Watzman), Metropolitan Books, Henry Holt & Co, LLC,

NY, 1999, 2000, pg 33. Lord Robert Cecil said, "I do not think that it is easy to exaggerate the international power of the Jews." pg 38. From the British Prime Minister's *Memoirs of the Peace Conference*, Segev quotes that Lloyd George called it a "contract," and that Lloyd George thought,

> "the Jews had every intention of determining the outcome of the World War—acting, he said, in accordance with their financial instincts. They could influence the United States to intensify its involvement in the war, and as the real movers behind the Russian Revolution, they also controlled Russia's attitude with Germany. ... The Jews of course offered themselves, of course, to the highest bidder ... Lloyd George believed that the friendship of the Jewish people would benefit Britain while Jewish hostility would harm it. **The British had thus no real choice—they had had to "make a contract with Jewry.""**
>
> Tom Segev, *One Palestine Complete, Jews and Arabs Under the British Mandate*, pg 38 (*bold emphasis added*)

There is, of course, much more to tell. Segev likewise hedges such information with insinuations that such British beliefs in Jewish power were naïve(??), a common evasion which you read in "serious" scholarship. [*Did they "Control the world"? No! Were they impotent to strike at their adversaries, or help their friends? Also, No! nf*] Even so, Segev's honesty and candor is seldom seen in World War I scholarship. Very few gentile historians have the courage to tell the truth about such matters, and many feign ignorance of what happened.

Naturally, the Germans felt they had as much call as anyone on Jewish fidelity and were very much surprised and disturbed by the wave of revolutionary violence which destabilized Germany during the armistice. The Allies benefited immensely from these revolutions, even though in the full sense they failed. But the Allies were never in a position to finance and direct these revolutions. The effect was such that by the time of the Versailles Peace Treaty the Germans were not able to offer any effective resistance to those onerous terms which led almost directly to ... the disintegration of Germany ... and the rise of Hitler ... and World War II. At the end, in Paris in 1919, the Zionist Mission came before "the Council of Ten" (of the League of Nations), and presented the Jews, not as neutrals, but "as citizens who had contributed toward winning the war." Reinharz, pgs 297-298.

In one way Balfour and the establishment of the state of Israel meant the greatest fruit of assimilation by the Jews so far. But some, like Lucien Wolf were afraid this meant the death of all the good fruits of assimilation. What then did Lucien Wolf think assimilation meant?

> "All that assimilation means, is that the Jews shall become good citizens in the same way as Roman Catholics are good citizens in England and Protestants are good citizens in France."

The Jewish Quarterly Review, Oct, 1904, pg 9.

I think that is a fair statement of the situation. To *many* Jews that is **all** it meant. Really though, as has been demonstrated, that was not what assimilation meant to some in Judaism. Also it must be admitted that many Jews were just plain tired of living in hostility to all nations, weary of living on the cutting edge of a knife, of living "like a fiddler on the roof" (if one wanted to coin a phrase!). Who would not want to escape from the ghastly demonic world in which many Jews lived, into the glorious light of God's beloved One and Only Son? So as an increasing tendency for assimilation became more organized and more aggressive, for more and more Jews it meant to treat Judaism/Pharisaism/Talmudism as irrelevant, obnoxious, and undesirable.

In fact, Lucien Wolf was deathly afraid that the invisible state, the assimilated Jews, would become visible. Many years before Balfour (1904) he was warning of the implications of these things.

> "The last attempt at the re-nationalization of Judaism by Sabbethai Zevi had failed disastrously, and even ignominiously. ... were now running riot in Cabalistical extravagance, were palsied by an ingrowing and stagnant bigotry or were engaged in mumbling the catchwords of misunderstood litanies as a sort of spiritual soporific."
> *The Jewish Quarterly Review*, Oct, 1904, Vol XVII, Macmillan and Co., NY, 1905, pg 5

> **"but the Zionist movement as it stands today** in its preliminary propaganda **is not without considerable danger to the security and happiness of the Jews throughout the world**."
> pg 19 (*bold emphasis added*)

He goes on to discuss Zionism as "an alien spirit." Alien that is to the spirit of living at peace with others. Wolf states this key objection even more clearly in a letter to Leopold de Rothschild, January 2, 1917.

> "I have no desire whatsoever to precipitate a controversy or schism but ... **our present policy of silence is** not likely to make for peace and **leading to perils infinitely worse than any public quarrel with the Zionists** ... in the higher interest of the Jewish community we cannot leave the situation as it is. **I am absolutely certain that when the preoccupations of this war have passed away, we shall find that the foolish things published by the Zionists will have seriously compromised the situation of the Jews all over the world."**
> *War, Jews, and the New Europe. The Diplomacy of Lucien Wolf 1914-1919*, by Mark Levene, Oxford University Press, London, 1992, pg 127 (*bold emphasis added*)

Of course, *although no one wants to admit it, that is exactly what happened.* In fact, I started to title this section, "Is Lucien Wolf among the prophets?" A century has gone by since these words were written, and many terrible things have happened, but the danger still lingers. **Balfour was clearly a crowning point of brilliant Jewish statesmanship** from a very disadvantaged position, **and it also inevitably carried with it those foreseen risks which are involved in violating neutrality in great conflicts**. These dangers will only end when there is 1.) a completion of the process of nationhood for the Jews, and 2.) when the predatory attitudes of many of the Jewish people toward the gentiles are neutralized by the Jews accepting the tenets of the Great Teacher of the Jews: Rabbi Yehoshua. **The real solution is Biblical Christianity.**

Assimilation as Success for the Jews

From time to time over the past 150 years Jewish books have appeared calling attention to their incredible successes. Such a recent work is Steven Silbiger's book, *The Jewish Phenomenon, Seven Keys to the Enduring Wealth of a People*, Longstreet Press, Atlanta, Georgia, 2000. Silbiger, gives some examples.

> "Jews make up only 2% of the total U.S. Population, yet 45% of the top 40 of the Forbes 400 richest Americans are Jewish

> "One third of all American multimillionaires are Jewish

> "The percentage of Jewish households with income greater than $50,000 is double that of non-Jews

> "On the other hand, the percentage of Jewish households with income less than $20,000 is half that of non-Jews

> "20% of professors at leading universities are Jewish

> "40% of partners in leading New York and Washington D.C. law firms are Jewish

> "25% percent of all American Nobel Prize winners are Jewish."
> (from the dust jacket. Compare pg 4.)

Might it be noted again that none of these figures include crypto-Jews. This assimilation has been accompanied with studious penetration of all centers of power with an incredible level of sophistication in politics, finance, international relations, education, entertainment, you name it. These "Court Jews" have had their ups and their downs, going all the way to Henry Morgenthau Jr. (President Franklin Delano Roosevelt's Secretary of the Treasury), and to today. Steven Silbiger's book, gives some examples, and a great deal of it being due to the Jews being motivated and working together.

> "On the campaign trail Jews are energetic volunteers. According to James Carville, outspoken Democratic consultant, "All you have in Democratic campaigns are Catholics and Jews. I don't know why, but

it's a standing joke. You show me twenty-five staffers in a Democratic campaign and you'll have maybe three Protestants."

"... Jews also have a greater direct representation to the houses of Congress than their population would dictate. In the 106th Congress of 1999, Jews were represented in the Senate at a rate five and one half times their representation in the population; in the house, the rate was three times greater. In the Senate there were eleven Jewish members (out of 100), one Republican, ten Democrats." pg 54

Silbiger is obviously proud of the accomplishments of the Jews, I might add, with considerable justification. The Jews *are* a very accomplished people. There is much more to tell from his book, and I am not just talking about politics. You might say, ***it is*** the *Jewish Phenomenon*. There is a tendency to see these sorts of things across the board down through the Christian Age, regardless of the type of government involved, from democracy to aristocracy, to oligarchy, to dictatorship. (In fact, because of their Platonic tendencies which have already been discussed, the Jews in one nation after another often *prefer* a dictatorship.) You can call it what you like, but it is indeed leverage.

One could go on and on, but there is no point to it. On a practical level, if you are talking to one of the leading heart or lung or surgical specialists in the world, or to one of the leading scholars in a phase of history or science, there is a very good chance you are speaking to someone who is of Jewish ancestry, even if he or she is not an active Jew. They are by no means in the majority, but their influence is very keen even at or near the top of many fields, if not most fields. Their pursuit of excellence and top positions is very tenacious. If you are speaking of biological-genetic-national drive, the only close parallels in the modern world would be some of the Asian nations, but they do not have the depth in the Western world that the Jews have, and they have not concentrated on politically dominating their hosts. As Jewish historian Dr. Josef Kastein observes in his introduction to his *History and Destiny of the Jews*, Garden City Publishing, Garden City, New York, 1936; "the mere fact of being different ... may lead to productivity." pg 5.

Even so, when you take a broad view, *one* of the factors in this success is systematic *concealed* direction toward unified purposes. These have often been very worldly purposes, but unified, nonetheless. They work together, in contrast to most of the gentile groups they encounter in which there is no such cohesiveness. The Jews have been able as a group to coordinate many of their activities and have been able to assign men to tasks or endeavors they have thought necessary or useful and mentored them to these ends. Often they have very astutely forecast major directions which societies have been taking socially, economically, scientifically, politically, and technologically. These things in themselves have been considerable achievements, especially when you remember that the Jews of the last 2,000 years have demographically been only a tiny sliver of the world population. Just to accurately forecast in the late 1800's, the direction of physics in the 20th century, so as to be able at the right times to have in place competent Jewish physicists at the heart of the developments for nuclear weapons *when they were developing*, is an astonishing accomplishment. They have not duplicated this level of insight in every field, but even so, their accomplishments have been spectacular.

Another advantage of the Jews has been that since they really had no homeland, and they were continually moving around, they continually had the "outsiders" advantage in looking at things. On many levels, we never really understand ourselves and the systems we live under, until we see them from the viewpoint of an outsider. Some people *never* move around, *never* read from people who are not like themselves, and *never* really come to see themselves or their systems objectively. That is often a very great loss. The Jews have never been like this as a group during the entire Christian age. Combine that with their Talmudic instincts for slicing and dicing ideas, and for hair-splitting, then you have all the tools for objectively looking at yourself and whatever situation you are in. These have been the finest intellectual tools one could ask for in order to be masterful merchants, politicians, scientists, professionals, or advisors.

As in every phase of this book, there is more to tell than there is space for telling. It would be enjoyable to discuss the Jewish influence on American culture, which for sure has not always been good, and only rarely could be described as showing Christian principles. However it has often been a tone setting role. In entertainment the discussion could range from Samuel Goldwyn, and George Gershwin, to many others. Admittedly many of these things have been enjoyable, but there is not space here for all of that.

Success in Israel, With Some Qualifications

It seems that Israel is completely dominant in the Middle East. In addition the United States has been fighting a series of devastating wars to ruin all of her would be enemies. The ultra-orthodox brag about these things in Hebrew in Israel and are quiet about these same things in America. It seems that no American administration can resist Israeli influence and still get elected. As Mersheimer and Walt demonstrate in *The Israel Lobby and U. S. Foreign Policy*, Farrar, Straus and Giroux, NY, 2007, Israel is very demanding in getting her way. Israel continually touts the righteousness of her cause, and the wickedness of any who would oppose her.

Still there are disquieting voices here and there, and sometimes the truth is acknowledged. Israeli war hero General Moshe Dayan has summarized the situation this way.

> ""It is not true that the Arabs hate the Jews for personal, religious, or racial reasons. They consider us—and justly from their point of view—

as Westerners, foreigners, invaders who have seized an Arab country to turn it into a Jewish state." Speaking at the funeral of a murdered friend, just before the Sinai campaign of 1967, Dayan said: "We must beware of blaming the murderers. Who are we to reproach them for hating us? Colonists who transform into a Jewish home-land the territory they have lived in for generations.""

Noam Chomsky, *Middle East Illusions*, Rowan & Littlefield Publishers, Inc., NY, 2004, pg 43

Chomsky is an interesting person. He is Jewish, a professed anarchist, a professor at MIT, an internationally recognized expert on linguistics, an extreme left-wing political activist, and a social and political commentator. As a young man, he and his wife considered moving to Israel and spent some time there living and working in one of the farming communes. He was turned off by much of the Jewish racism and mistreatment of the Arabs, and they returned to the United States. He fearlessly denounces whoever he thinks is in the wrong, including Israel. Consequently both conservatives and liberals tend to treat him as a pariah. He was a protest organizer against the Vietnam War and was at one time on Richard Nixon's "enemies list." But though from the extreme left, his research and comments are carefully reasoned and documented, and are well worth reading, even if you disagree with many of his basic positions. (Which I personally do.) I also thought at one point of titling that previous section as, "Is Chomsky Among the Prophets?" But Chomsky is too calculating to ever really be a prophet, too inclined to qualify his judgments, too much aware of how easy it is for anyone, including himself, to misjudge a situation. But he does seem to think that Israel is living in a world of illusions.

> "Guarantees of security do not exist. In the long run, Israel's security rests on relations with its neighbors. The policy of annexation rules out long-term security as unobtainable and thus virtually **guarantees further military conflict and the ultimate destruction of a state that can lose only once**." *Middle East Illusions*, pg 26 (*bold emphasis added*)

Ah! There you are: "**virtually** guarantees"! More than one person senses disaster in the making. Hubris does not go unpunished, even in this world,

> for "God resists the proud, but gives grace to the humble."
> 1Pe 5:5 WEB

Despite Israel's apparent ability to muffle all criticism, Lucien Wolf's warnings are still pertinent.

And Assimilation as a Threat to the Jews

"Assimilation" as it is called, has given the Jews their greatest opportunities and their greatest benefits during the last two thousand years, and especially during the last two hundred years. As has been shown, it really began following the Babylonian captivity, with operations like that of Esther becoming the queen of Persia and has been a continuous occurrence during the Christian age.

It has been discussed that infiltration is often a sword which cuts both ways. That those who are good at becoming part of foreign people, are also those most likely to be compromised by their work of infiltration. They often come to like, or even love, their targets. They have to learn the nuances of their target's culture and habits, and often come to appreciate what is good about those people ... often come to cross that line of separation, and become one with them. This is also true of Christians trying to reach out to the lost, so that to understand them often influences morals and values. Huge are the losses in modern Christianity of children subjected to what are really pagan cultures in government school systems. To prepare the children to operate as Christians in these cultures without it destroying them is a daunting task. One of the strategies of the rabbis was to keep *everyone* under close control, even tyrannical control. This *was* in one way effective and still is with the ultra-conservative Jews in Israel, but it is also suffocating and demeaning and hobbles intelligent human development. Also, it was detrimental to obtaining the best fruits of crypto-Judaism. In fact I think it is clear that the tremendous Jewish gains of the last 200 years would not have happened but for the loosening of rabbinical controls. Lastly, many Jewish writers today have expressed their apprehension that unless the ultra-conservative rabbis' grip over much of the modern nation of Israel is loosened, they may cause its unneeded and unnecessary downfall.

Additionally, it is clear that the Jews have suffered great losses during the last two thousand years. Part of this can be seen in the overall population figures, which can be found in resources like *A Historical Atlas of the Jewish People*. Their very worthwhile study begins on pgs xii-1 in a study and chart of Jewish demographics. The losses have been tremendous, and seemingly continuous throughout the entire Christian age. A more detailed treatment can be seen in various essays in Cecil Roth's *Personalities And Events In Jewish History*, 1953 (which will be abbreviated as *Personalities* in the following readings).

Roth is no stranger to this subject. He speaks of "assimilated Jews like ourselves," *Personalities*, pg 10. Then as a historian Roth tries to critically examine the evidence at hand. On one hand he estimates there were 4 to 5 million Jews in the Roman Empire, or as high as 10 million, pg 34. In another place he estimates the Roman Empire as having 55 to 100 million people, and the Jews in the time of the Emperor Claudius numbering 6,944,000, pg 39. But from the 10th century to the 17th century he says the Jews seemed to be as little as 1.5

million world-wide, pg 34. In another place he speaks of them ranging from 1 million to 1.5 million "at the outside," pgs 39-40.

During the same period of time the world population tended to steadily increase, but the Jewish population trended downward, despite what Roth calls the Jew's "legendary prolificness," pg 41. So it is only in modern times that the Jewish population has approached the huge numbers seen in the first century of the Christian age.

So what were the causes? As a historian Roth in *Personalities* ... points to assimilation, pgs 40-41, and to massacres, pgs 41-42. That fits the standard propaganda line pretty well to a point, but Roth also points to other things. Cecil Roth is an Italian Jew, and he points to continual conversions of Jews to Catholicism over many centuries. He supplies samples of the documentation and makes the point that much of this was not under any duress. Yes, he tells terrible stories of oppression, and even of kidnapping Jewish children to raise them as "Christians." Still, he also points to "continual attrition," "conversion from necessity, conversion from conviction, conversion from compulsion," pg 35. However, in the middle of all of this, is the reluctant admission that many Jews sneaked away, or just plain ran away from the control of the rabbis, who loved to keep them under their thumb, and still do!

Of course the prophets clearly pointed out that most Jews would reject their own Messiah. There are *many* passages to this effect, including,

> [14] And he shall be for a sanctuary; but for a stone of stumbling and for a rock of offence to both the houses of Israel, for a gin and for a snare to the inhabitants of Jerusalem. [15] And many among them shall stumble, and fall, and be broken, and be snared, and be taken.
>
> Isa 8:14-15 KJV

A "sanctuary" and "a stone of stumbling ... for a snare ..." Oh my! What a tragedy! As a Christian, even though the prophets clearly pointed to these things, I was also gratified that there was "at the present time a remnant according to God's gracious choice." Rom 11:5. I could see these things in the many conversions of the Jews both before and after the early church started preaching to the gentiles. I wondered about so many who stayed among the lost throughout the Christian age. Were there no Jews converted during those times. The answer of course is that there were. There were many. Many among even those sent to infiltrate Christianity, Gal 2:4, etc. Sometimes you can see these things among operatives, both Jewish and otherwise. You can almost see it written on their faces ... why am I trying to destroy these people ... I like these people. This is so much better than stultifying, suffocating, Pharisaism ... why am I here? Why am I doing this? So I think the answer is that many of those sent to assimilate among the gentiles ... finally crossed that line to firmly leave Judaism.

Roth points out that in Spain *many* did sincerely convert to Christianity. A wide range of historians point out that probably most Spaniards have at least some Jewish blood in their veins. After recounting these forces working in Germany he says,

> "The Jewish strain in the German people must necessarily be stronger than even the most fanatical Nazi is willing to admit."
> *Personalities*, pg 35

And when Roth goes on to speak of the assimilations since 1800, he says,

> "At the risk of repetition, I want to make it quite clear that assimilation was not due only to pressure; during the past one hundred years or so, it has been a spontaneous process." pg 49

Sometimes we get some insight into Jews who cross back and forth across the line between Jew and gentile, in studies like Michael Beschloss' *The Conquerors*, which is a study of "*Roosevelt, Truman and Destruction of Hitler's Germany, 1941-1945*," Simon and Schuster, NY, 2003. There are many interesting character studies in Beschloss's book, including many interesting sidelights on Roosevelt's Jewish Secretary of the Treasury Henry Morgenthau, Jr.

Morgenthau was a throughly assimilated Jew. He was not really a banking type, though he was Secretary of the Treasury for many years. Morgenthau was so secular that at age "fifty-two, he had never attended a Passover seder." *The Conquerers*, pg 43. At age five, someone had asked young Henry what his religion was. He did not know, so he asked his mom, and she said, "Just tell them you're an American." pg 46. His dad was a wealthy man in his own right, and said, "We Jews of America have found America to be our Zion. I am an American." Beschloss, pg 46.

As an aside I would comment that many Jews have viewed America this way, and many Jews who have seen both Israel and the United States cannot wait to get back to the United States. There are *many* ex-Israelis in the United States. I cannot help but think of one of the books in my library, titled *This Happy Land*, James William Hagy, The University of Alabama Press, Tuscaloosa and London, 1993, speaking of Jews in South Carolina. If you read much from Israeli Jewish writers, you cannot miss the comments which indicate they are wistfully looking at the many good things of America which cannot be reproduced in even a watered down Pharisaical culture.

Henry Morgenthau, Jr., had often been called on to represent the Jews, but he was not a Zionist until the late 1940's. If you read Zionist literature, it often treats Morgenthau as if he were some sort of idiot, but that is how some Jews treat *anyone* who disagrees with them. His dad had warned him, "Don't have anything to do with the Jews ... They'll stab you in the back." Beschloss, pg 251.

The son generally tried to stay away from Jewish issues while he was in government service, but at the height of World War II the terrible things that Hitler and his cohorts were doing in Germany to the Jews were coming to light.

Morgenthau did not learn these things from U. S. intelligence, but from Jewish intelligence links to Rabbi Stephen Wise. Wise would meet with Morgenthau to tell him what they knew about these things; Morgenthau would plead for Wise to spare him the details, but Wise would continue with the grizzly details. At some point, Morgenthau sort of snapped. He indeed became a zealous advocate in the Roosevelt administration for saving Jews. In fact, beyond all of that, at the end of World War II he put forth the notorious "Morgenthau Plan." It was a kind of reverse genocide plan. This plan envisioned isolating Germany, exporting all her means of manufacturing and production except farming and shepherding, etc., and starving off the rest of the population. Morgenthau's retort was, "Well, that is not nearly as bad as sending them to the gas chambers." Beschloss, pg 90. Secretary of War Stimson estimated that even after World War II, Germany had 30 million more people than she could support by agriculture. Not to ignore the guilt of many Germans in the genocidal plans of the Nazi, the plan was rightfully rejected, but Morgenthau is a good illustration of how those who have turned away from Judaism can sometimes be completely turned back to Judaism.

What then of assimilation today? Many Jews around the world, and especially in America, are so in love with their freedoms that there are realistic fears of the Jews as a group disappearing completely. For the past say 30 years, the *Wall Street Journal* has from time to time had articles about this very real danger. For instance Arnold M. Eisen's editorial "Wanted: Converts to Judaism," *Wall Street Journal, July* 25, 2014, pg A11. Even in Israel, the secular Jews have typical Western style birth rates, and many abortions. The Arabs in Israel already are 20% of the population, have high birth rates and do not practice abortion. Many books fearfully look at this dilemma.

So on one hand some gentiles may fear that anyone who is of Jewish descent may not be loyal to the nation of which they are citizens. On the other hand, Jewish publications run articles from time to time on some programs to retrieve assimilated descendants, for instance in Poland, to return to the religion of their ancestors. There are organized programs for Israel to reclaim many completely assimilated Jews. "Israel to spend billions on Jewish Diaspora initiative," *The International Jerusalem Post*, Jan 17-23, 2014, pg 9. Or again "Lazar's mission," *International Jerusalem Post*, May 16-22, 2014, pg 10ff. It says there, "Russia's chief rabbi says he stays out of politics to focus on bringing an assimilated generation of Jews into fold." So these and other articles you could cite are about bringing back to Judaism some of the many who sincerely assimilated and completely deserted Judaism. I think many Christians in America know some of Jewish descent who have sincerely converted to Christianity.

It is also easy to see there is definitely another side to this story. You can see articles like "Coming up for air," in the September 12-18, 2014, *The International Jerusalem Post,* about "Lt. Cmdr. Y. (full name withheld for security reasons)" who is retiring from heading Israel's submarine school. The Commander mentions that those who stay in the submarine service receive "a first-level security clearance," which means among other things that "we know they have no dual citizenship, and no problematic history that would prevent them from getting the highest security clearance."! So dual citizenship *can* pose a security risk! So says Israeli intelligence.

So assimilation cuts both ways. Literally. Could it be that the source of Israel's greatest gains, will also be her undoing?

Is it Assimilation or Human Bondage?

Is the alternative to extinction by assimilation going to be a Fundamentalists-Pharisee-Talmudic-Kabbalistic tyranny, with the rabbis ready to put to death anyone eating a cheeseburger or munching on grain on the Sabbath day (Mtt 12:1-3)? Maintaining order by endless minutia that goes beyond Scripture, and is more than anyone can possibly absorb or remember; and militantly denying the Messiah of the LORD our God?

That is the real dilemma for Israel today, as the fundamentalist sects in Israel today try to re-impose some sort of Talmudic-Kabbalistic-Halacha on the entire nation. These are terrible problems the still infant nation in Palestine is seeking to solve. In the Western media you can see the "sincere" ultra-orthodox by the Wailing Wall, bobbing their heads and reading and chanting something, and we think these are "real" Jews. But no! Almost all of these "ultra-orthodox" are Kabbalistic-occult sects with a veneer of Scripture. Their head bobbing is for some sort of self-hypnosis so they can draw nearer to God "for their much speaking." Much of this is so bizarre that many in Israel will not even come close to a synagogue. Is it "messianic"? Yes, but much of this is about a human-Kabbalistic-"messiah", *not* the LORD our God of Glory, Jesus of Nazareth.

This Halacha of God's Words, *with* men's words and traditions ruling **over** God's Word, was *never* part of the righteousness of God. It is still as true as it always was,

> Ye shall not add unto the word which I command you, neither shall ye diminish ought from it, that ye may keep the commandments of the LORD your God which I command you. Deut 4:2 KJV

> What thing soever I command you, observe to do it: thou shalt not add thereto, nor diminish from it. Deut 12:32 KJV

That was binding on the prophets of the Old Testament and is still binding today.

What is one of the things that could bring Israel down? Norton Merzinsky quotes Ze'ev Chafets from the *Jerusalem Report:*

> "The Arabs can't destroy Israel, but the rabbis can. The rabbis can do

that by turning Israel into ... a place governed by clerical law and clerical thinking which has become so backward and xenophobic that Israel won't be able to function as a state."
Shahak, *Jewish Fundamentalism in Israel*, pg x.

It is not that God's religion through Moses will not work. Instead, it is that it has been turned aside from its natural development, into a man made occult system. Moses will yet be truly honored in all of Israel, and so will their Great Prophet, Rabbi Yehoshua. It will be wonderful beyond all description, and successful almost beyond description, even on a worldly scale. But other things must happen first.

Micah: Sin, Repentance, Salvation, and Dominance, Yet to Come.

[28] For he is not a Jew, which is one outwardly; neither *is that* circumcision, which is outward in the flesh: [29] But he *is* a Jew, which is one inwardly; and circumcision *is that* of the heart, in the spirit, *and* not in the letter; whose praise *is* not of men, but of God. Rom 2:28-29 KJV

It is a common pattern in prophecy that the prophet starts with whatever is the situation in the present time, and goes all the way to the conclusion of these things, or even, all the way to the conclusion of ALL things. It is easy to see in Scriptures, for instance, in Jesus' letters to the seven churches of Asia in the book of Revelation. These letters go all the way from where the churches are now, through all the Christian age, to where this leads in eternity! Actually that is a common format for prophecy, both Old Testament and New Testament, and Micah likewise follows this format.

However, the prophets seldom describe these things in anything like a strict chronological order. Rather, it is more like a father describing to his children what they will be facing in a major move they are making, both the exciting and wonderful things and also some of the threats and trials they may face. Such discussions are often topical, and conversational, and seldom strictly chronological. The children could not understand it anyway. However the emphasis is on different things at different times.

In our present case, Micah talks first about where Jacob's sins (and yours and mine) end up when we wake up on the last days of this present earth and we see the Lord coming for judgment,

3   For, behold, the LORD cometh forth out of his place, and will come down, and tread upon the high places of the earth.

4   And the mountains shall be molten under him, and the valleys

shall be cleft, as wax before the fire, and as the waters that are poured down a steep place. Mic 1:3-4 KJV

These verses are not far from New Testament verses like 2Thes 1:7-8. And why will these things happen? It will be because of their sins.

> 5 For the transgression of Jacob is all this, and for the sins of the house of Israel. What is the transgression of Jacob? is it not Samaria? and what are the high places of Judah? are they not Jerusalem?
> 6 Therefore I will make Samaria as an heap of the field, and as plantings of a vineyard: and I will pour down the stones thereof into the valley, and I will discover the foundations thereof. Mic 1:5-6 KJV

But the Jews Have Been Pursuing Their Own Way.

Even so, despite the words of Moses and the prophets, the Jews have been pursing deliverance by human effort, by plan, procedure, formula and policy; by collusion and operatives. So when Christ came, and salvation by faith was more clearly declared, they stumbled. This was just as prophesied in Isaiah 7 and Isaiah 8, and especially in Isa 8:13-15.

> 13 Sanctify the LORD of hosts himself; and *let* him *be* your fear, and *let* him *be* your dread. 14 And **he shall be for a sanctuary; but for a stone of stumbling and for a rock of offence to both the houses of Israel**, for a gin and for a snare to the inhabitants of Jerusalem. 15 And many among them shall stumble, and **fall, and be broken**, and be **snared, and be taken**. KJV (*bold emphasis added*)

In other words, Isaiah says that both houses of Israel *will stumble* over God's salvation, over the Messiah to come. **He will be a trap for Jerusalem** and "**many**" will stumble and fall and be broken. *The Lord our God is a rock of help, or if you refuse to believe, a rock which will smash you.* The Jews had developed their own righteousness, *but it was like ours*, the self-righteousness of the nations. It was not, and is not, in itself, worth a mechanic's "damn!"

> 6 But we are **all** as an unclean *thing*, and **all our righteousnesses** *are* **as filthy rags;** and we **all** do fade as a leaf; **and our iniquities**, like the wind, **have taken us away**. 7 And *there is* none that calleth upon thy name, that stirreth up himself to take hold of thee: for thou hast hid thy face from us, and hast consumed us, because of our iniquities. Isa 64:6-7 KJV (*bold emphasis added*)

One of the key passages in Scripture concerning the Jews is Jesus' discussion with the Pharisees in Matthew 15.

> 7 "Hypocrites! Well did Isaiah prophesy about you, saying:
> 8   "*These people draw near to Me with their mouth,*
>   *And honor Me with their lips,*

> *But their heart is far from Me.*
> 9   *And in vain they worship Me,*
> *Teaching as doctrines the commandments of men.'* " Mtt 15:7-9 NKJV

Jesus was talking to the Pharisees here. He is saying that their traditions are not to be taken above Scriptures or even to be thought of as a foundation for serious thinking. Here then is the crux of the matter. They have refused to give up their own goodness, their own human "superiority," in order to accept the righteousness of God. Like many we may all know, they *do* have zeal, Rom 10:1-3, but it is not according to knowledge. But Paul says that Jesus is the end of the Law, Rom 10:4. That word "end" is the word *telos* τέλος, and it means the end or goal of something, that is to say, what the law aims at. Jesus is the Messiah at which the law aims. He is the goal, He meets the goal, and He becomes our goal, our objective, our purpose, *if we are to live.* Jesus fulfills the law,

> Think not that I am come to destroy the law, or the prophets: I am not come to destroy, but to fulfil. Matt 5:17 KJV

The law was a tutor to bring us to Jesus, to the Christ, (Rabbi Yehoshua, Jn 1:38, 3:2, etc.), so that we may be justified by faith, to replace the feeble marred righteousness that we have on our own, Gal 3:24. So having brought a righteousness we could not have on our own, Jesus brings the law to an end, and it was nailed with Him to the cross, Col 2:14.

Righteousness by law is impossible to obtain, that "by which a man may live if he does them," Lev 18:5. As can be seen from Romans 7, and from life, we just cannot do well enough. In contrast, the righteousness of faith is not difficult, as Paul points out in Rom 10:5-8. Paul here quotes Deut 30:11-14 to show that Moses around 1400 BC is declaring faith as the way. The basis of salvation has always been trusting, *obedient*, **faith**, *not* depending on human ability or plan or artifice or ritual to perform everything impeccably. The next part is that this salvation by faith is salvation *for all*, and yes, that does include the gentiles, that is to say the nations.

> 12 For there is no difference between the Jew and the Greek: for the same Lord over all is rich unto all that call upon him. 13 For whosoever shall call upon the name of the Lord shall be saved.
> Rom 10:12-13 KJV

What wonderful, abounding, generosity and grace God has given to all men! Paul in Romans 10:13 is quoting from Joel 2:32.

> Also There is Awesome Information About the Messiah,
> And Good Things Yet to Come for physical Israel.

What this Messiah will accomplish?

Of this ruler whose goings and coming are from everlasting, Micah says,

> "**He will be our peace** when Assyria invades our land,
>> And when he marches through our fortresses,
>> Then we will raise against him seven shepherds,
>> And eight leaders of men." Mic 5:5 WEB

Ah! "He will be our peace," truly even in trial. Assyria had invaded in Micah's time. In Isaiah chapters 36 and 37 it describes all of Judah being overrun, except Jerusalem. But when this ruler comes, He will raise up shepherds *against* the Assyrians. Shepherd is often a synonym for rulers in Scripture, as in 1Kgs 22:16-18. Of these later shepherds/rulers Micah says,

> "**They will rule the land of Assyria with the sword**,
>> And the land of Nimrod in its gates.
> **He will deliver us from the Assyrian**,
>> When he invades our land,
>> And when he marches within our border." Mic 5:6 WEB

So from the bounty of this future ruler it will be that **Israel will rule Assyria!** Now this has not happened yet! Still it should be noted that the Assyrian people, though small today, still exist, mainly in Iraq and Syria,

And a Future Dispersion for GOOD!

> "The remnant of Jacob will be in the midst of many peoples,
>> **Like dew from Yahweh,**
>> **Like showers on the grass,**
>> That don't wait for man,
>> Nor wait for the sons of men." Micah 5:7 WEB

When the Jews are converted to Jesus of Nazareth in the Great Distress, Scripture pictures the Jews as leading in the preaching of the gospel to an unsaved world. Could that be this?

Jacob will be like a lion among the nations, and will rule over many peoples.

> [8] The remnant of Jacob will be among the nations,
>> In the midst of many peoples,
>> Like a lion among the animals of the forest,
>> Like a young lion among the flocks of sheep;
>> Who, if he goes through, treads down and tears in pieces,
>>> And there is no one to deliver.
> [9] Let your hand be lifted up above your adversaries,

> And let all of your enemies be cut off. Mic 5:8-9 WEB

What is described as the survivors/escapees/the remnant from the time of great stress will then carry the gospel to the nations.

> I will set a sign among them, and **I will send such as <u>escape</u> of <u>them</u> to the nations**, to Tarshish, Pul, and Lud, who draw the bow, to Tubal and Javan, to the isles afar off, who have not heard my fame, neither have seen my glory; **and they shall declare my glory among the nations**. Isa 66:19 WEB

Further, Israel will bring the the nations to account.

> ... And **you** will beat in pieces **many peoples**:
> And I will **devote their gain** to Yahweh,
>   And their substance to the Lord of the whole earth. Mic 4:13b WEB

So the mid-Christian-age persecution by ALL nations, of first Christians and then including Jews (clouds of which may even be gathering now), will be avenged. Even in worldly terms. God will indeed care for His own, both temporally and eternally. So whose are you? And I? Are you really your own man? Or are you God's?

Wonderful promises! However the Jews have NOT been listening to God!

So Paul concludes it was because of their sins, that the Jews would not believe. "ALL THE DAY LONG I HAVE STRETCHED OUT MY HANDS TO **A DISOBEDIENT AND OBSTINATE PEOPLE**," Rom 10:21 NASB (*emphasis added*). The original from Isaiah is even better, and it tells vividly, why God turned to the nations.

> [1] I am sought of them that asked not for me; I am found of them that sought me not: I said, Behold me, behold me, unto a nation that was not called by my name. [2] **I have spread out my hands all the day unto a rebellious people, which walketh in a way that was not good, <u>after their own thoughts</u>;** [3] A people that provoketh me to anger continually to my face; that sacrificeth in gardens, and burneth incense upon altars of brick; [4] Which remain among the graves, and lodge in the monuments, which eat swine's flesh, and broth of abominable things is in their vessels; [5] **Which say, Stand by thyself, come not near to me; for I am holier than thou. These are a smoke in my nose, a fire that burneth all the day.**
> Isa 65:1-5 KJV (*emphasis added*)

Thus Isaiah says the same thing that Paul says, and makes special note of their occult practices even many centuries before Christ. So then God will call to others who will listen.

So in the end, of the losses and frustrations, **it is Israel's own fault**.

Only a Remnant will be Saved, Rom 9:27-29

This is a factor which affects both Jews and the nations. It is a fact of our age, every human age. In every generation, regardless of origin, it is only a remnant which survive, which will be saved. *The great mass of people end up paying for their own sins themselves:* a debt so great that men will never be able to touch the principal. We are indeed "fearfully *and* wonderfully made." Jeremiah compares the saved to the few grapes left on a vine. The gleaners have come through and only found a few worth keeping, Jer 6:9. So God is pictured as throughly searching for the few worth keeping.

> And there shall be an highway **for the remnant of his people, which shall be left,** from Assyria; like as it was to Israel in the day that he came up out of the land of Egypt. Isa 11:16 KJV (*bold emphasis added*)

He is speaking about the number who will survive the Assyrian conquest and deportation, and again be part of the true faith of God, and it describes them as a remnant, a surviving trace of the original number. Most of them did not survive. King Hezekiah urged the small remnant of his day to be faithful,

> ... Ye children of Israel, turn again unto the LORD God of Abraham, Isaac, and Israel, and he will return to the remnant of you, that are escaped out of the hand of the kings of Assyria. 2Chron 30:6 KJV

Later on Ezra urged the remnant from the first captivity to repent, Ez 9:14-15. There was only a small number left, and quite differently from the book of Esther, Ezra asked them why again would they break God's commandments and marry outside the faith? Ezra also indicates they have not been faithful in these things, and that they are in fact *a remnant **which is guilty** before the Lord*, as indeed they are even to this day.

So why is only a small number to be left? The answer of Scripture is that *it is not impossible to be otherwise,* rather it is because of our bad decisions. We can make other decisions. Elijah felt that he alone had been faithful.

> And he said, I have been very jealous for the LORD God of hosts: because the children of Israel have forsaken thy covenant, thrown down thine altars, and slain thy prophets with the sword; and I, even I only, am left; and they seek my life, to take it away. 1Kgs 19:14 KJV

God assures him that a few are left, a remnant.

> Yet I have left me seven thousand in Israel, all the knees which have not bowed unto Baal, and every mouth which hath not kissed him. 1Kgs 19:18 KJV

This is a pattern that can be seen down through history, that only a few are faithful despite *God's* faithfulness. In Hosea 13 the prophet gives the Lord's words to His people. They were to know no god but Yahweh the LORD. He cared for them in the wilderness, and in a deserted and desolate place He provided them with food and water. Even so, when they came to Canaan and had good pasture, they became complacent and contented and puffed up with themselves, and they forgot the Lord who had given them their pleasant pasture. So what will God do to Israel?

> [7] Therefore I will be unto them as a lion: as a leopard by the way will I observe *them*: [8] I will meet them as a bear that is bereaved *of her whelps*, and will rend the caul of their heart, and there will I devour them like a lion: the wild beast shall tear them. Hos 13:7-8 KJV

God is the lion in Hosea 13. After the lion has attacked, and the flock has been destroyed for unfaithfulness, the shepherd is only able to snatch from the lion's mouth a couple of legs, or a piece of an ear in Amos 3:12. Amos says this is the way it will be with unfaithful Israel in Samaria. They will be snatched away with the corner of a bed and the cover of a couch! The implications of these doctrines of a remnant are twofold.

First, it is only a remnant which is left, and it is those who are crippled. It is only the lame and outcasts and the afflicted which God gathers as a "remnant." This will be true of the final faithful at the Second Coming, and it will also be true of the remanent of Israel which will be delivered at the end of the first world -wide persecution of Christianity.

> [6] "In that day," says Yahweh,
> "I will assemble that which is lame,
> And I will gather that which is driven away,
> And that which I have afflicted.
> [7] **"And I will make that which was lame a remnant,
> And that which was cast far off a strong nation:**
> And the Yahweh will reign over them in Mount Zion
> **From now on and forever."** Mic 4:6-7 WEB (*emphasis added*)

So it is that the blessing really is on "the poor in spirit." Literally. ***Secondly,*** only a remnant is left ***so that*** God's people do not end up like Sodom and Gomorrah, again like Mic 4:6-7. It is clearly seen in Isaiah one, speaking of Judah.

> Except the LORD of hosts had left unto us a very small remnant, we should have been as Sodom, *and* we should have been like unto Gomorrah. Isa 1:9 KJV

The real point is that *this is the way it has always been,* and if a remnant had not been left, ***none*** *would have been left!* Look at the record. Look for instance at the flood. In the time of Noah only eight people out of the world had not given themselves over to violence and sin, Gen 7:13. It seems the world perished despite the preaching of Noah and despite God giving them an extra one hundred and twenty years to repent, as is indicated in Gen 6:3. Then out of a world of people that had again arisen in the generations following the flood, God called only Abraham from Ur, in what was later called Babylon, Gen 11:31-12:3. Why was he acceptable? He was willing to leave everything he had in this world. He was willing to believe God. Some of us, on the other hand, are not so willing.

The same thing happened with the twelve spies sent to spy out the land when they had first come out of Egypt. Israel was to go immediately into the land of Canaan. They could have had the good land *at that time*, and *could have kept it* until the end of time. Still they would not trust God and His promises. All of the spies had acknowledged the fruitfulness and plenty of the land, a plenty which does not remain after all these years of desolation and sin. Even so, only two of the spies said that they could capture the land as God had promised, and the other ten spies said that it was just beyond their ability to capture, despite God's promises.

> ²⁶ "Nevertheless you would not go up, but rebelled against the command of the LORD your God; ²⁷ and you complained in your tents, and said, "Because the LORD hates us, He has brought us out of the land of Egypt to deliver us into the hand of the Amorites, to destroy us."" Deut 1:26-27 NKJV

So refusing to trust God's willingness or ability to save, despite what they had seen in Egypt (for in truth, *seeing incredible things often has no more effect on our behavior than reading and believing those things in accounts written by the prophets*), so all of those men, including Moses, were forbidden to enter that symbolic heaven, Canaan the promised land. The exceptions were only the two faithful spies, Joshua and Caleb.

> ³⁴ And the LORD heard the voice of your words, and was wroth, and sware, saying, ³⁵ Surely there shall not one of these men of this evil generation see that good land, which I sware to give unto your fathers, Deut 1:34-35 KJV

Talk about only a remnant surviving! Of the original 600,000 men of the census in Israel, only two survived. **It wasn't because it was impossible!** It was because of moral decisions made by men, hearts departing from trusting in God. It was for resting and trusting only in themselves and their feeble abilities. They had no confidence in what God said He would do.

As the prophet John the Baptist told the men of Judah of his own day:

> ⁷ But when he saw many of the Pharisees and Sadducees come to his baptism, he said unto them, O generation of vipers, who hath warned you to flee from the wrath to come? ⁸ Bring forth therefore fruits meet for repentance: ⁹ And think not to say within yourselves, We have Abraham to *our* father: for I say unto you, that God is able of these stones to raise up children unto Abraham. ¹⁰ And now also the axe is laid unto the root of the trees: therefore every tree which bringeth not forth good fruit is hewn down, and cast into the fire. Mtt 3:7-10 KJV

It is still that way today, for both Jews and gentiles, but Paul speaks particularly about the Jews here.

> [27] Isaiah cries out concerning Israel, "THOUGH THE NUMBER OF THE SONS OF ISRAEL BE LIKE THE SAND OF THE SEA, **IT IS THE REMNANT THAT WILL BE SAVED;** [28] FOR THE LORD WILL EXECUTE HIS WORD ON THE EARTH, THOROUGHLY AND QUICKLY." [29] And just as Isaiah foretold,
>
> > "UNLESS THE LORD OF SABAOTH HAD LEFT TO US A POSTERITY,
> >
> > WE WOULD HAVE BECOME LIKE SODOM, AND WOULD HAVE RESEMBLED GOMORRAH." Rom 9:27-29 NASB

So it is, "Even so then at this present time also there is a remnant according to the election of grace." Rom 11:5 KJV. "**For many are called but few *are* chosen**," Mtt 22:14 KJV. Listen to God's greatest prophet Jesus of Nazareth, the Lion of the Tribe of Judah.

> [21] Not every one that saith unto me, Lord, Lord, shall enter into the kingdom of heaven; but he that doeth the will of my Father which is in heaven. [22] Many will say to me in that day, Lord, Lord, have we not prophesied in thy name? and in thy name have cast out devils? and in thy name done many wonderful works? [23] And then will I profess unto them, I never knew you: depart from me, ye that work iniquity.
> Mtt 7:21-23 KJV

Ritual is *not* the key. Listen to me Sodom and Gomorrah, who asked you to worship Me? is what God asks Judah in Isa 1:10-11. Who asked you to come to church?

> [12]   When you come to appear before me,
>   Who has required this at your hand, to trample my courts?
> [13]   Bring no more vain offerings.
>   Incense is an abomination to me;
>   New moons, Sabbaths, and convocations:
>   I can't bear with evil assemblies. Isa 1:12-13 WEB

Of the religious leaders of the first century Rabbi Yehoshua said,

> "But woe to you, scribes and Pharisees, hypocrites! For you shut up the kingdom of heaven against men; for you neither go in yourselves, nor do you allow those who are entering to go in." Mtt 23:13 NKJV

But the truth is, it is only a small number who are saved.

> And if the righteous scarcely be saved, where shall the ungodly and the sinner appear? 1Pe 4:18 KJV

God promised His people He would protect them. More than that, in Rom 8:38-39 He says that we are more than conquerers. He says that neither life nor death, nor angels nor demons, nor high places nor low places, nor things now nor things to come can separate us from the love of God. In the last days it says the Beast will make war on God's people, and even overcome them, Rev 13:7-10. However, *even then,* there is refuge, and the woman is pictured as fleeing to the wilderness where she is nourished by God during the time that the beast rules, during the "time, times and half a time," Rev 12:13-14. Will the Lord indeed care for His people? Yes, He will, Lk 18:6-7. But will the Lord find any faithful when He comes, Lk 18:8? He seems to ask this as an open question. It is not that it cannot be. **It is that we as men often *will not be*.**

But you and I and the Jews can be part of the remnant. Seek the Lord while you can.

> [1] Gather yourselves together, yes, gather together,
> > O undesirable nation,
> [2] Before the decree is issued,
> > *Or* the day passes like chaff,
> > Before the LORD'S fierce anger comes upon you.
> > Before the day of the LORD'S anger comes upon you!
> [3] Seek the LORD, all you meek of the earth,
> > Who have upheld His justice.
> > Seek righteousness, seek humility.
> > It may be that you will be hidden
> > In the day of the LORD'S anger. Zep 2:1-3 NKJV

"When You Are In Distress," **The Sixth Break**

> According to all the works which they have done since the day that I brought them up out of Egypt even unto this day, wherewith they have forsaken me, and served other gods, ... 1Sam 8:8 KJV

> <u>When</u> you are in oppression, and all these things are come on you, in the latter days **you <u>shall</u> return to Yahweh your God**, and **listen** to his voice: Deut 4:30 WEB (*bold emphasis added*)

I think the WEB (and other translations) of Deut 4:30 is a faithful rendering, in opposition to the KJV which treats the promise as conditional.[1] Even so, other passages show the correct intent. The prophet Zechariah tells Judah of a special day when the Lord will again choose Jerusalem, and again "possess" Judah.

> "And the LORD will take possession of Judah as His inheritance in the Holy Land, and will again choose Jerusalem." Zech 2:12 NKJV

---

[1] In Deut 4:30 it is a qual perfect with a leading vav conjunction, "you **shall return**" WEB וְשַׁבְתָּ. Compare (even in the KJV) similar useages in Gen 47:30 "But I **will lie** with my fathers," KJV וְשָׁכַבְתִּי, and a parallell passage Deut 30:6, "God **will circumcise** thine heart" KJV וּמָל.

Now one might be inclined to think that all of this speaks of the return from the Babylonian Captivity in the late 6th century BC. But the prophet Zechariah is writing *during* this first return from captivity, and the prophets do not view the returned Jews as anything but wicked formalists. Ezra records when the prophets Haggai and Zechariah first started to prophesy.

> [1] Then the prophets, Haggai the prophet, and Zechariah the son of Iddo, prophesied unto the Jews that *were* in Judah and Jerusalem in the name of the God of Israel, *even* unto them. [2] Then rose up Zerubbabel the son of Shealtiel, and Jeshua the son of Jozadak, and began to build the house of God ... Ezra 5:1-2 KJV

The returned Jews of the Babylonian Captivity were strictly tending to their own business and neglecting the commands of God and the rebuilding of the temple. The preaching of these prophets turned this around. Zechariah more precisely identifies the time of these prophecies.

> In the eighth month, in the second year of Darius, came the word of the LORD unto Zechariah ... the prophet, Zech 1:1 KJV

That would be about the year 520 BC according to our modern calendar, beginning in late August. Clearly Zechariah is preaching *after* the return from the Babylonian Captivity. However, Zechariah points to another *future* dispersion, and another *future* return from being dispersed among the nations.

> [8] "I **will** whistle for them to **gather them** together,
> For I have redeemed them;
> And they will be as numerous as they were before.
> [9] "**When I scatter them** among the peoples,
> **They will remember Me** in far countries,
> And they with their children will live and come back.
> [10] "**I will bring them back** from the land of Egypt
> And gather them from Assyria;
> And I will bring them into the land of Gilead and Lebanon
> Until no *room* can be found for them." Zech 10:8-10 NASB

So the prophet Zechariah, speaking sometime *after 520 BC*, conveys the Word of God that the LORD will *once more* **scatter the Jews** away from Palestine and will, a final time, *gather them* **again** and make them prosper, and "They will remember Me."

When did this second scattering happen, which Zechariah says was to be by God Himself? It obviously started in 70 AD, as was also prophesied by Rabbi Yehoshua in Lk 21:20-22, and many other passages. Look again at Zechariah. God says, "When I scatter them." And when does the final return occur?

A Bigger Holocaust Yet To Come?

> But if ye will not do so, behold, ye have sinned against the LORD, and be sure your sin will find you out. Num 32:23 KJV

The bottom line: the essential character of the Jewish people has not changed since Moses time, and the picture is not altogether a pretty one, though *they have produced some of the finest men and women in all of history, including the Messiah, Jesus the Christ, the Savior of the World.* Overall they have been and are a self-willed, arrogant and rebellious people. As a group they have often been hostile to both God, and to all men, and often even to each other.

As has been repeatedly pointed out, much of the most severe reactions against the Jews is because of their successes in their schemes. Most people do not recognize the strengths of their own position, and leave much on the table for the other side to gather. As a group, the Jews do *not* make these mistakes. They are *the* preeminent worldly negotiators. But there is a dark side to all of this. The back door to business success often quickly crosses the line to the unethical, the immoral, even illegal actions—actions which often have to be immediately disowned, if they are made known. The business news is all along sprinkled with stories of people caught up and destroyed by their "successes." Some delight in the forbidden fruits of a slick deal, but all too often these things lead to places neither side really wants to go. As Moses pointed out, these things always end up *being known,* or **accurately sensed**. "**Be sure your sin will find you out,**" Num 32:23. So these things end up leaving a bad taste in a lot of mouths, and alienating *those we did not realize we needed as friends.* So yes, you can underplay your hand and leave much on the table, and many do, but also you can make a career of *overplaying* your hand with disastrous results. This, one might be so bold to say, is a Jewish forte: pressing their luck *just a little* too far. One might say this is a strong suit of the Jews, a specialty of alienating friends and allies. The shameful human rights record of the Israeli's against the Palestinians could be cited. Why has it happened? They were sure they could get by with it. What will bring judgment? Rather, "Who" will?

> And **I will come near to you to judgment**; and I will be a swift witness against the sorcerers, and against the adulterers, and against false swearers, and against those that oppress the hireling in *his* wages, the widow, and the fatherless, and that turn aside the stranger *from his right*, and fear not me, saith the LORD of hosts.
> Mal 3:5 KJV (*bold emphasis added*)

Malachi is speaking to a remnant that has returned from the first captivity but has still not repented. The Lord told them in Ex. 19:6 "And ye shall be unto me a kingdom of priests, and an holy nation. These are the words which thou shalt speak unto the children of Israel." KJV. But like many of the nations they despise, they have not been and are not a holy nation. And they can *never* be a *nation* of priests under the Law of Moses, which restricts the priesthood to the lost tribe of Levi. The Messiah came to turn them into this nation of priests, by first changing the Law. When the Christ was going to his execution, He mourned the hard-heartedness of His fellow Jews, and yet pointed to a better day.

> ³⁴ O Jerusalem, Jerusalem, which killest the prophets, and stonest them that are sent unto thee; how often would I have gathered thy children together, as a hen *doth gather* her brood under her wings, and ye would not! ³⁵ Behold, your house is left unto you desolate: and verily I say unto you, Ye shall not see me, until *the time* come when ye shall say, Blessed is he that cometh in the name of the Lord. Lk 13:34-35 KJV

But Scripture *still* says, "And ye **shall be** unto me a kingdom of priests, and an holy nation," Ex 19:6, and states that as **a future fact**, but so far they have *NOT* been such. Only God will be able to mellow them, and He has promised that He will do that, but only after bringing them to their knees.

The bottom line is: they sought positions of trust among the gentiles, the nations, and argued for their patriotism and fidelity, and that they should have never in the first place been treated as second class citizens; and then they often betrayed those same positions of trust when it suited them. *And the sad conclusion*: the problems of the Jews are *not **all*** of someone else's origin. These problems are of such a spiritual and systemic nature for the Jews, that they do not seem likely to cure themselves. At some point the Jews will have to face their heritage. Not the traditions of men, nor the occult, nor the other spirits, but rather their real heritage. The One who called them out of Egypt. The same One who is now calling them out of their sins. As long as they, or we, are militantly unrepentant, both the offenses and the blow-back, will periodically flare up. God has laid a costly cornerstone: The Messiah.

> ¹⁶ Therefore thus saith the Lord GOD, Behold, I lay in Zion for a foundation a stone, a tried stone, a precious corner *stone*, a sure foundation: he that believeth shall not make haste. ¹⁷ Judgment also will I lay to the line, and righteousness to the plummet: and the **hail shall sweep away the refuge of lies**, and the **waters shall overflow the hiding place**. ¹⁸ And **your covenant with death shall be disannulled**, and **your agreement with hell shall not stand**; when the overflowing scourge shall pass through, then ye shall be trodden down by it. Isa 28:16-18 KJV (*bold emphasis added*)

It is speaking of an occult oriented Israel. It is clear from Scripture that *it will not happen all at once*. But the Jews ***will be*** captured and broken.

> But the word of the LORD was unto them precept upon precept, precept upon precept; line upon line, line upon line; here a little, and there a little; that they might go, and fall backward, and be broken, and

snared, and taken. Isa 28:13 KJV

We speak not as enemies, but as friends who dare to tell the truth. The Jews love to talk about the mythical "Judeo-Christian" ethic, but Pharisaism, Platonism, and the occult have not been conducive to righteousness. The Jewish influence in America, as in Europe and the Mohammedan world, has been at best mixed, and often even morally corrosive and debilitating, seeming to always trend downwards. If Jesus of Nazareth is the high point of morals, the Jews as a group have repeatedly been the low point. This is nothing on which to build a lasting empire, an enduring world order.

Men for sure end up being trapped by their deeds, and the Lord God does bring them to account, and these are not isolated things, but rather **continual things *in history***. American General Robert E. Lee spoke of it. Oddly enough the fullest expression of Lee's mind at the start of the American Civil War seems to be found in a letter to a little girl in the North, the daughter, no doubt, of prewar friends. She had asked for his photograph, which he sent her with a letter that concluded:

> "It is painful to think how many friends will be separated and estranged by our unhappy disunion. May God reunite our severed bonds of friendship, and turn our hearts to peace! I can say in sincerity that I bear animosity against no one. Wherever the blame may be, the fact that we are in the midst of a fratricidal war. I must side either with or against my section of country. I cannot raise my hand against my birthplace, my home, my children. I should like, above all things, that our difficulties might be peaceably arranged, and still **trust that a merciful God, whom I know will not unnecessarily afflict us**, may yet allay the fury for war. Whatever may be the result of the contest, I foresee that the country will have to pass through **a terrible ordeal, a necessary expiation, perhaps, of our national sins**. May God direct all for our good, and shield and preserve you and yours." Lee to "My dear Little H_," May 5, 1861; *New York Times*, Aug. 6, 1861, p3, col. 4. *R. E. Lee: A Biography*, Vol I, Douglas Southall Freeman, pgs 475-476 (*bold emphasis added*)

It is *national sins **that are not dealt with*** which bring the great disasters on nations, like the American Civil War. This was not just about the abuses in slavery, but also of drunkenness and adultery and fornication and covetousness and theft, and taking for granted the blessings of God, and on and on and on. (I am from the South, but do not think the Civil War was ***just*** about Southern sins. The North was twice the population of the South, with four times the white population, and their casualties were *roughly twice* those of the South.)

The trouble which is coming on the Jews, as described in Scripture, does not seem like a local event, with the curses which they try to bring on others, instead falling on themselves. It would seem to indicate punishments from God for betraying their own Deliverer, and punishments from God and the nations for defrauding and betraying them. The greater the blessings, the more strictly a people will be held to a standard of righteousness. These should be scary thoughts not only for the Jews, but also for unfaithful America as we enter the 21st century and as America, not Russia or China or Cuba, becomes the flagship leader of evil world revolution and desolation. Our being insensible will not necessarily protect us from gravity nor from the gravity of our sins.

Lucien Wolf, discussed earlier, was not a stranger to "normal" "diplomatic duplicity," nor was he totally at odds with the revolutionary tendencies of much of Judaism. Still he had a genuine angst and concern for the blow-back which he clearly saw coming from the World War I machinations. At one point he discussed with Russian Jew Baron Gunzburg the issuing of an Anti-Bolshevik Manifesto. He rejected the idea because it would only cause a Jewish Pro-Bolshevik Manifesto, so the net effect would be to leave additional evidence of the Russian Jews being drawn to Bolshevism, something he privately, but not publicly, admitted (Levene, *War, Jews, and the New Europe*, pg 247)

> He who digs a pit may fall into it; and whoever breaks through a wall may be bitten by a snake. Eccl 10:8 WEB

Rather than being a blessing to all nations, as prophesied to Abram in Gen 12:3, they have often been a curse, pushing the nations into the abyss, hooraying them into foolish and sinful overreach, into the very edge of despair. Arrogant abuse of others, whether by the Jews, or Israel, or the United States, breeds its own retribution. You cannot ignore the basics of righteous human conduct, as outlined in the book of Proverbs for instance, and not have it eventually come right back and smack you right between the eyes. The evil conduct of Israel in the centuries following Solomon, seemed at first to be sleeping, but not really. "... the way of transgressors is hard." Prov 13:15 KJV.

Other examples come to mind from history. The British Empire at first seemed to be able to exploit others with impunity, though much of the worst of her conduct was protested by good men in and out of Parliament. Even so, retribution does not sleep, and for all there finally comes our Ypres, our Somme, or what Robert E. Lee called "a terrible ordeal, a necessary expiation, perhaps, of our national sins." Such sometimes must come. Trumpets of warning! Yes! They are part of the four horsemen who ride through the Christian Age! Judgement for sins *within history* is not just a Jewish thing. The Lord judges the nationS, **and that _includes_ the Jews**.

It is strange that the modern road to the gospel for the Jews seems to have started with the sophisticated strategies to reach for greater power.

In the Valley of Trouble: Israel Below

The prophet Hosea, who was commanded by God to marry a prostitute, was discussed in some detail earlier. He was commanded to marry the worst kind, a religious prostitute.

> ... And the LORD said to Hosea, Go, take unto thee a wife of whoredoms and children of whoredoms: for the land hath committed great whoredom, *departing* from the LORD." Hos 1:2 KJV

It was discussed earlier that the prophet obeyed this command in Hos 1:3, and Hosea and his wife Gomer had a son with a symbolic name, Jezreel. For it was in the valley of Jezreel that Israel had fallen and was defeated.

Then we saw that they had a daughter named "not to be pitied," or "*Loruchamah*", לֹא רֻחָמָה, Hos 1:6. It was not clear whether this is the prophet's daughter or not. Still it was clear that she is symbolic of God's people no longer being pitied. Then Gomer has a son evidently not by Hosea. A son named, "Not My People," *Loammi* לֹא עַמִּי, Hos 1:8-9. Notice that God Himself is doing the naming, and *says in the long ago that Israel is no longer His people.*

So Gomer is a type, symbolic of unfaithful Israel. A disgraceful adulteress and not a faithful wife. She is symbolic of Israel having children by other gods, by other husbands rather than by the Lord her God. Hosea says to the children in his family, struggle with your mama, because she is not my wife any longer, and I am not her husband, Hos 2:2-3. (Talk about a current family situation!) **God was abandoning Israel**, *even then!*

God says He will no longer have pity on these children, for they are the children of harlotry, Hos 2:4-5. God says He will make her sin plain, Hos 2:10. I will put an end to all of her good times, God says, Hos 2:11. An end to all of her parties. God says He will destroy all of her prosperity, and the goodness in her life, Hos 2:12. I will punish her for all the days when she went to offer herself to the so-called gods of pleasure and prosperity, Hos 2:13.

The fact is that throughout Scripture, from the Old Testament to the New Testament, *True Israel* ("... those who are pure in heart," Psa 73:1) is contrasted with *Israel below,* which is called "Sodom ... Gomorrah," Isa 1:10. Also the *true Jew* of the heart (Rom 2:28-29, and Deut 10:16), is contrasted with those who "are not His children, because of their defect," Deut 32:5, but whose "vine is from the vine of Sodom, And from the fields of Gomorrah;" Deut 32:32 NASB.

Similar contrasts are made with Jerusalem also. It is Jerusalem below which is Sodom and Gomorrah in Isa 1:10; of which nothing but judgment is spoken. However, in contrast there is "the holy city" in Mtt 27:53, Jerusalem above with its citizens of righteousness, which God will "create," Isa 65:17. The True Israel, the pure in heart, those with circumcised hearts, it has been since the kingdom was established in the first century, when its citizens were translated (past tense) from the kingdom of darkness into "the kingdom of His dear

Son" (Col 1:13). It *always* has included many gentiles. It was *always* to be too small a thing for the Messiah to save just Jacob, but rather the Messiah was *always* to have been a light to the nations, Isa 49:6.

So when you read a prophecy of "Jerusalem," you must determine whether it is speaking of **"present Jerusalem**, for she is in slavery with her children," *or* **"Jerusalem above,"** Gal 4:25-26. And "Jerusalem above" will help lead the Jews out of disaster into the Glorious Light of God's Beloved Son, as shall be seen.

A Destruction Overflowing with Righteousness, Isa 10:22

Both during the time of Moses' leadership and before, Israel had always been stubborn and unfaithful.

> They have dealt corruptly with him, they are not his children,
>   it is their blemish;
>   They are a perverse and crooked generation. Deut 32:5 WEB

Notice Moses speaks of a crooked "generation." Does that mean only those of Israel of Moses time? No! For Moses also speaks of the Jewish people to come *and says that the worst was **not** past*. Look at the previous chapter.

> For I know thy rebellion, and thy stiff neck: behold, while I am yet alive with you this day, ye have been rebellious against the LORD; and **how much more after my death**? Deut 31:27 KJV (*bold emphasis added*)

So "generation" is used here, and other places, as one might use the words "tribe," or "people," or "nation," or even as one might loosely use the word "race." Those of a certain descent. There will be trouble for all evil doers, to the Jews first and then to the gentile.

> [9] Tribulation and anguish, upon every soul of man that doeth evil, **of the Jew first**, and also of the Gentile; [10] But glory, honour, and peace, to every man that worketh good, **to the Jew first**, and also to the Gentile: [11] For there is no respect of persons with God.
> Rom 2:9-10 KJV (*bold emphasis added*)

It will be a time of great stress when Israel finally turns to God and unbends her stiff neck. This time is described in Deuteronomy 4. It speaks of Israel being scattered because of her sins and worshipping many other spirits, and then the Lord says,

> "When you are in distress and all these things have come upon you, in the latter days you will return to the LORD your God and listen to His voice." Deut 4:30 NASB

That is a promise which was first made around 1400 BC. The King James Version does translate this promise as a *conditional* promise: "**if** thou turn to the

LORD thy God." Many modern translators translate this as a plain promise from God, just as in the New American Standard (Also see the note on the bottom of page 273). There are many *both* conditional *and* unconditional promises in the Bible. The key to correct translation here would be the grand context of prophecy. So what does the rest point to?

Other passages also point to repentance and a **change of character** of the people of Israel as **clearly** forecast. For instance, a regathering in which Israel has a change of heart is unequivocally forecast in Deut 30:4-6.

> ⁴ If any of thine be driven out unto the outmost parts of heaven, from thence **will** the LORD thy God gather thee, and from thence **will** he fetch thee: ⁵ And the LORD thy God **will** bring thee into the land which thy fathers possessed, and thou **shalt** possess it; and he **will** do thee good, and multiply thee above thy fathers. ⁶ And the LORD thy God **will circumcise thine heart, and the heart of thy seed**, to love the LORD thy God with all thine heart, and with all thy soul, that thou mayest live. KJV (*emphasis added*)

Notice very carefully that this is not a conditional statement of what God *might* do. *It is just stated as a matter of fact, this is what* God *will* do, and this should reflect the correct translation of Deut 4:30, as many translations show it. Once again, this also was written about 1400 BC. Isaiah *also* speaks of such a day in dogmatic terms, as an absolute statement of what God will do.

> ²² Thus saith the Lord GOD, Behold, I will lift up mine hand to the Gentiles, and set up my standard to the people: and they **shall** bring thy sons in *their* arms, and thy daughters **shall be** carried upon *their* shoulders. ²³ And kings **shall be** thy nursing fathers, and their queens thy nursing mothers: **they shall** bow down to thee with *their* face toward the earth, and lick up the dust of thy feet; **and thou shalt know** that I *am* the LORD: for they shall not be ashamed that wait for me. Isa 49:22-23 KJV (*bold emphasis added*)

Once again, it points to the nations (or "Gentiles," KJV, those whom the Messiah has drawn to Himself, Isa 49:6, which was referred to earlier), as among those whom God will use to bring the Jews to Jesus Christ. Again, **this is not a conditional statement** of what *might* happen, but an open statement of what *will* happen. On one hand, we *do* see a return from captivity after Isaiah's time, in the 6th century BC, but we *have NOT* seen kings becoming their guardians, and princesses becoming their nurses and them bowing low to the ground before them. Isaiah is clearly speaking of another time. **So either the prophecy is false, *or* it has just not happened yet.** Again we see a return from captivity forecast in Isaiah 14.

> ¹ The LORD will certainly have compassion on Jacob; he will again choose Israel as his special people and restore them to their land.

Resident foreigners will join them and unite with the family of Jacob. [2] Nations will take them and bring them back to their own place. Then the family of Jacob will make foreigners their servants as they settle in the LORD'S land. **They will make their captors captives and rule over the ones who oppressed them.** Isa 14:1-2 NET (*emphasis added*) [1]

Once again Isaiah is forecasting a return to Palestine (written *before* the first dispersion). Still it pictures several elements which have not happened in any return to date, including: the people of the world bringing them to Palestine, and then Israel possessing them as male and female captives, *and then ruling over their oppressors!* Such has *never* happened in history. But it will. **Isaiah also actually speaks of a second return,** *even before the first return has happened.*

> And it shall come to pass in that day, *that* the Lord shall set his hand again **the second time to recover the remnant of his people**, which shall be left, **from Assyria**, and from Egypt, and from Pathros, and from Cush, and from Elam, and from Shinar, and from Hamath, and **from the islands of the sea**. Isa 11:11 KJV (*bold emphasis added*)

So well before the first return to Palestine, that Isaiah says God will recover Israel a "**second time** with His hand." Jeremiah also speaks of a return.

> At that time they shall call Jerusalem the throne of the LORD; and all the nations shall be gathered unto it, to the name of the LORD, to Jerusalem: **neither shall they walk any more after the imagination of their evil heart**. Jer 3:17 KJV (*bold emphasis added*)

Remember God promised "And the LORD thy God **will** circumcise thine heart," Deut 30:6 KJV. But this change of heart did not happen in the time of Jeremiah or in the first returns. Jeremiah says,

> Egypt, and Judah, and Edom, and the children of Ammon, and Moab, and all *that are* in the utmost corners, that dwell in the wilderness: for all *these* nations *are* uncircumcised, **and all the house of Israel *are* uncircumcised in the heart**. Jer 9:26 KJV (*bold emphasis added*)

It has been demonstrated from Mal 3:5 and other passages, this circumcision of heart did not happened as a result of the Babylonian Captivity. The prophet Stephen speaking by the Holy Spirit, again he repremanded the Jews.

> Ye stiffnecked **and uncircumcised in heart and ears,** ye do always resist the Holy Ghost: as your fathers *did*, so *do* ye. Act 7:51 KJV

So prophecy of a return in which they have a change of heart, and follow God from the heart, has not happened *yet*.

---

[1] It is definitely possible to take Isa 14:1-2 in a way that is very harsh to the gentiles, and to so translate it, as many do. I think the NET translation strikes a good balance. Thus it pictures results so beneficial to all that the gentiles help Israel return, and thus help bring so much of a "blessing to all nations," that many foreigners become Jews!

So When Will All of This Happen?

"When you are in distress ... " Deut 4:30 NKJV. In the day of Jacob's distress.

> 'Alas! for that day is great,
> There is none like it;
> And **it is the time of Jacob's distress**,
> But he will be saved from it. Jer 30:7 (*bold emphasis added*)

When the prophet Zechariah pictures this future time of return, he also pictures it as a time of distress, when it says of Israel.

> **And he shall pass through the sea with affliction**, and shall smite the waves in the sea, and all the deeps of the river shall dry up: and the pride of Assyria shall be brought down, and the sceptre of Egypt shall depart away. Zech 10:11 KJV (*bold emphasis added*)

Ezekiel speaks of Israel's sins in terms that include many of Israel's current sins, and talks of a time when God will "consume" all of her uncleanness.

> [13] "Behold, therefore, I beat My fists at the dishonest profit which you have made, and at the bloodshed which has been in your midst. [14] Can your heart endure, or can your hands remain strong, in the days when I shall deal with you? I, the LORD, have spoken, and will do *it.* [15] **I will scatter you** among the nations, disperse you throughout the countries, **and remove your filthiness** <u>completely</u> from you. [16] **You shall defile yourself** in the sight of the nations; **then** you shall know that I *am* the LORD." Ezek 22:13-16 NKJV (*bold and underline emphasis added*)

Implied is that God will cleanse Israel *in the dispersion* throughout the world. Once again, Israel's sins have by no means been consumed, not even in human terms, even by our own time. When God says, "I will remove your filthiness completely from you," it seems to be speaking of that special time of distress. Nor should it be overlooked that this is the period during which "I will scatter you," that is to say, during the dispersion. And the "when" of these things seems similar to "the when" of the second coming of Christ. It is when there is no other way, and all of their strength is gone, and their hearts are not able to endure, nor can their hands be strong.

> "For the LORD will **judge His people**
> And **have compassion on His servants**,
> **When** He sees that *their* power is gone,
> And *there is* no one *remaining*, bond or free. Deut 32:36 NKJV

The Hebrew Apostle Paul tells us this will happen *after* the full number of Gentiles come into the church.

> For I would not, brethren, that ye should be ignorant of this mystery,

> lest ye should be wise in your own conceits; that blindness in part is
> happened to Israel, until the fulness of the Gentiles be come in.
> Rom 11:25 KJV

Paul is here contrasting physical Israel with the church which has been for most of the last 2,000 years composed mainly of gentiles, that is, the people of the nations. And when the full number of the nations has come in, *then* "the partial hardening" of Israel **will be** ended

The promise, the prophesy, is repeated (which has been cited from multiple passages in the Old Testament), that **God** will remove ungodliness from the Jews, from physical Israel.

> [26] ... the Deliverer, and shall turn away ungodliness from Jacob: [27] For
> this *is* my covenant unto them, when I shall take away their sins.
> Rom 11:26-27 KJV

This will not be because of their righteousness, but because of the Lord's promise to the Patriarchs Abraham, Isaac and Jacob.

> As concerning the gospel, *they are* enemies for your sakes: but as touching the election, *they are* beloved for the fathers' sakes. Rom 11:28 KJV

It will be glorious times.

> Now if the fall of them *be* the riches of the world, and the diminishing
> of them the riches of the Gentiles; how much more their fulness?
> Rom 11:12 KJV

At least one More Time in the Wilderness, Hosea 2.

Evidently God will rescue the Jews and convert them to Himself, one more time, in "the wilderness."

> Therefore, behold, I will allure her, and bring her into the wilderness,
> and speak comfortably unto her. Hos 2:14 KJV

It will be in that great day of trouble, in the Valley of trouble, the valley of Achor.

> I will give her her vineyards from thence, and the valley of Achor for a
> door of hope: and she shall sing there, as in the days of her youth, and
> as in the day when she came up out of the land of Egypt. Hos 2:15 KJV

None of what is presented in these verses has yet happened, to really turn the Jews to God. The Baals will no longer be mentioned, Hos 2:16-17. And God will make a covenant and abolish war.

> And in that day will I make a covenant for them with the beasts of the
> field, and with the fowls of heaven, and *with* the creeping things of the
> ground: and I will break the bow and the sword and the battle out of

the earth, and will make them to lie down safely. Hos 2:18 KJV

It is easy to take this as the immediate result of the valley of Achor, the valley of trouble, it seems to be speaking of the end of this world and the start of the new heavens and new earth. It is common to jump ahead in prophecy to see what the end of all these things will be. A good example is from Hebrews 1.

> [10] And, Thou, Lord, in the beginning hast laid the foundation of the earth; and the heavens are the works of thine hands: [11] They shall perish; but thou remainest; and they all shall wax old as doth a garment; [12] And as a vesture shalt thou fold them up, and they shall be changed: but thou art the same, and thy years shall not fail. Heb 1:10-12 KJV

Thus in three verses it jumps from the creation to the end of this world!

What are the indications in Hosea 2 that the stress of Achor is what will convert the Jews, and not the end of this world? At the last, Satan will gather all nations to make war on God's people, Rev 20:8-9. It is clearly *after* this that wars end permanently, thus Hos 2:18 *follows* Rev 20:8-9.

And God will marry His people in the following verses in Hos 2:19-20. The question then is: When does all of this happen? Once again, this does not happen until the second coming of Christ, when also hell receives her eternal load, Rev 20:13-14. Then, in the next chapter of Revelation, God will marry His people, Rev 21:2-3. At that point the betrothal will be consummated. But all of these things are too late for us to change our fate.

Thus Hosea generally seems to speak of blessings for Israel before the end of time, which it seems is the case. *A time of stress which results in conversion*, **not** the final time of stress which results in final judgment!

Clearly the conversion of the Jews **has to do with history *before*** the second coming of Christ, as has just shown. Naturally, if that is true, we should be able to demonstrate it in other passages. **It will <u>not</u> be about instituting the kingdom of God**, for it was started in the first century. "He ... transferred us," *past tense*, "to the kingdom of His beloved Son," Col 1:13 NASB. "For he must reign," *present tense,* "til he hath put all enemies under his feet." 1Cor 15:24-25 KJV. The *fullness* of the glory of Christ's rule, or the *riches* of a new universe in which sin and death are not operating principles (Isa 65:17, 2Pe 3:13, Rom 8:21), are yet to come. But Jesus has *already* received "All authority ... **in heaven** and **on earth**," Mtt 28:18 NKJV. *The present time* is one of *amnesty and grace*, to give us time to come to our senses, 2Tim 2:26, 2Pe 3:9.

What then of the time when the Jews as a nation turn to their own Savior? It will be an era of glory for Christianity before the end of time, and a period of blessings to a world still lost in sin, that we might all understand both the justice and the mercy of God, *before* He calls us all to account.

There is time in between, a time before the final day, reflected in Rom

11:12, a time of fulfillment and not of failure for Israel. A time when God blesses unfaithful Israel and will bring her to faithfulness, and He will bring blessings on her, Hos 2:21-23. God Himself will sow her in the land.

Paul Quotes Hosea 2 Concerning the Conversion of the Jews

Those He called "not my people" will be called the people of the living God, Hos 2:23. Paul quotes all of this about the conversion of the Jews and the gentiles, a time of mercy in the gospel for the Jews.

> ²⁵ As He says also in Hosea:
> *"I will call them My people, who were not My people,*
> *And her beloved, who was not beloved."*
> ²⁶   *"And it shall come to pass in the place where it was said to them,*
> *'You are not My people,'*
> *There they shall be called sons of the living God."* Rom 9:25-26 NKJV

Zechariah 12 and 13, Israel Turns to the Christ.

If there is a special point of emphasis in Zechariah chapters 12 and 13 it is the conversion of Judah to their Messiah, Jesus of Nazareth ...

> And I will pour upon the house of David, and upon the inhabitants of Jerusalem, the spirit of grace and of supplications: **and they shall look upon me whom they have pierced**, and they shall mourn for him, as one mourneth for *his* only *son*, and shall be in bitterness for him, as one that is in bitterness for *his* firstborn. Zech 12:10 KJV (*bold emphasis added*)

Zechariah is very emphatic that this is about Israel (Zech 12:1) and about Judah (Zech 12:2, 4, 6, etc.), and about their mourning the death of the Christ and it is plainly *all of Israel* that will mourn for the Christ.

> ¹² ... the land shall mourn, every family apart; ... ¹⁴ **All the families that <u>remain</u>, <u>every family</u>** apart, and their wives apart.
> Zech 12:12, 14 KJV (*bold and underline emphasis added*)

It is emphasizing that each part of Israel will repent "In that day."

> ¹ In that day there shall be a fountain opened to the house of David and to the inhabitants of Jerusalem for sin and for uncleanness. ² And it shall come to pass in that day, saith the LORD of hosts, that I will cut off the names of the idols out of the land, and they shall no more be remembered: **and also I will cause the prophets and the unclean spirit to pass out of the land**. Zech 13:1-2 (*bold emphasis added*) KJV

The passage is emphatically about a time when all of Israel/Judah as a group, all of the tribes, will accept the Christ who was slain, the One who was pierced. The passage associates this acceptance and repentance with time of great stress, when both Judah and Jerusalem are under siege, and the authority of men's traditions, and the Kabbalah, and other spirits will be purged from Israel, all things which have not happened to this very day. So what else might we learn from the passage? There will be,

A Serious Attack on the Church **and** Judah.

It is easy to miss, but *there is not just one period of great distress*; but there are multiple periods of stress, ***at least two really severe periods***. "This know also, that in the last days perilous **time₁** shall come." 2Tim 3:1 KJV. Not just a perilous "time" but perilous "times." One is the time in which the Jews are converted to Jesus of Nazareth in Zechariah 12 and 13, and Hosea 2, etc.; and at least one other is the final time of trouble, the final assault on Christianity, just before the Second Coming, as pictured in Zechariah 14 and various passages in the Old and New Covenant.

I think it can be shown that the *first time* of distress is a "type," symbolic, of the *final time* of trouble when the Lord will personally intervene to save His people, and "in flaming fire" will punish those "who know not God, and ... do not obey the gospel." 2Thes 1:7-9. **In the time of stress in Zechariah 12 and 13 those who would try to move "Jerusalem" injure themselves, and are not successful.** In contrast to this, **in the time of stress in Zechariah 14 "the city will be captured, the houses plundered, the women ravished and half of the city exiled, but the rest of the people will not be cut off from the city."** Zech 14:2 (*bold emphasis added*)

So I think that in this burden or oracle of the Lord concerning Israel it is picturing two different times or periods of great stress. They are separated by how much time? I do not know. It does not tell.

The final time of stress pictured is in line with the beast described in Revelation 13 who "overcomes" the true people of God, Rev 13:7, etc. So two very different results. Some would argue that this is all one "burden ... concerning Israel," in Zechariah chapters 12 through 14. I would not dispute that point, but would point out that such jumps in time are common in prophecy. Heb 1:10-12 jumps from the creation to the end of the universe in three verses, as we have just shown you (pg 285). Isa 2:2-4 jumps from the preaching of the gospel in the first century AD in Jerusalem in verse 1-2 to the final judgment and the ending of all wars at the end of time in verse 4. Prophecy does not have a built in time dimension, and similar jumps in time are common in prophecy, *thus showing how the immediate subject relates to the final end*. Many have argued the similarities in Zechariah 12-13 with chapter 14. I would agree, and would say that **I think the first time of stress is a "type,"symbolic of the second time of stress**, as it in other passages. *The thing to be noted is the differences*, some of which have just been pointed out. Notice carefully: in the first special time of stress "Jerusalem" is ***not*** conquered. In the second one she ***is*** conquered.

In the time of distress when Judah turns to the Lord, God's assistance is plain, but it is through intermediaries. "Israel" is mentioned just once in this passage, and the rest of the references are to "Judah," and "Jerusalem." There is a strange contrast in Zechariah 12 between "Judah" and "Jerusalem," and "Jerusalem" seems to be used in more than one sense in this passage. On one hand, it seems to speak of ordinary normal Jerusalem, which repents in great sorrow when it realizes how great their mistake has been in rejecting Jesus of Nazareth, for instance in Zech 12:10 and following. But then it seems to strangely *contrast* "Judah" and "Jerusalem," "and when the siege is against Jerusalem, it will also be against Judah." Zech 12:2. Now in normal military terms, you would *have to* attack Judah in order to attack Jerusalem, for Jerusalem is in Judah; but that is not how the passage is constructed, and it seems to picture "Jerusalem" as being attacked first, and *then* Judah is attacked.

Again let me point out that it is common in prophecy to use a single noun to refer to more than one person, place or thing. A double meaning in prophecy is very common. One example is from 2Sam 7:12-15. In this passage God is telling what He will do through David's "son." In for instance 1Kgs

Then there are books like Lo us and Aaron's, *The Secret War Against the Jews*, which is written as a lurid, tell all, spy story. Their stated thesis is that there is systematic plotting against the Jews among Western Intelligence agenices, and covert tracking of all Jewish activities. Lo us, according to the the back cover, was raised as an Irish Catholic. Aarons is of Jewish descent according to another Lo us book. They do not seem to write as Christians, but still almost as if present day "Israel" is some sort of holy entity which should be beyond any criticism. Even so, could this be speaking in part of those powers which will in time bring the great time of stress on Israel?

8:17-20 Solomon, as David's "son," fulfills this prophecy, although some parts of this prophecy clearly do *NOT* describe Solomon and his kingdom. On the other hand, according to Heb 1:5 the passage in 2 Samuel 7 applies to Jesus. As was pointed out in *Prophecy Principles*, page 77-79, parts of this passage apply only to Solomon, and parts of it apply only to Jesus, and parts to both of them, but in different ways. So in 2 Samuel 7 it switches back and forth between these two different "sons" with no clear line of division. And if you look around in Bible prophecy, such linguistic devices as these are common, from Genesis all the way to the book of Revelation. It is a conversational sort of syntax.

It seems
"Jerusalem"
in Zech 12:2-6 refers
to "Jerusalem above," as in Gal 4:26,
and Jerusalem the holy city, as it is in Isa 52:1,
and other passages, that is to say, the assembly, those
who are truly faithful to God and His Son Jesus the Christ.
So **it would seem** *that* **the church** *is attacked FIRST,* **then the Jews!**
However, Judah is delivered first, so that "Jerusalem" will not be exalted over
"Judah," Zech 12:7.

Notice the strange way "Jerusalem" is used in this passage. Judah in this passage is clearly pictured as fighting, and fighting very hard. "Jerusalem" is pictured as enduring a "siege," but is not clearly pictured as fighting. "... though all the people of the earth be gathered together against it," Zech 12:3 KJV. "And in that day will I make Jerusalem a burdensome stone" KJV for all of the nations, and all who try to move her will be "severely wounded," WEB, or "cut in pieces," KJV Zech 12:3.

> And the governors of Judah shall say in their heart, The inhabitants of Jerusalem *shall be* my strength in the LORD of hosts **their** God. Zech 12:5 (*bold emphasis added*) KJV

Look carefully, it does *NOT* say through the Lord of hosts **our** God. Rather it says that Jerusalem is a strong support for Judah through the Lord of hosts **"their"** God. It is strange wording and a strange contrast. So here is the implication in the passage itself that this "Jerusalem" *has a special relationship with God, a relationship which impresses Judah, a relationship* **which Judah does not have**, with **the** God which Judah does **not** serve, which is the source of "Jerusalem's" strength and survival. That my friend is the understatement of the day. Judah, as has been shown, has served many other gods, including Mammon. The fight will be huge, and by implication worldwide. Judah will be

> like a firepot among pieces of wood and a flaming torch among

sheaves, so they will consume on the right hand and on the left all the surrounding peoples, while the inhabitants of Jerusalem again dwell on their own sites in Jerusalem. Zech 12:6 NASB

Judah will flareup to the right and the left, but Jerusalem will "dwell on their own sites." It is quite a contrast, although the inhabitants of Jerusalem are pictured as being brave like David, Zech 12:8. And "though all the people of the earth be gathered together against" Jerusalem, God will set about to destroy them according to Zech 12:9.

Two-Thirds of the Jews Will Perish

There is a coming world-wide calamity. A calamity, shall we say, of Biblical proportions? A calamity which will lead the Jews to reassess their situation. The destruction of Jerusalem in 70 AD was a huge and calamitous event but failed to faze the Jews to turn them to their own Christ. The Holocaust of the 1940's was also a huge and calamitous event, but it also failed to turn the Jews to their very own Savior. Now this is speaking of a time of what seems to be a world-wide distress in which the Jews are converted to Jesus the Christ. If I am reading it right, two-thirds of the Jews world-wide will perish in this distress. The rest will be converted to Jesus the True and only Christ.

> 8 And it shall come to pass, *that* in all the land, saith the LORD, two parts therein shall be cut off *and* die; but the third shall be left therein. 9 And I will bring the third part through the fire, and will refine them as silver is refined, and will try them as gold is tried: they shall call on my name, and I will hear them: I will say, It *is* my people: and they shall say, The LORD is my God. Zech 13:8-9 KJV

The LORD was not their God prior to the traumatic events of Zechariah 12, but then they shall say, "The LORD is my God." There is more to tell here from Scripture than there is space to tell it, but to summarize: **It *appears* that this will be a time of stress for *both* Jews *and* Christians.** It appears that it will be gentile Christians who bring the Word of Life to the Jews in this special time of stress. Altogether, considering the history of the Jews, a very believable scenario. God will then ask them,

> 37 He will say: "Where *are* their gods,
>   The rock in which they sought refuge?
> 38   Who ate the fat of their sacrifices,
>   *And* drank the wine of their drink offering?
>   Let them rise and help you,
>   *And* be your refuge.

³⁹   "Now see that I, *even* I, *am* He,
And *there is* no God besides Me;
I kill and I make alive;
I wound and I heal;
Nor is there any who can deliver from My hand.
Deut 32:37-39 NKJV

Yes, where are these other gods? Where are those Sefirots, those emanations, those supposed transmitters of the Word, whom you trusted? Those spirits which by nature are no gods! Gal 4:8.

No! This is NOT the Second Coming of Christ.

These are events and trials *within history*, yet to come, clearly forecast in Scripture. Jesus *already* rules from the heavenly Zion, the heavenly Jerusalem, of which earthly Jerusalem is only symbolic, another Biblical "type." The pre-millenialists are ignoring clear Scriptures of the kingdom coming in the first century of this age. They are confusing prophecies of heaven itself with prophecies of the considerable benefits to the earth *and the gospel* which will come with the conversion of the Jews, and earthly Israel becoming a Christian nation.

Jesus **had already, *before*** leaving this earth in the first century AD, said "**All power** is given unto me in heaven **and in earth**." Mtt 28:18 KJV. Even the unclean spirits obey Him, Mk 1:27. "The Father loveth the Son, and **hath given all things** into his hand." Jn 3:35. Jesus is **now**, well before the Second Coming, "the ruler of kings of the earth," Rev 1:5. So rulers of the earth should take warning.

¹⁰ Be wise now therefore, O ye kings: be instructed, ye judges of the earth. ¹¹ Serve the LORD with fear, and rejoice with trembling. ¹² Kiss the Son, **lest he be angry, and ye perish from the way, when his wrath is kindled but a little.** Blessed *are* all they that put their trust in him. Psa 2:10-12 KJV (*bold emphasis added*)

That includes you and me, and even the great men of earth. You can see it on the evening news everyday. **For Jesus to step down from the rule of heaven _and_ earth to sit on an earthly throne is ludicrous.** So it was written by the Holy Spirit of God of one named Coniah, an ancestor of Jesus the Christ, in Jeremiah 22,

"Thus saith the LORD, Write ye this man childless, a man that shall not prosper in his days: **for no man of his seed shall prosper, sitting upon the throne of David, and ruling any more in Judah.** Jer 22:30 KJV (*emphasis added*)

But Jesus is a descendant of this "Coniah"/ Jeconiah, Mtt 1:17. This was discussed more fully in *Prophecy Principles*. But Jesus rules from heaven, not "in Judah." Nor will He ever, lest this prophecy fail! Compare Jn 10:35.

Jesus repeatedly warned that *many* impostors would come in His name and mislead many, Mtt 24:5. So if *anyone* says to you, Look here is the Christ, or there He is, *do not believe them!*

> [23] Then if any man shall say unto you, Lo, here *is* Christ, or there; believe *it* not. [24] For there shall arise false Christs, and false prophets, and shall shew great signs and wonders; insomuch that, if *it were* possible, they shall deceive the very elect. [25] Behold, I have told you before. [26] **Wherefore if they shall say unto you, Behold, he is in the desert; go not forth:** behold, *he is* in the secret chambers; believe it not. [27] For as the lightning cometh out of the east, and shineth even unto the west; so shall also the coming of the Son of man be.
> Mtt 24:23-27 KJV

So positively, Jesus will NOT *physically* be on earth again before the Second Coming and the end of this present universe. You have believed O man, many other verses! Why not believe these and give them their proper weight? This is NOT some sort of literal kingdom of God here on earth which will come with the conversion of the Jews. It will only be a very stubborn people who at last turn to their own Savior, become a militant Christian nation, and part of the kingdom of God, and receive great blessings from God. Jesus already rules now.

> [26] And hath made of one blood all nations of men for to dwell on all the face of the earth, and hath determined the times before appointed, and the bounds of their habitation; [27] That they should seek the Lord, if haply they might feel after him, and find him, though he be not far from every one of us: [28] For in him we live, and move, and have our being; ... Acts 17:26-28 KJV

Jesus will at the right time, draw the Jews to Himself, as He has said He would. Isaac Watts well summarized it some three hundred years ago.

"He rules the world with truth and grace,
And makes the nations prove
The glories of His righteousness
And wonders of His love,
And wonders of His love
And wonders, wonders of His love."
Joy to the World, 1719 AD

VII. The Great Break: Israel Turns to Her Great Prophet

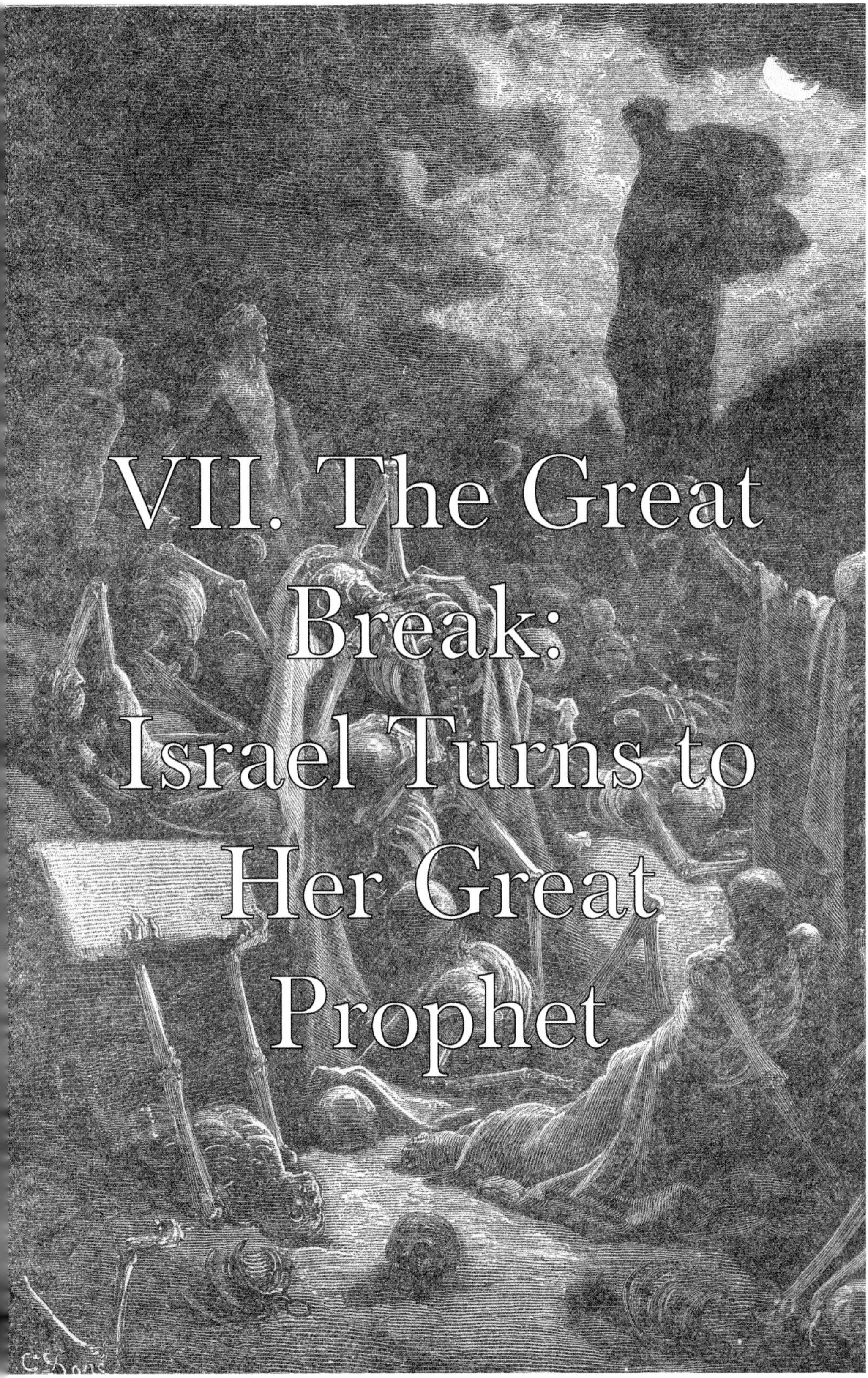

At the same time, saith the LORD, will I be the God of **all** the families of Israel, and they shall be my people. Jer 31:1 KJV (*emphasis added*)

"... The LORD *is* with you while you are with Him. If you seek Him, He will be found by you; but if you forsake Him, He will forsake you." 2Chron 15:2 NKJV

The moral degradation of the Jews throughout history we have discusssed all along in this volume, as it is well discussed throughout the Bible, both Old and New Testaments.

We have taken note under "Owning the Media?" on page 248, that the Jews do NOT actually own the media, but that they have and often do exercise considerable influence over the media, to make sure that the Jews are not badly portrayed in the media. In times past this has included protecting the Jews from accusations of immoral conduct, and often from accusations of sexual immorality. Since the first edition of this book came out in 2020, America anyway has been greatly surprised at the sexual revolution that the Western Establishment has been pushing. Pushing, in fact, all the way to the brainwashing, seduction and mutilation of even children as being good and wholesome. The Jews, of course, have been and are a significant part of the radical left in Western Europe and America, and perhaps that is in part a factor in the Jews no longer being shielded from accusations of even predatory sexual activities. Even some prominent Hollywood moguls, who were big Democratic Party contributors, have both been outed and prosecuted/sued and convicted of outrageous sexual predadations. Of course such things have been part of "Hollywood" from the first, but have often been hushed up in the mainline propaganda media.

Now we can even see books like *Genius & Anxiety, How the Jews Changed the World, 1847-1947*, by Jewish author Norman Lebrecht, Scribner, New York, 2019. The book concentrates on Jewish genius in multiple fields, and of their often anxiety that they might be persecuted in all of these things!

But other things are acknowledged in this book, like their "ineradicable sympathy with things Jewish and ... inveterate antagonism to the principles and results of Christianity." quoted of Emma Lazarus on page 112. These sorts of things the Jews historically have often been reluctant to acknowledge.

There is a muchf good discussion in the book of many Jewish influences. Lebrecht's disparagements of the now out of date Jewish psychoanylyst Sigmund Freud ("Sex in the City," pages 147-180) are enlightening, and right on, even in areas which even many gentiles would not have acknowledged very recently, much less a Jewish author.

But there is even more. This is a book that relishes Jewish immorality, and Lebrecht well documents the Jewish penchant for promoting immorality. These are all very sad things, but increasingly things which one cannot avoid noticing.

In fact, I even found myself wondering if Lebrecht should have named his book, *Genius & Degeneracy*!

Even so, the truth is that the roots of Christianity are hard and fast in what Christians call the Old Testament, and Christianity is the natural outcome of Moses and the prophets, unless you pervert it with outrageous unbelief. All of which the Jews in fact have done. Nevertheless, these things are not going to stay that way.

Now a look will be taken at the Great Break of Israel from her self-will and sinful past. It is a great and recurring theme of prophecy, that God will before the end draw the Jews to His one and only Son, and unite both Jew and gentile in Christ, Jesus of Nazareth, our Lord and our God.

All of the worldly understanding and influence and tenacity of the Jews will turn to God's account in righteousness, to the great glory of the Christ and His church, **and to the great glory of the Jews ... and to Israel as a country!**

Jeremiah, Zechariah And Spiritual Regeneration Yet To Come.

It needs to be emphasized here that this radical change of the Jews is NOT something which CAN happen, or MAY happen, but it is something which WILL happen, Jn 10:35. Jeremiah had been unsuccessful trying to get the Jews of his day to repent and turn to the Lord their God. Things were not going well spiritually, politically, or internationally. Jeremiah tells the Jews that they **wiil be** conquered by the Babylonians, and that they should submit to them.

Then the direction of the conversation changes. He has just told them they will be conquered, and then starts in chapter 30 to tell them that they will be redeemed and restored.

Now Moses law was not to be changed or amended, as in Deut 12:32 and other passages. Still, Moses himself speaks of the time when God will send the Great Prophet whom ALL **have to** listen to, Deut 18:15ff. He will thus have the authority to change the covenant brought to the Jews by Moses.

Then Jeremiah 31 describes the coming of that Great Prophet, the Messiah, Rabbi Jesus of Nazareth, and of one of the early attempts to murder him (which is quoted in Matthew chapter two), and of the new covenant which this special Prophet will bring, Jer 31:31-34. That prophecy of a new covenant coming is quoted twice in the book of Hebrews, and that is what happened in Jesus death on the cross, and in the first gospel sermon in Acts 2.

And notice what astonishing effects this gospel will have on the Jews. Jeremiah says,

> At that time, says Yahweh, will I be the God of **ALL** the families of Israel, **and they shall be my people**. Jer 31:1 WEB

The Jews of today are by and large an unbelieving people, and have actually been that way for most of the last 3,400 years or so. But this pictures the entire nation being faithful to God. Not necessarily every individual, but at least "**ALL the familes of Israel**". **Wow!**

This is clearly something which has not happed YET. *Never has there been this level of conversion to the New Covenant in any gentile nation to date!* This will truly be an awesome thing to behold. And, "Scripture cannot be broken," Jn 10:35.

Surely some extraordinary events must happen to bring about so radical of changes in such a stubborn and sinful nation.

Zechariah also is a witness to great changes which have not yet happened but which must happen.

Now the books Zechariah and Haggai were written in 520 BC. Moreover Zechariah was specifically written,

> In the eighth month, in the second year of Darius, the word of Yahweh came to Zechariah the son of Berechiah, the son of Iddo, the prophet, saying, Zech 1:1 WEB

All of which works out to be the period of October/November, 520 BC in our calendar. More important than that, this works out to be during the first Jewish return from captivity, from being prisoners of war (POW's) living in a foreign land, in mainly Assyria and Babylon. And *during* this **first return** from captivity, Zechariah speaks of bringing them **back from captivity a second time!**

> "I **will** strengthen the house of Judah,
>   And I **will** save the house of Joseph,
>   **And I <u>will</u> bring them <u>back</u>;**
>   For I have mercy on them;
>   And they **will be** as though I had not cast them off:
>   For I am Yahweh their God, and I will hear them."
> Zech 10:6 web (*bold and underline emphasis here and following*).

He writes further,

> "I will signal for them, and gather them;
>   For I have redeemed them;
>   And they will increase as they have increased." Zech 10:8 WEB

However, they were **<u>already</u> back in their own land**, and the truth was that things were not going so well. Then Zechariah deepens the mystery even more, by wriing,

> **"When I scatter them among the peoples,**

They will remember Me in far countries,
And they with their children will live and come back."
Zech 10:9 NASB

God is talking of scattering them, as one scatters seed they are sowing. God is talking about sowing them, scattering them among the nations **a second time** (as does Isaiah in Isa 11:11), **when they are just now recovering from being scattered the first time! Amazing!**

The **first scattering** of the Jews 586 BC when the Babylonians take Jerusalem, 2Kgs 25

Zechariah **520 BC**, during the **first** return, predicts a **second scattering** and a second **return**, Zech 10:9-11

The **second** scattering, predicted by Zechariah starts with the fall of Jerusalem, **70 AD**

600 BC   500 BC   300 BC   200 BC   100 BC

The **first return** from scattering starts **538 BC**, 2Chron 36:22-23

Isaiah about 700 BC says there will be a **Second Return** from the Jews being scattered, **Isa 11:11**

"and I will bring them, ... and they will be my people, and I will be their God, in truth and in righteousness." **Zech 8:8, Jer 31:1**

The Cross 30 AD

It is important to realize that the Scriptures speak of **two returns** from being dispersed.

We spoke briefly of this in ""When You In Distress," The Sixth Break."

And when would this second scattering / sowing start? Obviously with the fall of Jerusalem in 70 AD, nearly 600 years into the future.

Additionally Zechariah says this will have wonderful results for Judah and Israel. They, will become the key to everything! Yes, that is what it says, "From him," (Judah, verse 3)

"... will come forth the corner-stone,
From him the nail,
From him the battle bow,
From him every ruler together. " Zech 10:4 WEB

Breathtaking, striking, impressive! Things which have NOT happened YET!

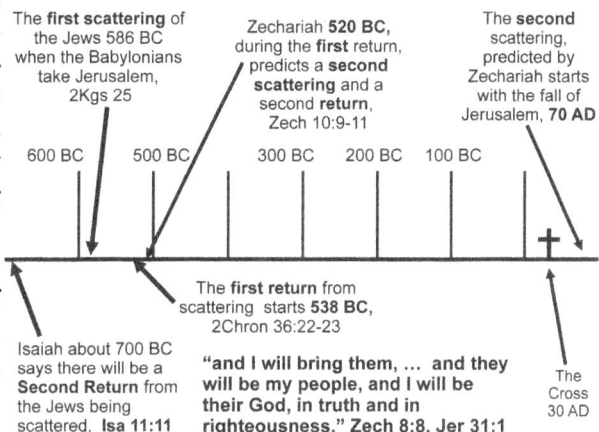

The Jews Return From the Dead, Ezekiel 37

Discerning Bible students over the past two thousand years have imminently expected the conversion of the Jews. So also the Jews have had continual "aliyahs" ("ascents") to Palestine and to Jerusalem. In particular they have been continually seeking their restoration to the land.

It must be pointed out again, that when Scripture is discussed, in particular prophecy, it is not using anything in which most modern Jews as a group have any faith. They may have faith in themselves as planners or fixers, or in rabbinic tradition as a source of the wisdom of the ages, or in the Kabbala and the Zohar as the "real" source of insight. But Scripture? No, not really, although they may speak patronizingly of a "Judeo-Christian" tradition (which in truth does not really exist), or may speak smilingly concerning Bible stories of which they know, but which they regard as children's fables. The Zionist linked groups continually work to shape gentile perceptions of modern day Israel prophetically ... but belief? It is not really there. As as has been shown, at least to some Zionists, almost any Jew will do as the Messiah. It is a child's story to be manipulated, but not truth, or a gospel to be obeyed. In fact, as soon as you turn to those passages among their own prophets which accurately describe the Jews of the last three thousand years, then their condescension quickly turns to rage, and they will be ready in an instant to accuse Isaiah, Jeremiah, Ezekiel, or even Moses of being ... well ... shall we say ... anti-Semitic! I would not be surprised to hear any day, that the Anti-Defamation League had filed suit against Moses. Indeed, many Jews would love to ban his books!

Then we see Ezekiel's vision of a valley of Dry Bones in Ezek 37:1-6. (pictured on the cover, and on page 293). The bones were very dry. The Lord asked if these bones could live, and Ezekiel answered, "O Lord GOD, You know." Ezekiel was commanded to prophesy over the bones so that flesh and sinews would grow back, and the breath of life would come back into them.

> [7] ... and as I prophesied, there was a noise, and behold a shaking, and the bones came together, bone to his bone. [8] And when I beheld, lo, the sinews and the flesh came up upon them, and the skin covered them ... [10] ... and the breath came into them, and they lived, and stood up upon their feet, an exceeding great army. Ezek 37:7-8, 10 KJV

Who then are these dead? "Son of man, these bones are the whole house of Israel:" Ezek 37:11 KJV. So the Lord God is picturing **all of Israel** <u>*as dead*</u>, as **spiritually** dead. And the Lord said

> "[13] ... when I have opened your graves, O my people, and brought you up out of your graves, [14] **And shall put my spirit in you,** and ye shall live, **and I shall place you in your own land: then shall ye know that I the** LORD **have spoken it, and performed it, saith the** LORD.
> Ezek 37:13-14 KJV (*bold emphasis added*)

So *the promise* was to return them to their land, and "put my spirit in you." These promises were given many places in Scripture. In Deut 30:3 it says "then the LORD your God will ... have mercy on you, and he will gather you again from all the peoples where the LORD your God has scattered you." ESV. So restoration from ***spiritual death***, <u>and</u> *restoration to the land of Israel* are related to each other in prophecy. Something which has **not** happened yet. In Jer 31:1 it says,

> **At the same time,** saith the LORD, **will I be** the God of **all** the families **of Israel**, and they shall be my people. KJV (*bold emphasis added*)

All the prophets spoke of Israel's return to God. Moses, like many of the prophets, had said "God **will** circumcise thine heart ... to love the LORD" Deut 30:6 KJV, (*emphasis added*). Zechariah implies that God will bring them back to their land, and *then* "I will be their God." In other words it implies that **God** will bring them back to their land and *at that time* they will be converted!

> 'And it shall come to pass
>> *That* **just as you were a curse among the nations**,
>> O house of Judah and house of Israel,
>> **So I will save you**, and **you shall be a blessing**.
>> Do not fear,
>> Let your hands be strong.' Zech 8:13 NKJV (*emphasis added*)

It might be asked, when did the Jews become "a curse among the nations"? I would be so bold as to say that it had not yet happened in the 6th century BC in Zechariah's day. It had not yet happened when the Messiah came, and when the tree was yet green Lk 23:31, in the first century. It was swiftly changing when Paul wrote that the Jews had become "hostile to all men" in 1Thes 2:15 NASB. It obviously came to have some of its modern significance in the revolts and Jewish massacres of gentiles in the first and second century AD.

Yet they will "become a blessing"? To whom? The answer is clear in Scripture: to **themselves** and *also* to "**all** families of the earth," Gen 12:3 KJV. There are of course two answers as to how "all families of the earth" will be blessed. The first of course is that the Messiah, who came by the seed of Abraham, will bring salvation to all the families of the earth, and that has happened. Secondly it speaks of God saving the Jews, "and **you** shall be **a blessing**," Zech 8:13. Or as it said in Ezek 37:14, "And **shall put my spirit in you**, and ye shall live, and **I shall place you in your own land**:" Or again,

> At the same time, saith the LORD, will I be the God of **all the families of Israel**, and they shall be my people. Jer 31:1 KJV (*emphasis added*)

Once again the Lord will be God "of **all** the families of Israel," not just bits and pieces of Israel as in the first century. You cannot read out of prophecy these statements that God will draw the nation of Israel *as a whole* to himself, so that *they* will become a blessing to the world, all of which has *never* happened. Not a curse will they be, but a blessing. It will be "**and they shall be as though I had not cast them off:**" Zech 10:6 KJV. So Zechariah accurately points to both the rejection of Israel, and God turning them around to righteousness.

And oh yes! The prophet Micah, speaking of the stress when the Jews are converted to Jesus of Nazareth, that of their defeated oppressors, they will "... pulverize many peoples, That you may devote to the Lord their unjust gain And their wealth to the Lord of all the earth." Mic 4:13 NASB.

So there will be some retribution against Mystery Babylon within history, and well before her defeat at the hands of the beast. Glorious days yet to come!

Jerusalem, The Great-Open-Unfortified-Mega-City

What would it be like if an earthly nation fully and completely committed herself to the Lord of hosts, and His Messiah, Jesus of Nazareth, and became a truly Christian nation? We shall see. It will happen, *within history*.

This is not about Jesus physically coming back to rule from an earthly Jerusalem. Nor about a theocracy of some sort, or some sort of literal-earthly-centered rule of God among men. God's throne, and Jesus' throne is and will be still in heaven, ruling over both heaven *and* earth. This is about an entire nation of mere men, repenting and becoming a nation righteous by faith: a truly Christian nation, and the wonderful fruits that will bring.

But men will still be men. The laws of gravity and of entropy, and of sin and death will still be operating principles. Men will still be tempted and stumble and fall and perhaps repent and stand again. And the Jews will just be men. The righteous will still rise from stumbling, but the wicked will still be destroyed by their fall, as it has always been. God will still be standing in the background, over-ruling in the affairs of men, and trying to make us finally face ourselves and our sins in time, if we will.

Jerusalem of those times will be the largest and greatest mega-city this world has ever seen or ever will see. That is quite a statement, I know, but I think I have told you the truth. So great will be the power and glory of this kingdom that it will serve as another "type," symbolic of the heavenly city yet to come in the new universe, the "new heavens and new earth" which will come, Isa 65:17, 2Pe 3:13. The greatest glories of *this* world will be realized in a *Christian* nation, and a *Christian* capital of breath-taking proportions.

Jerusalem will be a great, *unfortified*, *international*, *open* city.

> And said unto him, Run, speak to this young man, saying, **Jerusalem shall be inhabited as towns without walls** for the multitude of men and cattle therein: Zech 2:4 KJV (*emphasis added*)

Now **the heavenly city, the eternal city, *will have walls!*** They will be immense walls. Symbolically the heavenly Jerusalem is described as cubical, 1,400 miles on a side, and 1,400 miles high, Rev 21:16 NET, with walls symbolically of jasper and pure gold like glass, Rev 21:14-19. Even so, *it will have "walls."*

But there remains here on earth a city without "walls," a city on earth which is to be measured. And by such subtleties the two Jerusalems are differentiated.

> [1] Then I lifted up my eyes and looked, and behold, *there was* a man with a measuring line in his hand. [2] So I said, "Where are you going?" And he said to me, "To measure Jerusalem, to see how wide it is and how long it is." [3] And behold, the angel who was speaking with me was going out, and another angel was coming out to meet him, [4] and

said to him, "Run, speak to that young man, saying, '**Jerusalem will be inhabited without walls** because of the multitude of men and cattle within it. ⁵ 'For I,' declares the LORD, 'will be a wall of fire around her, and I will be the glory in her midst.'" Zech 2:1-5 NASB

Zechariah 2 is speaking of an incredible earthly city, a city of men here and now, yet to come *within* history, well before the end of time. Isaiah says (in a text overlapping this world and the world to come),

> ¹⁰ "Be joyful with Jerusalem and rejoice for her, all you who love her;
>> Be exceedingly glad with her, all you who mourn over her,
> ¹¹ That you may nurse and be satisfied with her comforting breasts,
>> That you may suck and be delighted with her bountiful bosom."
> ¹² For thus says the LORD, "Behold, I extend peace to her like a river,
>> And the glory of the nations like an overflowing stream;
>> And you will be nursed, you will be carried on the hip and fondled on the knees.
> ¹³ "As one whom his mother comforts, so I will comfort you;
>> And you will be comforted in Jerusalem."
> ¹⁴ Then you will see *this*, and your heart will be glad,
>> And your bones will flourish like the new grass;
>> And the hand of the LORD will be made known to His servants,
>> But He will be indignant toward His enemies.
> Isa 66:10-14 NASB

She will be an open city, unfortified. God Himself will be the source of the greatness of this people who will truly and fully commit themselves to the Lord *as a nation*. God Himself will be her defense, so it will be that if she turns from the Lord ... just as it was with ancient Israel ... she will be very vulnerable.

Judgment day will still be coming. The day will yet be when we personally appear in God's presence, "when He comes to be glorified in His saints on that day, and to be marveled at among all who have believed," 2Thes 1:10. The gospel will still need to be spread to a dying world.

Will Satan ever surpass this? The answer is no. That is not his purpose. His purpose is to destroy men and nations and souls, not to build. This will be the last and greatest super city. Satan desires, as Churchill noted, to reconstitute society on the basis of "arrested development"! Remember?

But Jerusalem as a city whose cords and roots will never be pulled up?

> Look upon Zion, the city of our festivals;
>> your eyes will see Jerusalem,
>> a peaceful abode, a tent that will **not** be moved;
> its stakes will **never** be pulled up,

nor any of its ropes broken.
Isa 33:20 NIV (*bold emphasis added*)

"*Never*" *again* is reserved for the heavenly city in a universe where sin and death and entropy are not operating principles. Similarly, I think that Isa 66:10-14 applies to physical Israel as a type, and heaven itself as the antitype, as the ultimate fulfillment. This is about,

Astonishing World Shaking Events.

There is a reign of glory for the Jews <u>and for Christianity</u> *in this present world* **which is yet to come.** No, this is not about the establishment of the kingdom, because the kingdom has already been established (Mtt 28:18, Col 1:13, etc.), and Jesus "must reign" until He puts all His enemies under His feet, 1Cor 15:25! Rather this concerns the Jews in repentance worshipping the Most High God of Glory, and His Son Jesus the Christ. They will bring a blessing to themselves, and to the world, both spiritual and material. This is speaking of **basic changes in national character,** needed so that they can become the kind of world citizens which they really should be, and become that prophesied **blessing to all of the world.** And,

... scripture cannot be broken, Jn 10:35 KJV

It is a strange thing about outstandingly stubborn people, the Bible often calls them "stiff necked" and "uncircumcised." You can never convert them. However, once they are converted, you can hardly sidetrack them. The only thing which will turn this into an engine of righteousness is the Only True and Living God ... His plans ... His mercy. So there remains a conversion of the Jews to God's One and Only Son, Jesus of Nazareth, in truth and righteousness, and they at some point in history will undergo *another* radical break, an extreme change and repentance, and they will be accepted by the Lord God. And the later glory of righteousness will be *greater than* the former glory of wickedness.

"Behold, I have told you in advance."
Mtt 24:25 NASB

When it all happens,
the whole world will be saying,
"Who would have ever thought it?"

Not a jot or a tittle of all of this will fail.

[19] "And when the LORD saw *it*, He spurned *them*,
Because of the provocation of His sons and His daughters.

²⁰   And He said: "I will hide My face from them,
        I will see what their end *will be*,
        For they *are* a perverse generation,
        Children in whom is no faith.
²¹   They have provoked Me to jealousy by *what* is not God;
        They have moved Me to anger by their foolish idols.
        **But I will provoke them to jealousy by *those who are* not a
        nation;**
        I will move them to anger by a foolish nation.
   Deut 32:19-21 NKJV

The prophets warned of these things, so God warned Israel by the mouth of Moses in Deut 32:21, that they had made God jealous by their images and seeking other gods, so God will make them jealous by those who are not really a people, by a "foolish" nation. How much more foolish can you get than us gentiles taken as a whole! And who are "*those who* are not a people," but those who are God's people in Christ? The consistent indication is that *God will use us, the gentiles, members of the nations in Christ, to stir the Jews to jealousy!*

So the survival under siege of those who are not a people (a spiritual people, yes! A literal people, no!) will change their perspective and make them desirous of this shield from beyond the human and beyond the demonic. And Israel will be changed.

What would it be like if an entire nation fully committed itself to Jesus the Christ? *The whole world will get to see it, and the glories and the power* which it will bring. The times of the Gentiles will have been fulfilled (Rom 11:25) and will fade away, Lk 21:24.Then Israel will truly become "the center" (literally the navel) "of the world," Ezek 38:12 NASB.

> Righteousness exalteth a nation: but sin is a reproach to any people.
> Prov 14:34 KJV

A Unity of Jew and Gentile in Jesus Christ Our Lord!

Now Paul notes in Ephesians chapter two that Jew and Gentile were formerly separated, and the Gentiles (the nations) had no hope.

> ¹¹ Wherefore remember, that *ye being* **in time past Gentiles** in the flesh, who are called Uncircumcision by that which is called the Circumcision in the flesh made by hands; ¹² That at that time ye were without Christ, being **aliens from the commonwealth of Israel**, and strangers from the covenants of promise, having no hope, and without God in the world: Eph 2:11-12 KJV (*bold emphasis added*)

Then Paul speaks of us Gentiles being drawn near in Jesus Christ,

> ¹⁹ **Now** therefore **ye are no more strangers and foreigners**, but

fellowcitizens with the saints, and of the household of God; ²⁰ And are built upon the foundation of the apostles and prophets, Jesus Christ himself being the chief corner *stone,* Eph 2:19-20 KJV (*bold added*)

This is dealing with the hateful thing which was so offensive to classical Pharisaism: Jews and the Gentiles being equal in the Messiah. Which we are. Also Paul speaks prophetically, of something which has NOT happened in history so far. That is the combining of both Jew and Gentile into one body in Christ.

¹⁴ For he is our peace, **who hath made both one**, and hath broken down the middle wall of partition *between us;* ¹⁵ Having abolished in his flesh the enmity, *even* the law of commandments *contained* in ordinances; for **to make in himself of twain one new man, *so* making peace**; Eph 2:14-15 KJV (*bold emphasis added*)

That emphatically has NOT happened to date. Jew and Gentile have NOT been *one*, **so far**, although Paul speaks of it as something Christ has already "made" to happen, past tense, in verse 14. We gentiles tend to read over this as symbolic and ideal, in a passage many do not even think of it as prophetic. It has NOT happened, but it *will* happen. This was firmly decided long ago, and after a period of time which is not much of anything in God's eyes, at the right time, it will be just as Jesus said.

Now *this will blur the distinction between Jew and Gentile* ... just as the Pharisees feared. **On the other hand** it should be noted:

1.) **this will actually strengthen the hand of the Jews in dealing with their enemies, because Jew and Gentile will be unified in Jesus Christ**, as was planned from the beginning!

2.) This will give **more cover to the Jews** *in dealing with their enemies* because Jew and Gentile will be indistinguishable in Jesus Christ!

3.) *This will* **not** be *heaven on earth*, but some incredible benefits will extend to all of mankind, including an incredible world-wide lengthening of human life on earth, as will be discussed a little later. Not really heaven on earth, but spectacular enough to be symbolic of those heavenly things yet to come, and glorious enough for it to be said that in these things "shall all families of the earth be blessed. " Gen 12:3 KJV. There are truly "types" yet to come in history.

Does Ephesians 2 imply an abatement of many of the divisions within Christianity? I do no know, but I am inclined to think it will be so to some degree. Even so, some divisions will still be necessary, 1Cor 11:18-19. However, in those future days when the Jews as a nation *turn in **faith** to Rabbi Jesus of Nazareth*, **and the Jewish nation becomes the most militant, and the most faithful, and the most successful, Christian nation of ALL history**, it will produce some dazziling results, far beyond anything men can accomplish by mere human effort.

Glorious Days in History, BEFORE the Second Coming.

The outlines of these things are clear. They will include,

1. The stubborn people Deut 9:6, will become submissive to Jesus Our Lord.

2. The Lord will again choose Judah, Zech 2:12.

3. The Jews will become a blessing to the nations instead of a curse.

4. There will be a widening of the preaching of the Amnesty for Our Sins. The Jews began the preaching of the Gospel in Acts 2, and they will complete the preaching of the gospel to all nations. This has not been studied here, but it is clearly part of the prophetic forecast.

5. Many health benefits will come to the entire world.

6. Many Gentiles will become Jews, Zech 2:11, etc.

7. Jerusalem will exist without walls, without fortifications, without defenses, Zech 2:4, 10.

And the Jews will at last become a nation of priests, for all Christians become priests to God, not just those of a certain tribe.

> Ye also, as lively stones, are built up a spiritual house, an holy priesthood, to offer up spiritual sacrifices, acceptable to God by Jesus Christ. 1Pe 2:5 KJV

There are many more people to be converted before the end of time, including the gospel coming with power to the Jews. The gospel must be preached literally to every nation tribe and people. There are many more to be converted to Jesus of Nazareth. Then the end will come, Mtt 24:14.

Is all of this Imminent?

The real answer to this is no one knows. Scripture tells us certain things will happen, but as Jesus tells us in Acts 1, "It is not for you to know the times or the seasons, which the Father hath put in his own power." Acts 1:7 KJV.

Your author is inclined to think it is "imminent," but imminent could still be some hundreds of years off in eternal terms, the real clock we are on. If you know anything about Christian history, then you know that these things have been known by the students of God's Word, and anticipated as coming "soon," all through the Christian age. **I have only brought the information up to date in terms of current history.** That being said, I would not be surprised if these things happened "soon" in human terms. It is the job of the faithful servant to "Watch," so that when our Lord is ready to act, we also are ready. Naturally, such watching, and preparation in readiness, changes how we live, and strengthens us in ways we scarcely understand. So comes the next question:

What Will This Mean? How Will It Work Out?

Is Neal Fain among the prophets? Hardly! So what is this section about?

NOT prophecy, but about how I personally
see all of this working out.

Reasonably looking at Scripture, how will some of this work out, when the Jews are converted to Christianity as a group?

Let me be emphatic that the Jews will NOT become some sort of gods in this world, with dazzling superiority to all others ethically and every other way. They will still just be men. They will be like many of us, with much bad background and "unlearning" to do from "the futile ways inherited" from our fathers, 1Pe 1:18 NASB. They will just be men, but now they will be Christians, and will begin the process of learning new ways of living. Just like us goyim in the Lord, they will have many tugs toward sin in their lives, but now, like those true believers among the goyim, they will have the Spirit of God living in them and helping them. Then as a nation that is being blessed by the Lord our God, they will be a very powerful and prosperous nation and they will bear some outstandingly good fruits. The general outline of the Christian age as seen in the book of Revelation will still be in place.

It might be worth noting that this does not necessarily mean that each and every Jew will become a Christian, any more than each and every American was a Christian when America was considered a Christian nation. Even so, Israel as a whole will become Christian, even **"all the families of Israel,"** Jer 31:1 KJV.

Among other things—it is clear that the Jews will have a great deal of sorting out to do. This will mean sorting out many things which they have ignored, or discounted or despised. Things which are both spiritual and worldly. Their conversion will lead to a complete social, cultural, spiritual, political and financial upheaval of gigantic proportions, and the results will take some time to sort out and mature. Again, **this is about world shaking events.**

The book of Hebrews will be the most hotly debated book in a new Christianized state of Israel. It will become pivotal to the Jews, sorting out the issues in their culture, which were sorted out by many gentile converts to Christianity by the end of the first century. The question will be rightly dividing the Word of Truth, and the book of Hebrews will be one of the most studied books. Galatians also will be right up there. Romans will be close behind in significance.

The bitterness and hatred will go away, and Jerusalem will become an international center for Christianity. The issues of Constantine and Cromwell and the Puritans and the early Americans, about how to create a truly Christian state, will once again come to life, but evidently in a more cohesive and organized manner.

Militant And Relentless Advocacy Will Survive.

What some have called the "tenacious advocacy" of the Jews will still be a factor, but now they will become advocates for Christianity. A corollary of this is that there will still be a certain amount of divisiveness, which is seen as an age long factor in 1 Corinthians chapters 1 through 3. This will still exist, in part, for as it says in 1Cor 11:19,

> For there must also be factions among you, that those who are approved may be recognized among you. NKJV

I expect the most noxious forms of divisiveness such as have been seen among the Jews down through history will be mellowed by the gospel. Christianity will bring character changes of such a fundamental nature, the effect of the Spirit of the Most High God working among them, and the most deplorable character traits of the Jews will disappear or be greatly mitigated.

> At that time they shall call Jerusalem the throne of the LORD; **and all the nations shall be gathered unto it**, to the name of the LORD, to Jerusalem: **neither shall they walk any more after the imagination of their evil heart**. Jer 3:17 KJV (*bold emphasis added*)

In context in Jeremiah 3 this is talking abut physical Israel, and here Jeremiah speaks of a day when they will no longer walk "after the imagination of their evil heart." Once again, this plainly something which has *not* happened *so far*. Clearly also, many of the links between Mystery Babylon, and the Mystery of Lawlessness (see the discussion of these things in *Prophecy Principles* and *Revealing the Christian Age*), and the Jews will be broken. These mysteries, though, will still exist, working their way to their own destinies.

Theologians, both Jew and Gentile, when they see all of this, will marvel that the Jews could have been *so blind so long* to the plain statements of Scripture. After it has been in place a while, the world will say, ah yes, we knew all along that it would come to this, but of course, they did not. Many have openly expressed their open doubts as to whether the prophecies of their conversion would ever happen. The true Jewish destiny will only be achieved through Rabbi Yehoshua, the One of their own whom they hated so long and so fervently.

World-Wide Influence And Leverage Will <u>Increase</u>.

The Jewish skills in writing, thinking, and perspective, in the arts and movies, finance, business, government and in advocacy, will all be employed in the service of Jesus Christ. The world will still be in darkness, and will still be opposed to God, but Jew and Gentile will be firmly bonded in Jesus Christ, as in Ephesians 2.

You might ask, why has this taken so long? I would answer, God knows what He is doing, and how to do it best. Remember also "that one day *is* with the Lord as a thousand years, and a thousand years as one day." 2Pe 3:8 KJV. So in eternity's grand plan, it has only been "a couple of days," and clearly God is using these things to save the maximum number of people.

From the Jews will come the great preachers and teachers of true Christianity, but not as "plants," nor as agents of subversion and destruction, as it has been at times during much of the last two thousand years. From the Jews will come the great martyrs of this new age of Christianity, including (I assume) those last two great martyrs against the beast, the two lamp stands and the two olive trees in Revelation 11. The Jews will bring the true completion of the Great Commission, Mtt 28:18-20. Then and only then will come the end things, Mtt 24:14.

They were and have been, *ipso facto*, a world nation without a country. In the present and into the future they will still be a world nation, but with a country, and it appears that a Christianized Israel will become heirs of many of the one-world tendencies of our modern age. It will become a "Christian" one-world of sorts, thus negating many of the present machinations of the Mystery of Lawlessness and Mystery Babylon the Great.

Evil men and seducers will still become worse and worse, 2Tim 3:13. Even so, the real game-changer will be when the Jews recognize their own Messiah, whom they have for so long rejected: Rabbi Yehoshua.

The nation of Israel will become a militant Christian nation. I did not say so, God said so, **and it will happen!**

Jews as an Ethnic Group Will Survive.

The Jews have had, and still have, a lingering fear of being assimilated out of existence in our modern world, which is part of the reason for their tenacious rejection of the nations of this world, and now I am speaking of all barriers between Jew and Gentile (the nations) being eliminated once and for all, eternally. So will the Jews disappear as a national group in this conversion? The answer is No! In fact **they will not only survive but they will prosper as a nation, even as prophesied by Moses and the rest of the prophets, and Jesus Himself.** In great part this will be just as gentile nations have become Christian and have survived as nations and even prospered.

Faith and generosity will replace pride and spitefulness toward others, and the fears of being assimilated to nothing will fade away in their incredible prosperity which is to come. The secret ingredient in all of this will be the teachings of Rabbi Yehoshua.

> And the LORD shall make thee the head, and not the tail; and thou shalt be above only, and thou shalt not be beneath; if that thou hearken unto the commandments of the LORD thy God, which I command thee this day, to observe and to do *them*: Deut 28:13 KJV

8 "I will whistle for them and gather them,
For I will redeem them;
And they shall increase as they once increased.
9 "I will sow them among the peoples,
And they shall remember Me in far countries;
They shall live, together with their children,
And they shall return.
10 I will also bring them back from the land of Egypt,
And gather them from Assyria.
I will bring them into the land of Gilead and Lebanon,
Until no *more room* is found for them."
Zech 10:8-10 NKJV (*bold emphasis added*)

Once again: Zechariah was written *after* the return from the *first* captivity! So they will be, until the end of time. **Jews as an ethnic group will survive until the end of time, Mtt 24:34.** So says Rabbi Yehoshua!

> Then He brought him outside and said, "Look now toward heaven, and count the stars if you are able to number them." Gen 15:5 NKJV

And strangely enough, I think,

The "Crypto-Jew" Will Survive.

I think he will remain. It is built into the situation and the turning of the hearts of the Jews toward the welfare of other nations and not just themselves, and their becoming even more effective.

> And I will make thy seed as the dust of the earth: so that if a man can number the dust of the earth, then shall thy seed also be numbered. Gen 13:16 KJV

I do not think the Christianizing of the Jewish nation will eliminate the presence of world-wide unrecognized Jews, and it might even increase them! Their religion will be Christian, *and most of the world will become "Christian," at least in nominal terms.*

> For the earth shall be filled with the knowledge of the glory of the LORD, as the waters cover the sea. Hab 2:14 KJV

It seems to be speaking here of this present world, and it clearly has not happened *yet!* **The line between Jew and Gentile will be even more blurred than it is today**, Ephesians 2, though the nation of Israel as such will prosper. In fact Scripture clearly says there will be many conversions to the Jews, and Christianity. Also,

Mystery Babylon and the Trade Cartels Will Survive.

The Jews will no longer be a primary player in Mystery Babylon, nor will they be able to destroy it. Mystery Babylon sits on too many "mountains" and "waters" for it to be easily destroyed by any one nation. Its destruction rather belongs to a later period and "the man of lawlessness" of the "mystery of lawlessness," but that is another subject. (See my second volume, *Revealing the Christian Age.*)

Some Jews have been members of, or have been complicit with, these mysteries. Even so, at that time the nation of Israel and the Jews as a whole, will be sincere, dedicated, militant Christians. The glory which they will bring to themselves, their nation, and the gospel, and the powerful influence they will have *against* Mystery Babylon and the Mystery of Lawlessness will be an awesome thing to behold. They will have the knowledge and the leverage to blunt many of these destructive influences. The Jews have been many of the leaders in the Platonic/communal assaults on the family, and they will roll back many of the assaults on the family in order to become the nation which they should become. This is regarding a world wide revolution for good which will come. Additionally,

The Mystery of Lawlessness Will Survive.

It will still be a destructive influence in our world, and indeed, it will *in time* again become a destructive influence in regenerated Israel. After all, even though some Jews partook of the Mystery of Lawlessness, that mystery was never really seated in Judaism. Judaism was *a* factor, but only *a* factor.

For sure, how great a part these twin mysteries will play in the great time of stress which will come on the Jews is still unknown, at least to this author. Mystery Babylon and the Mystery of Lawlessness are **NOT** Jewish organizations. It appears that Mystery Babylon is seated on many nations/waters (compare Rev 17:1 with Rev 17:15), and on seven religions (Rev 17:9). The Mystery of Lawlessness is seated on a more restricted seven to ten nations (Revelation chapters 13 and 17, etc.) It is true that some Jews have been member of these organizations, but so have some Americans, Germans, Englishmen, Irish, French, Asians, you name it. Will it be that these same organizations will come to consider the Jews as a group to be inimical to their well being, and organize the great time of stress which precedes their conversion? I would not be dogmatic, but to me it seems possible that this could become a factor leading to the conversion of the Jews.

It has been shown that the Kabbalah and the occult in their present form have a uniquely Jewish flavor and emphasis. Will this continue? It is possible that a so-called "Christian Kabbalah" will continue, but it so quickly degenerates into clearly "Black Magic," that a regenerate Israel may suppress it. I am inclined to think that the "Kabbalah" will simply morph still further into a more gentile form. **At its root, *the synagogue of Satan has no more use for the Jews* than they do for us gentiles.** All are mere *men* to be destroyed by Satan by any subterfuge available.

All of this aside, when the Jews as a group are converted, then Mystery Babylon and the Mystery of Lawlessness will come to consider Israel a primary target, and it seems (reading Scripture), will eventually subvert her into sin, but only after a long and bitter struggle. I project (but maybe wrongly) only after many centuries. Times and seasons? (Acts 1:7) I do not know any more of these things than you do, but if you read and study prophecy, there is more to come and to happen, not even counting the victory at the end of time which both Jews and Gentiles in Jesus Christ will share.

There Will Still be Those Who Say They Are Jews, but Are Not.

Nothing more needs to be said here than to point to Romans 2.

> [28] For he is not a Jew, which is one outwardly; neither *is that* circumcision, which is outward in the flesh: [29] But he *is* a Jew, which is one inwardly; and circumcision *is that* of the heart, in the spirit, *and* not in the letter; whose praise *is* not of men, but of God. Rom 2:28-29 KJV

That was and is and still will be.

Most Will Forget the Anti-Christ Days of the Jews!

One day, far before the end of time, everyone will forget that once, for over two thousand years, the Jews were the implacable enemies of their own Great Prophet, that they were part of the mechanisms of destruction. It will be *passé* that they would have finally have been converted, that they would finally become the most ardent, and the most successful, champions of Jesus Christ, leading the gospel to its most glorious heights yet in this present world, before the disasters leading to the very end of all things. Anyone who looks seriously at the Scriptures and who can read, should have known all of this would come to pass, and many did. Oh yes! Easy to see. *In retrospect!*

But a preliminary time of storm and stress must come first, a type of the end, but not the end. The storm and stress which will result in the Lord our God turning the hearts and minds of the Jews toward Himself. And, oh yes, it seems that:

The "Leaven of the Pharisees" Will Also Survive.

I do not say that Pharisaism will survive. I do not know that. Rather that some of a spirit of externalism, a spirit of rigid superficiality, a spirit of hypocrisy, will survive even among true Christians. That much seems clear from what Jesus has told us, and the teachings of the New Covenant. A tendency to drift in such directions, it seems will be an age long threat to the gospel, and that is the context in which our Lord discusses these things. Rabbi Yehoshua's warnings will still be pertinent ... even to the end of time!

Always keep in mind what Jesus said:

"My Kingdom Is Not Of This World," Jn 18:36

> Then if any man shall say unto you, Lo, here *is* Christ, or there; believe *it* not. Mtt 24:23 KJV

Rabbi Yehoshua will NOT return *before* the ***final* last day**, when He will return with the holy angels to bring vengeance on those who "know not God, and that obey not the gospel ..." 2Thes 1:8 KJV.

So if *anyone* tells you the Messiah is here or there or inside the house or out in the wilderness ... **do not believe them!** Those who look for Jesus to rule over a literal kingdom on this earth are looking in vain. The Jews will *NOT* establish the kingdom of God. The Jews will rather become a part of this embryonic kingdom which will reach it fullness in the new universe, the new heavens and the new earth which are to come.

> [17] For, behold, I create new heavens and a new earth; and the former things shall not be remembered, nor come into mind. For behold, I create Jerusalem *for* rejoicing And her people *for* gladness. ...
>
> [19] I will rejoice in Jerusalem, and joy in my people; and there shall be heard in her no more the voice of weeping and the voice of crying.
>
> [20] **There shall be no more there an infant of days, nor an old man who has not filled his days; for the child shall die one hundred years old, and the sinner being one hundred years old shall be accursed.**
>
> [21] They shall build houses, and inhabit them; and they shall plant vineyards, and eat the fruit of them.
>
> [22] They shall not build, and another inhabit; they shall not plant, and another eat: for as the days of a tree shall be the days of my people, and my chosen shall long enjoy the work of their hands
>
> [23] They shall not labor in vain, nor bring forth for calamity; for they are the seed of the blessed of Yahweh, and their offspring with them. Isa 65:17-23 WEB

You can see that most of this passage applies to the new universe, the "new heavens and a new earth" of Isa 65:17, which is yet to come, that is say what we call "heaven." It is the same thing noted many other passages, such as in Rev 21:1, "I saw a new heaven and a new earth: for the first heaven and the first earth have passed away, and the sea is no more." WEB But notice that part of this passage seems contradictory. On one hand it speaks of a time when, "there will no longer be heard in her the voice of weeping and the sound of crying," verse 19. Now that clearly points to something beyond our present world, when the laws of entropy and of sin and death are no longer operating principles. The conversion of the Jews, will bring some wonderful things, but NOT the end of all entropy to this present world. But then it talks about a youth dying in verse 20, and those being considered accursed who do not reach age 100. Still, it is clearly talking about people still dying ... so-o-o-o-o-o death is still there *somewhere*, and some weeping and crying *somewhere*. And that clearly does not fit the words, "And there will no longer be heard in her, The voice of weeping and the sound of crying," as said in verse 19. So what is going on? This seems contradictory.

I think it is **also** talking about the glories of the Christian age which are yet to come with the union of Jew and gentile, and radical extensions of the length of human life here on earth. Those glories will serve as a "type," symbolic, of heaven, which is yet to come. So the passage in Isaiah 65 which was covered above is talking about *both* the glories of the Christian age which are yet to come, **and** about heaven itself, and the former is a "type," is symbolic, of the latter. Such an approach to telling us things is common in Bible prophecy. Look back to the studies in *Prophecy Principles.*

The true Zion **is not material**. It is a mountain which *cannot* be physically touched. It is of another universe.

> [18] **For you have not come to *a mountain* that can be touched** and to a blazing fire, and to darkness and gloom and whirlwind, ...
> [22] But you have come to Mount Zion and to the city of the living God, the heavenly Jerusalem, ... [23] to the general assembly and church of the firstborn who are enrolled in heaven, ...
> Heb 12:18, 22-23 NASB (*bold emphasis added*)

And Ezekiel's temple?

I would not at this point in my studies be dogmatic about it, but if I am reading prophecy correctly, a physical temple to the Lord will be built one more time in Jerusalem. As the apostles and early Christians worshipped in Herod's temple in the first century following the resurrection of Jesus, so this new temple in Jerusalem will become a world-wide center for Christian worship. A coming temple will be built, *which will not quite be like Ezekiel's* ... mainly because it cannot be. It is a physical impossibility to build the temple which is described in those last chapters of Ezekiel. Parts of it may match Ezekiel's dimensions. However, the missing parts will clearly show that the temple yet to be built here on earth will be just another "type,"a "shadow," symbolic of heavenly things. Ultimately Ezekiel's temple speaks of the great temple in heaven, where the river of life flows from underneath the throne. The new temple here on earth, if such matches the glory and majesty of a rejuvenated Israel, will be incredible, mammoth beyond belief, but still not conforming to Ezekiel's temple, and never really able to match *all* of those criteria.

Moses' Letter to Apostate Israel, Deuteronomy 32

This is what is generally called the Song of Moses, and it is clearly meant to be a song. It is a long song, fifty-two verses. You might call it an ode. The saints in heaven sing, "the song of Moses the servant of God, and the song of the Lamb," Rev 15:3 KJV. Moses spoke all the words of this song before all the people of Israel and told them to take it to heart. This is not an idle word, he said, rather this is your life; and it was, and is. There are some key parts to the song.

First of all it asserts that: The Lord is perfect! He says first of all to listen, because he is going to proclaim the greatness of God. "... the Rock, his work is perfect:" verse 4 KJV. But there is more to the story, for God says of His people,

> They have dealt corruptly with him, they are not his children,
>   it is their blemish;
> They are a perverse and crooked generation. Deut 32:5 WEB

You can see clearly here: His people Israel are not really His. *Not even from the first.* They are not His children because of their defect. Instead they are a "perverse and crooked generation," a theme used with variations throughout the Scriptures.

You foolish people, he says. What do you think you are doing? Paying back God? What do they need to do but remember the ancient times, ask your fathers. It refers to the time when God parceled out the land to the nations. Paul referred to that in Acts 17, and even told the reasons for why He did these things.

> [26] And hath made of one blood all nations of men for to dwell on all the face of the earth, **and hath determined the times before appointed, and the bounds of their habitation;** [27] That they should seek the Lord, if haply they might feel after him, and find him, though he be not far from every one of us: [28] For in him we live, and move, and have our being; ..." Acts 17:26-28 KJV (*emphasis added*)

So in the active rule of this world God has Himself determined the specific "times ... and bounds of their habitation" of our nations, but not just arbitrarily. Rather it is to the purpose that all men would seek Him, and live for Him. So in this melee of divergent interests, the Lord chose Jacob to be His. He found Jacob in a desert, but He surrounded him and cared for him, even as an eagle circles about the nest. Moses is very specific. It was Yahweh alone who took care of Jacob. There was no other so-called "god" helping, and God made him prosper and cared for his needs. Nonetheless, when Jacob prospered he forgot. He forget what his fathers clearly knew. He lost sight of the heavenly care. Moses says that "Jeshurun" (*Yeshurun* יְשֻׁרוּן, literally "the upright one") grew fat and forsook his Lord, Deut 32:15.

God's people made Him jealous with other so-called "gods." What they actually had traffic with was demons, as has been discussed. It is well said in

1 Corinthians 10, and in Psa 106:37 of these same things. The Jews, like the gentiles, to use the words of the Apostle Paul, "... when ye knew not God, ye did service unto them which by nature are no gods," Gal 4:8 KJV. Consider the true nature of these spirits, for they are evil, and by their very "nature" they are not really gods. From a different realm? Yes? Still they are like us in that they too are limited beings, moral beings, but not really "gods." Still some sacrificed to these demons, even of their own flesh and blood, and forsook the Lord their God.

God then rejected them. This speaks of their defect. So God said that He would hide Himself from them in verse 20; and He did. He said "They have moved me to jealousy with that which is not God; ... and I will move them to jealousy with *those which are* not a people; ... a foolish nation," verse 21. The text seems to be speaking here of goyim like me: the gentiles who have accepted the true and only Messiah of the Jews: Jesus the Christ.

God says then through the mouth of Moses His prophet, that He will bring disaster after disaster on them, plague and famine and vermin. God Himself says He will do it. He will cut them to pieces. And He has. What are they like?

> ²⁸ "For they are a nation void of counsel,
>   Nor is there any understanding in them.
> ²⁹   Oh, that they were wise, that they understood this,
>   That they would consider their latter end!
> ³⁰   How could one chase a thousand,
>   And two put ten thousand to flight,
>   Unless their Rock had sold them,
>   And the LORD had surrendered them?" Deut 32:28-30 NKJV

So how could the Jews be beat around all these centuries unless God had sold them, had abandoned them? The answer here is that they could not have been defeated so throughly. So why is this? It is because they abandoned God. The "they" in verse 28 is physical Israel, "a nation void of counsel," and of them it says,

> ³¹ For **their rock is not as our Rock**, even our enemies themselves being judges. ³² For **their vine is of the vine of Sodom, and of the fields of Gomorrah**: their grapes are grapes of gall, their clusters are bitter: ³³ Their wine is the poison of dragons, and the cruel venom of asps. Deut 32:31-33 KJV (*bold emphasis added*)

So physical Israel became "Sodom and ... Gomorrah ... the venom of asps," and even Israel's enemies realize this, verse 31. Obviously that is nothing more nor less than the sober truth of the matter, even to our times, as has been shown. Really the most stunning and scorching condemnations of the Jews in all of world literature occurs in Moses and the Old Testament prophets!

Incredible! Literally "as their own prophets have said." I am glad Moses said that and not me! Still this book has tried to focus on the evidence from Scripture and the Jews themselves, whether that be acceptable or unacceptable. There are two things that are waiting. First God says through Moses that "To me *belongeth* vengeance, ... their foot shall slide in due time:" and *that He is the one who will repay*, Deut 32:35; and He will. All of this *is in* the context of punishing Israel after the flesh. Then the LORD adds that He will vindicate His people. It might be rightfully asked, who does this apply to? And when will it happen? Clearly in the perspective of Scripture this would apply to all who have become part of God's *holy* nation, and with the coming of the Christ, it also includes the nations, the gentiles, the *goyim* who have accepted the Christ.

> "I am the LORD; oI have called you in righteousness;
> > I will take you by the hand and keep you;
> I will give you as a covenant for the people,
> > a light for the **nations**," Isa 42:6 ESV (*emphasis added*)

and again,

> he says:
> "It is too light a thing that you should be my servant
> > to raise up the tribes of Jacob
> > and to bring back the preserved of Israel;
> I will make you uas **a light for the nations,**
> > that my **salvation may reach to the end of the earth**."
> Isa 49:6 ESV (*emphasis added*)

To "bring back the preserved one of Israel" and "the nations"! *So it was intended from the first* that the salvation of the Jews should have been *salvation for all men!* What Jew should have been surprised by what has happened? Or who should have been astonished as the prophets said they would be, and as they were. So when will physical Jacob be vindicated by God, redeemed from the world? This then is the answer to the question of when it will happen.

> For cthe LORD will vindicate his people
> > and have compassion on his servants,
> when he sees that their power is gone
> > and there is none remaining, ebond or free. Deut 32:36 ESV

Here again is the "when." When? When everything is absolutely hopeless; when there is in human terms absolutely no way out, so it is clear it is Yahweh who is delivering. It would not be hard for this to happen, but so far it has not happened on an international level. THEN the Lord will have compassion and deliver them. You may remember, this is the same answer which was discussed earlier from another text of Moses. Moses knew when it would happen.

> **When** you are in oppression, and all these things are come on you, **in the latter days** you **shall return to Yahweh your God**, and listen to his voice: Deut 4:30 WEB

The Messiah, Jesus of Nazareth, and the New Covenant apostles and prophets, add nothing new to the picture of the Jews. They merely confirm Moses and the prophets of old!

As you can see, this is exactly the same prophecy, and the same answer in both places. This is not about the Jews returning to the corrupt traditions of the Jewish nation, but of returning to God, and His special Holy Prophet, Deut 18:18-19. God will say at that time, okay where are your so called "gods" who promised to deliver you?

> See now that I, *even* I, *am* he, and *there is* no god with me: I kill, and I make alive; I wound, and I heal: neither *is there any* that can deliver out of my hand. Deut 32:39 KJV

and again

> Rejoice, O ye nations, *with* his people: for he will avenge the blood of his servants, and will render vengeance to his adversaries, and will be merciful unto his land, *and* to his people. Deut 32:43 KJV

The nations (plural) *will* rejoice with them. I hope you the reader have been following carefully and can see that these are consistent pictures of what will happen to the Jews, from both the Old Testament and the New Testament. Deuteronomy 32 was written well before the Jewish rejection of Jesus, and the conflicts of the gospel age. In fact, some 1400 years before Jesus came. It is not only in Romans and Luke and the letters. It is also in Moses and the Law and the prophets.

This is not a pretty picture Scripture paints of the Jews, but it is one that must be brushed out to its full. Indeed, the story told in full *of most peoples* is not pretty. Mine sure is not: English and Irish to America; though I, just like the Jews, am proud of my heritage. **But the Jews are too pivotal in history, both secular and religious, for us to neglect the truth. And the truth is seldom told of them, either by themselves or by others.**

Only if we see the Jews as they really are, will men preach to them tellingly, as they should. Only if the Jews see themselves as they are, will they listen in times of distress, repent and believe the gospel of Jesus Christ.

The Jews need to listen to their own prophets and their greatest teacher, Rabbi Yehoshua. The Jews need to come out of the dark into the light. **To really change things a moral revolution must come to the Jews.** Their own Messiah must be received: Jesus the Christ.

What is needed from the nation of Israel is **no less than national repentance**, and conversion to the Great Prophet like Moses: Jesus of Nazareth. To an unbelieving world, and an unbelieving Israel, such change is unthinkable, no more than a chimera, a delusion. It is rather more a dangerous fantasy than a possibility. Still, as has been shown it is something which is clearly forecast by the Lord our God. Then in some future crisis, one of those times of stress which Paul talks about; the mirage will become a reality, and the unbelievable will come to life; and the result will be part of the blessings to the world which were first promised to Abraham.

A call to the Christian scholar!

This work must continue until the time when God decides to rein in the Jews, and call them to His purpose. As has been in passing noticed, it seems it is the gentiles who will preach to the Jews on that fateful day. We as gentiles must be alert and ready for God's call when He decides to use us.

Before Israel will repent, she must realize she is lost.

Before we who are not a nation will preach to her, WE must realize she is lost.

Prophecy as a Command!

> Ye have not chosen me, but I have chosen you, and ordained you, that ye should go and bring forth fruit, and *that* your fruit should remain: that whatsoever ye shall ask of the Father in my name, he may give it you. Jn 15:16 KJV

Postscript

There are many things, both positive and negative, which have not been discussed. On every line of evidence presented, there is much more to say, all to be found, as seen here, mainly from publicly available Jewish sources. It may seem that I have concentrated on the seamier side of Judaism, but I have not, and have studiously avoided as much of such as I could. As has been emphasized previously, none of this is really secret or unavailable information. It is merely unknown to the general public, although it concerns all of us, Jews and the nations and the church.

This is an ongoing subject, which has not reached the glorious conclusions which it should and will reach. Not every question has been answered here, but as well as possible, some key answers have been given to some widely misunderstood issues. Which side of this story are you really on? In the end, the LORD of Hosts and His Son Jesus of Nazareth must inevitably emerge as victorious.

⁴⁰ **If** they shall **confess** their iniquity,
and the iniquity of their fathers, ... ⁴¹ ...
and they then **accept** of the punishment
of their iniquity: ⁴² **Then** will I
remember my covenant with Jacob, ... and
I will remember the land.

Lev 26:40-42 KJV

The Jews are no better than
the rest of us.
They too must repent and turn to
their own Messiah;
— or —
like the rest of us ...
bear the burden of their own sins
... forever!

A Select Bibliography

This list does not include all the works quoted in this book and not all of this list has been quoted in this book. Most of these books are still available in print or as "e-books", and a few (even some of the newer books cited) are available at this time as free downloads on the Internet. A couple of sources, for instance Koehler's *Hebrew Aramaic Lexicon of the Old Testament* (HALOT), will only be available to the average reader at a good university or seminary library, or perhaps in your minister's library, or computer resources.

These are by no means the only places to read. These are just places to start, to see how these things fit together. And, to take first things first, with this Trilogy's most quoted source, it would be ridiculous to leave it out.

Yahweh, The Lord God of Heaven and Earth, *The Bible, Old and New Testaments.*

Barclay, William, *The Letters to the Philippians, Colossians, and Thessalonians*, Westminster Press, Philadelphia, 1959.

Barclay, William,*The Letters to Timothy, Titus and Philemon*, Westminster Press, Philadelphia, 1960.

Barnavi, Eli, Gen. Ed. *A Historical Atlas of the Jewish People, From the Time of the Patriarchs to the Present*, Schocken Books, NY, 1992.

Beschloss, Michael, *The Conquerers, Roosevelt, Truman and the Destruction of Hitler's Germany, 1941-1945* , Simon and Schuster, N.Y., 2003.

Boyett, Jason, *Pocket Guide to the Apocalypse, The Official Field Manual of the End of the World*, Relevant Books, Orlando, FL, 2005.

Brown, F., Driver, S. R., and Briggs, C. A., *A Hebrew and English Lexicon of the Old Testament*, Coded with the numbering system from *Strong's Exhaustive Concordance of the Bible*, Hendrickson Publishers, 2000.

Buchanan, Patrick J., *Churchill, Hitler, and "The Unnecessary War", How Britain Lost Its Empire and the West Lost The World*, Three Rivers Press, NY, 2008.

Cavendish, Richard, *The Black Arts*, Capricorn Books, NY, 1967.

Charlesworth, James H., *The Old Testament Pseudepigrapha*, 2 Volumes, Hendrickson Publishers, Peabody, Massachusetts, 1983.

Chomsky, Noam, *Middle East Illusions, Including Peace in the Middle East? Reflections on Justice and Nationhood*, Rowan & Littlefield Publishers, Inc., NY, 2004.

Cornfeld, Gaalya, Editor, *Josephus, The Jewish War*, Zondervan, Grand Rapids, MI, 1982.

Durant, Will, *The Age of Faith*, Simon and Schuster, NY, 1950.

Durant, Will, *The Renaissance, A History of Civilization in Italy from 1304-1570 A.D.*, Simon & Schuster, NY, 1953.

Durant, Will, and Ariel, *Rousseau and Revolution*, Simon and Schuster, NY, 1967.

Durant, Will, and Ariel, *The Age of Louis XIV*, Simon and Schuster, NY, 1963.

Eban, Abban, *Heritage: Civilization and the Jews*, Summit Books, NY, 1984.

Elizur, Yuval, and Malkin, Lawrence, *The War Within, Israel's Ultra-Orthodox Threat to Democracy and the Nation*, Overlook Duckworth, NY, 2013.

Fain, Neal, *Prophecy Principles: The Background we Need for Bible Prophecy, and How it Works,* Second Edition, AngleOfEntry.Com, Lawrenceburg, Tennessee, 2018.

Fain, Neal, *Revealing the Christian Age, A Synthesis of the Prophets and Revelation,* AngleOfEntry. Com, Lawrenceburg, Tennessee, 2018.

Graetz, Heinrich, *History Of The Jews.* 6 Volumes, Jewish Publication Society of America, Philadelphia, 1895.

Finkelstein, Louis, *The Pharisees,The Sociological Background of the Their Faith*, 2 Volumes, Jewish Publication Society of America, 1940, Philadelphia, Penn.

Hess, Moses, translated by Meyer Waxman, *Rome and Jerusalem, A Study In Jewish Nationalism*, Bloch Publishing Co., NY, 1918.

Higham, Charles, *Trading With the Enemy, The Nazi-American Money Plot 1933-1949*, Barnes and Noble, NY, 1983, 1995.

Josephus, Flavius, *Antiquities of the Jews*, translated by William Whiston.

Josephus, Flavius, *Wars of the Jews*, translated by William Whiston.

Koehler, Ludwig, and Baumgartner, Walter, translated and edited under the supervision of M.E.J. Richardson *The Hebrew and Aramaic Lexicon of the Old Testament,* (HALOT) 1994, 1995, 1996, 1999, 2000 by Koninklijke Brill NV, Leiden.

Laqueur, Walter, *A History of Zionism*, MFJ Books, NY, 1972.

Lebrecht, Norman, *Genius & Anxiety*, Scribner, NY, 2019.

Levene, Mark, *War, Jews, and the New Europe, The Diplomacy of Lucien Wolf 1914-1919*, Oxford University Press, 1992.

Lotus, John, and Aarons, Mark, *The Secret War Against the Jews, How Western Espionage Betrayed the Jewish People*, St. Martin's Griffin, NY, 1997.

Mersheimer, John J., and Walt, Stephen M., *The Israel Lobby and U. S. Foreign Policy*, Farrar, Straus and Giroux, NY, 2007.

Patai, Raphael, *The Hebrew Goddess*, Third Enlarged Edition, Wayne State University Press, Detroit, 1990.

Ravitsky, Aviezer, *Messianism, Zionism, and Jewish Religious Radicalism*, translated by Swirsky and Chipman, The University of Chicago Press, Chicago, 1996.

Reinharz, Jehuda, *Chaim Weizmann, The Making of a Statesman*, Oxford University Press, NY, 1993.

Rosten, Leo, *The New Joys of Yiddish*, Random House, NY, 2001.

Roth, Cecil, *A History of the Marranos*, Shocken Books, NY, Fourth Edition, 1974.

Roth, Cecil, *Personalities And Events In Jewish History*, The Jewish Publication Society of America, Philadelphia, 1953.

Schneer, Jonathan, *The Balfour Declaration, The Origins of the Arab-Israeli Conflict*, Random House, NY, 2010.

Scholem, Gershom, *Jewish Gnosticism, Merkabah Mysticism, and Talmudic Tradition*, Jewish Theological Seminary of America, NY, 2012.

Scholem, Gershom, *Kabbalah*, New American Library, NY, 1978.

Scholem, Gershom, *Major Trends in Jewish Mysticism*, Schocken Books, NY, 1974.

Scholem, Gershom, *Sabbatai Sevi, The Mystical Messiah, 1626-1676*, Princeton University Press, Princeton, NJ, 1973.

Segev, Tom, trans. by Haim Watzman, *Elvis in Jerusalem, Post Zionism and the Americanization of Israel*, Metropolitan Books, Henry Holt, NY, 2002.

Segev, Tom, trans. by Haim Watzman, *One Palestine Complete, Jews and Arabs under the British Mandate*, Metropolitan Books, NY, 1999.

Shahak, Israel, *Jewish History, Jewish Religion, The Weight of Three Thousand Years*, Pluto Press, Sterling Virginia, 2002.

Shahak, Israel, and Mezvinsky, Norton, *Jewish Fundamentalism in Israel*, Pluto Press, Ann Arbor, Michigan, 2004.

Silbiger, Steven, *The Jewish Phenomenon, Seven Keys to the Enduring Wealth of a People*, Longstreet Press, Atlanta, Georgia, 2000.

Telushkin, Joseph, *Jewish Humor: What the Best Jewish Jokes Say About Jews*, William Morrow and Co., Inc., NY, 1992

Weizmann, Chaim, *Trial and Error*, Harper and Brothers, NY, 1949

Wurmbrand, Richard, *Marx and Satan*, Living Sacrifice Book Company, Bartlesville, OK, 2002.

Biographical Information

Neal Fain was born in Georgia and converted to Christ in Dallas, Texas in 1962. He attended Harding University from 1965 to 1967, preaching as a student, graduating with a degree in Bible and Biblical Languages. He lived in Alaska for over 30 years, both preaching and teaching, and much of that time self-supporting. He retired from a major oil company in 1999, followed by preaching in North Carolina. He is now retired to Tennessee, preaching, teaching, researching and writing.

This volume is an outgrowth of his study of Bible prophecy.

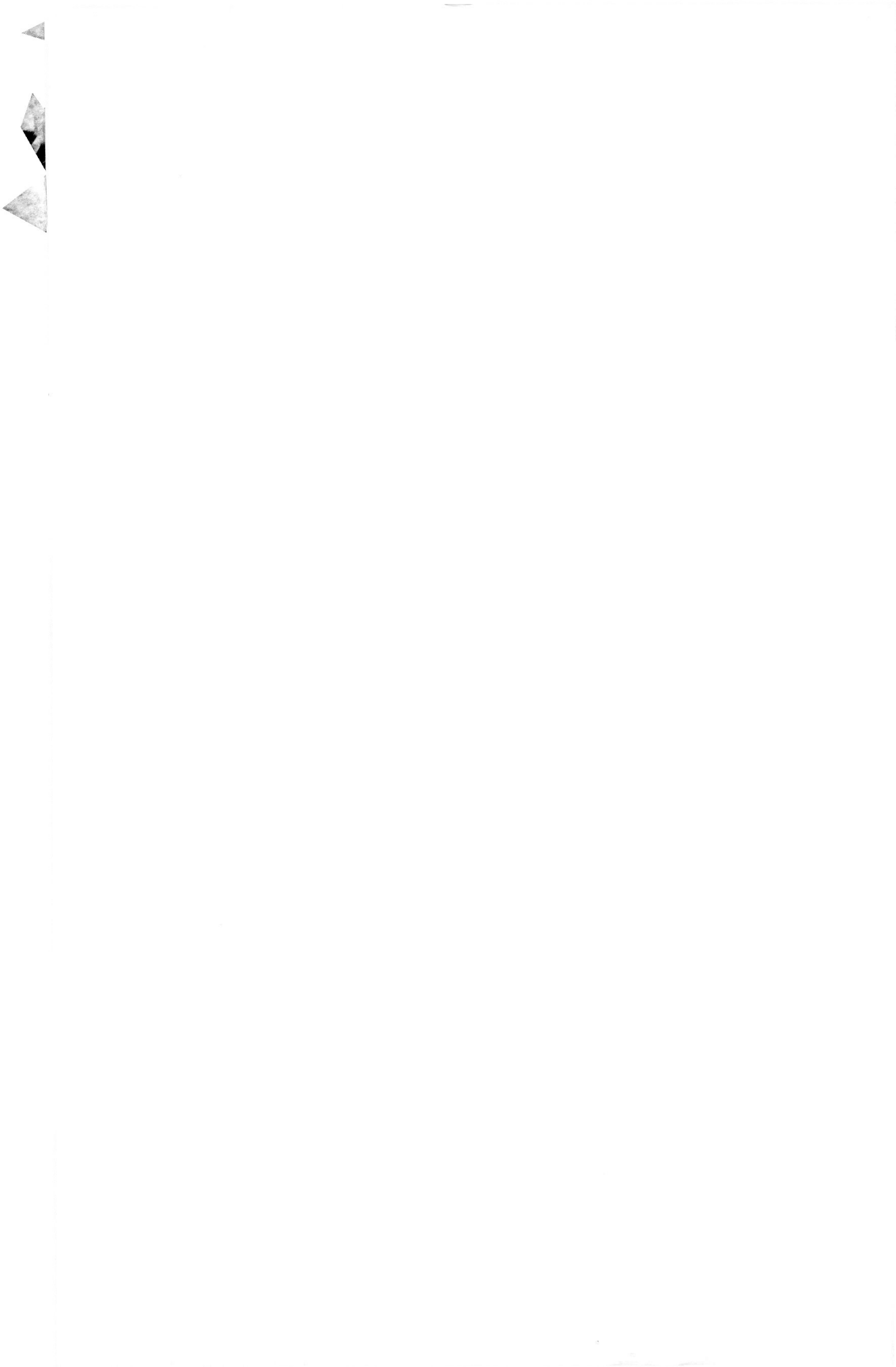

www.ingramcontent.com/pod-product-compliance
Lightning Source LLC
Chambersburg PA
CBHW060243100426
42742CB00011B/1619